nd the Best!

ATO

H'S ®

PS

HIGHEST QUALITY
1932 **70** 2002
YEARS
FRESHEST EVER

otato Chips in Australia.

the great australia
gazetteer™

2,422 places • maps • people • recipes

FOCUS PUBLISHING
PTY LTD

A FOCUS PUBLISHING BOOK PROJECT

Focus Publishing Pty Ltd
ABN 55 003 600 360
PO Box 518 Edgecliff NSW 2027
Telephone 61 2 9327 4777
Fax 61 2 9362 3753
Email focus@focus.com.au
Website www.focus.com.au

For enquiries regarding distribution and sales,
please contact the Marketing Manager.

Senior Editor and Gazettist: Kerry Davies
Designer: Jayne Wilson
Production Manager: Timothy Ho
Food Editor: Janet Little
Researchers: Cindy Luckman, Emma Sandall
Roving Reporters: Bruce Elder, Ron and Viv Moon,
    Susan O'Flahertie, Steve Starling, Peter Thoeming
Cartographers: Graham Keane, Melissa O'Brien
Editors: Alex Black, Leanne Croker,
    Sue Grose-Hodge
Proofreader: Derek Barton
Indexer: Michael Wyatt

Chairman: Steven Rich AM
Publisher: Jaqui Lane
Associate Publisher: Gillian Fitzgerald
Project Managers: Susan O'Flahertie,
    Bronwen Peters
Marketing Manager: Heather Boothroyd
Client Services Manager: Kate Sanday
Corporate Communications: Belinda Carson

ISBN 1 920683 03 8

contents

preface

A journey through Australia always reveals new wonders. The first edition of *The Great Australia Gazetteer*™ included a remarkable assortment of the interesting places, people and food that makes any trip outside the great cities of this nation such a memorable experience. That book became an instant best-seller Australia-wide. Now, this fully revised edition covers new territory, updated and expanded with the help of hundreds of contributors around Australia.

A 'gazetteer' is a book of places, people and food, three things that are close to the heart of regional and rural Australia. *The Great Australia Gazetteer*™ shows what lies beyond Australia's capital cities, in the country communities whose heritage and history is recorded here with affection.

This book was made possible by The Great Australia Partnership, a grouping of leading Australian companies with business in the bush and a deep commitment to the growth of the communities they work in. Companies such as Woolworths and Smith's Snackfoods joined The Great Australia Partnership to support the Gazettists in their search for Australian treasures—Outback festivals and great fishing spots, traditional recipes and natural wonders.

We hope you will get off the beaten track and enjoy the journey through real Australia.

Roger Corbett
Chairman The Great Australia Partnership

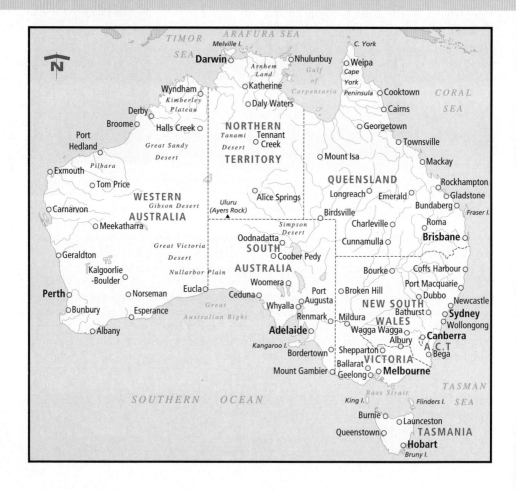

get off the beaten track

explore australia

about the gazetteer™

The real Australia is in the rural and regional communities and Outback places; the weird and wonderful stories, facts and histories; it's in Australia's culture and its character, its produce and its people. The real Australia is out there, and sometimes you have to get off the beaten track to really feel it.

The 2003 edition of the best-selling *Great Australia Gazetteer*™ (and its website) has been designed to help you do just that. It is packed with even more best-kept secret places in Australia's rural heartland, including 2,422 places, maps, 'don't miss' events and recipes from all over the country.

It is the ultimate guide to Australia's warmest, driest, wettest, biggest, longest, shortest, strangest … and all the ferret races you could possibly want to witness. This year we have added a special list of events for each region, with dates (when they have been set) and contact numbers (in case they haven't).

People from all over Australia have contributed to this book and, while every fact has been checked and re-checked, there may be something you disagree with or would like to share with others or see included in the next edition. If so, please send your comments, experiences, stories, travel tips, snapshots and recipes to **www.australiagazetteer.com** or mail them to PO Box 518 Edgecliff, NSW 2027.

We are grateful to the hundreds of contributors of content from around Australia, the people who dug up snapshots for us and who supplied their favourite recipes that they feel capture the flavour of their locality. We'd also like to thank The Great Australia Partnership for their generous support. And finally a very special thanks to the Gazetteer Team at Focus, who made it all possible.

Jaqui Lane, Publisher
Kangaroo Valley, NSW
November 2002

WOOLW
AUST

ORTHS'
RALIA

LOOK WHO'S BEHIND RURAL AUSTRALIA

Woolworths are one of the major employers in regional and rural areas. As the nation's number one buyer of primary products, Woolworths are proud to be the biggest supporter of rural Australia. And of course, we're Australian owned and proud of it. Which means we're particularly pleased to be a principal sponsor of *The Great Australia Gazetteer.*™

travelling with
the gazetteer™

There are many ways to get out there and see Australia. Many people choose the road to get to the best and the most places, to see the real Australia. *The Great Australia Gazetteer*™ takes you on a winding journey from state to state, region to region. From South Coast New South Wales you'll head all the way up the coast to the Northern Rivers, inland through tablelands and plains, down to the mighty Murray and the Outback. Hopping over the border to Queensland you'll again head north, from the South-east to the tropics, through the Gulf and Outback and on to Australia's Red Centre and the Top End of the Northern Territory.

Then you'll slip over to the Kimberley in Western Australia, down the great west coast to Australia's south-west corner, and across the Nullarbor to South Australia. You'll cruise around peninsulas, to ranges and wine valleys, down to the Limestone Coast. In western Victoria you'll again cross the Murray, up into the Grampians and down to the Great Ocean Road, to the ranges and down to Gippsland, the lakes and wilderness, and over Bass Strait to Tasmania. Then you can just do it all in reverse, or map out your own favourite road trip.

For each state there is a key map of its regions. For each region there's a detailed map highlighting the places to visit, with grid references to the maps, e.g. [A2]. Each map also has indicators to its adjoining maps. For complete road maps contact the state road authority, such as the NRMA in New South Wales, and visit the information centres in each region. Inside the Gazetteer you'll find symbols for the places we think are extra special (they'll be in red on the maps). DON'T MISS: means just that. Other symbols are for:

 wildlife

 diving

 ballooning

 whale watching

 four-wheel-driving

 rodeos

 fishing

 surfing

 lookouts

The Great Australia Gazetteer™ has its own website, including links to the members of The Great Australia Partnership, with all the information you need to get out there and see Australia. So even if you can't surf a good Aussie break you can surf us on the web.

Kerry Davies
Senior Editor and Gazettist

www.australiagazetteer.com

10

Ernie's holiday tip #1

Life is for living.
Take a holiday.

NP3311

Too many hard-working Aussies have forgotten how to take a holiday. And all work and no play is no way to live. Taking a holiday in our beautiful country lets you unwind, reconnect with your family and helps you get in touch with your inner nice person again. An Aussie holiday is so easy too, because a host of delights are right there in your own backyard. History, lifestyles and the chance to discover the tastes of local fair from equally unique characters. So what are you waiting for? Put in that leave form, jump on our website and get out there.

See Australia proudly acknowledges Premium Sponsors Accor Asia Pacific and MasterCard International and Partners AAA Tourism, Avis, Captain Cook Cruises, Hertz, lastminute.com, Qantas and travel.com.au

Go on. Get out there.

www.seeaustralia.com.au

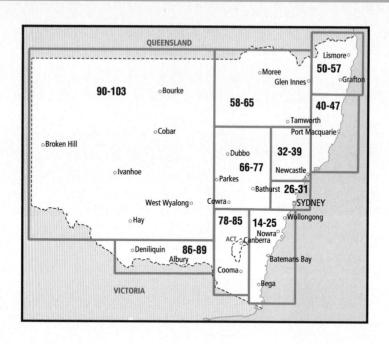

new sou

Rural and regional New South Wales is filled with landmarks that celebrate excellence, no matter what form it takes. This is a journey of discovery of the biggest, the smallest, the driest, the hottest, the wettest, the longest and the shortest of these landmarks.

You can surf at any one of the hundreds of beaches along the coastline, ski in an area of snow that is larger than Switzerland, wander through the farmland that separates the coast from the desert, or discover what it is about the colour and light of the desert that eventually brings Australians back to the land, even just to look.

th wales

Stretching from Eden to Bundeena, the South Coast and Illawarra regions contain many national and marine parks. Uncrowded beaches, top fishing, great surfing and outstanding bushwalking attract holiday-makers seeking an alternative to the more frequented holiday spots of the north. The Illawarra also serves as a respite close to southern Sydney, as well as a major economic zone for the state.

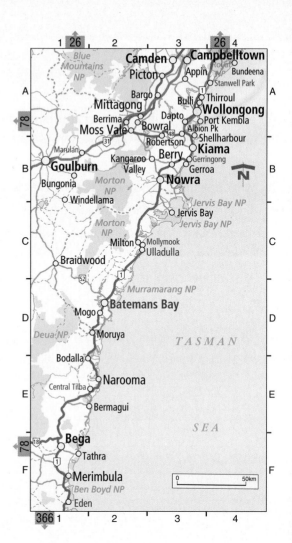

get off the beaten track

roam the south coast and illawarra

At **Albion Park** [B3] is the 1,059 ha **Macquarie Pass National Park**, a bush-walker's delight, with walking trails through untouched rainforest and abundant wildlife. Backpack camping is permitted as long as it is more than 1 km from any public access road.

The town of **Bargo** [A3], about 30 km north-east of Bowral, off the Hume Highway, is home to the Dingo Sanctuary (contact them on 02 4684 1156). The centre, on Arina Road, offers the opportunity to watch dingoes in a natural setting and is open Thursday to Monday. DingoFest is held each October. Activities include dingo parades and educational displays, and you can have yourself snapped with a dingo.

GO
RTESY OF
ONGA ZOO

 Near **Batemans Bay** [D2], at Pebbly Beach, on very hot days you are likely to see the resident kangaroos surfing on the beach, on the southern edge of **Murramarang National Park**, which also contains Pretty Beach and Depot Beach. The area is famous for its crayfish and oysters.

GAZETTEER

KANGAROO SALAD

This recipe comes from the Doncaster Inn, built about 1837 with convict-made bricks and boasting 33 rooms and a ballroom. The owner, Maria Badgery, sold the hotel to the Sisters of the Good Samaritan in 1879, who put the ballroom to use as a chapel. In 1907 the building was pulled down and the convent rebuilt, the new building being used as a boarding school until 1976, when it was deconsecrated. It has since been completely renovated as a guesthouse.

750 g kangaroo fillet
1 small red capsicum, seeded and sliced
1 small green capsicum, seeded and sliced
1 red onion, finely sliced
lettuce leaves
2 tbsp coriander, finely chopped, for garnish
2 tbsp mint, finely chopped, for garnish
cherry tomatoes, for garnish

DRESSING
1/3 cup lemon juice
2 garlic cloves, crushed
1 tbsp fish sauce
2 tsp sugar
chilli paste to taste

Preheat oven to 210°C. Sear meat to rare in a hot oiled pan, then roast in oven for a further 5 minutes. Top with capsicum and onion. Pour dressing on top and warm in oven for another 2 minutes. Remove meat from oven, then slice very thinly, arrange on lettuce leaves with capsicum and onion, pour dressing over and garnish with coriander, mint and tomatoes. Serves 6.

Daniel Villinger, BRAIDWOOD

BREAD IN A CAMP OVEN

This recipe comes from Moruya, the town where the stones of the granite piers and pylons of the Sydney Harbour Bridge were cut to size in a quarry and shipped to their destination. A camp oven can be as basic as a hole in the ground, hot coals and ashes and some bushes used as a wind break. Make sure the hole is deep enough that it can be covered and protected from the wind.

1 rounded tsp dry yeast
1 tbsp honey
1/4 cup milk, warmed
1 1/4 cups water
3 cups wholemeal plain flour
2 tbsp butter, melted
1 tsp salt

Stir the yeast and half the honey in half a cup of combined milk and water and let the mixture rise to fill the cup. In a large bowl, mix two cups of flour, the butter, salt and remaining honey, then add the risen yeast and the remaining cup of water. Knead in the third cup of flour. Form into a round or oblong shape on a baking tray, cover it with a cloth, and leave it to rise in a warm place for 30 minutes. Cook for 30 minutes in the camp oven, well bedded in ash and covered with hot ash. (Of course in the absence of the camp oven, you can bake in a preheated 190°C oven for 25–30 minutes.)

Von Klimpel
MORUYA

Bega [F1] began as a dairying centre in the 1850s; today 135 farms supply milk to the Bega Cooperative. To learn more about the history of the area and how cheese is made, visit the Heritage Centre, a reproduction of one of the early butter factory buildings. You can try the Bega range of products at the kiosk at Bega Cheese on Ridge Street, North Bega, open daily, 9 am to 5 pm.

Bermagui [E1], a rustic seaside port, is home to a thriving fishing fleet and is renowned as one of Australia's finest game and sport fishing centres, having been put squarely on the international angling map during the 1930s by the enthusiastic writing of cowboy novelist and adventurer, Zane Grey.

Bermagui and its coastal waters were also the setting for a large part of the movie *The Man Who Sued God*, starring Scottish comedian Billy Connolly. There are fishing tournaments from spring to autumn.

Berrima's [A2] Surveyor-General Inn on the old Hume Highway was built in 1834. Licensed in 1835, it claims to have the oldest continuously held licence in New South Wales. It has traded through renovations and even threatened demolition, a special Act of Parliament allowing its preservation.

Berry [B3] is known as the Town of Trees, a pretty country town set in rolling green hills, with the Cambewarra Ranges as a backdrop. The National Bank (1889) and the Court House (1891) are both architectural examples of the Victorian Classical Revival. The former English, Scottish and Australian Chartered Bank (1886) at 135 Queen Street, thought to be the only surviving building designed by William Wardell, is now a local history museum featuring local artefacts, photographs and archives (open Saturdays, Sundays and school holidays).

DON'T MISS: The pride of Berry's residents, their gardens, are open to the public only during the Berry Gardens Festival in October (phone 02 4464 1417).

Bodalla's [E1] St Edmunds and Our

Lady of the Assumption Catholic Church, on the corner of the Princes Highway and Potato Point Road, is the only timber shingle-walled church designed by leading 19th-century architect John Horbury Hunt. The church was purpose-built for the large number of Catholics on the estate of J Laidley Mort and his wife Mary. Its design is based on the little church in the grounds of the Convent des Dames Anglaise at Bruges, where Mary Mort had gone to school in 1859. Also a dairying centre, it could be said that Bodalla is famous for Mary and the baby cheeses.

Bowral's [A2] Bradman

Museum, opposite the legendary cricketer's childhood home, has memorabilia from the 18th to the 20th centuries. The oldest item there is an oak cricket bat from the 1750s.

In **Braidwood** [C1] is St Bede's Roman Catholic Church, erected in 1856 from local granite and noted for its large bell, whose fine tone may be heard on clear mornings at a distance of 15 km. At the southern extremity of Wallace Street is the

cemetery, which contains a large and distinctive monument to four 'special' constables killed in pursuit of local bushrangers Thomas and John Clarke in 1867. The constables, posing as surveyors, had been tracking the Clarke gang in the Jingera Range and were originally buried where they died. Later their

bodies were dug up and buried in the cemetery with a monument erected to their memory.

DON'T MISS: During the annual Airing of the Quilt, on the last weekend in November, quilts are displayed on the verandahs of Braidwood's Main Street and exhibited at the National Theatre.

On the Princes Highway in **Bulli** [A3] is what used to be called the Bulli Family Hotel (now the Heritage Hotel), which opened in 1889. This huge three-storey Victorian public house includes a turret that enabled the hotelier to see customers coming down treacherous Bulli Pass by coach.

The small community of **Bundeena** [A4] lies on the northern headland of the **Royal National Park** south of Sydney. The

160 sq km park was gazetted as a national park in 1879, making it the second oldest in the world, after Yellowstone in the United States. The 'Royal' tag was added after a visit by the queen in 1954. There's a lot to enjoy here: picturesque beaches, surfing, hang-gliding and bushwalking among the abundant native flora and fauna. The **Otford Lookout** offers spectacular views north along the rugged coastline of the park, south to Port Kembla where the massive Port Kembla smokestack is the dominant distant landmark and looking straight down to **Bulgo**, a most unusual coastal settlement. It is a tiny village of about 12 shacks with no road access, electricity, sewerage or reticulated water. The shacks are perched on a

rock shelf just above the high-water mark. All materials used to build and furnish them, including kerosene refrigerators, were skidded down the mountain or brought by boat.

Camden [A3] is

home to the largest koi breeder and dealer in the Southern Hemisphere, the Australian Koi Farm. Here Japanese koi carp are bred, with some 25,000 fish on display and for sale, including show champions. They are open from 9 am until 5 pm.

Campbelltown [A3] was the first

district to be settled outside Sydney, and many of its historic buildings still stand. Visit the Quondong Visitor Information Centre, housed in the original 1840s Catholic school.

The entire village of **Central Tilba** [E1], built from 1894 to 1919, is classified by the National Trust. Stay in the century-old postmaster's quarters, now the Two Story Bed & Breakfast. The historic town is on a signposted scenic route.

GAZETTEER

In **Dapto** [A3], remnants of an old railway line built in 1893 are still visible off Marshall Street and on the eastern side of Bong Bong Road. The 8 km line was built by the Illawarra Harbour and Land Corporation to run from Fleming's Mine in the escarpment to the lake in anticipation of the Lake Illawarra Harbour scheme. The scheme was dropped just after the railway opened—the official train ran on opening day but the line was never used again.

GAZETTEER

In **Eden** [F1], one of Twofold Bay's famous killer whales, 'Tom', was found dead in the bay in 1930. His skeleton has been preserved in the Killer Whale Museum at the corner of Imlay and Cocora Streets. A particular group of killer whales visited the area each year, using the south of the bay as their base for the season. Locals, recognising them by distinctive markings, gave them names and found them to be a great help in hunting and bringing other whales into the bay. The killer whales cooperated closely and intelligently with the local whalers. If they detected whales about, they would travel to the whaling station, make a great deal of noise, wait for the boats to launch, then lead them to the whales. The combination of killer whales and humans increased the certainty of a kill, ensuring a meal for the killer whales. They were fed almost exclusively on the lips and tongues of the whales; the whalers kept the blubber and anything else of use. North and south of Eden is **Ben Boyd National Park** and the small and delightful Bittangabee Bay. Tucked into the bush, just a short walk from the bay, are the stone ruins of a European-style building thought to pre-date the discovery of the east coast of Australia by Captain James Cook in 1770.

GAZETTEE

In **Gerringong** [B3], at the northern end of Seven Mile Beach, there is a memorial to pioneer aviator Charles Kingsford Smith—this is where he took off on his historic flight to New Zealand in the

GAZETTEER

Southern Cross in 1933. The Gerringong Hotel featured prominently in the Australian feature film *Mullet*, starring Ben Mendelsohn and Susie Porter, which in 2001 had its world premiere in the Gerringong Town Hall.

In **Gerroa** [B3], at the end of Stafford Street, is Black Head. The rock platform below (there are tracks from the carpark) has one of the best displays of fossils on the New South Wales coast. Breaking or removing the rocks is forbidden. Just lower your eyes and you will see exposed fossils.

The Old **Goulburn** [B1] Brewery on Bungonia Road is Australia's oldest surviving brewery, and was designed by ex-convict architect Francis Greenway. The building of the mill was begun in 1833, the castellated brewing tower and malt houses in 1840.

Small extensions were added later. Australia's oldest industrial complex, it includes a cooperage and a tobacco-curing kiln. The brewery makes its own ales, still using old methods and recipes and is open daily from 11 am (02 4821 6071). If you were sauntering in the countryside south-east of Goulburn in 1924 you might have witnessed the first Australian Motorcycle Grand Prix. It was four laps of a long triangular course—at least 90 km. It began on the outskirts of Goulburn, ran to **Windellama**, across to **Bungonia** and back. Outside Goulburn, the waters of **Pejar Dam**, on the Wollondilly River, have a

reputation for producing some of the state's largest trout. The fishing here is rarely easy, but for those anglers willing to invest the necessary time and effort, the rewards can be outstanding.

Hyams Beach on **Jervis Bay** [C3] is said to have the whitest sand in the world. Jervis Bay is one of the largest and best anchorages on the east coast—and one of the most pristine. The fishing and diving are

OYSTERS MAE WEST

Along the Illawarra coast numerous river inlets make perfect habitats for oysters to grow. This recipe is a local variation on the usual oysters mornay.

2–3 cloves garlic, crushed	salt and pepper to taste
1 tbsp butter	12 oysters on the shell
1 tbsp plain flour	
1 cup milk	1 sheet puff pastry
3 tbsp cheddar cheese, grated	1 egg, lightly beaten

Preheat oven to 190°C. Sauté garlic in butter over low heat for 1 minute. Add flour and cook for 2–3 minutes, stirring. Slowly add milk, a little at a time. Stir constantly, until it becomes a thick sauce. Add 2 tbsp cheese and salt and pepper. Allow to cool in the fridge. Top oysters with the chilled sauce and then with the remaining cheese. Cut pastry sheet into 12 pieces and place a piece over each oyster. Press the pastry around the top of the oyster shell and remove excess. Glaze with a little beaten egg and bake for 10–15 minutes. Serves 2.

Flicks Cinema Restaurant, KALARU (via Tathra)

superb as the bay, enfolded in the great pincer-like arms of its northern and southern headlands, juts out toward the 50-fathom line, the Continental Shelf and the waters of the East Australian current. There are a number of marine preservation zones within and adjacent to the bay. **Lake Wollumboola**, near Jervis Bay, is the smelliest lake in New South Wales. Research into the cause of the bad smell has found that the lake's sediments contain extremely high levels of hydrogen sulphide, commonly referred to as rotten egg gas.

Kangaroo Valley's [B3]

magnificent stone Hampden Bridge opened in 1898, making it the oldest suspension bridge in the country. It spans the Kangaroo River on the main road from Kangaroo Valley north-west to Moss Vale. It has castellated towers at the ends to support the cables. The bridge was named for then Governor of New South Wales Lord Hampden.

Kiama [B3] has two blow-

holes. The Big Blowhole can shoot spray 60 m into the air, depending on the pressure of the swell in its underwater tunnel; erosion of the tunnel mouth has made its performance less than reliable. Two kilometres south is the Little Blowhole. It shoots a thin jet of water up to 30 m, but far more consistently. In the 1840s chains were fixed to the

rocks on either side of **Black Beach** to provide secure moorings. The iron post that functioned as an anchor pin for the securing chain is Kiama's oldest surviving historic artefact. It can be seen, still with some chain remnants, from the concrete walkway on the north-western side of the harbour. On the northern side of **Bombo Headland** is 'The Boneyard', where basalt quarrying has left a legacy of remarkable hexagonal basalt columns. The site is protected by a permanent conservation order.

Marulan [B2] is the only town

in the world situated on the 150° meridian. Here you are in the exact middle of the Eastern Standard Time zone, a place where the sun rises at 6 am and sets at 6 pm precisely every equinox.

GAZETTEER

Merimbula's [F1] Old School

Museum was built as a school in 1874 and operated as such until 1946. The local minister, the Reverend Mr Thom, was married to Henry Parkes's daughter, and it was her influence over her father that ensured that the school was built. Merimbula Wharf is a popular diving spot because of its easy access and the diversity of fish and plant life.

Other shore dives include Bar Beach, Short Point, Tathra Wharf, Kianinny Bay and Ross Bay. Just south of Merimbula off Haycock Rock is an impressive shipwreck. The *Empire Gladstone* ran aground here on 5 September 1950 and now lies in 10–12 m of water. Divers can explore the wreckage, now transformed into a spectacular artificial reef. For information call Merimbula Divers Lodge on 02 6495 3611.

At **Milton** [C2] Donovan's Cottage Gallery features works from local artists, including paintings, photography, hand-blown glass, woodturning and furniture. The cottage, built in the early 1870s, was saved from demolition by shipwright and carpenter Murray Pollock, whose restoration of the cottage featured on national television in 2000. It's open 10 am to 4 pm.

DON'T MISS: Milton's Settlers Fair is on the October long weekend, when the town revives its pioneer spirit and celebrates Milton's agricultural and heritage significance.

Visit **Mittagong** [A2] in spring and autumn. In spring the blossoms will be out on Cherry Tree Walk, a memorial planted in honour of those who served and died in Vietnam. The main street of Mittagong comes alive for the Tulip Time Street Festival held each year in late September or early October. For details phone 02 4861 3133. The gardens of Kennerton Green, a series of outdoor 'rooms' with an 1860s cottage at their centre, are particularly beautiful in autumn. Some of the trees date back 100 years.

At **Mogo** [D2] it is still possible for fossickers to pick up the odd speck of gold from an official fossicking area on the Tomago River. Mogo had its heyday as a goldrush town in the late 1850s, but the gold was gone within 30 years and the town slipped into gentle obscurity. All that's left of the halcyon days is an underground gold mine, which is open for inspection (phone 02 4474 2123).

Mollymook's [C2] name is thought to be derived from the mollymawk albatross. The area's GAZETTEER first settlers built a house called Molly Moke in 1859, at today's Garside Road. Mollymook is a popular family holiday spot, with something for everyone it

CRUNCHY PECAN CAKE

Employees of Woolworths, nationwide, recently took part in a bake-off to select a recipe to be produced in the company's bakery and sold through their stores. The winning entry, a family favourite, is delicious as an afternoon tea cake or as a winter dessert served with custard or a caramel sauce.

BUTTERCAKE	FILLING
250 g butter	1 cup pecan nuts,
1 tsp vanilla	finely chopped
essence	2 tbsp brown sugar
¾ cup castor	½ tsp cinnamon
sugar	¼ cup coconut
2 eggs	
170 ml sour cream	**CRUNCHY TOPPING**
130 ml milk	1 cup pecan nuts,
1½ cups plain flour	finely chopped
½ cup self-raising	2 tbsp brown sugar
flour	½ tsp cinnamon
1 tsp bicarbonate	50 gm butter
of soda	2 tbsp self-raising
	flour
	¼ cup coconut

Preheat oven to 150°C (fan-forced). Grease a 20 cm round cake pan. Cream butter, vanilla essence and sugar in small bowl until light and fluffy, then beat in eggs one at a time until combined. Transfer mixture to large bowl, stir in sour cream, milk, then sifted flours and bicarbonate of soda. Spread half the mixture into prepared pan, sprinkle with combined filling ingredients. Spread remaining cake mixture evenly on top. Combine topping ingredients and sprinkle over. Bake for 1 hour and 40 minutes. Let the cake stand for 5 minutes before turning out and cooling on wire rack.

Vicki Geyer, KELLYVILLE

seems. The large beach caters for the surfers and anglers. You might even spot a whale in migration, usually around June, from the bay at Mollymook. Bogey Hole is a protective ring of rocks on the headland, providing a safe tidal pool for children to play in. There are also two golf courses: a 9-hole beachside course and the 18-hole championship Hilltop course, for more serious golfers. The fairways are surrounded by trees and there are also plenty of waterways to make this course challenging.

DON'T MISS: Mollymook, Milton and Ulladulla each host events in the Tabula Rasa Contemporary Arts Festival,

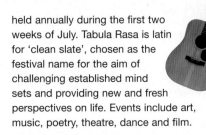

held annually during the first two weeks of July. Tabula Rasa is latin for 'clean slate', chosen as the festival name for the aim of challenging established mind sets and providing new and fresh perspectives on life. Events include art, music, poetry, theatre, dance and film.

Moruya [D2] is a good base for exploring **Deua National Park**, the largest

in the south-east region. This scenic area provides fantastic walking with pockets of wilderness and easy canoeing trips along the Deua River, where you can camp. For those with a 4WD, camping at secluded Bendethera is well worth it (access via the Dampier Mountain fire trail, off

BARBECUE CHILLI SEAFOOD

All along the south coast you'll find an abundance of both seafood and idyllic locations for a barbecue. For this recipe you might want to stop in Tathra to sample the products of the Tathra Beach Pickle Factory, including chilli seasoning, chilli oil, coriander and chilli jam and preserved lime.

1½ tbsp chilli seasoning or cajun seasoning
1 tbsp chilli oil
2 tbsp olive oil
3 tbsp lemon juice
1 tbsp garlic, finely chopped
salt and pepper to taste
½ kg baby octopus, cleaned
½ kg green prawns, peeled

bamboo skewers
fresh coriander leaves, for garnish
rocket or baby spinach leaves
4 cups cooked jasmine rice
preserved lime wedges
coriander and chilli jam

Mix seasoning, oils, lemon juice, garlic, salt and pepper. Marinate seafood for 1 hour. Soak skewers in water for 30 minutes. Thread 3 or 4 prawns and some octopus on each skewer and barbecue briefly over hot coals (about 1 minute per side). Do not overcook—the seafood will toughen. Serve seafood on fresh rocket or spinach leaves and rice. Garnish with lime wedges and coriander and chilli jam. Decorate plates with a few drops of chilli oil. Serves 4.

Tathra Beach Pickle Factory, TATHRA

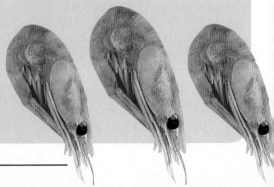

Snowball Road, or via Western Boundary and Sugarloaf Roads off the Princess Highway).

Outside **Moss Vale** [A2], on Meryla Road, Indigo Jones, one of Australia's early weather forecasters, is commemorated in a lookout. From a small hut on what is now The Pines pastoral property he forecast sunspots in the southern highlands. A pine believed to have been planted by Jones remains on the property today but all that's left of his hut is one wall dating back to the 1890s. The property has self-contained cottages for rent (phone 02 4868 3523).

DON'T MISS: Moss Vale Golf Course is a world-class championship course regarded as one of the state's prettiest. Accommodation is available at Dormie House, right on the golf course.

At Wagonga Head, **Narooma** [E2], near the mouth of the river is Australia Rock, which features a naturally occurring hole with an uncanny resemblance to the map of Australia (minus Tasmania).

To the west of **Nowra** [B3] 'Bundanon' is a historic two-storey sandstone homestead built in 1866. It is situated on 400 ha of land next to the Shoalhaven River and was the home and studio of noted painter Arthur Boyd for many years. Along with the gardens, grounds, some antique furniture, the studio and some artworks, it was recently given to the Australian people by Arthur and Yvonne Boyd. It is open on Sundays. Nearby at Riversdale is the new Arthur and Yvonne Boyd Education Centre, designed by renowned architect Glenn Murcutt. Tours

are available by appointment (call Bundanon on 02 4423 0433).

Historic **Picton** [A3], in the foothills of the southern highlands, dates back to the 1860s. Find out the background of some of the town's pioneers on a tour of the old section of the Upper Picton Cemetery. One of them was the pirate and convict Antonio Manolis, the first Greek settler in New South Wales. If you believe in the supernatural, a two-hour walk around the town at night visits sites of reported ghost sightings.

Port Kembla [A3] has a tour with a difference. The integrated steelmaking plant, one of the most modern and efficient in the world, can be inspected up close in tours run by Australia's Industry World. They are based at the visitors' centre, at the main gate of the plant.

DON'T MISS: The area around **Coomaditchie Lagoon**, between Lake Illawarra and Port Kembla Beach, was used by the local Aboriginal community, who shared their knowledge of bush tucker in a guided walk. Since then fires have swept through, destroying some of the vegetation. It is now part of a regeneration project run by volunteers in conjunction with BHP. Call Coomaditchie United Aboriginal Corporation (02 4274 7477) for information.

The lush green hills of **Robertson** [B3] provided the idyllic setting for *Babe*, the film about a talking pig who saves the farm. No special effects were needed to paint the countryside, which is every bit as beautiful as it was on screen. Potatoes are also important in Robertson, celebrated by the Big Potato on the main street.

Shellharbour [A3] is a

great spot for both fishing and surfing. Launch a boat in the harbour or try fishing at the popular Windang Bridge at the mouth of Lake Illawarra a few kilometres from Shellharbour at **Warilla**. There are bream, blackfish and flathead, and prawns in the summer months.

Stanwell Park [A4] was the site

of the world's first successful attempt at flight. In 1894 Lawrence Hargrave was lifted 5 m above the beach here on a seat attached to a string of four tethered box kites. Nine years later America's Wright Brothers applied Hargrave's theories to their own successful, powered, sustained and controlled aircraft flight at Kittyhawk. **Bald Hill Lookout** is now a major international hang-gliding spot with a memorial to Hargrave there.

Tathra [F1] wharf, built in 1868, is the

only remaining coastal steamer wharf in New South Wales and one of only six historic timber wharves listed on the Register of the National Estate. Once the wharf was built the town replaced Merimbula as the port for Bega. Tathra got its wharf before its residents. They didn't arrive until 1876.

Thirroul [A3], one of Wollongong's

northern suburbs, was once the residence of novelist DH Lawrence, who lived at 3 Craig Street in the California-style mission bunga-low 'Wyewurk'. It was here that Lawrence lived from May to August 1922 and wrote most of the novel *Kangaroo*, in which the town based on Wollongong was called 'Wollona'. The house is not open for inspec-tion. North of Thirroul, Austinmer Beach is one of the top surfing beaches along this coastline, which offers 17 surf beaches and numerous headlands.

DON'T MISS: Thirroul Seaside and Arts Festival is on the first weekend in April, a two-day spectacular of visual and performing arts as well as beach and surf events, camel rides, helicopter rides and much more (phone 02 4267 4700).

Ulladulla [C2] has some of the

best fishing, diving and surfing spots along the south coast. Deep-sea fishing is available through the many different boat charters. Experience the history of the Shoalhaven from an Aboriginal perspective on One Track For All, a trail on the northern headland of Ulladulla Harbour. Each carving or painting along the 2 km track tells a story of how the development of the timber and the fishing industries affected the local Aboriginal people. The track includes four lookouts with fantastic views of the coast and harbour. The track starts at the end of Dolphin Street on the north side of the harbour.

DON'T MISS: The Blessing of the Fleet at Ulladulla at Easter is an old Italian tradition originating in Sicily that has been continued by the Italian fishermen who settled in Ulladulla. The first ceremony took place in 1956

and it now attracts about 80,000 people. The festival also includes the Fleet Princess Ball, held two weeks before the blessing ceremony, yacht races, a breakfast by the harbour and lantern parades.

Wollongong [A3] is home to the

largest Buddhist temple in the Southern Hemisphere. Dominating Nan Tien is an eight-storey pagoda containing three shrines lined with more than 10,000 Buddhas. The temple offers meditation retreats, vegetarian cooking classes, tai chi courses and lessons on Buddhism. A new museum features an indoor river, and one of the displays is a single strand of human hair on which an elderly Taiwanese Buddhist has engraved 28 words using a sharpened grain of rice.

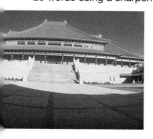

Wollongong is also the staging point for offshore observation of the world's largest array of albatrosses. The giant seabirds are attracted by cuttlefish, which breed at depths of up to 20 fathoms (a fathom is 1.83 m) within 10 km of the Illawarra coast. After breeding, the cuttlefish die and float to the surface, providing a smorgasbord for the annual albatross inshore migratory convention through July and August. Varieties of seabird can be seen from Hill 60 in Port Kembla during the albatross migratory season, and in rookeries on the Five Islands off Port Kembla during the seabird and little penguin breeding season. The giant albatrosses stay just off the Wollongong coast until November/December, and can also be viewed during research and banding trips. Call the Southern Oceans Seabird Study Association on 02 4271 6004.

DON'T MISS: Viva La Gong is an annual 10-day celebration of cultural diversity and creative innovation in various locations around Wollongong in late September (phone 02 4227 7389). You can go to market four days a week in Wollongong. Wollongong Markets are held every Thursday and Saturday at Harbour Street. Gipps Street Markets are Fridays, Saturdays and Sundays.

Diary of Events

Town	Event	Date	Contact
Bargo	DingoFest	October	02 4684 1156
Berry	Gardens Festival	October, 3rd weekend	02 4464 1417
Braidwood	Airing of the Quilt	November, last weekend	02 4842 2626
Merimbula	Jazz Festival	June	0417 445 011
Milton	Settlers Fair	October long weekend	02 4454 1916
Mittagong	Tulip Time Street Festival	September	02 4861 3133
Mollymook	Tabula Rasa Contemporary Arts Festival	July, 1st 2 weeks	02 4454 1916
Moruya	Deue River Bush Races	June	02 4478 8582
	Jazz Festival	October	02 4474 4462
Nowra	Shoalhaven Stamp Fair	July	02 4421 4624
Thirroul	Seaside and Arts Festival	April, 1st weekend	02 4267 4700
Ulladulla	The Blessing of the Fleet	Easter	02 4454 1975
	Food and Wine Festival	August, 3rd weekend	02 4455 4505
	Scrabble Competition	May, last weekend	02 4455 1269
Wollongong	Viva La Gong	September	02 4227 7389

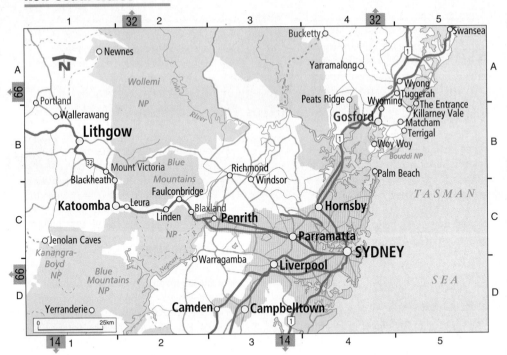

From the Blue Mountains to the Central Coast is a vast array of scenic delights. The towns and villages of the Blue Mountains are strung through a vast bushland of cliffs, gorges, waterfalls and rivers. Toward the coast an unspoilt, timbered hinterland gives way to pristine beaches.

get off the beaten track

cross the blue mountains
to the central coast

Blackheath

Blackheath [B1], the highest town in the Blue Mountains, was named twice by Governor Macquarie within 16 days. Passing through on his way to Bathurst in 1815 he named the place Hounslow. Returning, he renamed it Black-Heath, because of its charred, open, wild appearance.

Blaxland

Blaxland [C2] is the site of Australia's second-oldest stone arch bridge, Lennox Bridge, completed in 1833. To get to the bridge leave the highway at McDonald's in Blaxland and take Mitchell's Pass Road.

GAZETTEER

Bucketty

Bucketty's [A4] Koolang Observatory (turn off the motorway toward Peats Ridge) has the largest privately owned public telescope in Australia. Guided tours (30 or 45 minutes) are conducted during the day to study the sun, with longer sessions at night when the sky is more interesting (phone 02 4998 8216).

GAZETTEER

Faulconbridge

In **Faulconbridge** [C2] Cemetery is the grave of the 'Father of Federation', Sir Henry Parkes, who died in 1896.

Gosford

Gosford's [B4] Forest of Tranquillity hosts the Firefly Festival from mid-November to mid-December. It offers a chance to see hundreds of these glowing yellow-green, enchanting insects. It runs from 6 pm to 8 pm, Fridays to Sundays. Upon a rock in **Kendalls Glen**, west of Gosford, are the

INDIAN LAMB CURRY

In the Central Coast hinterland, the road winds through beautiful forests and valleys. One of the gems of the highlands, Yarramalong has some of the oldest buildings in the shire. Among the area's frequent inhabitants is the Laws family. This is a favourite recipe of Caroline Laws, which she loves to cook when at their Yarramalong property.

1 kg lamb fillet	2 tbsp OSEM
2 to 3 brown	chicken soup
onions, chopped	seasoning mix
2 tbsp oil	1 stick cinnamon
2 tbsp vindaloo	2 star-anise
curry paste (or	12 curry leaves
more to taste)	1 tbsp red wine
1 x 440 g can	vinegar
peeled tomatoes	salt to taste

Cut lamb into cubes, trimming all fat. Fry onions in oil until soft and transparent. Put to one side. Brown lamb in the remaining oil. Add curry paste and cook for a minute or two until aromatic. Add onions and stir into lamb and curry paste. Add peeled tomatoes. Cover with water and add chicken soup seasoning mix (or chicken stock if seasoning mix is unavailable). Add cinnamon, star-anise, curry leaves and red wine vinegar. Simmer gently for one hour, or until tender. Note: This is best cooked the day before, removing all fat when cold, then reheating. Serves 6.

Caroline Laws, YARRAMALONG

carved initials of Henry Kendall, one of Australia's best-known 19th-century poets, at a spot that allegedly inspired some of his poetry. Turn off the Pacific Highway at Coorumbine Creek, park and follow the creek west until you reach

GAZETTEER

NSW

the rock (a 10–15 minute walk). At **Wyoming**, beside the Pacific Highway in Gosford's northern precinct is the grave of Frederick Hely, a Superintendent of Convicts in New South Wales in the 1830s. At that time, he owned a large amount of land here. A government township was laid out at the head of Brisbane Water, to be called

Point Frederick in honour of Hely, who died in 1836, but Governor Gipps, who approved the town plan, insisted that it be changed to honour his friend the Earl of Gosford.

Jenolan Caves [C1] are the best

known limestone caves in Australia, though not the biggest—the Nullarbor's Abrakurrie Cave is bigger. Jenolan Caves do feature two of Australia's biggest holes—the Bottomless Pit and the Devil's Coachhouse—and largest open cave, the Grand Arch. Nearby are the clifftops of Kanangra Walls, affording spectacular views over **Kanangra Boyd National Park**.

Katoomba's

[C1] scenic railway is the steepest in the world—it is 415 m long, dropping 178 m into the Jamieson Valley (the grade is at times as steep as 52 per cent). The railway was originally built to haul coal and coalminers up and down the cliff face. That colliery closed in 1895. In the 1920s Katoomba Colliery was back in business and in 1930 began using their coal skip (a container attached to a crane or cable) to give bushwalkers and tourists the ride of their lives.

 DON'T MISS: The Winter Magic Festival is held on the weekend closest to 21 June, the winter solstice.

Olympian Parade in **Leura** [C2] is home to the historic art deco mansion Leuralla, which now contains Australia's biggest collection of toys. Leuralla is a private home owned by the Evatt family, who began the

NUTELLA CREAM CHOCOLATE CUPS WITH STRAWBERRIES

Lithgow is the home of Ferrero, makers of fine chocolate, as well as Nutella (that magical hazlenut spread) and Tic Tacs. This is a no-fuss dessert with lots of eye appeal.

2 tbsp Nutella
300 ml cream
6 chocolate cups
1 punnet strawberries, hulled

Combine Nutella and cream in a bowl and beat with an electric mixer until stiff. Spoon mixture into chocolate cups and top with strawberries and a little shaved chocolate if desired. Note: Chocolate cups are available from some supermarkets and specialty food stores. Serves 6.

Jodie Rayner, LITHGOW

collection 17 years ago. The Leuralla Toy and Railway Museum also includes a large number of model railway exhibits.

Linden [C2] was

once called 17 Mile Hollow—this referred to its distance from Emu Plains. Bulls Camp was known as 18 Mile Hollow and Woodford was 20 Mile Hollow. Handy to know if you're pacing yourself.

Around 30 km north of **Lithgow** [B1] is the Glow Worm Tunnel, on the Glow Worm Tunnel Road in the Wollemi National Park. The hand-tooled tunnel was the former rail link down to the Newnes oil shale works. You can still see the pick marks and the old rail line as you walk through the tunnel. Remember to take a torch! The tunnel is a 45-minute drive from Lithgow's Zig Zag Railway, a masterpiece of 19th-century engineering. A series of cuttings, embankments and viaducts were cut into the western escarpment of the Blue Mountains to allow the rail line access to the rich western plains. Now the same hair-raising journey can be taken by steam train enthusiasts. Two well-established man-made lakes close to Lithgow—Lake Wallace at **Wallerawang** and Lake Lyall via **Donnybrook**—offer excellent trout fishing at other times, as does the newer Porters Creek, to the north-west of Lithgow. The Lithgow Workmen's Club, on Tank Street in Lithgow, is the oldest registered club in Australia. Blast Furnace Park, off Inch Street, contains the only surviving relics of Australia's first modern iron and steel industry.

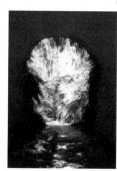

William Sandford opened it in 1886 and was awarded a contract to supply iron and steel for the NSW government in 1907. It continued to produce large quantities of iron until 1928.

In **Matcham** [B5], at the Ken Duncan Gallery, you might see a few images familiar from calendars and posters, especially of the northern beaches. This is the largest privately owned collection of his photographs.

At **Mount Victoria** [B1] is the Toll Keeper's Cottage, built in 1848. Each coach with springs that passed along the road was required to pay one shilling and six pence. Heavy vehicles were not charged because it was believed they helped crush the loose stones.

GAZETTEER

The old **Newnes** [A1] shale works features 24 dome-shaped ovens set back-to-back, in two rows of 12. They are one of only two remaining sets of coke ovens in New South Wales shale oil plants. Other ancient-looking remains of the works are litterered through the surrounding bush. Newnes nestles on the edge of **Wollemi National Park**, a wilderness of almost 5,000 sq km, with no roads or tracks. What it does have is one of the world's rarest species of pine tree, belonging to a genus of plants previously known only as fossils. The genus dates back 150 million years; only 43 adult trees have ever been seen, all here in three small stands. Nobody knows how old the pines at Wollemi really are, but estimates range from 500 to 1,000 years. Although the original stands are closed to public access, you can see young Wollemi pines at the **Mount Tomah Botanical Garden**, the cool-climate garden of the Royal Botanic Gardens, Sydney, on

Bells Line of Road, 12 km west of Bilpin, open 10 am to 4 pm daily.

Portland [A1], about 20 km north-west of Lithgow, had the first cement-making kilns west of the Blue Mountains. They were built in the early 1890s and are subject to a preservation order. The bottle kilns are at the northern edge of the Blue Circle Southern Cement Works—turn north off Laurie Street into Kiln Street, which becomes Carlon Road. **Mount Piper** Power Station, 5 km east of Portland, has an energy expo centre including machines that allow you to generate your own electricity.

GAZETTEER

The bridges at ## Swansea [A5] provide good diving sites, especially for a drift dive, the best time being low tide. Night dives are also possible here but make sure you take a torch. Remains of the second bridge provide old pipes that now house various marine inhabitants. Visibility varies from 0 to 15 m.

Terrigal's [B5] beach has excellent diving, accessible from the shore. Sites include Terrigal Cave and the Pinnacle. About 15 km north of Terrigal is another dive site, Sweep City, known for its large schools of fish.

Pelican feeding at ## The Entrance [B5] began about 20 years ago when staff at a waterfront fish and chip shop threw scraps to the birds when business closed for the day. The pelicans became so tame that if the staff were late the pelicans would cross the road to the shop to be fed. The birds are now fed punctually, and checked for any injuries, at 3.30 pm at the Waterfront. There's commentary about

the pelicans and other birdlife in the area. Nearby, the Waterfront Markets are held every Saturday. It's not just people who thrive in the Central Coast's mild climate. Between The Entrance and Tuggerah you will come to **Killarney Vale**, which has the light alluvial soils needed for growing the high-quality potatoes that Smith's Crisps look for.

DON'T MISS: The Scarecrow Competition in September at The Entrance Waterfront Memorial Park. Entrants compete for the best-dressed scarecrow. Call 02 4333 5377 for details.

The ## Tuggerah [A5] Lakes Mardi Gras Festival is one of the longest-running events in New South Wales. Buy a duck in the Ducks for Bucks race and cheer your choice across the lake—the first one who feels like crossing the line is the winner. It's held each year on the first weekend in December at The Entrance foreshore, phone 02 4333 5377.

Warragamba Dam [D2] is one of the largest domestic supply dams in the world. The dam itself is 351 m long, 142 m high, 104 m thick at the base and 8.5 m thick near the top, impounding 2,057,000 megalitres, almost four times the capacity of Sydney Harbour (a measurement colloquially known as Sydharbs) and providing a 7,500 ha lake.

Woy Woy's [B4] tunnel used 10 million bricks in its construction—when the railway arrived in 1889 they were unloaded at Brickwharf Road, then shipped along a rail line to the construction camp at the tip of Woy Woy Peninsula. The 1,793 m rail tunnel has long been known as the longest in Australia, though the Sydney Airport rail tunnel may now vie for the title.

NSW

The **Wyong** [A5] courthouse foundation stone was laid by then New South Wales Minister for Justice Thomas John Ley in 1924. A year later he won the federal seat of Barton when his opponent mysteriously disappeared after accusing Ley of attempting to bribe him. Three years later another adversary who had threatened Ley with legal action was found dead—at the foot of a cliff in Sydney. Another of Ley's associates disappeared on his way to Newcastle. The decrease in the population surrounding Ley had some impact on his re-election chances—he lost his seat in the 1928 election. He then went to England, had some involvement in the black market during World War II and was eventually found guilty of murder in 1947. Four months later he died in Broadmoor, a British asylum for the criminally insane.

 DON'T MISS: On the lawn of the Alison Homestead Museum in Cape Road, West Wyong, are two enormous anchors salvaged from the wreck of the *Suffolk*, washed ashore on Tuggerah Beach during a violent storm in 1859.

Yarramalong [A4] Macadamia Nut Farm is the largest plantation this far south. The Macadamia Café has plenty of samples and a great view of the Yarramalong Valley.

The ghost town of **Yerranderie** [D1], was bought lock, stock and barrel 30 years ago by conservationist Valerie Lhuede, who has since worked on restoring the old silver-mining town to its former glory.

A suit of clothes made by the town's original tailor, Gallipoli veteran Slippery Norris, is on display. Slippery's false teeth are in the pocket. Yerranderie is deep in the southern section of the Blue Mountains National Park, just over two hours from Oberon on the Oberon–Colong Stock Route, a dirt track usually suitable for conventional vehicles, though you'll need a 4WD if it's wet.

Diary of Events

Town	Event	Date	Contact
Blackheath	Blue Mountains Fine Food and Wine Festival	May	02 4787 6999
	Rhododendron Festival	November	02 4787 8695
Gosford	Firefly Festival at the Forest of Tranquillity	Nov/Dec	02 4362 1855
Katoomba	Winter Magic Festival	June	02 4782 5257
	Blue Mountains Music Festival	March	1800 651 322
Leura	Gardens Festival	October	02 4757 4043
The Entrance	Tuggerah Lakes Festival	December, 2nd weekend	02 4333 5377
	Scarecrow Competition	September	02 4333 5377

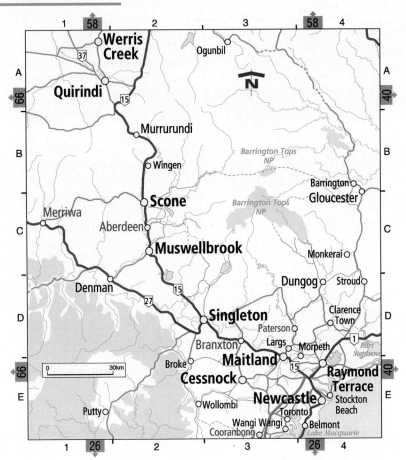

The Hunter's rich soil has attracted winemakers since the early days. The region is steeped in history, and towns like Maitland, Morpeth and Newcastle are noted for their 19th-century elegance and charm.

get off the beaten track

enjoy the hunter

Aberdeen

Aberdeen [C2] is the birthplace of Australia's legendary cattle dog, the blue heeler. The original crossbreed was a

dingo with a Northumberland blue merle drover's dog. Australia's oldest remaining steam mill, built around 1840, still stands at Aberdeen, on Rouchel Road.

GAZETTEER

DON'T MISS: The Highland Games, over the first weekend in July, are the culmination of a week-long celebration of all things Scottish, starting with International Tartan Day on 1 July. This is celebrated by Scots worldwide to mark the lifting of a 36-year ban on the wearing of tartan (among other Scottish traditions) imposed after the loss of a battle at Culloden in 1746. The

Games include tug-o-war, the 'best set of legs' competition (for both men and women), haggis hurling, egg throwing and the kilted dash (a three-legged race).

To the west of **Barrington** [B4] are the two sections of the **Barrington Tops National Park**. On Dilgry Circuit near the junction of Dilgry Circuit Road and Barrington Tops Forest Road there is a signpost to 'The Rock'. This amazing formation is known locally as Phallus Rock or Cock Rock, for obvious reasons. There is a series of walking trails detailed in a brochure available from Dungog Visitors' Centre (call 02 4992 2212). Follow the Allyn River Rainforest Trail to see

COCKFIGHTER'S LEGENDARY LEG OF LAMB

In the early 1820s Governor Macquarie sent an expedition to establish an overland route to the Hunter Valley. As the travellers were crossing Wollombi Brook the lead horse, named Cockfighter, became bogged and drowned, giving birth to the legend of Cockfighter's Ghost. In 1994 David Clarke acquired property at Wollombi Brook, naming it after that phantom horse. He is now proprietor of Cockfighter's Ghost wines.

1 x 2 kg leg of lamb
2 garlic cloves, cut into slivers
1 tbsp salt
1 tbsp pepper
2 red onions, peeled and roughly chopped

5 medium ripe peaches, peeled and chopped (or 1 large can peach halves in natural juice)
1 bottle Cockfighter's Shiraz

Preheat oven to 220°C. Pierce leg in about 8 places and insert slivers of garlic. Cover leg generously with salt and pepper. Place leg in a baking dish, scatter red onions and peaches in the dish and pour in half the bottle of shiraz. Bake for 30 minutes at 220°C, then 1 hour at 190°C. Check every 30 minutes, and add extra wine or water if needed. Remove leg and leave to stand on a plate for 30 minutes. Meanwhile, place baking dish with remaining juices on a hotplate and add rest of wine (and a little water if sauce is becoming dry). Reduce slightly, stir and simmer (add juices from standing lamb). Slice lamb and serve on platter topped with sauce. Serves 6.

Cockfighter's Ghost & Poole's Rock Vineyards, BROKE

the largest small-leafed fig tree in New South Wales—50 m high with a crown of 40 m across—and the largest river oak in the state—at 53 m tall. The Barrington Tops are an aeroplane graveyard—many have gone down here and never been found again.

SMOKED FISH

Smoked fish is considered a delicacy, and the procedure is not as difficult as you might think. Following is how to hot smoke a fish using a stove (gas or electric). Once the fish is smoked it should be kept refrigerated and treated as a perishable product. Some prized fish for smoking are trout, Atlantic salmon and tuna.

2 baking trays of equal size
1 cake cooling rack
sawdust or woodchips
fish
oil for basting
herbs and spices (optional)

Sprinkle a layer of sawdust over the bottom of the baking tray, sit the rack on the sawdust and lay the fish on the rack. Brush the fish with oil. Put the other baking tray upside down on top and place this little smokehouse over a gentle flame or electric hotplate. To maintain a steady source of smoke, the heat needs to be a low 80–90°C. The smoking process can take 30–60 minutes, depending on the size of the fish. Fish should feel firm to touch. Oil can be brushed on several times during the process to maintain moisture in a dry-fleshed fish. Herbs and spices in small quantities can be added to the smoking wood to impart flavour.

The Fish Shed,
MURRURUNDI

The area that is now **Belmont** [E4], on the eastern side of Lake Macquarie, was the site of an Aboriginal mission, established in 1826 by the Reverend Lancelot Threlkeld. He reportedly had a high regard for the Aboriginal people, learning their language in order to translate the scriptures for them (an early landmark in Aboriginal studies). The mission house overlooked Belmont Bay and was connected to Newcastle by a rough dray track. Threlkeld also started the first coal mine around the lake, at Coal Point, in about 1840. Cane Point, in Belmont South, is a small peninsula jutting into the lake, with a caravan park, boat ramp and pleasant views of the lake. Hire a boat and go fishing for tailor, bream, whiting and flathead, plentiful in summer, along with the odd blue swimmer crab. In winter it'll be mainly bream, some mullet, tailor and garfish.

Near **Branxton** [D3], in Dalwood, the Wyndham family settled in 1828, planting vineyards on the bank of the Hunter River.

GAZETTEER

The family still has what are among the oldest surviving records of farming in Australia. George Wyndham built a house of stone with Doric columns, inspired by his visit to Italy a few years earlier. Wyndham Estate today is located at 700 Dalwood Road, near the corner of Branxton Road and the New England Highway.

DON'T MISS: Enjoy the vintage while being entertained with Opera in the Vineyards at Dalwood Wyndham Estate every October. A 'feature' event of the Hunter, you'll need to book (for more information phone 1800 675 875).

In **Cessnock** [E3], the memorial to the Bellbird mining disaster stands opposite the former site of the Bellbird Colliery, at the corner of Wollombi Road and Kendall Street.

Here on 1 September 1923 explosions and fires underground killed 20 men and their horses. Also on this corner is a signpost to The Lookout, the starting point for the Great North Walk, extending 190 km to Sydney. Cessnock also has a monument to the Rothbury Riots, on Branxton Road at North Rothbury, commemorating the death of Norman Brown in 1929. He was shot when police opened fire on thousands of miners protesting against scab labour during a lockout. The Cessnock region takes in the Watagan State Forest, where there are some good 4WD trails, and the spectacular Brokenback Ranges.

In Clarence Town

[D4] in 1831 the first wholly Australian-built steamship was launched. The *William IV* was named for the former Duke of Clarence, who had become King William IV. Locals called the ship 'Puffing Billy'.

In Cooranbong

[E3] is the Sunnyside and South Sea Islands Museum, which features a large and fascinating collection of South Sea Island artefacts, gathered by the Seventh Day Adventist church during its extensive missionary work there. The material includes an enormous war canoe and items used by South Sea Island priests during human sacrifices.

GAZETTEER

Dungog

[D4], gateway to the Barrington Tops National Park, was also once a base for chasing bushrangers. The old courthouse, near the intersection of Brown and Lord Streets, was built between 1835 and 1838 as a barracks and stables for the troopers who drove bushrangers such as Thunderbolt from the area.

Gloucester

[B4] hosts the Shakespeare-on-Avon Festival, held at the showground in May (it used to be in the nearby village of Stratford on the Avon River). As well as performances by the Railway Theatre Company, there are feasts where you're welcome to don your best medieval costumery on Friday and Saturday nights, markets, a fair and more.

The public school at **Largs** [D3] is the state's oldest school, officially opening in 1849 but operating for 11 years before that as a Presbyterian church school. The schoolhouse has been preserved as a museum. It is open to the public during the school year by arrangement, call 02 4930 1050.

Maitland

's [E3] Walka Waterworks complex, on Scobies Lane in Oakhampton, is one of the largest and most intact 19th-century industrial complexes in the Hunter Valley. Constructed between 1879 and 1885, it was the first permanent, clean water supply. The water was pumped with engines supplied by James Watt in England. The *Maitland Mercury* is the oldest provincial newspaper in New South Wales, established in 1843. Maitland is also the site of the world's first speedway track, dating back to the 1925 agricultural show. Grossman House Museum and Brough House (Maitland City Art Gallery) are uniquely inverted mirror images of one another. These two elegant red-brick Victorian townhouses were built simultaneously (1860–61) by Samuel Owens and Isaac Beckett, partners who established a large general business in High Street in 1838.

DON'T MISS: The Hunter Valley Steamfest is held on the last weekend in April each year at the Maitland Railway Station and adjoining streets. The two-day festival of steam includes the 'Great Race' from Newcastle to Maitland between Loco-motive 3801 and a Tiger Moth aircraft.

In the town of **Merriwa** [C1] is the Battery Picnic Area, named after a very interesting basalt rock formation produced by a phenomenon known as columnar jointing. Lava cooling after an eruption many

millions of years ago formed fractures, resulting in clumps of cylindrical columns that protrude at right angles to the vertical rock face. Some say they look like a series of densely clustered pencils; others see the cylinders of a battery—hence its name. The site is 14 km east of town on the Golden Highway.

DON'T MISS: The Running of the Sheep provides the extraordinary sight of 200 sheep in red woollen socks running down Merriwa's main street. The spectacle is part of the Festival of the Fleeces, held on the June long weekend.

The **Monkerai** [C4] bridge is the oldest timber truss bridge in New South Wales, built in 1877. Its three spans feature flat sloping end diagonals and an extra timber midspan on the upper chord.

The whole town of **Morpeth** [D4] is covered by a permanent conservation order, which keeps its buildings exactly as they were at the turn of the 20th century.

DON'T MISS: If you like it hot get along to the Morpeth Fiery Food Festival on the last weekend in April. Prepare to be warmed up with tastings of chilli mustards, curry powders, jams and other assorted condiments. If you're there in late October, check out the Morpeth Gallery's Festival of Mugs (02 4934 2107).

The **Murrurundi** [B2] Bushman's Carnival on the October long weekend has one of the best rodeo and campdraft displays in the Hunter region. For kids, the Upper Hunter Billy Cart Championships are held on the first weekend of the September school holidays (02 6546 6205).

From **Muswellbrook** [C2] you can hook up with a tour of the best thoroughbred horse studs of the district. Meet famous horses such as Octagonal and learn all there is to know about the workings of a stud (phone 02 6547 2442 for details).

GAZETTEER

The guns of **Newcastle**'s [E4] Fort Scratchley were among the few to fire shots in hostility from the Australian mainland—in June 1942 when a Japanese submarine attacked Newcastle (as a coal port, it was a target). The military relinquished the site in 1972 and it is now the Newcastle Region Military Museum. Its displays include the Time Ball, which stands atop Customs House, one of only two on Australia's east coast. It was lowered at exactly 1 pm each afternoon to allow ships to check their chronometers. At the corner of Bolton and Church Streets is Newcastle East Public School, Newcastle's first school. It was established in 1816 by Commandant Thompson—the teacher then was a convict—and moved to its present site in the 1830s, becoming a public school in 1883, the oldest school operating in Australia. The present building dates from 1908.

Near **Ogunbil** [A3], on Dungowan Creek, there is good trout fishing. The season runs between the long weekends of October and June. The size limit for trout and salmon is 25 cm and the bag limit is five. Contact NSW Fisheries for a licence on 1300 369 365.

The area around **Paterson** [D3] was settled by Scots—St Ann's Presbyterian Church in Paterson, built in the late 1830s, is said to be the oldest continually operating Presbyterian church on mainland Australia. When the first minister advertised for a teacher in 1837 skills in Gaelic grammar were a requirement. An atypical portrait of Napoleon in which he did not pose with his arm in his jacket was painted by Frederick Bedwell, who is buried in St Paul's Anglican Church in Paterson. He was first officer on the HMS *Northumberland*, which escorted the defeated Napoleon to his exile on St Helena. John Tucker Park, on Maitland Road in Paterson, features two intriguing structures—

GAZETTEER

an open, rectangular timber box elevated on stumps and a dilapidated old brick shed. An adjacent plaque states: 'From the 1860s to the 1920s this site was the base of Frys Coaching Enterprise, which served the Hunter Valley and New South Wales.' The former business used the brick building to house the town's hearse and the timber structure was a corn straddle, a dry, vermin-free store for fodder.

The **Putty** [E1] Road offers an alternative and scenic route into or out of Sydney that avoids the Newcastle

MINER'S CRIB SCONES

Coal mining is synonomous with the Hunter region. But this recipe, a classic snack for a miner's lunchpack, in fact comes from Ackland, north-west of Oakey in south-east Queensland. Ackland's coal mine is the smallest and oldest continually worked coal mine in Queensland, having opened in 1930. Taking coals to Newcastle …

3 cups self-raising flour
1/2 tsp mixed spice
1 cup sultanas
1 cup ginger ale
1 cup cream

Preheat oven to 210°C. Grease a scone tray. Place flour, spice and sultanas in a large bowl and add the ginger ale and cream. Gently mix to form a scone dough. A little extra ginger ale may be needed. Turn onto a floured board and knead lightly. Cut into scones, place slightly apart on baking tray, brush with a little milk or cream and cook for 10–15 minutes or until golden brown. Makes 20 small scones.

John Carey, ACKLAND

BEER DAMPER WITH FLY-BOB TREACLE

Treacle has its origins in an idea similar to 'hair of the dog'. In classical Greece the antidote to a bite from a wild animal was called theriake or 'poisonous beast'. By the 14th century the English word 'triacle' was in use and evolved to mean any healing remedy. To make them easier to swallow the mixtures were sweetened and soon the word 'treacle' meant not only the medicine but also the thick syrup that contained it.

3 cups plain flour
1/2 tsp baking powder
1/2 tsp salt
2 tbsp butter
375 ml flat beer
butter and treacle, for serving

Preheat oven to 230°C. Combine all dry ingredients in a large bowl. Add butter and rub through, then add enough flat beer to mix into a dough. On a floured board knead dough lightly, forming an oval. Place on a floured oven tray and bake 20–30 minutes, or until browned. When cool, slice damper, butter it and top with treacle.

Cuttabri Wine Shanty, NARRABRI

Motorway. It might be a more sedate pace but it can still be hair-raising, with spectacular views over the ranges and some pretty tight corners. It's a 150 km trip (but you'll need fuel for 3 hours running) through the Wollemi and Yengo National Parks between Windsor and Singleton.

Quirindi

Quirindi [A1], on the New England Highway, was home to one of the first polo clubs in Australia, established in 1888. The annual polo carnival began in 1893 and is still held every August. The very substantial police station at Carinda, a tiny town about 70 km south-west of Walgett [see Tablelands and Plains], was intended for Quirindi but ended up in Carinda when a clerk misheard the town's name. It is now used as a clinic.

Raymond Terrace

[E4] has two large trees halfway along King Street with a sign that says 'marriage trees'—weddings were celebrated under the trees before the town had churches. King Street was the business centre of Raymond Terrace from 1840 until 1955, when a flood immersed it.

East of **Scone** [C2], on the Allan Bridge Road off Segenhoe Road, is the Kia Ora stud, which has produced eight Melbourne Cup winners, 16 Derby winners and 14 Oaks winners since it opened in 1910. Among its most famous equine residents was Gunsynd, who stood at stud at Kia Ora from 1973. He is buried there, along with Midstream, Magpie and Channel Swell, among others. The stud is open to visitors by appointment (02 6543 7105). About 15 km north of Scone, on the road to Murrurundi, is **Mt Wingen**, the burning mountain. Early settlers believed it was an active volcano. It is, in fact, a coal seam 30 m below the surface, which has been on fire for 5,000 years—it may be the oldest and largest of its kind in the world.

Singleton

In **Singleton** [D2], in Gowrie Street, is Rose Point Park. It contains the largest monolithic sundial in the Southern Hemisphere, which was presented to the town

as a bicentennial gift (in 1988) by the Lemington Mine.

Stockton Beach [E4] stretches

for 32 km, the largest continuous mobile sand mass in the Southern Hemisphere. Sand from here was used on Hawaii's famous Waikiki Beach. Stockton Beach is mostly a 4WD recreation area. In places—mostly on the northern end—you can still find tank traps built to stop a Japanese invasion.

In **Stroud**'s [D4] St John's Anglican Church is a tiny piece of carved stone from the Parish Church of St Lawrence in Stroud, England—it is 600 to 700 years old.

DON'T MISS: The towns of Stroud in England, the United States, Canada and Australia hold an International Brick and Rolling Pin Throwing Competition on the same day in July each year. It originally started as a brick throwing competition in 1960 when the American and English towns of Stroud discovered they had brickworks in common. Two years later Stroud Australia included women in the competition, and so suggested adding rolling pins to the list. The rolling pins are now all made in Australia and shipped overseas so that no one Stroud has an unfair advantage.

Toronto [E3] celebrates every Sunday

with Music in the Park, performances from musicians from rock to classical. It's held on the beautiful **Lake Macquarie** foreshore on Victory Parade from midday. Lake Macquarie was first called Reid's Mistake, after Captain William Reid sailed his 30 tonne schooner *Martha* into the lake, thinking it was the Hunter River.

Wangi Wangi [E3] is the former

home (in Dobell Place) of noted Australian painter William Dobell, who lived here from the 1940s until his death in 1970. He won the Archibald Prize in 1943, 1948 and 1959. There are prints of his work on display.

A previous owner of **Wollombi** [E2] Tavern, Mel Jurd, is the inventor of Dr Jurd's Jungle Juice, a dubious alcoholic beverage created in 1949. After an explosion wrecked the pub in 1960, leaving Mr Jurd in need of some quick cash, he started to sell it. While there is a considerable degree of mythology surrounding its supposed potency, it can still be purchased here.

Diary of Events

Town	Event	Date	Contact
Branxton	Opera in the Vineyards	October	1800 675 875
Cessnock	Hunter Valley Harvest Festival	May, 1st weekend	02 4990 4477
Gloucester	Shakespeare-on-Avon Festival	May, 1st weekend	02 6558 1408
Maitland	Hunter Valley Steamfest	April, last weekend	02 4934 1439
Merriwa	Festival of the Fleeces	June long weekend	02 6548 2109
Morpeth	Fiery Food Festival	April, last weekend	02 4934 2107
	Festival of Mugs	October	02 4934 2107
Murrurundi	Bushman's Carnival	October long weekend	02 6546 6205
	Billy Cart Championships	September	02 6546 6205
Stroud	Brick and Rolling Pin Throwing	July	02 4994 5221

The North Coast of New South Wales is filled with unspoilt villages and peaceful fishing and surfing spots. Port Macquarie now bills itself as an affordable family holiday destination, which is a far cry from its beginnings as New South Wales' third penal and military settlement.

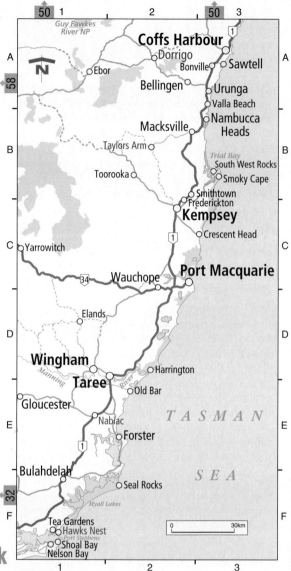

get off the beaten track

relax

on the north coast

Bellingen

Bellingen [A2] was the setting for the film of Peter Carey's book *Oscar and Lucinda*. Bat Island is home to a large colony of flying foxes—up to 40,000 at some times. The island is in north Bellingen. In dry weather, follow the path from the caravan park; in the wet, it may be submerged.

 DON'T MISS: Jazz lovers should put the Bellingen Jazz Festival in August in their diaries. The arts are celebrated over the October long weekend in one of Australia's most popular festivals, the Bellingen Global Carnival, when regional, interstate and international artists showcase music, arts, dance and theatre for three days and nights. Also on the October long weekend in the Bellingen/Bowraville region the Tallowood Community School organises for a range of handmade houses in the area to be open to the public. The Community Markets, on the third Saturday of the month, is one of Australia's largest regional markets.

Bulahdelah

In the **Bulahdelah** [F1] National Park, 14 km north of the town on Stoney Creek Road heading for Wootton, stands *Eucalyptus grandis*, an 87 m flooded gum, the tallest tree in the state. It is estimated to be 400 years old.

Coffs Harbour

Coffs Harbour [A3] is home to the Big Banana. At 11 m long and 5 m high, you won't miss it towering above the Pacific Highway. There's a monorail tour of a banana plantation,

CHEESY BAKED BANANA

Coff's Harbour's Big Banana was one of the earliest of Australia's 'big things', and is probably one of the best known.

- **60 g butter**
- **1/2 tsp salt**
- **1/2 tsp paprika**
- **3–4 large firm bananas**
- **1/2 cup fresh breadcrumbs**
- **30 g parmesan cheese, grated**
- **60 g cheddar cheese, grated**
- **extra butter**

Preheat oven to 180°C. Melt butter, add salt and paprika. Peel and thickly slice bananas and place in a shallow greased casserole dish. Spoon melted butter over bananas. Combine bread crumbs with the two cheeses and spread two thirds over the bananas. Dot with extra butter and add remaining cheese mixture. Bake for approximately 15 minutes until golden. Serve as a side dish for fish, chicken or pork.

M. Rubie, COFFS HARBOUR

a skywalk to a lookout, toboggan rides and an ice rink. Also on the Pacific Highway, between High Street and Orlando Street, is the Clog Barn, a miniature Dutch village with buildings, waterfalls, canals, windmills, a locomotive and clog-making demonstrations. At **Bonville**, 9 km south of Coffs Harbour, the Butterfly House has one of Australia's largest displays of live butterflies.

DON'T MISS: At the Buskers Festival on the October long weekend Australian and international artists perform in various locations around Coffs Harbour.

TENDER CROCODILE IN VEGETABLE SAUCE

Just north of Kempsey is Frederickton [C2], the site of Nora Turnbull's Fredo Pies & Icecreams shop. You can get a crocodile pie here. Nola started making fresh pies with family dinner leftovers—steak casserole and sweet and sour pork. When people came back for more she tried a few more exotic ingredients, hoping for a bit of shock value. Crocodile, camel, emu, buffalo, venison and kangaroo were just some of the meats she added.

500 g best cuts crocodile, diced
1 tbsp extra virgin olive oil
1 large onion, diced
1 cup mixed vegetables, diced
1 garlic clove, crushed
2 cups vegetable stock
2 bay leaves
dash of tabasco sauce
salt and pepper to taste
2 tbsp cornflour in a little water,
   for thickening

In a large frying pan, sauté crocodile meat in oil until opaque. Add onion, vegetables and garlic and stir over medium heat for 2 minutes. Add stock, bay leaves, tabasco, salt and pepper. Gently simmer for about 20 minutes, or until meat is tender. Remove bay leaves. In a cup, mix cornflour in water. Add this gradually to the frying pan mixture, stirring continuously until mixture reaches the required consistency. Serve hot on a bed of rice or pasta, or use as a pie filling. Serves 2.

Nora Turnbull, FREDERICKTON

Crescent Head [C3] is famous

for its Malibu waves and has played host to the Australian Malibu Titles. Every year in May, the Crescent Head Malibu Classic is attended by many surfing legends.

Dorrigo [A2] Steam and Railway

Museum in Tallowood Street (to the west of town) has the largest collection of railway rolling stock in the Southern Hemisphere. It is not open to the public yet, but they are easily seen from the road.

GAZETTEER

Ebor [A1] Falls consists of two waterfalls,

one 100 m downstream from the other, together creating a spectacular effect. Ebor Falls are part of the **Guy Fawkes River National Park**, a vast, secluded wilderness encompassing 356 sq km of rugged river country. The Bicentennial Trail, for horse-riding, runs along the western bank of the Guy Fawkes River, which cuts through the middle of the wilderness. The park has long been a favoured haunt for brumbies. However, there is increasing concern about how to balance the heritage value of the horses against their detrimental effect on native flora and fauna. There is also research into how to humanely remove them from the park.

Near the village of **Elands** [D1], on Tourist Drive 8, is the second-longest single-drop waterfall in the Southern Hemisphere. Ellenborough Falls is a spectacular 160 m single-drop waterfall over the edge of the New England Tableland. It's easily viewed from several platforms. Take the steps to the bottom of the falls for a memorable, if slightly damp, view.

Off the coast at **Forster** [E2] is the largest dive wreck on Australia's east coast. The SS *Satara*, which sank in 1910, lies at around 42 m—a dive strictly for the experienced.

At **Harrington** [D2] is one of two river mouths of the Manning River, making it a very rare river system—the other mouth is near **Old Bar**. The Manning is the only delta river system of this type in Australia.

Hawks Nest [F1] and Tea

Gardens are connected by the 'Singing Bridge', so named because of the sound made by the wind as it passes through the rails of the bridge. House boating on Myall Lakes provides the perfect opportunity to see dolphins up close. You can moor your boat in a private cove, with nothing but nature for company. There are plenty of good dive sites in the area, including the Looking Glass, where you dive right through the middle of an island that has been split in half, Bubble Cave, a large air pocket in the cliff face, and the Grey Nurse Shark Gutters, with a resident population of up to 40 of these marine wonders on the north-eastern point of Broughton Island, among many others. Hawks Nest Dive Centre, at 13 Maxwell Street, can give further information (02 4997 0442).

Kempsey [C2] is

where Australia's national hat, the Akubra, is made. They also grow perfect potatoes for Smith's Crisps at Stewarts Point, just outside Kempsey.

The entrance to the **Myall Lakes** [F1], the largest system of freshwater lakes in the state, is on the northern side of Port Stephens Harbour. The Myall River passes through the twin towns of Tea Gardens and

Hawks Nest before meandering 55 km or so into the first of the lakes. Myall River prawns are best eaten after they have been boiled in Myall River water for 90 seconds, then cooled quickly in Myall River water, covered in rock salt and left overnight in the fridge.

The town of **Nabiac** [E1] has Australia's only Amish Country Store, established in 1995 by the Weerheim family. The store, a modest but interesting craft shop cum eatery with some lovely handmade wooden toys, is housed in the National Trust-listed Hancock Buildings. An old-style buggy sits out the front of the shop.

GAZETTEER

Nambucca Heads [B3] sea wall

has been turned into an informal graffiti gallery by enterprising holiday-makers and locals. Rather corny poems, declarations of love for both the town and other human beings, and in one case a joyful declaration of divorce, have been painted. There is an 18-hole golf course in the middle of the Nambucca River on an island, the only golf course in Australia completely surrounded by water. Golfers claim the best design for a golf course is one surrounded on three sides by water; locals claim that this must be even better. Cross over a small causeway from Riverside Drive.

Port Macquarie [C2] is

famous for its urban koala population. It is also home to the Koala Hospital in Macquarie Nature Reserve, Lord Street, where between 150 and 200 koalas are treated each year. Open all year, seven days a week. Feeding times are between 7.30 am and 3 pm. Surfing is popular here and Flynns Beach is the venue for both local and state competitions. Other good locations are the river mouth and Nobby's Beach, also good for rock fishing.

BARRINGTON PERCH FILLETS

The north coast abounds with fresh local produce and seafood. The macadamia industry has expanded in the region in the last two decades and occupies more than 6,000 ha of land. This recipe poaches the Barrington perch in a delicate combination of lemon myrtle, macadamia and cocunut.

50 ml good olive oil
2 brown onions, finely chopped
3 cloves garlic, crushed
2 kaffir lime leaves, finely chopped
1¹/₂ tsp lemon myrtle, ground
2 tsp lemon grass, finely chopped
120 g macadamia nuts, chopped
400 ml can coconut cream
salt and pepper to taste
4 silver perch fillets, skinned
2 tbsp shallots, finely chopped
2 tbsp leek, finely chopped
¹/₂ bunch coriander, finely chopped
4 portions of arborio rice, steamed
according to cooking instructions

Heat oil in a large pan, add onions and garlic and cook gently for 5 minutes. Add lime leaves, lemon myrtle, lemon grass, nuts and coconut cream, season to taste. Stir to combine and bring close to the boil. Add fish and simmer for 5 minutes or until fish is cooked through. Add shallots and leeks, simmer for one minute. Sprinkle with coriander and serve with rice. Serves 4.

Tellers Restaurant, WINGHAM

Port Stephens [F1] is home to

a very old olive tree, in the gardens of the convict-built house Tanilba—it was planted in 1831 and is still flourishing. It is reputed to be the oldest olive tree in Australia. Tanilba is open to the public on weekends, Wednesdays, public

and school holidays from 10.30 am to 4.30 pm. The house has an extensive library of antique books, among them a handy tome called *Enquire Within Upon Everything*. Written in 1881, its multifarious suggestions cover the efficient use of food and clothing, fresh air and good manners. It even suggests that 'there is not anything gained in economy by having very young and inexperienced servants at low wages; the cost of what they break, waste and destroy, is more than an equivalent for higher wages, setting aside comfort and respectability'. Port Stephens hosts the largest game and sport fishing tournament in the Southern Hemisphere. The Port Stephens Inter-Club Competition is run over consecutive weekends (the last weekend in February and the first weekend in March) and typically attracts well in excess of 200 boats and 1,000 keen anglers. Prime targets are the marlin and sharks that frequent the offshore waters east of Port Stephens in the

summer and autumn. Today the emphasis is firmly on tag and release, and the vast majority of game fish caught during the annual event are returned to the water alive. Another big event is the Trailer Boat Fishing Tournament, the largest in Australia. Held at Nelsons Bay during the weekend before Easter, it also attracts more than 1,000 local and international contestants.

Storyland Gardens at **Sawtell** [A3] features sculptures of favourite children's storybook characters. To add to the magic, the owners, like the old woman in the poem, actually live in an old shoe, although this one has a kiosk and theatre. It's open Thursday to Saturday and daily during school holidays.

DON'T MISS: At the Sawtell Chilli Festival in July choose from a range of chilli dishes or enter an eating or drinking competition. But be warned, all contestants are required to eat six red bell chillies followed by 10 ml of habañeros paste.

Seal Rocks [F2] takes its name from the series of rocks that break the sea's surface several kilometres off the coast and provide a sunbathing area during the winter months for fur seals. The underwater caves at Seal Rocks attract divers from all over the world. The caves are sometimes packed with up to 40 grey nurse sharks, and massed schools of mulloway, black cod and kingfish.

Smoky Cape's [B3] 17 m high lighthouse is one of the tallest and oldest in the state, first lit in 1891. Its light can be seen 23 km out to sea.

South West Rocks [B3] has the Fish Rock Cave, one of the largest ocean caves in the Southern Hemisphere and considered the best ocean cave dive in Australia. It's world renowned for its coral, and tropical and cold water fish. You can also

COMBOYNE BLUEBERRIES FLAMBÉ

Marrook Farm yoghurt is made at Marrook Farm in the beautiful lush hills north-west of Taree. They make their yoghurt in the traditional way, in small batches, using unhomogenised milk and live cultures. If you're in the area pick up some of their Bush Honey, Wattle Seed or Lemon Myrtle yoghurt and try out this recipe.

130 g Marrook Farm Country Style or flavoured yoghurt
130 g crème fraîche
juice of 1 lime
50 g icing sugar
3 tsp or 1 sachet gelatine dissolved in a little hot water
130 ml whipped cream
2 egg whites
20 g sugar
1 tbsp butter
2 tbsp brown sugar
3 punnets Comboyne blueberries
60 ml Cassegrain's Old Port

For the mousse, mix yoghurt, crème fraîche and lime juice in a bowl. Add icing sugar, gelatine and whipped cream and fold through. Beat egg whites and sugar until stiff and fold into yoghurt mixture. Fill individual moulds or one large mould and allow to set in the fridge. Once the mousse has set, melt butter and brown sugar in a pan, add the blueberries and toss until coated. Add the port and flame. Turn out individual moulds onto serving plates and spoon blueberries around mousse.

Tellers Restaurant, WINGHAM

take a coastal track all the way south to Port Macquarie and along the way enjoy some beach driving (4WD and a permit required).

South of **Taree** [D2] is Tallwoods Village, an 18-hole championship golf course designed by the world's leading course architect, Michael Hurdzan. In **Tinonee**, a short drive from Taree, is a tiny cottage housing Australia's smallest cinema.

Taylors Arm's [B2] Cosmopolitan

Hotel (1903) was the subject of the song 'The Pub With No Beer', the story of the regulars who used to drink at this old and isolated timbergetters' watering hole in the 1940s. The World Championship Egg Throwing Competition is held here in June, a precarious spectator sport. To win, your egg must be caught unbroken by your partner, after being lobbed 40 m over the pub roof. Nearby **Macksville** hosts an annual trek to the pub in May. About 7 km south of Macksville, the Way Way Forest Drive includes blackbutt forest,

Mount Yarrahapinni Lookout, the Pines Picnic Area and the Way Way Creek forest walk. It's a 29 km round trip with markers starting where Rosewood Road leaves the old highway at Warrell Creek.

From **Toorooka** [B2] to Sherwood and back is an 80 km round trip through the forest, but you'll need a 4WD. From Toorooka take the unsealed road to Moparrabah then turn left on the Willi Willi Road. Another good 4WD track is from Toorooka to Daisy Plains. Cross Toorooka Bridge, turn right into Warbro Brook Road and onto Carrai Road through the Carrai State Forest to Kookaburra, where you can walk to the waterfall and drive on to Daisy Plains.

The **Trial Bay** [B3] jail, where the Macleay River empties into Trial Bay at South West Rocks, started as an experiment in prison reform. In 1886 prisoners were

GAZETTEER

MUESLI BARS

Australia's famous drink, Milo, is made at Smithtown [B2]. Milo is produced by Nestlé and by 1906 Australia had become this Swiss company's second-largest export market. In 1908 the company set up business in Australia and it was here that Milo was born, in 1934. Not only does it taste great but it's also a good source of vitamins A, B and C, calcium, iron and other essential minerals. It also makes great muesli bars.

60 g butter
¹/₂ cup honey
2 tbsp glucose
4 cups toasted muesli
1 cup Milo

Line an 18 cm x 26 cm cake tin with baking paper. Combine butter, honey and glucose in a pan and stir over low heat until butter is melted. Add butter mixture to muesli and Milo, mix to combine and press into prepared tin. Refrigerate until firm and cut into slices to serve. Store in the refrigerator.

Helen Way,
SMITHTOWN

organised to build a breakwater, which was wiped out by a storm three years later. The jail was closed in 1903 and reopened in 1915 as an internment camp for German nationals during World War I. It closed again in 1917. There are said to be two ghosts at Trial Bay: one haunts the jail, the other haunts nearby German Bridge. Visitors to the area shouldn't miss the opportunity to cast a line into the Macleay River, with good catches of flathead, bream, whiting and mulloway in its lower reaches as well as some fine Australian bass upstream from Kempsey.

Urunga [A3] has a European straw
beehive, a replica made of concrete. Inside is a display of the honey-making process.

East of **Wauchope** [C2] along the Oxley Highway (turn left into Redbank Road) climb the 14 m Big Bull to get a bull's-eye view of the Hastings River. It's also a working dairy farm. **Timbertown**, 2 km west of Wauchope, recreates a pioneer village of the 1880s, with a blacksmith's forge, railway station and steam train, steam sawmill, shops, bakery, a pub and arts and crafts.

Wingham Brush [D1] is part of the last
10 ha of subtropical floodplain rainforest left in New South Wales. During the 1980s it was regenerated by a team of volunteers led by a local dentist; it has since been recognised as a world-class example of successful rainforest regeneration. The techniques developed have become a model for national rainforest regeneration projects. If you look up into the branches of the huge Moreton Bay fig trees in Wingham Brush you may well see the grey-headed flying fox giving birth. It is one of their most significant maternity sites in the state.

The Apsley–**Yarrowitch** [C1] river system, part of the Macleay Gorges Wilderness, with its spectacular, rugged gorges, is home to 12 threatened species. These include the brush-tailed rock wallaby, koala, squirrel glider and tiger quoll. It is also home to a recently discovered species, the Macleay tortoise, and the rare Hastings River mouse, thought to be in imminent danger of extinction.

Diary of Events

Town	Event	Date	Contact
Bellingen	Jazz Festival	August, 3rd weekend	02 6655 1053
	Global Carnival	October long weekend	02 6655 3024
Bowraville	Back to Bowra Festival	October long weekend	02 6564 7135
Coffs Harbour	Buskers Festival	October long weekend	02 6652 8266
Crescent Head	Malibu Classic	May	02 6566 0183
Port Stephens	Inter-Club Fishing Competition	Feb/March	0417 770 900
	Trailer Boat Fishing Tournament	April	02 9976 3544
Sawtell	Chilli Festival	July	02 6653 1403
Taylors Arm	Egg Throwing Competition	June, 1st Sunday	02 6564 2101

Fatigue is a factor in 1 out of 5 fatal crashes.

CRASH BEFORE YOU DRIVE

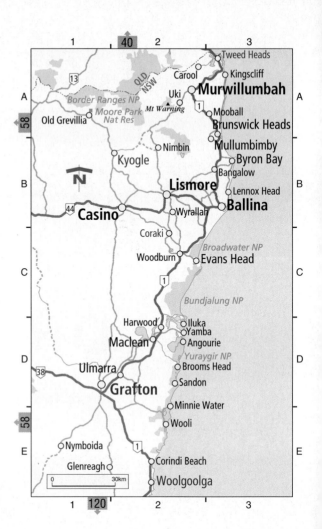

The Northern Rivers region is broken into three distinct parts, the heart of each is one of its rivers—the Clarence, the Richmond and the Tweed. The people who live here believe it to be as close to paradise as anywhere on Earth.

get off the beaten track

cruise

the northern rivers

Ballina

[B3] is the final resting place of what was then—in 1975—the longest-serving riverboat in Australia. The MV *Florrie* now lies on the banks of the Richmond River. It was built in 1880 at Brisbane Waters, wrecked two years later, then repaired and run without incident until being decommissioned. Ballina Lighthouse, built in 1879, is one of the oldest in the state. In 1928 Black Head was the first land Charles Kingsford Smith and Charles Ulm saw at the end of their historic flight across the Pacific in *Southern Cross*. One of the three rafts involved in a quite different Pacific crossing from Ecuador in 1973, *Las Balsas,* is in the Naval and Maritime Museum here. The museum also has photographs, artefacts and a video about the journey. The Big Prawn (20 m high, 4.5 m wide, 27 m long and weighing 8 tonnes), on the Pacific Highway, houses an Opal and Gem Museum.

MACADAMIA AND DAVIDSON PLUM PAVLOVA ROLL

As you travel along the Bruxner Highway from Lismore to Ballina you'll pass a number of macadamia and fruit farms. Not only do macadamias grow well in this tropical region but also Davidson plums, small rainforest trees that bear an edible plum-like fruit.

CRUST
1/2 cup caster sugar
2 tsp ground aniseed myrtle (omit if not available)
200 g macadamia nuts, roasted

MERINGUE
6 egg whites
1 tsp lemon juice
1 1/4 cups caster sugar

CREAM FILLING
4 Davidson plums, stones removed
125 g caster sugar
250 ml cream

Preheat oven to 150°C. To make crust, combine sugar and aniseed myrtle in a food processor, then add the macadamias, using the pulse button in short bursts. Mix until fine.

To make meringue, line a large flat baking tray with shallow sides, 29 cm x 44 cm, with baking paper. In a large bowl, whisk egg whites with lemon juice until soft peaks form. Slowly add sugar and beat until stiff. Spread onto tray. Sprinkle crust on top and bake for 20 minutes. While cooking, make cream filling. Place plums in a small stainless steel saucepan with enough water to cover, add sugar and bring to the boil. Reduce heat and allow to simmer for 30 minutes. Remove from heat and leave to cool. Drain and finely dice plums. Whip cream until very thick, then fold in chopped plums. (Use fresh strawberries if plums are not available.) When meringue is cooked, remove from oven, place a tea towel over it and invert. Remove paper and spread cream evenly over meringue. Using the tea towel, roll up the meringue like a swiss roll, from the shortest side. Allow to cool.

Peter Ilic, BALLINA

CHOCOLATE MACADAMIA CAKE WITH GANACHE

World-class coffee is grown at Carool. The crisp mountain nights, rich volcanic soil and ideal balance of sunshine and rain provide perfect conditions for growing coffee. This recipe is recommended by Zeta Grealy, owner of Carool Coffee.

275 g dark chocolate, chopped	1 tsp baking powder
275 g butter	1 cup macadamia nuts, roasted and chopped
1 short black coffee (1/4 cup) (preferably Carool Coffee)	**CHOCOLATE GANACHE**
2 nips Tia Maria	1 dsp butter
1/2 cup caster sugar	3/4 cup cream
5 eggs, separated	220 g dark chocolate, chopped
2/3 cup plain flour	

Preheat oven to 170°C and line a 26 cm springform pan with baking paper. Gently melt chocolate and butter in a saucepan over low heat. Stir in coffee and Tia Maria. Cool slightly. In a bowl, beat sugar and egg yolks till fluffy. Add to chocolate mixture. Fold in flour and baking powder. In another bowl, beat egg whites till stiff. Gently fold into mixture, with nuts. Pour mixture into pan and bake for 40–50 minutes, then cool in tin. When cold, turn out onto wire rack. To make ganache, in a small saucepan, bring butter and cream to the boil. Remove from heat and stir in chocolate. Mix until smooth and cool. Spread over cake.

Zeta Grealy, CAROOL

Bangalow [B3] is the only intact Federation village on Australia's east coast. The Billy Cart Derby is in May and markets are on the 4th Sunday of every month at the showground.

The Brunswick Heads [A3]
Fish and Chips Festival, held over the second weekend in January, celebrates two important commercial activities—the chips commemorate the old timbergetters who helped build the town, and the fish signify what the town does now.

Byron Bay's [B3] Cape Byron
Lighthouse marks mainland Australia's most easterly point. It's a great place for spotting whales as they migrate north in July and August and return in September and October. Cape Byron Headland Reserve is now part of the **Arakwal National Park**.

DON'T MISS: Byron hosts the internationally acclaimed East Coast Blues and Roots Festival annually on the Easter weekend.

The village of **Carool** [A2], behind Tweed Heads, grows some of Australia's best coffee. The crisp mountain nights, rich volcanic soil and ideal balance of sunshine and rain are perfect conditions to grow Arabica beans. The volcanic soils give the coffees less caffeine. Carool Coffee Traders in Blissett's Road conducts small tours by appointment (07 5590 7836).

Casino [B2] Beef Week, held every
year in May, includes an old-fashioned family bush dance, a toe-tapping hoe down, talent quest and poetry in the pub.

Coraki [C2] calls itself the Tea
Tree Capital. Tea-tree oil has long been used as an antiseptic and cure-all, and the industry originally harvested the natural forests. Plantations were established as demand increased, the

GAZETTEER

first successful one in the mid-1980s. The Northern Rivers Tea Tree Group's Coraki plantation has more than 16 million tea trees, with an annual output of more than 150 tonnes of oil.

At Corindi Beach [E2] the
Yarrawarra Aboriginal Cultural Centre on Red Rock Road provides a walkway through the surrounding bushland with guided bush tucker tours. Try the organic bush tucker on offer at the café.

Evans Head [C2] is said to have
been the first prawning port in Australia, and commercial and recreational fishing here is still going strong. **Broadwater National Park** has 8 km of beaches and large sand dunes that date back 60,000 years. Surfing is good here too, the swell around Goanna Headland providing one of the most popular in the area. Try Gumma Garra Picnic Area on the Evans River in **Bundjalung National Park**— cross the bridge at the bottom of Elm Street and turn right.

Glenreagh [E1] has the smallest
post office still operating solely as such in New South Wales. It was built in 1947. It's 3.3 m wide and perhaps twice that deep.

Despite its tiny size it still offers a full range of postal and banking services and sells a few very small souvenirs. It's open 9 am to 5 pm Monday to Friday but closes for lunch between 12.30 and 1.30 pm.

Next to # Grafton 's [D2] main
street, in the rainforests of Susan Island, a nature reserve in the Clarence River, is a flying fox colony said to be the largest in the Southern Hemisphere. On the south side of the Clarence River, a few hundred metres upstream from the Grafton Bridge, are the rusty remains of the SS *Induna*, an old boat that saw service as a train ferry and as a wharf on the banks of the Clarence River. In an earlier life in South Africa the *Induna* had been a weekly steamer and had played a part in the escape of a young war correspondent—in 1899 Winston Churchill escaped from a prison in Pretoria and rode the *Induna* to safety in Durban.

GAZETTEER

DON'T MISS: In October to
November, Grafton holds Australia's oldest floral festival, the Jacaranda Festival being part of Grafton since 1934. Call 02 6642 4677 for details.

Iluka [D2] Nature Reserve is the largest area of subtropical littoral rainforest in New South Wales. It has been included in the World Heritage listings. A designated walk takes around half an hour.

South of **Kingscliff** [A3], on Duranbah Road at Duranbah, is Tropical Fruit World, a 65 ha farm that started as a family home and has since developed into one of the world's largest tropical fruit plantations and research parks, growing more than 500 varieties of tropical and rare fruit. The fruit safari, running between 10 am and 5 pm daily, shows visitors a series of fruit gardens of the world. Tropical Passion jams, sauces and chutneys, and the Tropicology avocado oil skin care range, are sold here.

Kyogle [B2] is surrounded by one of the largest remaining areas of rainforest in New South Wales, the **Border Ranges National Park**. If you prefer to enjoy the scenery from the comfort of your car, the 64 km Tweed Range Scenic Drive runs along the edge of Mt Warning. To get there, follow the Barkers Vale sign from the Kyogle–Murwillumbah road. Kyogle is linked to Beaudesert in Queensland by the Lions Road. Originally there were two unconnected roads until the Lions Clubs in both towns collaborated to build this one, right off the beaten track. For the drive, turn right at Wilson Avenue, 19 km from Kyogle (there's a short stretch of unsealed road).

Lennox Head's [B3] Lake Ainsworth is a freshwater lagoon coloured brown by tannins that leach from the nearby tea trees. The water is believed to have health-giving and rejuvenating properties.

The history of **Lismore** [B2] and its environment can be found driving through the city's streets. More than 20 roundabouts that reflect the city's heritage have been planned and planted. Of special note is one of the city's largest, on Rotary Avenue at the Ballina turn-off. The 26 m roundabout combines plant species typical of the local 'dry' rainforest with an Art Space where students from Lismore's Southern Cross University display their work.

DON'T MISS: The Northern Rivers Herb Festival—Celebrating Natural Living takes place in August during National Herbal Medicine Week at various venues in and around Lismore. It includes the Hot'n'Spicy Ball, much food and education about growing herbs, using herbs in cooking and using herbs in health products such as soap and body oils. Call 02 6622 1036 for details.

Maclean [D2] calls itself the Scottish town in Australia, and boasts a network of power poles painted in clan tartans throughout the town. It's also the place to try haggis and rumble de thump, a traditional haggis accompaniment. Sugar fever struck the area around Maclean and nearby **Harwood** after initial experiments in the mid-1860s. Several mills were set up and Harwood has the oldest operating sugar mill in Australia (1874).

Moore Park [A1] Nature Reserve is near **Old Grevillia**. It might be tiny but within it is the most important black bean rainforest in New South Wales.

Mt Warning [A2] (1,157 m) receives the first rays of sunlight on the Australian mainland each day. The centre of a World Heritage listed park, Mt Warning was the magma chamber and central vent of a volcano that covered 4,000 sq km, when Mt Warning was twice its present height. The harder rhyolite from the magma chamber has formed a core—this has remained while the basalt deposits of the surrounding area have eroded away, leaving the present basin, the largest erosion caldera in the Southern Hemisphere and the second largest in the world.

South-west of **Mullumbimby** [B3], perched on a hillside, is Crystal Castle. Housed within is a display (said to be Australia's largest) of crystals—violet amethyst, clear and rose quartz, banded agate, etc—in natural and artificial forms.

South of **Murwillumbah** [A2], **Mooball** holds the annual Fish'n'Nana Carnival in May, including family activities, a fishing competition and a banana cake competition.

Nimbin [B2] is the counterculture capital of Australia. The Cullen Street shops reflect this, with colourful shopfronts and unusual stock.

DON'T MISS: Nimbin Mardi Grass Festival celebrates the joys of cannabis, with the Hemp Olympics judging the fastest and most artistic joint rolling.

SCOTTISH LION RUMBLE de THUMP

Maclean is famous for its Scottish heritage and and what could be more Scottish than haggis? Perhaps its traditional side dish, rumble de thump. This recipe was contributed by Alastair McIntyre, who manages a website that brings together Scots from all around the world (www.electricscotland.com/australia), where you can find out more about Scottish history and trace your family roots.

- **6 medium potatoes, peeled and quartered**
- **5 cups chopped cabbage (half a large head)**
- **4 tbsp butter**
- **$\frac{1}{2}$ cup milk**
- **2 tbsp black olives, seeded and chopped**
- **salt and pepper to taste**
- **$1\frac{1}{2}$ cups cheddar cheese, grated**

Preheat oven to 180°C. Grease a medium-size baking dish with butter. Cook potatoes until tender and drain. Cook cabbage until tender and drain. Mash potatoes, butter and enough milk to make a light texture. Add olives, cabbage, salt and pepper to potatoes and combine. Spoon into baking dish, sprinkle with cheese and bake for 15–20 minutes or until cheese melts and browns.

Alastair McIntyre, GRANGE-MOUTH (Scotland)

Nymboida National Park [E1] offers plenty of opportunities for action: canoeing, kayaking, orienteering and abseiling abound.

The Nymboida and Mann Rivers provide some of the best whitewater rafting in the country and some of the canoe courses are used for championship events. Nymboida Canoe Centre on Armidale Road has equipment and information.

Sandon

Sandon [D2] is a small village of 30 houses at the mouth of the Yuraygir River and is one of three villages enclosed by the **Yuraygir National Park**, which provides excellent bushwalking and secluded beaches. The river has been formally acclaimed as the most pristine environment of its kind by the state's Fisheries Department. Sandon can be reached by a dirt road from **Brooms Head**, further north, or a 4WD track from **Minnie Water**, to the south. There are also camping facilities in the park.

Tweed Heads

Tweed Heads [A3] (actually Point Danger) is home to the Captain Cook Memorial. The lighthouse lays claim to being the first in the world to experiment with laser technology (1971), but the experiment was unsuccessful and it returned to the more conventional mirrors, magnifying glass and powerful electric lamps. Both Point Danger and Mt Warning were named by Captain Cook, who felt that he should leave a message for future sailors after the *Endeavour* almost ran aground on offshore reefs here. The ship's capstan that stands at the base of the memorial was actually made from the *Endeavour*'s cast iron ballast. Cook dumped it overboard when the *Endeavour* did run aground later on the Great Barrier Reef.

Uki

Uki [A2] is a heritage village at the foot of Mt Warning. From here you'll see stunning views of the mountain and the rock formation known as the Three Sisters. Uki Buttery Bazaar is held on the 3rd Sunday of every month in the grounds of the old Norco Butter Factory.

Ulmarra

Ulmarra [D2], on the Clarence River, has excellent fishing. It's the largest river system in New South Wales and is the habitat of the much sought-after Australian bass. The best time to catch a bass is in the summer months in the early morning or late afternoon. For the rest of the year you can catch shrimp, herring and mullet. Even though Ulmarra is in New South Wales, the Commercial Hotel looks like a typical old Queensland pub, so authentic that it appears in the television series Fields of Fire, set in 1920s Queensland.

Woodburn

Woodburn [C2] is a riverside mining town with a beach and many good bushwalks close by at the Broadwater and Bundjalung National Parks. Visit in August for the Woodburn Flower Show. South of Woodburn is the New Italy Museum, which celebrates the contributions made by 19th-century Italian pioneers in this area.

Woolgoolga

Woolgoolga [E2] is home to a large Sikh population, decandants of the Punjabi migrants who originally came to Australia to work on the Queensland canefields. Today they represent about 25 per cent of the population of the Woolgoolga area. The Guru Nanak Sikh temple, on the hill above the Pacific Highway, was the first Sikh temple to be built in Australia. Visitors are welcome to the temple on weekends. You'll

GAZETTEER

GAZETTEER

need to remove your shoes and cover your head (cloths are provided). One of the more exotic spots in Woolgoolga is the Raj Mahal Emporium, complete with minarets and elephant sculptures, and a fine restaurant.

DON'T MISS: The Sikh Vaisakki Festival, held in Woolgoolga in April each year, celebrates the birth of Guru Nanak, the founder of the Sikh religion, which combines elements of Islam and Hinduism. The festival includes a street parade for which the Sikh community turn out in full traditional costume.

Wooli [E2] holds the Goanna Pulling

Championships in June each year. It's a tug-o-war between pairs of contestants joined by a belt looped around their necks. Don't worry, the contestants aren't really goannas—just people who resemble the reptiles a little while they're doing this. It's held each year on the June long weekend.

In the village of **Wyrallah** [B2] is a signposted turn-off to a fine example of an Aboriginal bora ring (22 m in diameter), a ceremonial site that is a circular cleared area bounded by a low bank of earth. The bora ring lies to the rear of the Tucki Tucki village cemetery, overlooking the Steve King's Plain and a portion of the Richmond Valley.

Surfing conditions at **Yamba** [D3] are among the best on the north coast. Australian world champion surfer Nat Young put **Angourie**, 5 km south of Yamba, on the surfing map years ago when he came here to escape the crowds at Byron Bay. Today, the crowds are here too. Try other beaches such as Turners, Pippi, Whiting and Convent. There's also good fishing and prawning.

Diary of Events

Town	Event	Date	Contact
Bangalow	Billy Cart Derby	May	0412 111 111
	Markets	4th Sunday each month	02 6687 1314
Brunswick Heads	Fish and Chips Festival	January, 2nd weekend	02 6685 1385
Byron Bay	East Coast Blues and Roots Festival	Easter long weekend	02 6685 8310
Casino	Beef Week	May	02 6662 8181
Coraki	Markets	4th Sunday each month	02 6683 4739
Grafton	Jacaranda Festival	Oct/Nov	02 6642 4677
Lismore	Northern Rivers Herb Festival	August, 3rd weekend	02 6622 1036
Mooball	Fish 'n' Nana Competition	May, 1st weekend	07 5536 4244
Nimbin	Mardi Grass Festival	May, 1st weekend	1300 369 795
Woolgoolga	Sikh Vaisakki Festival	April	02 6654 8080
Wooli	Goanna Pulling Championships	June long weekend	02 6649 7575

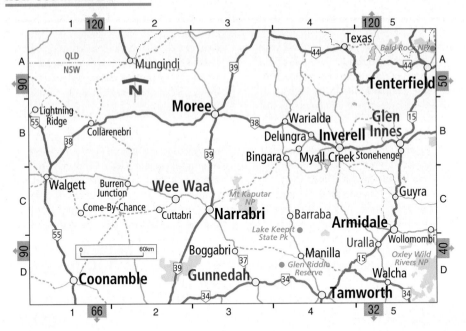

The region surrounding the New England Tableland is also known as Big Sky Country, so named because here the stars seem to touch the Earth. While still dominated by agriculture, the region is diversifying into tourism with the clever nurturing of local national parks and specialist Aboriginal cultural tourism.

get off the beaten track

travel the
tablelands and plains

Around 43 km east of **Armidale** [C4], off Waterfall Way in the **Oxley Wild Rivers National Park**, is one of Australia's highest waterfalls, and the fifth highest in the world, Wollomombi Falls, which drops 470 m in two stages. Dangars Falls, closer to Armidale, has a long history of public recreation, starting in 1866, when a Signor Vertelli walked a tight-rope across the falls, crossed again with a wheelbarrow, and again turning somersaults. According to the *Armidale Express*, the crowd was enchanted … but not enough to raise more than £11 to pay him for his trouble.

Barraba [C3] has been

described as the bird capital of New South Wales. The Birdman of Barraba, Russ Watts, says

GAZETTEER

'twitchers'—birdwatchers

to the rest of us—would find 165 species of bird in this region, including the endangered regent honeyeater. He says there are 12 bird routes that follow the old stock routes of the area. In this belt of country the dry interior joins the wet east coast and provides an ideal habitat for birds and plants. Regent honeyeaters can sometimes be seen perched on the wing mirrors of cars, busily attacking their own images. The information centre, in a large heritage building on Queen Street, can give advice about the best spots, or call 02 6782 1255. If you're interested in geology, the country around Barraba is an encyclopaedia of rock formations. To make it easy, there's a new driving tour taking in various sites along the district's geological belts (the drive is signposted but detailed brochures are available from the information centre). Here you'll see evidence of the Peel Fault, active in the area for more than 350 million years,

THUNDERBOLT PIE

The Ly family recipe for Thunderbolt Pie is a secret. This is our adaptation.

8 dried Chinese mushrooms	$1/2$ cup frozen baby peas
2 tbsp oil	$1/2$ cup baby corn, chopped
1 onion, finely chopped	220 g can water chestnuts, sliced
1 clove garlic, chopped	2 tbsp soy sauce
1 tbsp ginger, grated	1 tbsp oyster sauce
1 small red chilli, finely chopped	3 tsp cornflour
250 g pork mince	$1/2$ cup water
$1/2$ small red capsicum,	2 tbsp dry sherry
3 baby bok choy, shredded	puff pastry sheets
	1 egg, beaten (for egg wash)
	sesame seeds

Preheat oven to 200°C. Cover mushrooms with boiling water, stand for 30 minutes, drain, remove stems and chop mushrooms finely. Heat oil in pan, add onion, garlic, ginger and chilli and cook for 3 minutes to soften. Add pork mince and cook, stirring until it changes colour. Add chopped capsicum, bok choy, peas, corn, water chestnuts, soy sauce and oyster sauce. Cover and cook for 10 minutes. In a small bowl mix together cornflour, water and sherry. Add to pork mixture and stir to thicken. Allow mixture to cool for 30 minutes. Line a pie or flan dish with puff pastry, add pork mixture, top with puff pastry, sealing edges with a little egg wash. Brush top with egg wash and sprinkle with sesame seeds. Cut 2 slits in pastry to allow steam to escape during cooking. Place in oven and bake for 20–25 minutes or until golden brown. Serves 4.

Helen Ly, URALLA BAKERY

NSW

layers of mudstone with traces of ash and lava, volcanoes, the Ruby Hill fossicking area and old gold mines. There's good fishing at the **Glen Riddle Reserve** at the northern end of Split Rock Dam, with a variety of fish species, including golden perch and Murray cod. Bushwalks are a feature of **Mt Kaputar National Park**, about 40 km west of Barraba. On clear days the view from the Mt Kaputar peak, at 1,524 m, takes in one-tenth of the state. There is a 2 km return summit bushwalk that leads off the easy-grade Dawsons Spring Nature Trail, a 1.4 km circuit from the camping ground.

DON'T MISS: Australia's Smallest Country Music Festival is in Barraba on the second last weekend in January. It's an opener to the big one in Tamworth. The entertainment is held on the lawn outside the RSL club on Friday and Saturday. The Barrarbor Festival of Barraba, held on the first weekend in November, is a celebration of music and trees.

Bingara

Bingara [B4] is an old goldmining town. It's a popular place for fossicking, as many old mine shafts are within walking distance of the town. You'll find some of the best fishing in the region here, especially at Gwydir River and Copeton Dam. The Bingala Museum in the old Post Office Hotel has a collection of gemstones and rocks and information on local history. About 20 km north-east of town is **Myall Creek**, the scene of the massacre of 28 Aboriginal men, women and children in 1838 that led to the first case in Australian history of white men being tried and convicted of crimes against Aboriginal people. The murderers' justification for their crime—that they believed they acted with the support of the community—was initially accepted, with 11 defendants acquitted by the jury. However, seven were later retried, convicted and hanged. Today a 500 m path overlooking the site of the massacre tells the story on information plaques illustrated by an Aboriginal artist.

HOP BEER

Home-brewing is popular for a number of reasons, including being able to produce cheap beer specifically to your own tastes. Generally the ingredients needed for a good home brew are malted barley, hops as flavouring agents, and preservatives, yeast and water. Sugar boosts the alcohol level.

20 ltr water in a kerosene can, bucket or boiler
1 x 75 g packet of hops
1 small handful raisins
12 pieces root ginger, lightly bruised with a hammer
1.4 kg sugar
1 tsp Dri-balm

Wash bottles (on the day of boiling), then drain in rack upside down. Boil water, hops, root ginger and raisins together for 3 hours, topping up with water as it boils away. Place sugar in a large container and pour in strained liquid. When cooled, add Dri-balm, cover well and leave till next day. Strain mixture through a tea towel carefully (tie towel around top of bucket with string), then bottle and cork. Let beer stand for 5 days before drinking. If bottles begin popping, reduce quantity of raisins in next mixture. Makes 24 bottles.

Helen Allerton, COME-BY-CHANCE

Boggabri

Boggabri [D3] lies between the Namoi River and the foothills of the Nandewar Range. There are many great fishing spots along the meandering Namoi River. At the foot of a sheer rock face is the site of Grover's Rock Inn. Today, a vault containing the  remains of the Grover family and a grave of a servant girl are all that is left of the old inn. The Boggabri Museum has memorabilia of the town's history. Nelson's Honey Factory sells delicious light honey produced from local white and yellow box and iron bark.

At **Burren Junction** [C2] hot mineral water has been channelled from an artesian bore into the town baths. They're also floodlit for use at night.

Collarenebri

Collarenebri [B1] on the Barwon River has some of the best inland fishing in Australia. It also has the distinction of possessing the largest cotton gin (a machine that separates the cotton seeds from the plant) in the Southern Hemisphere. An Aboriginal cemetery at Collarenebri, a registered sacred site, has more than 100 individual graves, some symbolically marked with shells and artefacts. Research is being conducted to identify the older graves and to record the cemetery's significance to the contemporary Aboriginal community.

Come-By-Chance

Come-By-Chance [C1], population five, was once the only privately owned village in the Southern Hemisphere. In 1862 William Colless came upon the property by chance, discovering it had been overlooked during selection—when small farmers were allowed to take up Crown land and pay for it in instal-

ments. He selected it and built his station—eventually building a post office, hotel, police station, blacksmith's and cemetery. The town's picnic races are held in September.

Coonamble

Coonamble [D1] is a small town in arid country on the Castlereagh River. Some say the town's name derives from the Aboriginal word gunambil, or 'full of bullock's dung', others reckon it means 'full of dirt'. Either way, this part of the country has suffered from droughts and the river bed is dry most of the year.

The **Cuttabri** [C2] Wine Shanty in the **Pilliga Forest**, is the oldest in New South

Wales. The original Beehive Hotel burned down in the 1890s. Rebuilt on the same site, the pub had only four owners in its first hundred years of operation. The Pilliga Forest is home to one of Australia's largest populations of koalas. There are some pleasant 4WD tracks in the area, plus Yarrie Lake, formed a few thousand years ago by a meteor strike.

The **Glen Innes** [B5] brickworks in Thomas Street have been in continuous operation since 1886. Although no longer steam-powered, the old equipment is still in working order and group tours can be organised (phone 0438 667 926).

New South Wales

DON'T MISS: The Australian Celtic Festival is held during the first weekend in May at the **Australian Standing Stones** in Centennial Park on the Gwydir Highway just outside Glen Innes. The feature events are Celtic Yard Dog Trials, Strongman Events and the Kirking (Blessing) of the Tartans. Call 02 6732 2397 for more information. The Standing Stones were placed by the Celtic Council of Australia as a monument to Australia's Celtic pioneers. Officially opened in 1992, they were inspired by the Stones of Callanish on the Scotish Isle of Lewis, which were first used as calendars and later acquired religious significance. The Australian stones average 17 tonnes. The main feature is 24 granite stones set in a circle, representing the 24 hours of a day. Outside this circle are four 'cardinal' stones, pointing to the true compass points. These four stones, plus one more just inside the circle, make a Southern Cross. Like earlier stone circles, this one also functions as a seasonal clock; other stones mark the summer and winter solstices.

Balancing Rock is 12 km south of Glen Innes on the New England Highway. It is a natural rock formation that appears to be poised precariously on a 300 mm point. Nearby is the **Stonehenge Recreation Reserve** with picnic facilities (it is not a Celtic site). There are also some beautiful rock formations at the back of this reserve and magnificent granite rocks all around this area. On **Old Grafton Road** a 20 m tunnel was carved through solid rock by convicts when the road was constructed. The road heads south off the Gwydir Highway about 35 km east of Glen Innes. Once the main access road to the coast, it was cut by wood haulers and timbergetters in the 1840s. The tunnel is about 64 km from the highway. Around 8 km further on is the abandoned settlement of Dalmorton. At Jackass Creek, a little further on, you can find goldmining relics.

Gunnedah

Gunnedah [D3] is proud to identify itself as the town of 'My Country', the quintessentially Australian poem by Dorothea Mackellar. The poet spent time there from 1905, and the sunburnt country, sweeping plains and rugged mountain ranges she refers to were perhaps inspired by the Liverpool Plains and Great Dividing Range. Her memorial, a life-size bronze statue, is in Anzac Park. For anglers there are opportunities to catch golden and silver perch, Murray cod and catfish at nearby **Lake Keepit State Park** or you could try the increasingly popular sport of fly-fishing for carp. Unusual events in Gunnedah include the National Tomato Contest, a competition for the biggest, the heaviest, the most unusual and the most tasty tomatoes, held in January each year, and the Grey Mardi Gras, a celebration for seniors every April.

Guyra

West of **Guyra** [C5], on the historic Ollera property is a cemetery that holds the remains of a dray driver who carried his coffin wherever he went, with instructions that wherever he fell he should be placed in the coffin and returned to Ollera for burial. The cemetery (established in 1843) is still 'open' to descendants of the original pioneers. Ollera, settled in 1838 by the Everett brothers, is today a sheep and cattle station—still run by the Everett family.

Inverell

[B4] is also known as Sapphire City, because 80 per cent of the world's blue sapphires are mined here.

Lightning Ridge

[B1] has the world's largest supply of black opals. The town also has a mineral and mining museum built in a house made entirely of beer bottles. The Bottle House, in Opal Street, first took shape in the 1960s, when German artist Tex Moekel gathered the bottles together and started building. Take a look at Amigo's Castle,

too. Every rock in this ironstone castle has been hand placed or hauled up by rope. It's on a dirt track off Black Prince Drive on the outskirts of town. It's not open to the public but it's interesting to see from the outside and best photographed in the late afternoon.

Manilla

[D4] is home to Dutton's Meadery, on Barraba Street. Mead is an alcoholic beverage made using honey. The Duttons use their own honey (which they also sell) to make dry, medium and sweet varieties. They also make Melamol, a blend of grapes and honey. Call 02 6785 1148.

Moree

[B3] sits on part of the Great Artesian Basin, the waters of which, at 41°C, work wonders in a spa bath. The place to go is Artesian Spa Baths—02 6752 7480—on the corner of Anne and Gosport Streets. On Greenbah Road (the Gwydir Highway), at the western outskirts of Moree beyond the golf club, is a cemetery. To the left of the main gates is the grave of Charles Dickens'

BEEF BURGUNDY

Come-By-Chance, at the junction of two rivers, is in good cattle country. There were so many cattle runs in 1862, when William Colless arrived, there was little unsettled land. Finally finding a plot, he couldn't believe his luck, and called it Come-By-Chance.

2 tbsp oil	200 g mushrooms
1 kg blade steak, cubed	1$^1/_2$ cups beef stock
3 rashers bacon, diced	salt and pepper to taste
1 tbsp brandy	1 bay leaf
3 small onions, diced	$^1/_2$ tsp thyme
1 clove garlic, chopped	$^1/_2$ cup red wine
1 carrot, sliced	1 tbsp finely chopped parsley, for garnish

In a large saucepan or frying pan sauté onion, bacon and meat in the oil until browned. Warm brandy in a small pan, ignite, then pour into onion and bacon mixture. Add garlic, carrot and mushrooms. Pour in stock, seasonings and wine. Simmer covered for 1$^1/_2$–2 hours. Serve garnished with parsley. Serves 6.

Helen Allerton, COME-BY-CHANCE

youngest son, Edward Bulwer Lytton Dickens, who arrived in Australia in 1868, two years before his father's death. Once the Mayor of Wilcannia, he worked for the Lands Department in Moree from 1900 until his death— almost a pauper by then—in 1902.

DON'T MISS: The Moree Club in Frome Street in 1900 was the home of a Dr McGill, who owned Australia's first motor car. He bought it in Sydney, driving it back to Moree, but soon returned to horse power.

New South Wales

The locals at **Mungindi** [A2] can celebrate the stroke of midnight twice every New Year's Eve, with half of the town in Queensland and half in New South Wales. In summer, when daylight saving starts and New South Wales moves ahead an hour, if you stand on the bridge you can have one foot in each of the time zones. The town also has a police station on either side of the bridge.

Narrabri [C3] is a rich agricultural shire, thanks to cotton, oilseed, cereals, wool, livestock and timber. The Australian Cotton Centre features interactive, entertaining and educational exhibits produced by Canberra's

National Science and Technology Centre. Narrabri also boasts the CSIRO's Australia Telescope on Yarrie Lake Road. The telescope is actually an array of six linked 22 m wide telescopes that, with the help of other dishes at Coonabarabran and Parkes, offer a detailed view of the universe. It is the leading telescope of its kind in the Southern Hemisphere. Narrabri also has its own bright pink slug—*Triboniophorus graeffei*. This slug, about 20 cm long, is found nowhere else.

Tamworth [D4] was the first town in the Southern Hemisphere to have electric street lighting supplied by a municipal council, in 1888.

DON'T MISS: That Tamworth is the Country Music Capital of Australia is

not in dispute. For 10 days in January (starting on the second to last weekend) the city's population swells with more than 40,000 visitors, as hopefuls and fans come together to celebrate

everything from bluegrass to gospel. There are Country Music Awards, Golden Guitar Awards, Hands of Fame and Winners Walkway. Less well known, but as hotly contested, is the Noses of Fame Award in Joe Maguire's Pub on Peel Street.

In **Tenterfield** [A5], on the corner of Manners and Rouse Streets, is the Sir Henry Parkes Memorial School of Arts. The building began its life as a Working Man's Institute in 1876. It was here, in 1889, that five-times premier of New South Wales Henry Parkes delivered his famous Federation speech, calling for a united and cohesive nation. The speech is credited with sparking off the chain of events that culminated in the declaration of the Australian Commonwealth in 1901. Along the Mt Lindesay Road, 12 km from town, is a sign pointing to Thunderbolt's Hideout, used by the bushranger Captain Thunderbolt (Fred Ward). Tenterfield also lies at the hub of some great fishing territory, especially for anglers pursuing the mighty Murray cod, which makes its home in the deep, granite-lined pools of the local rivers. Tenterfield fishing lure maker, Peter Newell, handcrafted his earliest products from Australian hardwoods specifically to target these fish, and Newell Lures are now famous throughout Australia. **Bald Rock National Park**, 29 km north of Tenterfield, has Australia's biggest granite monolith—measuring 750 m by 500 m, and rising 200 m above the surrounding bushland. There are walks to the top—the long way and the short way—and several other longer walks and trails in the park.

In **Uralla** [D5] there is a statue of the notorious bushranger Captain Thunderbolt (Fred Ward) astride his horse. East of the statue (20 m) a mere plaque memorialises the policeman who killed him in 1870. The grave of the bushranger is clearly marked on the eastern side of the cemetery. The **Deeargee Woolshed**, 11 km south-east of Uralla, was a forerunner of good workplace design in 1851. The octagonal shearing chamber has a tiered roof allowing maximum air flow, while the building's layout allowed sheep to move through at a rapid pace. The woolshed is still in use on the Deeargee property.

In **Walcha** [D5], at the Plane Shed of the Pioneer Cottage and Museum Complex, is a 1930 Tiger Moth biplane used by AS Nivison at a local property in 1950 to spread super-

phosphates over his crops. It was reputedly the first time this had been done in Australia and was certainly one of the earliest instances of aerial fertilising, or crop-dusting, in the country.

Walgett [C1] is on what used to be the north-eastern border of the sheep run Euroka. The property was owned by Frederick Wolseley, who in 1877 invented the sheep shearing machine.

About 8 km east of **Warialda** [B4] is Cranky Rock Reserve. Cranky Rock is a tall rock with a series of boulders perched atop. It is said that, in the goldmining days, a 'cranky' Chinese miner jumped to his death from the uppermost rock after being accused of some wrongdoing.

If you visit **Wee Waa** [C2] in April you'll see a magical landscape of snowy white fields of cotton as the harvest begins. The town is Australia's cotton capital and from April to July tours depart daily from the Wee Waa Coffee Shop on Rose Street. The tours include a viewing of cotton picking and a visit to Namoi cotton gin and classing rooms.

Diary of Events

Town	Event	Date	Contact
Barraba	Smallest Country Music Festival	January, last week	02 6782 1255
	Barrarbor—Festival of Barraba	November, 1st weekend	02 6782 1255
Come-By-Chance	Picnic Races	September	02 6822 1982
Coonabarabran	Festival of the Stars	October, last 2 weeks	02 6842 1441
Glen Innes	Australian Celtic Festival	May, 1st weekend	02 6732 2397
Gunnedah	National Tomato Contest	January	02 6742 0400
	Grey Mardi Gras	April	02 6742 1957
Guyra	Lamb and Potato Festival	January	02 6772 4655
Lightning Ridge	Opal and Gem Festival	July, last weekend	02 6829 0429
Tamworth	Great Country Music Awards	January, last 2 weeks	02 6755 4302
Walgett	Walgett Rodeo and Campdraft	August, 3rd weekend	0418 259 165

get off the beaten track

discover

settler country

Abercrombie Caves [F3]

contain Abercrombie Arch—at 221 m long and 30 m high in the centre, the largest natural limestone tunnel in the Southern Hemisphere. The stage in the Caves was built

by miners in the 1880s; the Baltic pine it is made from probably came from a packing case for mining equipment or ship's ballast. A few kilometres south, at **Tuena**, is the Goldfields Inn.

In **Albert** [C1] is the famous Rabbit Trap Hotel, the inspiration for cartoonist Joliffe's Saltbush Bill cartoons. Nearby **Dandaloo**, now only a church, might well have been the inspiration for a Dr Seuss story.

In the centre of **Bathurst** [E4] is the carillon in Kings Parade, one of three in

Australia (the others are in Canberra and at Sydney University). The Bathurst carillon is the only one of its kind in the Southern Hemisphere, its internal structure being based on a classic 17th-century Flemish design. In what was the village of **Kelso**, now a suburb

of Bathurst 2 km from the city centre, on Gilmore Street off the Great Western Highway is Holy Trinity Church, the first church in Australia to be consecrated by a bishop. While you're in the area, why not drive the Mt Panorama race circuit, and visit the motor racing museum?

Blayney [E3] is the site of Australia's

biggest wind farm, with 15 wind turbine

ELIZABETH CHIFLEY'S SCOTCH SHORTBREAD

This recipe takes its name from Elizabeth Chifley, the wife of Prime Minister Ben Chifley who spent much of his childhood in Bathurst. Elizabeth was renowned for her work in the community.

250 g butter
125 g caster sugar
500 g plain flour, sifted

Preheat oven to 180°C. In a large bowl, cream butter and sugar until light. Add flour and knead well. Roll to 1 cm thickness and cut into desired shapes. Crimp edges and prick well. Bake for 20–25 minutes.

Felicity Baines, BATHURST

generators set in three groups on elevated ridges between Lake Carcoar and Mt Macquarie beside the Midwestern Highway. In its lifetime—the land on which the turbines have been built has been leased for 22 years, with an option for another 22 years—the $18 million facility is expected to reduce carbon dioxide emissions equivalent to taking 88,000 cars off the road, and to supply the annual electricity needs of 3,500 homes—a shire about Blayney's size. It has a capacity of 10 megawatts.

The **Bylong** [C4] Mouse Races are held in late March each year. The card features 10 races with 10 mice in each. The winners of each race go into the final event, the prestigious Bylong

GAZETTEER

New South Wales

Cup. Local kids catch the entrants in haystacks (they're said to be very quick off the blocks). The races are held in a 10 m long, 10-track Perspex-sided race box. Call 02 6379 8254 for specific dates.

Byng [E3] cemetery holds the remains of William Tom, the man who, contrary to popular belief, first discovered gold at Ophir and so sparked the first Australian goldrush. In April 1851 Tom spotted a 14 g nugget near the intersection of Summer Hill Creek and Lewis Ponds Creek. He, his brother James and John Lister turned their attention to the adjacent creekbed, turning up 113 g over the next three days, including a 55 g nugget. Then they told Edward Hargraves, who's had the credit for the discovery ever since.

Around **Canowindra** [E2], 360 million years ago, a large lake or river teeming with tens of thousands of fish dried up during a severe drought. In 1961 council workers straightening a bend in the Gooloogong Road west of the town pulled up a slab of rock and propped it against a fence out of the way. A few weeks later a local apiarist fencing off his beehives saw the rock, noticing it was thick with fossils. In 1993 the fish mother lode was struck. Eventually 3,000 fossil fish specimens were recovered—from 80 tonnes of rock—some of them completely new to scientists. Among the many specimens in the Age of Fishes Museum in Gaskill Street is the *Canowindra grossi*, the only one of its family group in the world.

DON'T MISS: In April each year Marti's Balloon Fiesta is held in Canowindra, and the town's population swells by several thousand as national and

NANNA SMITH'S BOILED CHOCOLATE CAKE

Euchareena was originally named Warne but was renamed in October 1899. The broad accent of an Irish or Scottish porter (no one's any longer sure which) at the railway station confused travellers into getting off at Warne instead of Warren, some 150 km north-west. One of the first settlers in the area had come from a Queensland property and named the town Euchareena after a Kanaka worker there.

Preheat oven to 180°C and line a 26 cm springform pan with baking paper. Combine butter, sugar, water and cocoa in a large saucepan. Bring to the boil, remove from heat and slowly add bicarbonate of soda. Leave to cool. When cool, add flour and eggs. Pour into prepared pan and bake for 45–60 minutes. Makes a very large, moist cake. Serve with whipped cream.

Kim Frazer, EUCHAREENA

250 g butter
2 cups sugar
2 cups water
3 tbsp cocoa
1 tsp bicarbonate
   of soda

4 cups self-raising
   flour, sifted
3 eggs, beaten
whipped cream,
   for serving

international hot-air balloonists descend on the town—in order to sail over it.

The town of **Carcoar** [E3] is listed by the National Trust in its entirety, a complete example of 19th-century Australian architecture. Settlement began in the 1820s, but its official birthdate is 1839. 'Daylesford' on Belubula Street, now a private residence, was used for a time as premises for the Commercial Bank. It was here, in 1863, that Johnny Gilbert and John O'Meally conducted Australia's first recorded daylight bank robbery; however, they fled empty-handed when a teller fired a shot into the bank ceiling.

Coolah [B4] is one of several towns claiming to be the mythical 'Black Stump'. In the early days of settlement in sparsely populated regions (no fences, no road signs) 'black stumps' were fire-blackened markers used as local landmarks in uncharted territory. According to Susan Butler, of the *Macquarie Dictionary*, there is no one Black Stump.

GAZETTEER

DON'T MISS: Coolah Tops National Park, east of Coolah, claims a stand of the largest snow gums in existence. They are on the right-hand side of the Forest Road as you head east, 22 km from Pinnacle Road.

In **Coonabarabran** [A3] there was a time when, as there was no police lock-up, offenders were locked up in the local pub instead. The **Skywatch Observatory** west of town has guided telescope viewings of the night sky. Open daily from 2 pm, the observatory also has Astro Mini Golf for the kids, a nine-hole course in outer space with aliens and black holes. Down the road is the **Siding Spring Observatory** where the real astronomers carry out their studies through Australia's largest optical telescope. Both observatories are in the **Warrumbungle National Park**, which has

one of Australia's most popular walks, the Grand High Tops Track. The Warrumbungles (originally called Arbuthnot Range after a British civil servant), also features the Breadknife, a 90 m rock wall that measures just one metre thick.

DON'T MISS: Coonabarabran Festival of the Stars is held in October each year. Call 02 6842 1441 for details.

During World War II **Cowra** [F2] was home to a Japanese POW camp. When the prisoners tried to break out, 231 Japanese and four Australian soldiers were killed. The Japanese War Cemetery on Doncaster Drive in Cowra contains the remains of all Japanese who died in the breakout, and of all other Japanese nationals who died on Australian soil during World War II. Sakura Avenue, which connects the Japanese and Cowra War Cemeteries, the POW campsite and the Japanese Garden and Cultural Centre on Binni Creek Road, will eventually be an avenue of 2,000 cherry trees. Cowra is the only non-capital city in the world permitted to hold a replica of the United Nations' World Peace Bell, at the entrance to the Council Chambers in Darling Street. Cowra won that honour in 1992 for its

GAZETTEER

contribution to world peace and international understanding. Just a short distance out of Cowra is **Croote Cottage**, one of the oldest buildings west of the Great Divide and one of Australia's oldest residences. This four-room pisé (rammed-earth construction) cottage was built by convict labour in 1827.

Awassi Australia, the nation's only intensive sheep dairy, is on the Midwestern Highway at Cowra. Awassi comes from the name of the breed of sheep—most people know them as Desert Fat Tails. They're considered the best milking sheep in the world, with pure Awassi ewes producing up to 6 ltr daily. Sheep milk products such as cheese, milk and yoghurt (called Ewegurt) are ideal for people with lactose intolerance.

DON'T MISS: Cowra's Festival of International Understanding is in March (call 02 6342 4333 for exact dates). The National Bush Tucker, Home Brewing and Billy Boiling Championships are held in **Morongla Creek** in the first weekend in May.

On the outskirts of **Dubbo** [C2] is the Western Plains Zoo, Australia's first open-range zoo, where animals and their visitors can study each other in safety, separated by moats and ditches rather than by bars and wiremesh.

Dunedoo

[B3], the gateway to the Warrumbungles, is on the Talbragar River

where you can fish for rainbow trout, carp, catfish and yellowbelly.

Euchareena

[D3], on the main rail line between Orange and Wellington, is the only place of that name in the world. A postmaster in Norway, helping two Euchareenans send a postcard back home, checked the international register of post offices to confirm the address. That's how they know.

At **Eugowra** [E2] Frank Gardiner pulled off the biggest gold heist in New South Wales colonial history. In 1862 he and his gang, which included Ben Hall, commandeered two bullock teams and blocked the road, making the drivers lie on the road feigning drunkenness. When the gold escort arrived, the gang sprayed the troopers with a hail of gunfire, wounding one. The gang made off with 77 kg of gold and £3,700 in cash.

In 1872 in **Forbes** [E2], Australia's (and possibly the world's) first sheep dog trials were held. In 1865 bushranger Ben Hall was buried in Forbes Cemetery, across the way from Ned Kelly's sister Kate, who drowned in the Lachlan River in 1898. Captain Cook's great-granddaughter, Rebecca Shields, is also buried here.

Forbes' first cemetery was destroyed by floods, but a list of people possibly buried there has been posted on the site.

Gilgandra

[B2] was home to Arthur 'Cliff' Howard, who, in 1912, invented the Howard Rotovator, a rotary cultivator used to break up the soil before planting—since adopted worldwide. Gilgandra was also where the Cooee recruiting march started during World War I, following the setbacks suffered at Gallipoli, which had made recruiting drives difficult. Marching from

Gilgandra to Sydney, recruiting from the towns they passed through, the march gathered a group of 263 men into uniform. The Gilgandra Museum contains memorabilia relating to the march, as well as artefacts and pictures relating to the murders of 1900 at **Breelong**, 18 km south-east of Gilgandra. Jimmy Governor and Jacky Underwood, both in the employ of Jack Mawbey, murdered Sarah Mawbey, three of her children and Helen Kurz, the local school teacher. The tragedy forms the basis of Thomas Keneally's novel *The Chant of Jimmie Blacksmith*.

DON'T MISS: The Cooee Festival, a four-day event including the NSW State Cooee Calling Championship, is held over the October long weekend each year. Competitors cooee across the Castlereagh River to judges armed with a sound meter.

Grenfell

[F2] is home to the Pinnacle Guinea Pig Races. The races are held on Easter Sunday and the Sunday of the June long weekend, in conjunction with the Henry Lawson Festival of the Arts. The races attract enthusiasts and visitors from all over Australia. The Grenfell goldfields, although short-lived, produced

GAZETTEER

FRESH TOMATO SOUP

Tomatoes contain the antioxidant lycopene, which gives tomatoes their red colour and is thought to decrease the risk of heart disease and prostate cancer. When cooking fresh tomatoes make sure you choose smooth-skinned, brightly coloured tomatoes that have a bit of weight in them. If you are not going to cook them immediately don't store them in the refrigerator as they will lose flavour.

1 dsp butter	600 ml chicken or
500 g fresh	vegetable stock
tomatoes,	1 bay leaf
chopped	1 dsp soaked sago
2 bacon rashers,	salt and pepper to
diced	taste
1 onion, diced	600 ml milk

Melt butter in saucepan, add tomatoes, bacon and onion, cook for 3 minutes. Add stock and bay leaf and bring gently to boil. Simmer until vegetables are soft. Remove from heat and discard bay leaf. Blend soup in blender. Add sago and seasoning, and simmer until sago is clear. Add milk and heat through, but do not allow to boil. Serves 4.

Margaret Smith,
BARMEDMAN

$3 million worth of gold, attracting both prospectors and bushrangers. Bushranger Ben Hall didn't have far to commute to the takings. He lived here. A sign in a paddock outside Grenfell marks the spot of his childhood home, which is said to have burned down in 1862. Its location offers an insight into rural life (and isolation) in the 1860s. To get there, head west on the Midwestern Highway. After 23 km turn right,

heading toward **Pullabooka**. After another 12 km turn right again, toward Forbes. The site is 250–300 m along the road. Also out of town is Ben Hall's Cave, which, it is now widely accepted, Hall used for shelter, also providing an ideal vantage point. Head south-west to **Bimbi** from Grenfell, then turn north 2 km after Bimbi on Nowlands Road. The cave, a half-hour walk from the carpark, is clearly signposted.

In the 1870s **Gulgong** [C4] was known as 'the hub of the world'. The Prince of Wales Opera House on Mayne Street was built in 1871 as a theatre to entertain the estimated 20,000 people on the surrounding goldfields. Renowned boxer Les Darcy fought an exhibition bout there just before heading to the United States in 1916. The theatre's predecessor, Cogdon's Assembly Rooms, had the largest edifice ever constructed entirely of bark. Thomas Alexander Browne (who wrote *Robbery Under Arms* under the nom de plume Rolf Boldrewood), the town's police magistrate from 1871 to 1881 and perhaps Australia's first novelist of any distinction, initially held court at Cogdon's Assembly Rooms, using a piano as a bench. In the town's heyday it was not unknown for female performers at the venue to have gold nuggets thrown at their feet. Among the people who performed there was an unknown soprano who had bombed in Bathurst—audiences were far smaller than expected and she had two nights spare. Mrs Armstrong sang for the Gulgong miners in 1886. Two months later she left Australia for voice training and 19 years later returned as Nellie Melba.

In **Mendooran** [B3] the walls of major buildings feature life-sized murals of shearing sheds, horseracing, bullriding, camp-drafting and rodeos—the work of local artist Karin Duce.

The town of **Montefiores** [C3] was built by a rich tea merchant to take advantage of people crossing the Macquarie River. Australia's last duel was fought there in 1854. The duel was between two police magistrates—both were so drunk that the one shot that was fired hit no one.

Narromine [C2] calls itself the gliding capital of Australia. The local aerodrome (on the Mitchell Highway) is home to the oldest country aero club in Australia, formed after World War I. Visitors to the club have included Australian aviators Charles Kingsford Smith, Charles Ulm and Nancy Bird Walton, and US pilot Chuck Yeager, the first man to fly faster than the speed of sound. It has a large collection of memorabilia, which can be seen on weekdays. Narromine's Lime Grove, the largest lime orchard in the Southern Hemisphere, grows giant yellow limes. Visit between February and July.

GAZETTEER

CRISP-SKINNED SILVER PERCH WITH SAUTÉED VEGETABLES

Viticulture was established in the Mudgee region in 1858 by German vignerons and today it has a reputation for producing premier red wines. While in the area pick up a Mudgee muscat, a liqueur made from muscat grapes and aged brandy spirit. It tastes like warm caramel with a hint of spices and adds a wonderful flavour to this recipe.

1 or 2 fillets silver perch, skin on
salt and pepper to taste
olive oil
2 tbsp butter
200 g mushrooms, sliced
1 garlic clove, crushed
2 baby bok choy, washed
1/2 small red capsicum, cut in strips
juice and zest of 1/2 grapefruit
2 tbsp Mudgee muscat
1 tbsp parsley or basil, chopped

In a hot pan, season perch and seal quickly in a little olive oil, skin side first. Remove and keep warm. In same pan melt butter and sauté mushrooms over high heat. Reduce heat and add garlic, bok choy and capsicum. Combine gently until bok choy is just wilted. Add juice and zest of grapefruit, muscat and parsley or basil. Place vegetables in a pile in the centre of a warmed plate. Return pan juices to high heat and reduce by half. Top vegetables with silver perch fillets. Pour juices around plate. Serves 1.

Central Ranges Food & Wine, RYLSTONE

Oberon [E4] benefited from a touch of Shakespeare when the town's name was changed from Bullock Flats and the hamlet of Fish River Creek was renamed Titania. Big Tom (the fish that keeps getting away) is rumoured to live in Lake Oberon, renowned for its trout fishing. Oberon is surrounded by pine forests, the source of exotic wood mushrooms. Between January and late April visitors can pick Saffron Milk Caps (bright orange with distinctive darkening rings and reddish-pink gills on the underside) and Boletes or Slippery Jacks (dark brown on top with bright yellow spongy gills) free. Take an identification kit from the Oberon Visitors Centre (137 Oberon Street) before you start, and remember the warning: if in doubt, throw

it out. To make the most of your mushrooms remember the following rules:

1. Always carry a pocket knife to cut the mushroom stems (cover them over with pine needles so they will come again next year).
2. Walk slowly, but look quickly.
3. If you see a little mound, push the pine needles away gently and there will be your mushroom.
4. If you find a mushroom, look nearby; it will have neighbours.

DON'T MISS: Flickerfest, Australia's premier international short-film festival—all 16 mm and 35 mm film, not video—is held at the Oberon RSL Club (Oberon Street), in February or March.

If you can't take a trip to Oberon to **pick your own mushrooms**, there are a variety of cultivated mushrooms available all year round from your supermarket—oyster, enokitake, Swiss brown, to name a few. Mushrooms have a very high moisture content and need very little cooking. Store them in a paper bag in the refrigerator (they will sweat and deteriorate quickly in plastic). Mushrooms don't need to be washed; all they need is a quick wipe with a damp cloth, or at the most a light peel of large dark mushrooms. Use the stems whole or chopped in stews and soups. Cook mushrooms quickly over a high heat in butter or olive oil. Delicious with lemon juice, nutmeg, bacon, eggs, chives, parsley, goat's cheese, asparagus, onions, shallots, toast, garlic, ham, or barbecued with a steak.

The time changes each year so call the Oberon Visitor Information Centre—phone 02 6336 0666. To hear chamber music with a distinctly local flavour, come to Oberon and Bathurst in the last two weeks of March when international musicians give a series of concerts in caves, cattle sheds, halls and churches. Kowmung Music Festival is coordinated in Oberon. For more information call 02 6336 2022.

The **Ophir** Reserve [D3] is where Australia's first payable gold was discovered in 1851. Some of the gold used for the medals at the 2000 Sydney Olympics was sourced from here. From Ophir you can head across to historic **Hill End** and its Heritage of Gold, while keen 4WD enthusiasts will enjoy the steep hills and creek crossings of Madman's Territory, a large property open to campers and four-wheel-drivers.

In the heart of **Orange** [E3] is Cook Park, named after the famous captain. The caretaker's cottage, built in 1887, and many of the original trees, planted in the 1870s, still stand today. Including deodar cedars, elms, oaks, poplars, redwoods, lindens, cypress and ash trees, they give the park a distinctly English air. The heritage walk provides an interesting lesson in park design and colonial history. A fountain was built in 1891, a bandstand in 1908, an aviary in 1948 (since considerably extended) and a fernery in 1938 and restored 50 years later. On display are a German gun, captured in France during World War I, and an 18th-century cannon. About 5 km from Orange, at **Narambla**, is a simple white monument—this

was where Australia's most famous bush poet, Andrew 'Banjo' Paterson, was born. The great 20th-century poet Kenneth Slessor was also born in Orange. Oranges don't grow in Orange. It's apples and cherries and pears and peaches country. The area was named after the Prince of Orange by Major Thomas Mitchell, who had served with the Prince (as a surveyor) in the Napoleonic Wars in Spain.

DON'T MISS: In October at **Borenore**, 15 km west of Orange, the Australian National Field Days are held, with Australasia's biggest selection of agricultural machinery and equipment on display (phone 1800 069 466

for exact dates). **Millthorpe**, on the road from Blayney to Orange, celebrates the humble spud every March at the Millthorpe Murphy Marathon. There's an award for the longest potato peel and a race in which contestants carry a 50 kg bag of potatoes.

The **Parkes** [D2] telescope, the famous 'Dish', standing in an old sheep paddock on the north side of town, is the best radio telescope in the Southern Hemisphere for making radio pictures. It electronically listens to, collects and analyses the feeble, naturally created radio waves emanating from stars.

DON'T MISS: The Elvis Revival Festival is held on a weekend close to 8 January, the King's birthday. Call 02 6862 4365 to check the date. There are several must-do events: breakfast at the Gracelands Restaurant, a rock'n'roll dance competition, a display of Elvis memorabilia, a sound-alike and look-alike competition, plus concerts and a parade.

You can still visit the **Peak Hill** [D2] goldmine on Mingelo Street, though all that's left are two big holes. Different colours highlight the remaining trace elements in the walls. View the mine from nearby lookouts to appreciate the scale of the work, done entirely by hand. On the Baldry Road south-east of Peak Hill is **Goobang National Park**, which, until the fires of 2001, held the largest remnant of original forest and woodland in the Central

APPLES ROASTED WITH QUINCE JELLY

Apples and quinces come from the pome, or fake, fruit family. Quinces must be cooked before eaten and contain pectin, a substance that gels when heated, which makes wonderful jams, jellies and preserves. They come into season from August to December. Apples are also a good cooking fruit, in season from January to October.

ROASTED APPLES
6 medium apples
60 g butter, in knobs
1 x 250 g jar quince jelly
thickened cream, crème anglaise
  or vanilla ice-cream, for serving
icing sugar

PIKELET BATTER
2 cups self-raising flour
2 tsp ground cinnamon
3 eggs
50 g butter, melted
3 cups buttermilk

Preheat oven to 180°C. Quarter and core apples, place in a baking dish with knobs of butter and quince jelly. Bake, basting occasionally, for about 30 minutes. Mix batter ingredients together in a bowl and leave for about 30 minutes. Cook tablespoons of batter in a greased pan until golden brown on both sides. Serve 3 per person, topped with the apples, thickened cream, crème anglaise or vanilla ice-cream, and dust with icing sugar. Serves 6.

Central Ranges Food & Wine, RYLSTONE

NSW

PEANUT AND CARAMEL SLICE

This recipe has been handed down through generations of Shirley Morrish's family, who have lived in the Warren district for 35 years.

BASE	TOPPING
125 g butter	1/2 cup brown
1/2 cup caster	sugar, lightly
sugar	packed
1 egg yolk	1 tbsp golden
1 cup plain flour	syrup
1/4 cup self-raising	100 g butter
flour	125 g unsalted
2 tbsp custard	roasted peanuts,
powder	roughly chopped
1/4 tsp salt	

Preheat oven to 180°C. Grease an 18 x 28 cm lamington tin. In a large bowl, cream butter and sugar until light and fluffy. Add egg yolk and mix well, then add flours, custard powder and salt, and work with a fork to combine. Press mixture into base of tin. Bake for 15 minutes, until golden brown. To prepare topping, place brown sugar, golden syrup and butter in a small saucepan, stir over low heat until butter is melted and sugar dissolved. Simmer gently for 5 minutes. Stir peanuts through. Remove base from oven and spread with topping. Return to oven for 5 minutes. Remove and allow to cool in tin. Cut into squares.

Shirley Morrish, WARREN

West. More than 300 plant species had been recorded there, including 40 species of orchid. The fires destroyed about a quarter of the park (mostly in the northern end) and work is under way to assess the extent of long-term damage.

West of **Rylstone** [D4] is Joe Horner's Flora Glen Queens, a world renowned bee-breeding establishment. To ensure the comfort of the bees during summer, they are kept cool—between 15°C and 17°C. Group bookings can be made by phoning 02 6379 4528. From Rylstone south to Capertee is the **Capertee Valley**, Australia's largest enclosed valley and second only (in size) to the United States' Grand Canyon. It is 30 km wide. The best view is from Pearson's Lookout on Capertee Valley Road.

About 25 km north-east of **Trangie** [B1] is the Gin Gin Weir, built in 1896, on the Macquarie River. It's a good spot for picnics, fishing and bushwalking.

The village of **Trundle** [D1] is said to have the widest main street in western New South Wales. Forbes Street is approximately 60 m wide and was built so that a bullock team could comfortably do a U-turn on it. People now drive from one side of the street to the other. The Trundle Hotel once claimed the longest balcony in New South Wales—approximately 70 m of it fronts Forbes Street, then another 20 m wraps around the corner into Parkes Street. It is now the second longest, being 10 m shorter than that of Cobar's Great Western Hotel.

DON'T MISS: At the Trundle Bush Tucker Day in September each year competitors must cook their meals on site in camp ovens in the ground. Entries vary from pavlova to emu, crocodile, muffins and ox tongue. The day attracts up to 3000 people and includes bush poetry, a Billy Boiling Competition, Damper Throw and Cross-cut Saw Competition. Camp on site to make

GAZETTEER

the most of it. For further information call 02 6892 1046.

Trunkey Creek [F3] (a town that
used to be called Arthur) has the Grove Creek Observatory, on Grove Creek Road. It is one of the largest privately owned observatories in the country. At the moment it is not set up for the individual day visitor. The idea is essentially to take up accommodation at the observatory and then use the telescope at your leisure; larger group tours can be arranged. All visits must be booked in advance 02 9438 1757.

About 50 km north of **Warren** [B1], are the Macquarie Marshes, one of the most significant wetland areas in Australia and listed as a wetland of international importance. Birdlife in the area was affected by the construction of the Burrendong Dam in 1968 and the Tiger Bay Wildlife Park at Warren aims to recreate the abundance and diversity of wildlife activity the marshes once enjoyed. This region is also home to some of Australia's premier merino studs and in

September each year they participate in the Macquarie Merino Field Days, displaying sheep and wool on their properties and at the Warren Showground.

Wellington's [C3] Burrendong
Arboretum, 22 km south-east of town, is one of Australia's major regional botanic gardens. Its 160 ha have 2,500 species of native plants. On Parkes Road, 20 minutes out of Wellington, there is an Angora Farm—if you've ever wanted to watch a rabbit being shorn, this is your chance. The Lion of Waterloo Hotel on Montefiores Street in Wellington was licensed in 1842 and is said to be the oldest licensed hotel west of the Blue Mountains still standing. Along the road to **Wellington Caves** are the Great Western Crystal Cottage (an exhibition of crystals, gold, amethyst and gemstones) and the Bottle House (made of 9,000 bottles). Behind Crystal Cottage is the garden railway, an unusual piece of engineering in landscaped gardens.

Diary of Events

Town	Event	Date	Contact
Borenore	Australian National Field Days	October, 3rd week	1800 069 466
Bylong	Bylong Mouse Race	March	02 6379 8254
Canowindra	Marti's Balloon Fiesta	April, 3rd weekend	02 6344 2422
Cowra	Festival of International Understanding	March	02 6342 4333
Gilgandra	Cooee Festival	October long weekend	02 6847 2709
Millthorpe	Millthorpe Murphy Marathon	March	02 6366 3033
Morongla Creek	The National Bush Tucker and Billy Boiling Championships	May, 1st weekend	02 6297 7539
Oberon	Flickerfest	Feb or March	02 6336 0666
Parkes	Elvis Revival Festival	January	02 6862 4365
Trundle	Bush Tucker Day	September	02 6892 1046

T he rolling green country and heritage settlements surrounding the Australian Capital Territory contrast sharply with the wild country of the Australian Alps to the south. Both attract numerous visitors, the former for the rigours of antique shopping, the latter for the ski slopes, hiking and riding trails, and swift mountain streams.

get off the beaten track

trip

the alps and foothills

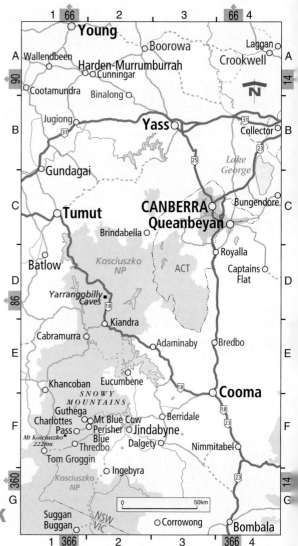

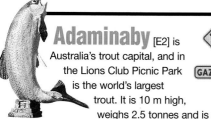

Adaminaby [E2] is

Australia's trout capital, and in the Lions Club Picnic Park is the world's largest trout. It is 10 m high, weighs 2.5 tonnes and is made of fibreglass. The idea for the trout came from local Leigh Stewart, who then happened upon Andy Lomnici, a Hungarian artist who was on a fishing holiday. Lomnici created it, sketching a frozen trout on the floor of the local bowls club then moving to ever bigger quarters as the fish took shape.

A perfect temperate climate is **Batlow**'s [D1] secret to producing some of Australia's best apples. Here, in the foothills of the Snowy Mountains, the climate is neither too cold nor too mild for apple-growing, and the cold nights trigger an enzyme that increases the colour of the fruit. Pick your own during picking season (usually March until May) or stop at a roadside stall for apples just off the tree.

Near **Berridale** [F3], the Snowy River Winery prospers in what might seem less than promising climatic conditions.

Binalong [A2] has two graves of

interest. The first belongs to bushranger Johnny Gilbert, a member of Ben Hall's gang, buried in the police paddock in 1865. In the local cemetery, buried with the righteous, is poet Banjo Paterson's dad, Andrew.

Bombala's [G4] art deco style Olympia

Theatre was built between 1915 and 1918. The town has the biggest platypus population in the state. There's a Platypus Viewing Platform 4 km south of town on Delegate Road. The best viewing times are early morning and at dusk.

In Boorowa [A2],

St Patrick's Church has a special stained-glass window depicting Daniel O'Connell (1775–1847), the 'Liberator of Ireland'— the man who fought for Catholic emancipation.

LAVENDER AND GINGER BISCUITS

Bombala's lavender cooperative was the first in Australia. Lavender is an anti-depressant, anti-spasmodic relaxant. Tip: Using too many lavender flowers in cooking can make the food taste bitter.

1 tbsp dried *lavendula angustifolia* (English lavender)
1 cup caster sugar
120 g butter
1 egg
3/4 cup glacé ginger, chopped
2 cups self-raising flour

Preheat oven to 200°C and grease 2 baking trays. Add the dried lavender to the sugar the day before making biscuits. In a bowl, cream butter and sugar. Add egg and combine, then add ginger and flour and combine. Roll mixture into balls, place on prepared baking trays and press the balls with a fork. Bake for 10–15 minutes or until golden. Cool on a wire rack. Makes 36 biscuits.
Note: Try replacing ginger with chocolate chips for a sensational combination.

Monaro Country Lavender
Co-op, BOMBALA

It was imported from Ireland in 1881. The Irish connections in Boorowa go deep: a Catholic nun was asked early in the 20th century whether she had been to Ireland. 'No,' she replied, 'but I have been to Boorowa.'

You can have a beer at the **Bredbo** [E4] Inn, where poet Banjo Paterson was a regular. Also at Bredbo, Monaro Wood World showcases Australia's native timbers, exhibiting fine contemporary Australian woodwork, from bowls to boardroom tables.

Brindabella [C2] nestles in an isolated valley on the edge of the Snowy Mountains. It was here that Miles Franklin, author of *My Brilliant Career*, grew up. The Franklin family home, however, is not open for inspection.

MOONBAH GOAT'S CURD SOUFFLÉ WITH BLACKCURRANTS

Moonbah is a very old village about 11 km south of Jindabyne along the Barry Way. If you are in the area between September and June you can visit Hobbitt Farm and purchase some of their traditional French-style mountain-goat cheese to try this recipe.

60 g butter
60 g plain flour
350 ml warm milk
75 g Hobbitt Farm
  goat's curd
  cheese
1 tbsp freshly
  grated parmesan

4 eggs, separated
salt and pepper
  to taste
a little cream

SALSA
400 g sugar
200 ml water
1 kg blackcurrants
1 bunch mint
zest and juice of
  1 lemon
juice of 1 orange
1 red onion, finely
  chopped
100 ml extra virgin
  olive oil
salt and pepper
  to taste

Preheat oven to 180°C and butter 12 quarter-cup moulds. In a large saucepan, melt butter and stir in flour. Cook over low heat for 2–3 minutes and gradually whisk in warm milk. Whisk over low–medium heat until sauce thickens and boils, then remove. Stir goat's curd cheese into hot sauce, then parmesan. Set aside to cool for 3–4 minutes. Mix in egg yolks thoroughly and season. In a bowl, beat egg whites until firm peaks form, and fold quickly and gently into the yolk mixture. Spoon into moulds and place in a baking dish. Add water to halfway up sides of moulds and bake for about 15 minutes, or until firm and well puffed. Remove from oven. The soufflés will deflate. Let stand for a few minutes before gently easing from moulds and inverting onto a buttered ovenproof dish. (They can be allowed to cool.) Meanwhile, make salsa. Caramelise sugar, then add water and blackcurrants. Cook until soft. Cool, then add remaining ingredients. Before serving, pour enough cream over soufflés to moisten, and bake at 180°C for 10 minutes, or until heated through and slightly puffed. Serve immediately on a bed of salad greens with salsa drizzled around. Serves 12.

Mike Corbett, JINDABYNE

In **Bungendore** [C4], on the south-western corner of Molonglo and Gibraltar Streets, is a building erected in the 1870s as the Orient Bank. It was used in the filming of

Ned Kelly (Mick Jagger had the leading role) in 1969. Note the stables and the tiny cottage built for the boy who tended the bank manager's horses. The Royal Hotel on Gibraltar Street was built in 1882 during a boom period. Under the front verandah are death masks of John McMahon, the hotel's owner, who died in 1889, age 63.

Cabramurra [E1], in the
Kosciuszko National Park, is the highest town in Australia, at 1,465 m above sea level. Built for the workers on the Snowy Mountains Hydro-electric Scheme in the 1940s, the town had a population of almost 2,000 (today there are less than 200 people living there). This was the largest engineering project in the world, a massive system of dams, power stations, tunnels and aqueducts that now generates about 5,000 gigawatt hours of environmentally clean electricity annually.

The hotel in **Captains Flat** [D4] claims to have the longest bar in Australia, built during the town's second mining rush, in the 1930s.

Charlottes Pass [F1] village
holds the record for the coldest temperature ever recorded in Australia at -23°C. Established in 1930 as one of the first ski resorts in Australia, it also holds the record as the highest resort in the country, at 1,760 m.

On the road to **Collector** [B4] in 1865 bushranger Ben Hall and his gang bailed up 50 people before he rode into town to rob the local store and pub. One man, Samuel Nelson, a local constable, took him on and got shot for his trouble. There is a memorial to Constable Nelson outside the (now renamed) Bushranger Hotel, and he is buried in the Church of England cemetery. By the 1880s Collector had five pubs and two cemeteries.

The climate of **Cooma** [E3] is close to that of the Andes—there are now a few llama farms growing superfine wool. Llama World, just outside town, has alpacas, llamas and guanacos. You can go on a llama sulky ride, tractor ride and even a llama bush picnic.

Cootamundra [A1] was the birth-place, in 1908, of Australia's most famous cricketer, Sir Donald Bradman. The house where he was born, in Adams Street, was then being used as a nursing home. The town is also home to Australia's oldest country golf club, established in 1895. Cootamundra's silvery grey wattle has become one of the most widely cultivated of the acacia species, to the point of becoming an invasive plant species in some areas.

Crookwell

Crookwell [A4], in 1922, was the site of the first branch meeting of the Country Women's Association. About 20 km north of town, at Binda, is the Funny Hill Racecourse. The oldest country racecourse in New South Wales, it has hosted the Binda Picnic Races every year since 1848. They're now held in March.

Visit **Dalgety** [F3] and imagine what it would have been like if it had been chosen as the site for the federal capital. Instead, it was passed by in favour of Canberra. Today Dalgety remains a tiny settlement, though its location—a picturesque riverside site with great views—shows its potential.

Lake **Eucumbene** [E2] is the largest artificial lake in the Southern Hemisphere and part of the Snowy Mountains Hydro-electric Scheme. Its 240 km of shoreline enclose the best trout fishing in Australia. There's also fishing and horse riding at Eucumbene Trout Farm on Eucumbene Dam Road, Berridale.

While **Gundagai** [B1] is better known for a dog that sits on a tuckerbox, the Visitor Information Centre in Sheridan Street houses a miniature cathedral. Rusconi's Marble Masterpiece was created by monument mason Frank Rusconi using 20,948 pieces of New South Wales marble and taking 28 years to complete. Rusconi's other work includes the aforementioned dog on the tuckerbox, 8 km north of Gundagai on the western side of the Hume Highway. The Gabriel Gallery, on the first floor of the Butcher & Roberts Mitre 10 store in Sheridan Street, features the photographs of

Dr Charles Gabriel, who lived in Gundagai and died there in 1927. Cliff Butcher, who established the gallery, found about 1,000 10 cm glass negatives after the doctor's death, and now prints showing Gundagai at the turn of the 20th century line the gallery walls. Gundagai is also the site of Australia's worst flood disaster, in 1852, when 89 people lost their lives.

From **Guthega** village [F1] skiers have a choice of 20 ski runs. Come here for the day or book in at Guthega Lodge, the only accommodation available.

Harden-Murrumburrah

[A1] men were the first to sign up for the 1st Australian Light Horse. Permission had been sought from the NSW government to assemble a regiment of the colony's best horsemen, and 3,000 answered the call.

Just past **Ingebyra** [G2] the Barry Way becomes an unsealed 4WD route that winds its way south to **Suggan Buggan** [see Victoria, Lakes and Wildnerness] over the Victorian border. Stop at the Wallace Craig Lookout for the fantastic views before descending to Jacob's River. The road then follows the Snowy River.

OFFICER, 1st AUSTRALIAN HORSE—18

Jindabyne

Jindabyne [F2] is known as the 'Heart of the Snowy Mountains'. The Snowy Region Visitor Centre on Kosciuszko Road has displays on the natural and cultural features of Kosciuszko National Park and the history of the Snowy Mountains. Lake Jindabyne is the second-largest reservoir of the Snowy Mountains Scheme, holding water from the eastward-flowing Snowy and Eucumbene Rivers, which is then diverted for irrigation and power generation for south-eastern Australia.

DON'T MISS: Shout About Trout is held in the first week of December to celebrate the popularity of mountain trout.

In the town of **Jugiong** [B1] is the Sir George Tavern, built by Irish settler John Philip Sheahan in 1845 on the banks of the Murrumbidgee River. It was washed away by the floods of 1852 and rebuilt in its current form by stonemasons from Ireland. The walls are half a metre thick. It is still run by the Sheahan family, making it the oldest Australian pub to stay in the hands of one family.

GAZETTEER

At **Khancoban** [E1] on the Alpine Way the autumn leaf colours are spectacular. Travelling south toward Thredbo there are two worthwhile lookouts. The one at Scammell's Spur, halfway to Geehi, provides spectacular views of the western face of the main range; the other is Pilot Lookout, just before Dead Horse Gap. Khancoban is a good base for horse trail rides, flyfishing and exploration of the Kosciuszko National Park.

Kiandra [E2] is the home of the world's first ski club, formed in 1880 (it seems elsewhere skiers just hadn't thought of

FRUIT LEATHER TREAT FOR THE LUNCH BOX

Snacks are an important part of travelling, relieving boredom on the long open road, providing energy on the walking trail or rounding off a satisfying picnic lunch. Try making your own to take on your next trip.

1 kg washed, peeled and stoned fruit (any in season—cherries, apricots, peaches, nectarines, strawberries)
2 tbsp water

FLAVOURINGS TO ADD:
apples (cinnamon, nutmeg, brown sugar)
apricots (brandy, honey, lemon juice)
bananas (vanilla, ginger, lemon juice)
cherries (lemon juice, almond essence)
oranges (cinnamon, lemon juice)
peaches (honey, cinnamon, nutmeg)
pears (lemon juice, nutmeg)
pineapples (cinnamon, honey)
plums (honey, lemon juice)
rhubarb (honey, sugar)
strawberries (Cointreau, lemon juice, honey)
watermelon (lemon juice)

Cut fruit into small pieces. Place in a saucepan with the water. Bring to boil, reduce heat and simmer until mixture is soft and pulpy. Liquid should have reduced and mixture should be quite thick. Stir regularly to stop mixture sticking to base of pan. Remove saucepan from heat, then purée or mash fruit. Place mashed fruit in food dryer or smooth into a thin layer on a baking tray lined with baking paper and place in oven—on lowest heat setting and with door slightly ajar. Cook until fruit is dry to touch and not sticky. This can take some hours, depending on fruit.

Lorraine Brown, HARDEN-MURRUMBURRAH

forming a club). Skiing was introduced into the area by snowbound Scandinavian gold miners here for Kiandra's short-lived goldrush. These days Cabramurra is the nearest ski field.

Laggan's [A4] Willow Vale Restaurant is

operated by a man with a potato passion. Of the 20 new potato varieties Graham Liney has introduced to Australia, the one called sapphire is the most unusual. It's purple, both skin and flesh, making for an interesting chip.

Lake George [B4] is a huge, flat

body of water, at times 25 km long, 10 km wide and covering 155 sq km, the largest freshwater lake in Australia when it's full. However, it has the disconcerting habit of appearing and disappearing, apparently almost at random. It was first sighted by Joseph Wild in 1820. At the time it was so full that Wild felt he had reached the Pacific Ocean. That same year it was named after the king by Governor Macquarie. By 1837 it was totally dry, but it was full again in 1852. It was dry again by 1870, full in 1897, dry by 1902, full in 1925, dry in the 1930s, full in the 1950s, dry in the early 1980s and full again in the mid-1980s. At the moment it's dry.

DON'T MISS: Weereewa is a triennial festival celebrating Lake George's mysterious disappearing act, and is also the Aboriginal name for the lake, which is sacred to the indigenous people of the area. The festival showcases works by regional artists and performers and the lake bed is used as a stage for dancing. The next festival will be held in 2004.

Mt Kosciuszko [F1], Australia's

highest mountain, is 2,228 m, but a great view of the surrounding alps can be had from the top of **Mt Blue Cow**. Kosciuszko National Park is the largest alpine park in Australia, with 7,000 sq km of diverse natural

landscape. **Yarrangobilly Caves**, in the north-west of the park, feature the Glory Cave, the first 'self-guided' cave in Australia and one of four open to the public within the area. In the north-east of the park, a reasonable dry-weather road (open only in summer, with a 4WD recommended for the last 8 km) across Long Plain, reaches the historic and well-preserved **Coolamine Homestead**. Nearby are the spectacular Blue Waterholes, which offer chilly swimming, even in the middle of summer. In the very south of the park, near the **Tom Groggin** picnic area at the southern extremity of the Alpine Way, a 4WD track crosses the shallow but fast-flowing waters of the River Murray into the remote high country of Victoria. You will need a good map and some experience, as the mountains are steep and rough—better to join a 4WD tag-along tour to experience this wild beauty.

Nimmitabel [F4] was a location

for the 1960 movie *The Sundowners*, about a family on a sheep property. A number of 19th-century buildings still stand, including the police station, flour mill, the Tudor Inn, Commercial Hotel, an emporium and Gelchmacher House. The cemetery has gravestones dating back to 1842. There is excellent trout fishing here and a 9-hole sand golf course.

Perisher Blue [F2] is Australia's

largest ski resort, with more than 50 lifts and about 100 km of marked runs. Of greatest interest to non-skiers is the remarkable Skitube, claimed to be Australia's highest rack railway and the longest rack system in the Southern Hemisphere. It is an 8.5 km journey (6.3 km through the tunnel). Bullocks Flat terminal is at 1,120 m

elevation and the Mt Blue Cow terminal is 1,875 m—a total climb of 755 m.

In **Queanbeyan**'s [C4] Queen Elizabeth Park are Napoleon's Willow Trees, which allegedly began as cuttings from Napoleon's grave on St Helena.

Thredbo's [F1] Eagles Nest restaurant, at the top of the Crackenback chairlift, is Australia's highest restaurant and the town's golf course is Australia's highest golf course. It's a picturesque, 9-hole, PGA-rated course that is hilly and challenging. Unique features are the snake pit and Wally's wombat house.

GAZETTEER

Tumut's [C1] Blowering Dam has two main claims to fame—it was where the world's longest water-ski run, 1,673 km, took place, and in 1978 it was where Ken Warby set a world speed record when he travelled at 510.45 km/h in a jet-engined boat.

DON'T MISS: Autumn in Tumut is said to offer the most spectacular display of colours anywhere in New South Wales. The town's Festival of the Falling Leaf has become a hugely popular event and is held every year on the last weekend of April.

Wallendbeen [A1] is a mustard seed oil centre. The oil from the

specially developed seeds is integral to Indian cooking. The Yandilla Mustard Oil Enterprise on the Olympic Highway is open to visitors. Tours are available by appointment—02 6943 2516.

Yass [B3] railway station (1892) has the shortest platform in Australia, now housing a railway museum. The bells of St Clements Anglican Church, designed by Edmund Blacket (who designed the Sydney University Quadrangle) and built in 1847, are said to be the only full peal of bells in rural Australia.

The Lambing Flat Museum in **Young** [A1] (Campbell Street) has the famous 'Roll Up' flag carried by miners protesting the presence of the Chinese on the Lambing Flat goldfields in 1861. The museum also houses the world's only operational Auto-gengas Light Machine, a gas-powered light that gives a brilliant white light—it was first used to give light to a hand-powered film projector in 1905. There's also a stuffed three-legged chicken, the result of an experiment conducted by a local man trying to breed one with four legs. Young has the largest cherry orchard in Australia, planted by Austrian Nicole Jasprizza. The first commercial orchards were planted in 1878, and the town now produces 75 per cent of the state's cherries.

Diary of Events

Town	Event	Date	Contact
Crookwell	Binda Picnic Races	March	02 4832 1988
Jindabyne	Shout About Trout	November	02 6456 2424
Thredbo	Legends of Jazz Festival (www.thredbojazz.com)	May, 1st weekend	02 6457 6882
Tumut	Festival of the Falling Leaf	April	02 6946 4482
Young	National Cherry Festival	December, 1st week	02 6382 5996

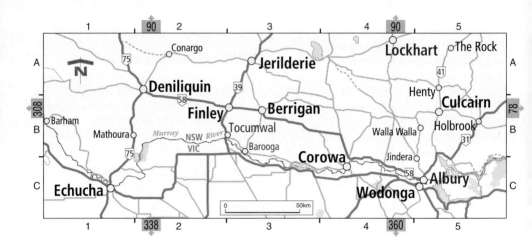

Historically the Murray River has been Australia's most important river. It not only waters the vast western plains of New South Wales and Victoria but, during the 19th century, was a vital transportation link serviced by a large number of paddle steamers.

get off the beaten track

meander

through the murray

Albury

[C5] railway station has the longest covered platform in the Southern Hemisphere, a relic of the days when Albury was the changeover point and customs station

between Victoria and New South Wales. Because the two states had different rail gauges, a bridge to accommodate both gauges was sent out from England in 1883. This is the old iron lattice bridge on the Wodonga side of the Murray, and it still carries the main rail line. About 30 piers from the temporary wooden bridge erected for use during the 12 months the new bridge took to be shipped can still be seen when the Murray River has been 'turned off' at the end of the summer irrigation season to store water in the Hume Dam. On the north bank of the Murray, off Wodonga Place, is a series of parks, among them **Hovell Tree Reserve** (it's signposted), where you can see an old Murray gum in which the explorer William Hovell carved his initials in about 1824, and the Botanical Gardens, which has a pine tree grown from a seed taken from Lone Pine in Gallipoli.

GAZETTEER

The bridge linking **Barham** [B1] to Koondrook is one of the oldest bridges on the Murray River, built in 1904. There's a good golf course on Moulamein Road.

Barooga's [B3] Daveile

Gallery has an unusual specialty, a collection of antique oil lamps.

GAZETTEER

On Oatlands Road in **Berrigan** [B3] the Sojourn Station Art Studio features the works of local artist Jan Barnett and historical displays including vintage cars, household goods and other historical memorabilia. The irrigation waters from

EXPRESS LAMB BIRYANI

The Murray Valley Irrigation district is one of the only rice-growing regions in Australia. If you're in Deniliquin stop in at the Peppin Heritage Centre in George Street for a cooking demonstration from the SunRice Centre.

2 tbsp oil
1 onion, chopped
2 garlic cloves, crushed
2 tsp tikka curry paste or $1/2$ jar
   Sharwood's Tikka Masala Sauce
1 tbsp mild curry powder
1 tsp each cinnamon, cumin
$1/4$ tsp ground cloves
1 tbsp fresh ginger, grated
$1/3$ cup fresh coriander, chopped
500 g lamb backstrap, sliced thinly
2 cup SunRice long-grain rice
2 cups chicken stock
1 cup frozen peas
310 g can corn kernels
$1/3$ cup sultanas
1 tomato, chopped, for garnish
extra coriander, for garnish

Heat oil in wok, then add onion, garlic, tikka paste, all spices and herbs. Cook until onion is soft. Add lamb and cook until brown. Stir in rice, stock and peas. Simmer, covered, until liquid is absorbed (about 6 minutes). Add corn and sultanas. Serve sprinkled with chopped tomato and extra coriander. Serves 4.

SunRice Centre, DENILIQUIN

the Murray make a mighty contribution to Australia's food lands and the area is famous for its citrus. Potatoes thrive in the light alluvial soils and are an important local crop—Smith's use them for their crisps. The most important factor in the choice of

potatoes for crisps is the sugar content.
If it's too high the crisps discolour in cooking.
The Drop, 14 km south of Berrigan, is an
interesting water-flow control set-up that is
part of an irrigation system providing water
to the town. The Drop is a 4 m fall along the
Mulawa canal. It is here that Pacific Hydro
captures the unharnessed energy created
from the fall of the water to produce renewable
energy with a 2 mW turbine. This project is
expected to replace about 11.5 million tonnes
of green-house gasses annually.

The bar of the **Conargo** [A2] Pub, a
popular local watering hole in merino country,
has an intriguing collection of stickers and
photographs on its walls, including one taken
at Davis Station, the Australian base in
Antarctica. The sign in the photograph, which
warns people to 'keep left', points the way to
Phillip Island, Mallacoota and Conargo.

Corowa [C4], just on the New South

Wales side of the Murray River, is known as the
birthplace of Federation. Proposals from the
1893 Corowa Federation Conference
supporting Federation as a
means of promoting free trade
were put to the 1895 premiers'
conference and were instru-
mental in Australia becoming a
Federation on 1 January 1901.

Culcairn [B5] in years

gone by was known as Round
Hill Station, famous for a hold-up by
bushranger Dan 'Mad Dog' Morgan in June
1864. You can still see the original Round Hill
homestead and the grave of the overseer
Morgan shot is clearly signposted on the road
leading to Holbrook. Further along the road
are the original Cobb & Co. stables.
Morgan's Lookout, west of Culcairn
opposite Walla Walla Station, was Morgan's
hideout and provides great views.

Deniliquin

[A2] is the 'ute'
capital of the world
and hosts the annual
Deniliquin Ute Muster
on the Labour Day
long weekend in
October. In 2000 more than 2,990 utes showed
up, enough to win Deniliquin a place in the
Guinness Book of Records—once the
organisers explained precisely what a ute was
and why anyone would want to gather them in
one place. Deniliquin also boasts the biggest
rice mill in the Southern Hemisphere.

Henty [A5] Machinery Field Days, in

September, has been held since 1963 and has
grown into the most successful mixed farming
expo in the Southern Hemisphere.

In **Holbrook** [B5] there is a 90 m
submarine parked alongside the Hume Highway. It is a reconstruction of the above-water
section of the decommissioned HMAS *Otway*,
one of six Oberon class submarines operated
by the Royal Australian Navy. Although
Holbrook is 400 km from the
kind of water a submarine
needs, the town adopted a
submarine connection when,
during WWI, it changed its
name from Germanton to
Holbrook to honour a British
submariner whose exploits in
the Dardanelles won him the
Victoria Cross. Holbrook has another
submarine, too, an 8.5 m scale model of Commander Norman Douglas Holbrook's 43 m B11
submarine. It is on display in the Commander
Holbrook Memorial Park.

The windmill in **Jerilderie**'s [A3] Luke
Park is easy to see from quite a distance—it is
one of the largest in the Southern Hemisphere.
It was built in 1909–10 and used for irrigation

on nearby Goolgumbla station. It is 15 m high, with a wheel of 12.5 m diameter.

In Jindera's [C5] Pioneer Museum

the painstakingly restored Wagner's Store recreates the interior of a 19th-century country store. Outside is the hitching rail and inside is a huge cedar counter; behind it antique canisters, containers and packages bearing the labels of period products are stacked on shelves to the ceiling. There is a ladder for the shopkeeper's use and a tall chair on which customers sat while they called out their orders. Hand-

made nails secure the old floorboards, a wooden staircase leads to an attic. There is a cellar for storage and a cupboard for the safe storage of explosives. German books and pictures of the Kaiser remind visitors that many of the town's earliest settlers were German.

Lockhart [A4] is known as the

'Verandah Town' because of its wide verandahs. At night, the verandahs along the main street are lit up, **GAZETTEER** giving the place a magical look. Etched into the pavement below, thousands of images depict the life and times of the town.

Mathoura [B1], dating back to the

1840s, was originally known as Red Bank. Mathoura Forest, the world's largest river red gum forest, covers 215 sq km. The gums thrive here because of periodic flooding from snow melting in the Snowy Mountains to the east.

The Rock [A5] is a small town named

after a hill of the same name. The Rock nature reserve is a haven for birds, with more than 100 species recorded in the area. The view from the hilltop is well worth the walk: on clear days you can see Kosciuszko, some 200 km away.

Tocumwal [B3] boasts a giant

Murray cod made from fibreglass, which stands on the river foreshore. It was **GAZETTEER** commissioned by the Ladies Auxiliary of the Tocumwal Chamber of Commerce in 1967, when fibreglass was new and its potential seemed enormous. The Murray cod—or Goodoo, to use the Aboriginal term— was once plentiful in the Murray–Darling River system. Early records tell of specimens weighing up to 112 kg.

Today their numbers are much reduced, with few fish of 10–45 kg caught each year. Tocumwal offers some of the Southern Hemisphere's best thermals (rising currents of heated air—magic to the ears of glider pilots, who head here from all over the world). If you love camping and water, enjoy the delights of camping along the Murray in state forests that stretch for kilometres on both sides of the border.

Walla Walla's [B5] Zion Lutheran

Church was built in 1924 and is reputedly the largest Lutheran church in New South Wales. It can seat 500 people and can be opened for visitors on request.

Diary of Events

Town	Event	Date	Contact
Deniliquin	Ute Muster	Labour Day long weekend	03 5881 2878
Henty	Henty Machinery Field Days	September, last week	02 6929 3305

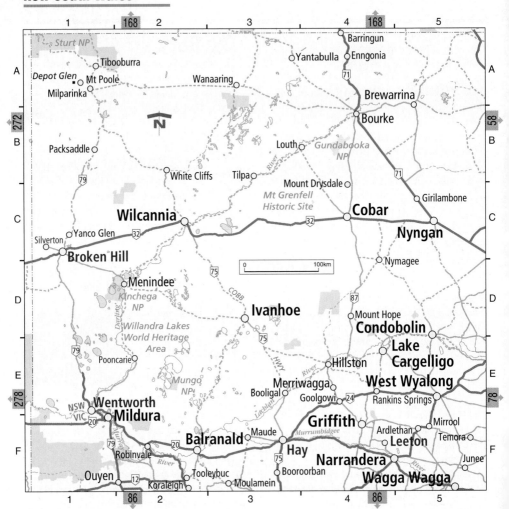

get off the beaten track

roam the riverina

to the outback

Ardlethan [F5] is the birthplace of the Australian kelpie, to which there is a bronze memorial in Stewart Park. The Kelpie Dog Festival is held in March every year.

About 8 km south of **Balranald** [F2] is Yanga Homestead, said to be the oldest freehold property in the Southern Hemisphere, dating back to the 1850s, and is still in almost original condition. Yanga also received one of the first telephones in Australia. The telephone line was installed by Alexander Graham Bell's nephew and connected the homestead to the men's quarters.

The pub in **Barringun** [A4] once grooved to the funky beat of soldier and poet Breaker Morant, who played the comb in a local band. Marking the border between New South Wales and Queensland is the dingo fence—the longest fence on Earth, designed to keep wild dingoes away from the sheep flocks of south-eastern Australia.

Booligal [E3] had its reputation—for heat, dust, flies, rabbits, mosquitoes, snakes and drought, not to mention poor shearing conditions—immortalised in AB Banjo Paterson's poem, 'Hay and Hell and Booligal'. Every October (the exact date varies each year) locals attempt to determine the fastest wether in the west with the Booligal Sheep Races. In the tradition of great racing there's a sheep fashion parade as well. On the road from Booligal to Hay is the **One Tree Hotel**, which even the locals say is in the middle of nowhere. There's in fact nothing to drink and no one to serve you, but you might catch a

LEMONADE CAKE

Lemonade fruit is a non-acidic fruit whose origins are unknown. It is thought to be a natural hybrid between a lemon and possibly a tangelo, and tastes like lemonade, being juicy and sweet yet not bitter. As it is becoming more popular, you should be able to get it through good fruit markets.

1 lemonade fruit or lemon, whole	1/2 cup self-raising flour
1 orange, whole	1/2 cup plain flour
100 g ground almonds	1 tsp baking powder
5 eggs	1/2 cup extra virgin olive oil
pinch of salt	
1 1/4 cups caster sugar	

Preheat oven to 180°C and line a 20 cm springform pan with baking paper. Place the lemonade fruit or lemon and the orange in a saucepan and completely cover with water. Bring to the boil, then drain. Add fresh water, bring to the boil and cook gently until the fruits are quite tender (45–60 minutes). Drain and leave to cool. Cut away both ends of the fruit and remove seeds. Pulse remainder in a blender for a few seconds and then transfer to a sieve and leave to drain. Place citrus mixture in a bowl and add ground almonds. In another bowl, beat eggs with salt and sugar until very thick and pale. Fold the flours into the eggs. Add the fruit mixture and the oil. Pour mixture into pan and bake for about 1 hour, or until firm to the touch. Leave to cool in the pan and then invert onto a plate. Peel away the paper carefully. Sift some icing sugar over the cake and serve.

Paula Clarke, INVERELL

New South Wales

glimpse of the ghost who is said to live there. The hotel was built in 1862 as a staging post for Cobb & Co. and is now a famous landmark. It is called One Tree because of a large gum that grows about half a mile away, in some of the flattest terrain on Earth.

Booroorban [F3], on the Cobb

Highway, is where the headless horseman ranged in the mid-19th century. The Royal Mail Hotel has a Headless Horseman bar. The horseman was said to be the ghost of a drover who died in a nearby swamp. He would appear suddenly at drovers' campsites, scaring the daylights out of the men and stampeding the cattle. It then emerged that an entrepreneurial butcher from Moulamein, seeing an opportunity

for free cattle, had put a wooden frame over his shoulders, wrapped himself in a cloak and helped himself to the strayed animals.

In the cemetery at ## Bourke [B4] the

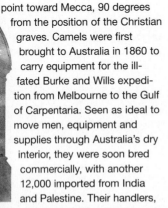

graves of the Afghan camel drivers all point toward Mecca, 90 degrees from the position of the Christian graves. Camels were first brought to Australia in 1860 to carry equipment for the ill-fated Burke and Wills expedition from Melbourne to the Gulf of Carpentaria. Seen as ideal to move men, equipment and supplies through Australia's dry interior, they were soon bred commercially, with another 12,000 imported from India and Palestine. Their handlers, most of whom were actually from Pakistan, lived in shanty 'ghantowns', often on the edge of railhead settlements. Bourke has a mosque in Bourke Cemetery. The town is also the site of Fred Hollows' grave—this is where he began his ground-breaking eye operations. South of Bourke is the **Gundabooka National Park**, with its fine Aboriginal art sites. There is good bush camping but you need permission from the National Parks Service (02 6872 2744). The North Bourke Bridge over the Darling River is the oldest bridge in New South Wales built with a span able to be raised to allow paddle steamers through. It was built in 1883. The Bourke weir was the first to be built on the Darling River and the lock was the first in Australia. Bourke is on the rim of one of the world's major natural phenomena, the Great Artesian Basin, which has about 1,657,600 sq km of underground water. Visit the Pera Bore Artesian display to see the site of the first experimental artesian farm.

DON'T MISS: The Mateship Festival in October—02 6872 2035—celebrates the bond Outback pioneers had, a bond that ensured they helped each other through tough times. The word 'mateship' was coined by Henry Lawson, so the festival is built around bush poetry.

The ## Brewarrina [A5] Aboriginal

Fisheries on the Barwon River are the oldest man-made fish traps in the world; in fact, at an estimated 40,000 years old, they are thought to be among the oldest built structures on Earth. They are low-walled stone pens, open at one end, with stones alongside ready to close the pens once full of fish. The Brewarrina Aboriginal Cultural Museum above the fish traps, on the corner of Darling and Bathurst Streets, has a display of bones of the diprotodon (giant wombat), which became extinct half a million years ago.

Fishing in the **Barwon River** is still popular today. Try your luck at the Lion's Club camping reserve, known locally as the Four Mile, where you can barbecue your catch of Murray cod, golden perch (yellow-belly), black bream or catfish on the spot. The **Darling River** is the largest river system in Australia, measuring 2,735 km and draining an area of 647,500 sq km in two states. Keen anglers also have a good chance of a catch from the waters of the Darling around Brewarrina and further downstream toward Bourke and Louth, although, sadly, introduced carp are today the river's most abundant and conspicuous inhabitants.

DON'T MISS: The Darling River Outback Surf Boat Classic, which attracts entrants from all over Australia, is held in Brewarrina every October over the Labour Day long weekend.

Broken Hill [C1] has the state's
only legal school for traditional two-up. The Broken Hill Musicians Club on Crystal Street (almost opposite the Railway Station) runs the game from 10 pm on Friday and Saturday nights. There may be other games in back streets and old buildings in town but there are hefty fines if you're caught playing in them. The musicians of Broken Hill have played a great part in the town's history. It was they who inspired the city fathers to build a monument to the musicians of the *Titanic*. Situated in Sturt Park, the memorial consists of a broken marble column, standing 5.8 m above the ground. During the legendary 1909 mine

YABBIES À LA BALRANALD

The Balranald Shire is known to anglers as the Heart of the Riverland, with four main river junctions within its boundaries. Near Balranald the Murrumbidgee offers some great fishing with good-sized perch, redfin, Murray cod and yabbies.

green yabbies
cheese
bacon

Drop yabbies into boiling salted water. When cooked they will float (around 8 minutes). Shell tails. Place a piece of cheese on each tail and wrap with a piece of bacon. Place about six on a skewer and grill.

Des Biske, BALRANALD

lockout, what was then the Broken Hill City Band led the miners each day to the pickets outside the mines along the Line of Lode, the ore body situated in the town centre. Broken Hill was the scene of an 'enemy attack' on Australian soil when, on 1 January 1915, only four months before the Anzacs fought the Turks at Gallipoli, two Turkish sympathisers shot at a trainload of picnickers, killing four people. They took

refuge in a cottage on the northern edge of town, where they were eventually shot by police. The White Rocks Historical site at Schlapp Street commemorates the final shoot-out. Threats of a Japanese invasion on

the eastern seaboard during WWII caused the largest single movement of gold ever in Australia—the nation's gold was moved to the old Broken Hill jail, on the corner of Talc and Gossan Streets. Locals were convinced the jail was to house German war criminals until they noticed that the reinforcements were designed to keep people out, not in. Broken Hill is also home to one of Australia's first mosques. It was built in 1891 by a community of Moslem camel drivers on the site of a former camel camp.

Broken Hill's City Art Gallery on Blende Street is the oldest gallery in Australia after the NSW Art Gallery in Sydney. It opened in 1904 when George McCulloch donated some paintings. He was one of seven people who staked claims to land that is now Broken Hill, forming the Broken Hill Mining Company (now BHP) in 1883. Today the arts are playing an increas-

ingly important role for Broken Hill's economy, with no less than 26 art galleries in the town. Silver City Art Centre and Mint is the home of the 'The Big Picture', by artist Peter Anderson. This is the world's largest painting on canvas, being 100 m long, more than 12 m high and painted with 9 tonnes of paint.

Although quandongs (wild peaches) are native to Australia and are a popular bush food, their propagation is a challenge, mainly due to the parasitic nature of the plant. Quandongs are famous for their ability to adapt and grow in arid conditions, but young plants must not be allowed to dry out. Broken Hill residents Bill and Lyn McAllister took up the challenge in 1993, establishing the Santalum Quandong Orchard primarily with voluntary labour. Rainfall in the area is approximately 200 mm per annum so they have had to set up a twin watering system using town water for all seedlings in the field and bore water for the older established trees. Water is reticulated, under computer control, to each plant and at present they have 150 seedlings under dripper irrigation and 600 established trees. If you would like to take a tour of the farm contact the Visitor Information Centre on 08 8087 6077.

The **Cobar** [C4] Shire, covering just over 44,065 sq km, is about two-thirds the size of Tasmania. The Great Western Hotel (1898) in Marshall Street has a timber verandah with cast iron balustrades and a lacework balcony—at 100 m long it is the longest in New South Wales. The Grand Hotel on Marshall Street holds another record, and this one's global: according to the *Guinness Book of Records*, it has the distinction of possessing the world's largest beer can. This monument to the hop stands 5 m high and 2.5 m wide. The historic gold mines of **Mount Drysdale**

once rivalled Cobar, to the north, for size and growth potential. From 5,000 people in

its heyday, Mount Drysdale has been reduced to just one family. The town has Australia's best examples of rock wells. Aborigines created them by heating the rock and breaking bits of it away to catch what water there was.

 DON'T MISS: The Festival of the Miner's Ghost has been held for the past three years. A curator at the Cobar Museum had been disturbed on many occasions by voices and apparitions of what he believed to be the ghosts of disgruntled miners. Tourists on self-guided tours can now imagine and appreciate the back-

breaking and soul-destroying work of a miner. The Festival of the Miner's Ghost is held on the last weekend in October.

Just 8 km north of **Condobolin** [D5] is **Mount Tilga**, thought to be the geographical centre of New South Wales. The locals celebrate this at the Heart of New South Wales Festival at Condobolin Showground in April. Climb the mountain for a fantastic view of the lower Lachlan Valley. In the town there is an interesting old Chinese cemetery, restored as a Bicentennial project by local high school students.

West of **Enngonia** [A4] is the unmarked grave of Captain Midnight, a bushranger who terrorised the local area until he was cornered at Irrara Creek. He died at a cottage near his burial site. It is possible that author Rolf Boldrewood modified Midnight's nom de plume to Captain Starlight for his famous novel *Robbery Under Arms*. Turn west off the Mitchell Highway at the sign marked Yantabulla and Irrara Creek and

TRIPE ITALIAN STYLE

Harnessing the Murrumbidgee River transformed vast arid plains into a fertile agricultural region. Two of the towns of this district, Leeton and Griffith, were designed by Walter Burley Griffin, who also designed Canberra (Griffith even shares its radial design). Almost half of the citizens of Griffith are of Italian descent. This recipe originally came from Florence.

800 g tripe
3 tbsp olive oil
1 large onion, finely chopped
1 carrot, finely chopped
1 celery stick, finely chopped
60 g pancetta (or bacon), finely chopped
1 x 60 g sachet tomato paste
1 kg tomatoes, peeled and roughly chopped
1 1/2 teaspoons dried marjoram
salt and pepper to taste

Place tripe in a large saucepan and boil for 30 minutes. Drain and cut into very thin strips. Pour olive oil into a large saucepan and brown the onion, carrot, celery, pancetta and tomato paste for 10 minutes. Add the tomatoes, marjoram, salt, pepper and tripe and cook covered for 40 minutes. Remove lid and continue cooking to reduce sauce for another 20 minutes. Serve tripe in bowls topped with grated parmesan and a good crusty Italian bread on the side. Serves 4.

Janet Chapel, GRIFFITH

continue for 35 km until you cross Irrara Creek just before Wirrawarra Station. There is a cottage on the south side of the road before the southern turn-off to Wapweelah Station. The grave, west of the cottage, is

SAVOURY BREAKFAST PANCAKES

A great many English and Australian recipes have been produced through the use of leftovers. These simple and tasty pancakes have the added bonus of using up whatever bits and pieces you have in the fridge.

- **2 cups grated raw potato, squeezed of all excess liquid**
- **1 small onion, grated**
- **3 eggs, well beaten**
- **1 tbsp flour**
- **1 tsp salt**
- **pepper to taste**
- **1 cup chopped or minced cooked meat, bacon or cheese (or any leftovers)**
- **1 tbsp finely chopped parsley**

Combine all ingredients. Have frypan very hot, butter well. Place in tablespoons of mixture and brown on one side before carefully turning and browning other side.

Kim Frazer, STUART TOWN

unmarked and distinguished only by a nearby pine tree and four pine logs marking the grave's perimeter.

Girilambone [C5], on the way to

Bourke, has a reminder of one of Australia's most famous murders. In the cemetery is the grave of schoolteacher Helena Kurz, one of the victims of Jimmy Governor, around whom Thomas Keneally based his novel *The Chant of Jimmie Blacksmith*.

At # Goolgowi [E4] you can gain a good understanding of life in pioneer times, as depicted in the extensive Goolgowi Wall Hanging produced by the local community.

To view the hanging call the Carrathool Shire Council on 02 6965 1306.

Griffith [F4] is

the site of Hermit's Cave, just below Sir Dudley Dechair Lookout on Scenic Drive. It was created by Valerio Riccetti in the early 1930s, when he took shelter from the rain in a cave. He lived there for more than 20 years, building rooms, gardens, furniture and a chapel, all using hand tools. The Regional Theatre in Griffith has a curtain designed and made by 300 local residents to represent the town, the surrounding villages and local industry.

DON'T MISS: The Festival of Gardens is held every October when sculptures made entirely of citrus fruit are on show. The idea was inspired by a similar event in Menton, a town in France.

The # Hay [F3] Jail, on Church Street, was established in 1878 and has been used variously as a jail, maternity hospital, a lock-up for the insane,

GAZETTEER

compound for the internment of Japanese and Italian prisoners of war and maximum security institution for girls. Now it's a museum, open from 9 am to 5 pm every day except Christmas. Bishop's Lodge House Museum, once the official residence of the Anglican bishop of the Riverina, has features designed specifically to cope with the extremes of the Outback climate, being made from corrugated iron and timber, with sawdust for insulation. Stop and smell the roses while you're there. The garden is nationally renowned for its fine collection of late 19th and early 20th century blooms. The old Hay Railway Station is now the site of the

Hay Internment and POW Camp Interpretive Centre, documenting the era in WWII when almost 3,000 prisoners of war and internees were 'housed' here. New to Hay is Shear Outback (the Australian Shearers Hall of Fame), an interpretive centre and museum that tells the story of Australia's wool industry. A few kilometres east of Hay, on the Mid Western Highway, is Sturt's Marked Tree, a box tree famous because Charles Sturt carved markings into it in 1829.

 DON'T MISS: On Australia Day Hay hosts its Annual Surf Carnival at Sandy

Point on the banks of the Murrumbidgee River. Key events include the Murrumbidgee Belly Flop Compet-

ition; the Save the Whale Mission, which involves large men stuck in shallow water; cow pat and thong throwing; and the Hay Duck

Race, when thousands of yellow plastic ducks are sent speeding downriver. If you're in Hay at the full moon, drive 16 km north on the Cobb Highway to the Sunset Viewing Area to see simultaneously the setting of the sun and rising of the full moon. It's unforgettable.

From Booligal to **Hillston** [E4] is a pleasant drive on the Lachlan Valley Way along the banks of the Lachlan River. If the kids need a break stop at the swinging bridge and Hughie Cameron Park in High Street. Local sculptors have carved animals from timber, including a redback spider, a crocodile and a prehistoric monster. Continue the journey to Lake Cargelligo.

About 25 km south-west of **Ivanhoe** [D3] is Kilfera Station, where the shearers' union is thought to have made its first stand, in July 1887. The station had 82 shearers (plus 82 shed hands, 4 wool pressers, 4 wool scourers and up to 200,000 sheep), and when union terms were ignored by management, the shearers upped and left, setting up camp at Ivanhoe. They heard that the station had hired 10 non-union men—a night visit brought these men into the union camp. Two weeks later, the company agreed to union terms and shearing began. The shearing shed at Kilfera was originally an Exhibition Hall in Melbourne and was moved to Kilfera in the late 1870s.

Typically in Australian country towns, the locals pull together to support community services. In the mid-1960s Hay locals compiled the *Hay Days Cookbook* to raise money for a retirement village, called Hay Days, which opened in 1968. Among its gems of wisdom is a cooking tip for witchetty grubs: 'Collect Witchetty Grubs from saplings of *Eucalyptus camaldulensis*

and place upon a clean shovel. Place shovel above the coals sufficiently to cook but not burn. When they cease to wriggle and have sizzled for approxi- mately 2 minutes (bubbling slightly), remove from heat. When sufficiently cool to hold in hand, pull off head with attached entrails and commence to eat from other end.'

Junee

Junee's [F5] Red Cow Hotel, at the corner of Crawley and Junction Streets, was named in honour of a local who tethered his red cow

outside the hotel so that patrons could mix fresh milk with their rum. The Roundhouse Rail and Transport Museum in Harold Street reflects the railway's histori-cal importance to Junee. The 32 m train turntable, built in 1947, was the largest loco-motive roundhouse in the Southern Hemisphere. Other features are the massive original workshop, with 42 repair bays, locomotives and other rolling stock, a working steam crane, an old wooden mail van, a breakdown van and other memorabilia. A new addition is an enormous model railway that takes up several rooms.

Koraleigh

Just outside **Koraleigh** [F2] (about halfway to Tooleybuc) there is a direction to the Ring Tree, a rare surviving example of an old Aboriginal boundary marker in which the branches of a tree have been tied together so that they grow in a ring. The tree is on the left about 10 m off the road.

Lake Cargelligo

Lake Cargelligo's [E4] District Museum displays local artefacts including old farm machinery. Naradhan Woolshed, built in 1888, is a working woolshed, (visit by appoint-ment 02 6896 9802). At the tourist centre is the Alf Tyack collection, a fascinating stone butterfly exhibit (a rock and gem collection, many of which are cut into the shape of butterflies).

DON'T MISS: The Lake Cargelligo Day Outback and Rodeo is the genuine article, held on the October long weekend. Events include rabbit trap setting, fire lighting, billy boiling, and whipcracking.

GAZETTEER

Leeton

Leeton's [F4] Roxy Theatre (1929) on Pine Avenue is one of the few remaining rural movie palaces of the 1920s and a fine example of modified Spanish-style architecture. The neon lighting is especially effective.

Screenings take place on Friday and Saturday nights. Inspections of the theatre at other times are by appointment (02 6953 2074).

DON'T MISS: Each Easter the Leeton Camel Stakes attracts riders and camels from all over Australia to compete in the Australian Camel Cup.

Maude

Maude [F3] Weir, built in 1939, provides water for the Lowbidgee area. It's a pictur-esque spot with well-kept green lawns and barbecue facilities. The road to Maude takes you past market gardens where fruit and vegetables are grown for the Melbourne markets and export trade. Camp amid the river red gums at Four Mile Reserve.

Menindee

Outside **Menindee** [D2], west of town, are the Menindee Lakes, a huge amount of water at the edge of one of the driest areas of the continent and responsible for the surprising sight of orchards, flowers, cotton, barley and wheat thriving in the desert. Nearby is **Kinchega National Park** with its superb wildlife and historic woolshed.

Merriwagga

Merriwagga [E4] is one of two sites in New South Wales claiming to be the real Black Stump. The other is Coolah [see Settler Country], its reason being the traditional 'last outpost' story. A plaque at Merriwagga's Black Stump picnic area has another explanation for the term, dating back to 1886 when a man named Blain found his wife burned to death at their campsite and observed that 'she looked just like a black stump'.

The **Mildura** [F1] International Balloon Fiesta is held every July and includes aviation workshops and other activities.

Milparinka

Milparinka [A1] is the remotest ghost town in New South Wales. It had only a brief spurt of life, from the early 1880s, when gold was

discovered there, till 1893, when its mini goldrush ended. The old pub is licensed again, and you can get a drink and fuel there— if there is anybody around. Across the wide dusty road is a kangaroo shooters' camp, while north of town is Charles Sturt's **Depot Glen**. Here Sturt and his men were trapped for

nine months during his 1844 expedition, and on **Mt Poole** he engaged his men in building a huge stone cairn—just to keep them busy. Both can be reached across a marked 4WD track.

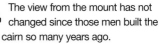

The view from the mount has not changed since those men built the cairn so many years ago.

Mirrool

Mirrool [A2] is the site of the Annual Brownless Mirrool Silo Kick Challenge. The event began in 1970, when a skinny 18-year-old Aboriginal kid from Darwin kicked a football, barefoot, over the 30 m high (and 20 m wide) silo across the road from the Royal Hotel. It became an event in 1992 when Bill Brownless repeated the feat. Several AFL champions and some US gridiron players have risen to meet the challenge. The event is held in October—call the pub on 02 6974 1237 for details.

BILLABONG BREAKFAST

The Riverina and Outback regions support substantial sheep populations, many of which are the descendants of the first merino flocks developed in New South Wales by John Macarthur and the Reverend Samuel Marsden, among others. This recipe comes from Historic Mamre Homestead at St Mary's in Sydney, the Reverend Marsden's original model farm.

1 loaf white toast bread (large size)
butter
1/2 kg bacon rashers, chopped
12 small eggs
sprigs of parsley, for serving

Preheat oven to 150°C and grease a large 12-cup muffin tray. Cut crusts from bread and spread one side lightly with butter. Line muffin tray with bread slices, buttered side down. Cook in a low oven for approx. 20 minutes (until starting to crisp and just beginning to brown—this can be done the day before). Add a layer of bacon to the bottom of each bread case (use half the bacon for this), then break in an egg and cover with another layer of bacon. Return to a moderate oven (180°C) and cook for 10–15 minutes. Run a spoon around the edge of the bread case to remove, and serve with sprigs of parsley. Serves 12.

Mary-Louise Petro, Mamre Homestead, ST MARYS

On Easter Saturday the **Moulamein** [F3] Yabby Races take place. Yabbies compete in a number of different classes, with the fastest, most strategic yabby winning Supreme Champion. Some yabbies are bred specially for the race; others are captured and pressed into immediate service. Moulamein is the oldest town in the Riverina and was once an important river port for paddle steamers plying the Edward River.

The **Mount Grenfell** [C3]

Historic Site, 32 km north of the Barrier Highway on an unsealed road, contains three rock shelters that between them have more than 1,300 richly coloured motifs—paintings of human and animal figures, abstract linear designs and hand stencils. These are among the most spectacular Aboriginal rock paintings in New South Wales.

At **Mount Hope** [D4] ask at the hotel or general store for directions to the old copper mines if you fancy your luck fossicking for crystals.

In **Narrandera**'s [F4] Memorial Gardens, among the memorials to those who died in conflicts from the Boer War to the Vietnam War is a Royal Doulton ceramic fountain, one of only two in the world (the other is in India). It was presented to commemorate all those from Narrandera who served in the Great War (1914–18). In the Parkside Cottage Museum are the Macarthur Opera Cloak, which was made from the first

LEG OF LAMB WITH PLUM JAM AND BLACK PEPPER SAUCE

This recipe took several years to develop, starting with the old concept of sweet and sour and a combination of traditional family ingredients. A cutting from an ancient plum tree was handed down to each generation and was said to make the best plum jam ever.

- 1¹/₂–2 kg leg of lamb
- 1 large garlic clove, slivered
- soy sauce
- 1¹/₂ rashers bacon
- 1¹/₂ rashers bacon, diced
- 1 x 340 g jar plum jam
- 1¹/₄ cups boiling water
- 2 tsp cracked black pepper
- 2 spring onions, chopped
- ¹/₂ bunch parsley, chopped
- 4 large garlic cloves, finely chopped
- 1 tbsp plain flour
- water

Preheat oven to 180°C. Stud lamb with slivered garlic, then pour soy sauce into the cuts with garlic. Place in a baking dish. Place bacon rashers in a herringbone pattern over lamb and diced bacon in bottom of pan. Meanwhile, place two-thirds of jam (225 g) in a bowl and mix with boiling water and pepper until all the jam is dissolved, pour over lamb. Top with spring onions and parsley. Place remaining garlic (and another splash of soy sauce) in liquid around lamb. Cover lamb well with foil and bake for 11/2 hours, then uncover and cook for a further 30–45 minutes to brown. In the meantime, prepare gravy. In a bowl, mix enough flour to thicken pan juices with a little water, rest of the jam and a reasonable amount of black pepper. Let stand for 15 minutes before adding it to pan juices. Serves 6.

Garry Thomas, AUBURN

bale of wool ever sent to England—by the Macarthur family in 1816—and a snow shoe and wooden snow ski from one of Robert Scott's Antarctic expeditions. In Narrandera Park you can see a 5.8 m long guitar—and it is playable—and a restored Tiger Moth aeroplane. Narrandera Fisheries on Buckingdong Road is responsible for the propagation of well over a million native fish fry each year. To arrange tours call 02 6959 9021.

Nymagee [C4], an Aboriginal word
meaning 'surrounded by hills', aptly describes the town's location. The Overflow, home of Clancy the drover in Banjo Paterson's poem, is 32 km from town.

DON'T MISS: Nymagee Music Festival, a three-day celebration of music, entertainment and outback culture, is held annually on the October long weekend.

The Packsaddle [B1] Roadhouse
on the Silver City Highway is decorated with memorabilia from the wool industry. It also hosts Quickshear, an annual shearing competition, in March.

East of **Pooncarie** [E2] is Mungo National Park, part of the Willandra Lakes World Heritage Area. The archaeological treasures of the area prove that Aboriginal people lived on the lake shores more than 60,000 years ago. The cremated remains of a

woman, discovered in 1968, make it the oldest cremation site in the world. If you had visited 50,000 years ago you might have seen buffalo-sized *Zygomaturus* grazing at the edge of Lake Mungo, which dried up around 15,000 years ago. Today the Walls of China, a great crescent-shaped dune that once encircled the lake, covers material dating back 40,000 years—anything you find must be left where it is.

The Rankins Springs [E4]
Worm Drowners Fishing Club celebrates Yabby Day on Good Friday. West of the town on the Mid Western Highway is Cocoparra National Park. The scenery includes the eroded cliffs of the Cocoparra Range. If you go bushwalking you might see parrots, cockatoos, honeyeaters and wrens, as well as kangaroos, echidnas, goannas and geckos. The Whitton Stock Route, travelled by Cobb & Co. coaches in the late 19th century, runs along the western boundary of the park. The road is graded but not sealed and becomes slippery and boggy after rain.

Silverton [C1] has become a haven
for filmmakers looking to capture the spirit of the outback. It has been the setting for films such as *Wake in Fright, Mad Max 2, A Town Like Alice, Hostage, Razorback, Journey into Darkness* and *Golden Soak*, as well as many commercials and documentaries. The old jail (1889), at Burke and Loftus Streets, is now a local history museum. It contains the coroner's bath, used to preserve the dead until a coroner arrived, usually from Sydney, sometimes taking three months. There is also a copy of the bill of sale by which James Poole exchanged his share in the Broken Hill mine for 10 steers, before the riches of the lode had been established. At the corner of Layard and Sturt Streets, you will find Andy Jenkins,

GAZETTEER

the only person in Australia who has a licence to deface the currency. Andy is a coin carver who fashions money into interesting pieces of jewellery.

Temora [F5] is a must for World War II

plane enthusiasts. The airport was the site of the biggest RAAF training school in Australia, established in 1941. The 2,741 student pilots learned their flying skills on Tiger Moth planes. Today the airport houses an Aviation Museum. Among its exhibits are Austalia's only flying Spitfire and oldest airworthy Tiger Moth, and the only Australian-built Vampire. Open from 10 am to 4 pm, Wednesday to Sundays. On regular Flying Days you can see the planes in action. Call 02 6977 1088 for details.

Tibooburra's [A1]

Family Hotel in Briscoe Street was built in 1883 and its walls are covered in paintings by artists such as Clifton Pugh, Russell Drysdale, Rick Amor and Eric Minchen. Pugh arrived in the area in the 1960s, fell in love with the place and became friends with the publican. When other artists joined him in 1970 they started drawing on the walls. Richard Amor painted a portrait of Pugh on one wall; it was valued by a Melbourne art dealer at $1.5 million—if it had been on canvas and hanging in a gallery. The 9 m whaleboat sculpture in Tibooburra's Pioneer Park is a replica of the boat Charles Sturt hauled across inland Australia on a wagon, hoping to row across the continent's inland sea. He abandoned the original near Depot Glen. Tibooburra is the gateway to nearby **Sturt National Park**. A good dirt road leads to Cameron Corner, in the park's far north-west—the meeting place of Queensland,

South Australia and New South Wales. The corner post is also where the Dingo Fence changes direction to head along the South Australian and Queensland borders.

Wagga Wagga's [F5]

Shakespearian Garden, in the Botanic Gardens, is a knot garden, with formal beds planted in patterns and clipped into shape. The Museum of the Riverina, on Lord Baden Powell Drive opposite the Botanic Gardens, possesses a bullet fired by bushranger Dan 'Mad Dog' Morgan in 1863.

Wanaaring [A3] became home

to apiarist Stan Hughston in 1964. He then built up what was to become the largest bee-keeping enterprise on a permanent site in the Southern Hemisphere. Today the 4,000 hives yield about 100 kg of honey a year. Capilano and Allowrie honey comes from here.

In Fotherby Park, ## Wentworth [E1],

is a statue of local legend David James Jones, known as 'The Possum' owing to his habit of sleeping in trees. The statue's inscription reads: 'David James Jones 1901–1982. A will-o'-the-wisp nomadic recluse who lived for 54 years in the bushland downstream of Wentworth.' The Wentworth Museum has fossil remnants and replicas, found at Perry Sandhills, of extinct Australian megafauna, including the diprotodon (giant wombat), a giant emu, a giant marsupial lion and a giant kangaroo, as well as an example of the world's first outboard motor. Wentworth has the distinction of possessing the only monument to a tractor in Australia, at the corner of Adelaide and Adams Streets. It commemorates the occasion in 1956 when

GAZETTEER

locals worked a fleet of about 35 Ferguson tractors day and night to form large levee banks in order to save the town from flooding.

West Wyalong [E5] is home to

the World Mallee Root Throwing Champion-

ship. The current championship throw is a 9 kg root thrown 11.6 m, by Michael Crowe. The root is dense, knotted and bulbous, and comes from the bull mallee tree. At the moment the competition gets tacked on to other town events.

Opal mines at **White Cliffs** [B2] have uncovered an astounding variety of opalised marine specimens. An almost complete skeleton of a 100-million-year-old plesiosaur (a marine reptile) now has pride of place at the Queensland Museum in Brisbane.

In 1885 the **Wilcannia** [C2] courthouse heard a case concerning cruelty to animals. One of the police magistrates was Edward Bulwer Lytton Dickens, the son of Charles Dickens, and one of the prosecution witnesses was Frederick James Anthony Trollope, the son of the novelist Anthony Trollope. Along the all-dirt River Road that heads north-east to Bourke you'll pass through **Tilpa** with its famous bush pub and **Louth** with its Turf Club. On the second weekend in August more than 4,000 people gather from near and far for the local race meet, a week of racing and socialising.

Diary of Events

Town	Event	Date	Contact
Ardlethan	Kelpie Dog Festival	March	02 6978 2040
Booligal	Sheep Races	October	02 6993 8119
Bourke	Mateship Festival	October	02 6872 1321
Brewarinna	Outback Surf Boat Classic	October long weekend	02 6993 4600
Cobar	Festival of the Miner's Ghost	October, last weekend	02 6836 2448
Condobolin	Heart of NSW Festival	April	02 6895 4120
Griffith	Festival of Gardens	October, 3rd weekend	02 6962 4145
Gundagai	Dog on the Tuckerbox Festival	November, 3rd week	02 6344 1450
Hay	Surf carnival	Australia Day	02 6993 1390
Hillston	Hook, Line and Sinker Fishing Festival	August	02 6967 2555
Lake Cargelligo	Day Outback and Rodeo	October long weekend	02 6898 1501
Leeton	Camel Stakes	Easter	02 6953 2005
Louth	Louth Picnic Races	August, 2nd Saturday	02 9993 4600
Mildura	International Balloon Fiesta	July, 2nd week	03 5021 4424
Moulamein	Yabby Races	Easter saturday	03 5887 5246
Narrandera	John O'Brien Bush Festival	March	02 6959 1766
Nymagee	Music Festival	October long weekend	02 6837 3667

At home a

Wherever you travel, from Abels Bay in Tassie to Zilzie in Queensland, you
juicers and health grills, Breville make portable appliances that make

ver Australia.

ome with Breville. With kettles and sandwich makers, blenders, e fun. That's why we've been part of Australian life since 1932.

Breville
Better ideas sooner

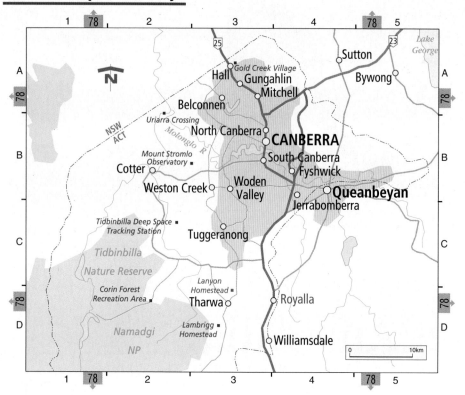

When the six Australian colonies federated in 1901 a national capital was needed. Because of the intense rivalry between Sydney and Melbourne it was to be neither of these cities. After much consideration, 2,359 sq km of sheep-grazing lands on the Monaro Plains were transferred to the Commonwealth on 1 January 1911 to become the Australian Capital Territory, commonly referred to as the ACT.

get off the beaten track
amble
around the territory

The **Corin** Forest Recreation Area [D2] in the **Tidbinbilla Nature Reserve** has Australia's longest bobsled slide—it's 800 m long.

At **Gold Creek**

[A3] is the National Dinosaur Museum, which has Australia's largest dinosaur display. There are 10 full-size replica skeletons of dinosaurs, including stegosaurus, chasmosaurus and deinonychus along with muttaburrasaurus, an Australian dinosaur that roamed around Queensland and was named after the outback town of Muttaburra, the only dinosaur to have been named in that manner. You can even touch the 150-million-year-old shin bone of apatosaurus and walk under the flying reptile pterandon. The museum is on the corner of Gold Creek Road and the Barton Highway at **Gold Creek Village**. It's open daily 10 am–5 pm (9 am–5 pm during ACT and NSW school holidays). It is closed only on Christmas Day.

Lambrigg [D3] Homestead, on the

Murrumbidgee River near Tharwa, is the site of scientist William Farrer's final resting place. It was on Lambrigg that Farrer's scientific experiments resulted in the development of rust-free and then disease-resistant wheat, which greatly expanded Australia's wheat industry. In 1924, William's wife, Nina, sold the property to the Commonwealth government who leased it back to her for an annual rent of one peppercorn. It is not open to the public.

GAZETTEER

The **Lanyon** Homestead [D3], a neighbour of Lambrigg, also on the banks of the Murrumbidgee, does give public access. It is one of Australia's best historic pastoral proper-

BRONZED AUSSIE CHICKEN

Various bush herbs and spices are now popular in Australian cooking and available from specialist shops. In Canberra you can pick them up at Cooking Coordinates in Belconnen Markets (02 6253 5133), an outlet for Herbie's Spices. This recipe uses a mix including lemon myrtle leaf (or lemon ironwood, sweet verbena tree, sand verbena myrtle, tree verbena). It has a lemongrass-like flavour and the aroma of lemon verbena. Use sparingly and add toward the end of cooking, no more than 10–15 minutes before serving, as any longer than this will destroy the delicate lemon notes.

2 chicken breast fillets
1 tbsp olive oil
salt
1/4 cup orange juice or pouring cream

NATIVE SPICE MIX
1 tbsp coriander seed, ground
1 tsp wattleseed
1/2 tsp akudjura (desert raisin)
1/2 tsp lemon myrtle leaf ground
1/4 tsp mountain pepperleaf
1/2 tsp salt (more or less to taste)

Sprinkle 1/2 tsp native spice mix over each side of the chicken breasts, pressing on firmly. Heat olive oil in a pan and cook the fillets until golden brown on each side. Remove chicken to a warm plate and deglaze the pan with the liquid of your choice. Add salt to taste, stir until smooth and well coloured, then pour sauce over cooked fillets. Serve immediately. Serves 2. This recipe is also delicious using kangaroo loin fillet, tuna or salmon steaks instead of chicken.

Ian Hemphill, Herbie's Spices, ROZELLE

SALMON QUICHE

If you hear the phrase 'Real men don't eat quiche' in your travels then Canberra, being the power base of Australia's politicians, may be a place that springs to mind. This phrase is defined in the *Macquarie Dictionary* as referring to a man who is kind, gentle and who has a politically correct social consciousness.

puff pastry sheets	**salt and pepper to**
1 tbsp olive oil	**taste**
1 medium leek,	**2 eggs**
thinly sliced	**$1/2$ cup thickened**
2 cloves garlic,	**cream**
finely chopped	**$1/2$ cup milk**
415 g can pink	
salmon, drained	

Preheat oven to 180°C and grease a standard quiche dish (or a 20 cm x 28 cm oblong flan pan with removable base). Line with pastry sheets, joining sheets where necessary. Heat oil in a pan and cook leek and garlic for about 5 minutes, or until leek is soft and golden. Add salmon to leek mixture and season. Mix gently to combine and remove pan from heat. Place eggs, cream and milk in a bowl and whisk until combined. Spread salmon mixture over pastry base and pour egg mixture over it. Bake for 45–50 minutes, or until quiche is set and lightly browned. Serves 6.

Roshani Payne, QUEANBEYAN

ties, and is protected by the National Trust. The main house dates from 1859 and some of the nearby farm buildings were built by convict labour in the 1840s. A few metres from the homestead, though only accessible by prior arrangement, is a well-preserved Aboriginal 'scar' tree, with a long mark where a large section of bark was removed to make a canoe. A short stroll from Lanyon is the Nolan Gallery, which has some of Sidney Nolan's most important paintings, including the Ned Kelly originals. Both the homestead and the gallery are open Tuesday to Sunday (02 6237 5136).

At **Mount Stromlo** [B2]

Observatory you can touch a meteorite. The observatory, established in 1924, is run by the Australian National University's Research School of Astronomy and Astrophysics. There are hands-on exhibits and guided tours and three working telescopes, including the largest, the 74-inch. During the day (in fine weather) you can see the moon and Venus; night viewing is by appointment only. Open seven days (except Christmas Day) 9.30 am to 4.30 pm.

Namadgi National Park

[D2] covers 1,060 sq km of country—around 45 per cent of the total land area of the Australian Capital Territory.

Queanbeyan Nature Reserve [B4]

protects the button wrinklewort, a grassland daisy that is endangered. Public access to this small area is restricted, as it is the only place in New South Wales where the species is formally conserved.

GAZETTEER

Royalla [D4] is now the terminus of

the Spirit of Tugerranong tourist railway from Canberra. The line first began

ACT

running in the 1880s, and until 1989 it ran all the way to Cooma, and now gives passengers a bird's-eye view across the Tuggeranong Valley as it climbs to the old **Tuggeranong** siding then winds around the Melrose Valley. If you're lucky you might spot a kangaroo leaping alongside the train. It is run by the Australian Railway Historical Society (phone 02 6284 2790).

Tharwa [D3] is a village with a weatherboard church and a wooden bridge. Built in 1895 to ford the Murrumbidgee River, the bridge is the oldest in the ACT. South of Tharwa is Cuppacumbalong, a large homestead with a pleasant garden that now houses an arts and crafts centre.

Tidbinbilla [C2] Deep Space Tracking Station, off Paddys River Road at Tidbinbilla, is one of only three such stations in Australia, all of which are operated by the government in partnership with NASA. It opens 9 am–5 pm. Call 02 6201 7800 for further details.

Uriarra Crossing [B2] is a popular spot with wombats. This nature reserve beside the Molonglo River is also popular with humans for picnics, barbecues and swimming.

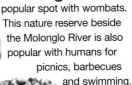

PRESERVED LEMON MAYONNAISE

This recipe includes the chopped skin of half a preserved lemon. You can buy jars of preserved lemon or make it yourself, although this will require a month to allow time for it to mature. To preserve a lemon, soak it in water overnight. Then cut in quarters from the top to within 2 cm of the bottom. Sprinkle plenty of fresh sea salt onto the flesh. Place lemon in an airtight container and refrigerate for one month.

5 egg yolks
30 g Limelight seeded chilli mustard
juice of 1 lemon
300 ml light olive oil
100 ml extra virgin olive oil
chopped skin of ½ preserved lemon

Place egg yolks, mustard and half the lemon juice in the bowl of a food processor and blend. With the motor running, add both the oils in a slow constant stream. Finish with the chopped preserved lemon and a little more lemon juice if required. The mayonnaise should not need any salt, as the preserved lemons are quite salty.

Sven Hossack-Smith,
CANBERRA

Diary of Events

Town	Event	Date	Contact
Queanbeyan	Charity Rodeo	March	02 6298 0211
	Show	November	02 6298 0211
	Country Music Festival	December	02 6298 0211

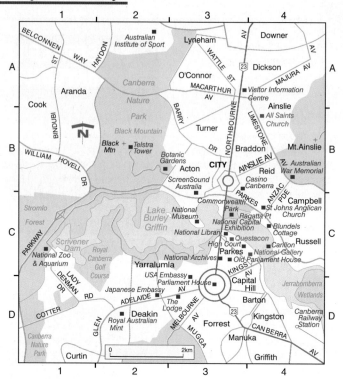

Also in 1911, the year the ACT was declared, a competition was launched internationally for the design of a city for 25,000 people. American landscape architect Walter Burley Griffin won the competition with a design based on a series of circles and axes similar to the street patterns of Paris and Washington. Canberra is now a beautiful modern city of more than 300,000 people, centred around Lake Burley Griffin.

get off the beaten track
cruise
through canberra

All Saints Church [B4]

was once a funeral parlour. An attractive Gothic building, it started life in Sydney in 1860 as the railway station for Rookwood cemetery. In those days trains brought grieving relatives and coffins to the cemetery.

GAZETTEER

The Australian War Memorial

[B4] has received extensive renovations enabling the first-time display of a number of classic aircraft that have till now been in storage. A Zero, Japan's most feared fighter plane from WWII, is on

display, along with planes such as a Mosquito, Kittyhawk, Mustang, Wirraway, Sea Fury and MiG-15. The extra space at the museum now allows it to display large items such as the Japanese midget submarine that attacked Sydney Harbour in 1942. It had previously been housed in the Treloar Technology Centre in Mitchell. A small plaque on a rock behind the Australian War Memorial commemorates Australia's Aboriginal war dead. Go across the road behind the War Memorial and you will see a track. Follow that track into the bush and when you have gone about 100 m turn left. Along the track is the rock and its plaque, acknowledging the contribution made by all those Aborigines who fought for Australia in the wars of the 20th century.

At Blundell's Cottage [C4], near

Regatta Point, you can see what Canberra was once like—the stone and slab cottage is a reminder of the area's farming heritage.

Canberra's **Carillon** [C4] is one of only three in the country, with the others in Bathurst and at the University of Sydney. This one is 50 m high and has 53 bells.

At Commonwealth Park [C3] on

Lake Burley Griffin Captain Cook's water jet sends up to 6 tonnes of water 140 m into the air at a speed of 200 km/h, every hour, on the hour. The Floriade Spring Festival in September and October provides a spectacular sight of millions of massed flowers. It's floodlit at night and has entertainment on weekends.

ROSEWATER POACHED NASHI

Nashi is the Japanese word for pear. The Nashi pear was first planted in Australia in 1980 at Orange Agricultural Institute and it is a great cooking pear. Nashis are available all year round but are at their best and cheapest from May to August.

750 ml water
300 g sugar
3 tsp rosewater
20 slices semi-dried Nashi pear

In a saucepan, bring water to the boil, then add sugar and stir to dissolve. Add rosewater and Nashi pear slices. Simmer 3–5 minutes, then remove from heat. Leave fruit to cool in syrup. Serve with lavender panna cotta [see following page].

Sven Hossack-Smith, CANBERRA

ACT

The **High Court** [C3] is at the top of Australia's judicial system and is the final court of appeal. Its first sitting was in Melbourne in 1903. In 1973 it moved to Sydney and then to its permanent home in Canberra after the impressive building to house it was completed in 1980. Seven justices sit on the bench and hear cases regarding the interpretation of the Australian Constitution and appeals against decisions made by the states and territories. One of the most significant of these in recent times was the 1992 Mabo decision, in which the High Court recognised traditional owner-ship of the land and paving the way for Aboriginal rights to native title.

LAVENDER PANNA COTTA

A lavender field in full flower is a spectacular sight; if you're in the Canberra area visit Crisp Galleries located on the Hume Highway. There you can enjoy the Lavender Walk among the beautiful lavender gardens. The owner of the gallery, Peter Crisp, is an artist who works with glass moulding techniques and you will notice a glass mosaic among the gardens. You can purchase some lavender and try this recipe.

- **2 cups fresh cream**
- **60 g caster sugar**
- **2 vanilla beans, split**
- **6–8 lavender flower heads**
- **2 leaves gelatine, softened in cold water**

Place cream, sugar, vanilla beans and lavender flowers in a saucepan and heat to simmering. Remove from heat and allow to infuse for 10 minutes. Strain into a clean bowl and stir in the gelatine. When dissolved, pour into mould and chill overnight.

Sven Hossack-Smith, CANBERRA

Jerrabomberra Wetlands [D4], on the edge of Lake Burley Griffin, is a refuge for water birds during droughts in the inland. Paths give access to the wetlands and you can watch the birds from hides. There are some 77 bird and animal species here. You might even see a platypus.

The **Lodge** [D3] is the official residence of the prime minister, although when it was built in 1926–27 it was intended to be temporary until something more appropriate could be designed. The first prime minister to move in was Stanley Bruce, in 1927. Humble though it was considered by some, the first Australian-born Labor prime minister, James Scullin, thought it too grand and refused to live there, prompting suggestions that it could house the National Library or be turned into a private hospital. It was occupied again when Joe Lyons came to office in 1931.

The **National Zoo and Aquarium** [C1], opened in 1989, is now one of the world's leading aquariums. There are thousands of fish from giant cod to tiny luminous reef inhabitants as well as sharks and turtles. The complex also includes a rainforest area, water gardens and a fly-fishing pond.

The **National Capital Exhibition** [C3] at Regatta Point tells the story of the Australian Capital Territory from Aboriginal occupation to the arrival of the British through audiovisual displays, photographs, laser maps and artefacts.

The **National Archives** building [C3] on Queen Victoria Terrace was built in 1927 and is one of Canberra's oldest government offices. The unmarked green door on the north-western side of the building was once the 'secret' entrance to ASIO (Australian Security and Intelligence Organisation). The new **Federation Gallery** here displays Australia's 'birth certificates', including the original decree, signed by Queen Victoria, proclaiming Australia an independent nation. The building was originally Canberra's GPO. It now holds ephemera such as lighthouse plans, theatre scripts, flag designs, old photographs and the early designs for the national capital and Old Parliament House. The gallery made Australian constitutional documents available to the public for the first time when it opened in January 2001.

The **National Botanic Gardens** [B2], on the lower slopes of **Black Mountain**, has the largest collection of native plant species in the country. They are grouped by species to re-create Australia's major ecosystems. Higher up in Black Mountain Nature Park, one of several such reserves around the city, is the landmark **Telstra Tower**.

At the **National Gallery** [C4] is a restaurant with a very special entrance. Past Auguste Rodin's statue of 'The Burghers of Calais' and a setting by Japanese artist Fujiko Nakaya that is almost a piece of performance art is the Juniperberry Restaurant, in the Sculpture Garden. The restaurant is on the far side of a marsh pond with clouds of mist drifting across it. The mist is machine-produced and blows quite dramatically if there is a breeze—a remarkable piece of moving sculpture.

The **National Library** [C3] has constantly changing exhibitions. They reflect the varied and eclectic contents of the library, such as the diaries of famous Australians.

The **National Museum** [C3] uses state-of-the-art technology and interactive exhibitions to tell the story of Australia and the people who live here. It has the world's largest and one of the most significant Aboriginal bark painting collections. Here you can see 20,000 years of environmental change come to life in the rock art of Kakadu, and celebrate two of Australia's icons—the Hills Hoist and Vegemite.

ACT

DON'T MISS: The National Poker Championships, are held in February or March each year at **Casino Canberra** [A2]; the National Capital Dancesport Championships, featuring Ballroom, Latin American and New Vogue dancing, are held in June or July annually at the AIS Arena, **Australian Institute of Sport** [A2]. Canberra Festival is held over 10 days in March and includes food and wine, hot-air ballooning, art and craft exhibitions, a street parade and mardi gras.

Old Parliament House [C3]

(1927–88), now houses the National Portrait Gallery, which is one of only four such galleries in the world. It celebrates the people who have helped shape Australia, with portraits of Sir Donald Bradman, Captain James Cook and Cathy Freeman, for example, along with one of the five death masks of Ned Kelly.

GAZETTEER

AUNTY OLIVE'S PRIZE WINNING PASSIONFRUIT BUTTER

Aunty Olive, still going strong at 83 years old (she was just eight years old when Old Parliament House was new, and remembers all the pomp), won a prize at the Royal Easter Show in Sydney with her delicious passionfruit butter recipe.

225 g butter
900 g caster sugar
rind and juice of 6 large lemons
pulp of 10 passionfruit
6 eggs, beaten

In a large saucepan melt the butter slowly and add the sugar, lemon rind and lemon juice. Stir and bring to just under boiling point. Remove from heat and add passionfruit and beaten eggs. Return to a low heat and stir constantly (do not allow to boil), until the mixture coats the back of the spoon (about 5 minutes). Be very careful not to boil, as the mixture will separate. Pour into warm sterilised jars. Delicious on croissants or toast, or as a filling for tarts and scones.

Olive Artindale, BELCONNEN

The Parliament House [D3]

Members' Hall has some of Australia's most important historical documents on display. The original *Commonwealth of Australia Constitution Act 1900* (UK) is there, along with one of only four surviving copies of the Magna Carta, made in 1297. One of the world's largest tapestries hangs in Parliament House. The Great Hall Tapestry is based on an Arthur Boyd painting. It measures 20 m by 9 m—except for the large chunk that was removed so the doors behind it could be used. In all, 70 new art and craft works were commissioned for the new Parliament House and another 3,000 were bought.

Questacon [C3] has a disaster every

few minutes. It experiences tornadoes and 55 earthquakes every day and it's not built on a previously undiscovered fault line. Questacon is a science and technology centre that combines education and entertainment. Visitors experience earthquakes, get up close to 3 million volts of lightning and paint pictures with their own brainwaves. One exhibit, Sideshow, captures the culture and history, the biology, psychology, maths and physics of sideshow exhibits and fairground rides.

GAZETTEER

The Royal Australian Mint [D2]

on Deakin Street at Deakin opened in 1965 and has produced over 11 billion circulating coins. It has coins from the earliest days of Australian settlement until modern decimal currency, and you can see the production process from an elevated gallery. There's even an opportunity to make your own money. Open seven days a week.

The Royal Canberra Golf Course

[C2], established in 1926, is one of Australia's most popular golf clubs. Access is restricted to

ACT

members, guests of members and interstate and overseas golf club members.

St Johns Anglican Church [C4]

and Schoolhouse Museum is one of the few old buildings in Canberra. The Church was built by Robert Campbell and consecrated by Bishop Broughton on 12 March 1845. The tower was struck by lightning in 1851 and Edmund Blacket (Colonial Architect 1849–54 and architect of the Quadrangle at the University of Sydney) was commissioned to design a new one. It is a simple three-stage stone tower with corner buttresses. The graveyard near the church has gravestones dating back to 1844. St Johns Schoolhouse, the first schoolhouse in Canberra, was built in the late 1840s and restored in 1969.

ScreenSound Australia [A3], the

National Film and Sound Archive, has Australia's finest collection of old films and sound recordings. It is a treasure trove of Australian audiovisual material dating back to the 1890s and regularly shows historic films and documentaries. It also holds Australia's first Oscar, awarded for the 1942 documentary, *Cinesound Review: Kokoda Front Line*. The ScreenSound building once housed the Institute of Anatomy, and at one stage stored the body of the then unidentified murder victim, the Pyjama Girl, in its basement. Because of the mystery surrounding her identity and her death (she was found in a culvert in Albury in 1934) she was placed in preserving liquid and kept at the institute for 10 years, until she was identified, as Linda Agostini, and buried. Her husband was eventually convicted of her killing. Her ghost has been reported in the building on several occasions since.

Many of the embassies in **Yarralumla** [C2] are interesting, built to reflect their countries' culture. When viewed together they create a display of architecture from around the world. Two of particular interest are the US Embassy at Moonah Place, a stately red brick mansion modelled on those designed by Sir Christopher Wren for Williamsburg in Virginia, and the Japanese

Embassy at 112 Empire Circuit, which is distinguished by its formal Japanese garden and traditional Japanese tea house.

Diary of Events

Town	Event	Date	Contact
Canberra	Summernats Car Festival	January	02 6205 0044
	Royal Canberra Show	February	02 6250 0044
	National Poker Championships	Feb/Mar	02 6257 7074
	Canberra Festival	March	02 6205 0044
	National Folk Festival	Easter	02 6250 0044
	Australian Science Festival	April/May	02 6250 0044
	National Capital Dancesport Championships	Jun/Jul	02 6214 1111
	Floriade Spring Festival	Sept/Oct	02 6205 0044

Australian hotels for all budgets

Hotel accommodation in Australia is remarkably cheap compared to most other countries.

Australia's largest hotel company, Accor, is the leader when it comes to providing you with quality accommodation, value for money and friendly service.

You can stay with Accor's deluxe 5-star brand Sofitel in Melbourne, Cairns and Sydney (the renowned Wentworth hotel will be launched as a Sofitel in mid-2003). The Sofitel name is synonymous worldwide with refined elegance, exceptional cuisine and first-class service.

Novotel is the most famous Accor hotel brand, and you will find them in all the key cities as well as the most popular resort areas, such as Palm Cove and the Sunshine Coast in Queensland and in the wine districts of the Barossa Valley and Swan Valley. Their Dolfi Club is ideal for kids and up to 2 children can share their parents' room for free.

Make sure you visit the Observation Deck at the Novotel at Sydney Olympic Park. The hotel (and adjoining Ibis) were the first hotels ever to be built in an Olympic precinct and the views are stunning.

A hotel name that you will see not only in cities, but throughout regional areas is Mercure. There

are three levels of Mercure—Grand, Hotels and Inns. For a truly unique indulgence you can't go past the heritage Mercure Grands such as Mt Lofty House

in the Adelaide Hills or the Hydro Majestic in the Blue Mountains—living history with 5-star service. Mercure Hotels offer great city value while the budget-conscious Mercure Inns in Outback Western Australia, Northern Territory and Queensland offer local character and low rates.

Also watch out for All Seasons hotels in locations such as Sydney, Melbourne and Coffs Harbour. For genuine no-frills value, the 3-star Ibis and 2-star Formule 1 brands

lead the pack. You know exactly what you'll be getting and the one price per hotel policy makes it easy to budget for your accommodation around Australia.

And watch out for Accor's pioneering backpacker brand called Base. Already popular in New Zealand, it is set to expand rapidly in Australia, including cities and resort areas such as the Whitsundays.

When you come to Sydney, two must-dos ... cruise on the Harbour with Accor's Magistic Cruises or Sydney Showboats, and combine stunning views and cuisine at the Summit Restaurant on top of Australia Square.

For great rates visit our 'Hot Deals' section at **accorhotels.com.au** or call 1300 65 65 65.

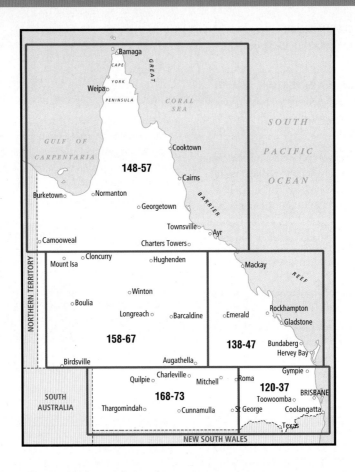

queen

Queensland is one of the world's best eco-tourism destinations, with the world's largest coral reef, the world's oldest rainforest, a huge swathe of the Outback and an enviable stretch of coastline.

Dutchman Willem Jansz was the first European to set foot on Australian soil. In 1606 Jansz, in his ship the *Duyfken*, landed near the Wenlock River close to present-day Weipa. His report convinced the Dutch authorities that there was nothing worth having there. He was on the wrong side of the state.

QLD

sland

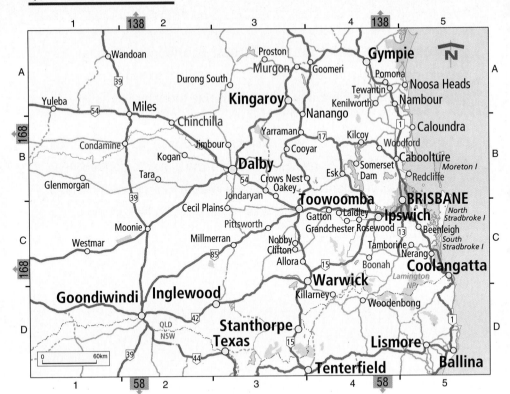

South-east Queensland is rural Australia at its best. Pretty inland cities such as Warwick, Killarney and Stanthorpe are complemented by boutique wineries, pristine national parks and breathtaking scenery.

get off the beaten track

roam

the south-east

In the **Allora** [C3] museum in the old court house (1860) is a replica of the Talgai skull, an Aboriginal cranium estimated to be 15,000 years old. The town's name comes from the Aboriginal 'ngallorah', meaning swampy place. The town began as an out-station of Neil Ross's Goomburra grazing run.

The **Beenleigh** [C5] Rum Distillery (the town was named after the distillery, not the other way around) on Distillery Road beside the Pacific Highway is the oldest registered distillery in Australia, holding Commonwealth Distiller's Licence No. 1. It also houses the oldest copper pot, made in 1863, and the country's oldest surviving still, built in 1884. There is an interesting series of displays and guided tours of the works—for details call 07 3807 4970. About 10 km east of Beenleigh is the **Rocky Point Sugar Mill**, built in 1879 and still operating, run by the fourth generation of the Heck family. It is the only privately owned sugar mill in Australia. Most others are run as cooperatives. The mill is on Mill Road, **Woongoolba**.

Boonah [C4] is one of several towns of the region that were settled in the late 1800s by German farmers. About 8 km to the north-west is Templin Historical Village, which has a rare heavy iron pump manufactured in Melbourne in the 1860s and used to wash sheep. It survived the scrap metal merchant only because its underground pipe was buried too deep for anyone to shift.

POTATO CHRISTMAS PUDDING

Many early Australian recipes were developed in times of adversity, using ingredients such as potatoes instead of eggs and milk, with surprisingly good results. Try this variation on the traditional Christmas pud.

750 g plain flour
500 g sultanas
125 g mixed peel, finely chopped
500 g seeded raisins, chopped
500 g currants
1 cup firmly packed brown sugar
1 cup firmly packed grated carrot
1 cup grated potato
1 cup treacle, warmed

Mix all ingredients well in a large bowl. Pour into a large greased pudding basin. Cover with foil and secure with string. Place pudding in a large saucepan and pour boiling water halfway up side of basin. Cover pan with a tight-fitting lid and boil for 4 hours. Serves 12.

Templin Historical Village, BOONAH

Caboolture's [B4] Abbey Museum, on Old Toorbul Point Rd, is a private collection of art and archeology, one of the finest in Australia. Every June it hosts the Medieval Tournament, with jousting, mock combats, archery, dancing, music, crafts and live theatre—phone 07 5495 1652 for details.

At **Caloundra**'s [B5] Dicky Beach is the rusting skeleton of the SS *Dicky*, which ran aground there on 1 February 1893. Attempts to relaunch it proved unsuccessful. Legend has it that the vessel was used for local dances until someone knocked over

QLD

a kerosene lamp and it was burned out. The ship's propeller is propped up near the caravan park. Around the headland, just north of Kings Beach is a memorial to the 268 people,

mostly medical staff, who died when the HMA Hospital Ship *Centaur* was capsized off Moreton Island by a Japanese submarine during World War II.

DON'T MISS: The Great Dunny Race Celebrations are held at Aussie World, **Palmview**, on the Bruce Highway just north of the Caloundra turn-off—the full-size working replica of the Ettamogah Pub marks the spot—on the Australia Day weekend. Other events include thong throwing and cane toad racing.

Cecil Plains [C3] was without a

pub until 1938. The town's teetotallers twice voted against a drinking establishment; when the imbibers finally won they called the hotel 'Victory' to mark the triumph of thirst over adversity. The Victory Pub is on Taylor Street.

Chinchilla [B2] is the centre

of Queensland's polocrosse life. It is also famous for having one of the largest petrified wood areas in the world. Chinchilla wood was formed during the Jurassic Age, 140–180 million years ago. There are some good examples at the museum, but the best is in the main street next to the library in Fuller Park. There have also been finds of now extinct pentoxlin trees. The only other finds of these fossilised trees have been in Peru. The Chinchilla Folk Museum in Villiers Street specialises in transportation and has a copy of the first ticket ever issued by Qantas (originally the Queensland and Northern Territory

GAZETTEER

Air Service)—to a Mr A Kennedy, for the first flight from Longreach to Cloncurry. The original is in the local ANZ Bank. The Boonarga Cactoblastis Memorial Hall is 10 km east of Chinchilla on the Warrego Highway. The local farmers dedicated the hall to the South American moth larvae that

had saved their farmlands from the invasion of the prickly pear cactus. Prickly pear was planted in Australia as a cheap source of fodder and an ornamental hedge as early as 1839. Declared a noxious weed in 1900, by 1925 nearly 25 million ha of agricultural land in Queensland and northern New South Wales were infested.

DON'T MISS: The Chinchilla Melon Festival is held every two years. The next one is on 10–16 February 2003—call 07 4662 7056 for details. Major events include melon skiing, melon seed spitting and the melon heads competition.

In 1868 **Condamine** [B2] blacksmith Samuel William Jones invented the Condamine 'Bullfrog' cowbell to help find cattle in the bush. On a clear morning the bell could be heard up to 4 km away. It was so successful, according to poet Dame Mary Gilmore, that it made the cattle deaf. Bell Park in Condamine features a 2 m high replica of the bell.

Coolangatta [C5] is the southern-

most town of the Gold Coast, and one of its earliest resorts. It was named for a steam ship that was wrecked off the coast in 1846.

In **Crows Nest** [B3], in the centre of the village green, is a statue of Jimmy Crow, after whom the town was named, and nearby is the tree that was his 'nest'. The inscription on the tree reads: 'In the early

days when teamsters visited this area Jimmy Crow, an Aborigine named by early settlers, used a hollow tree as his gunyah. He was relied on for information and directions. This place was used as a camping place by teamsters and travellers and became known as Jimmy Crow's Nest, hence the name Crows Nest.' **Cabarlah**, a tiny hamlet south of Crows Nest, has the Farmers Arms, licensed in 1863, the pub claims to hold the longest continuous liquor licence in Queensland. Bowen disputes this with a licence awarded in 1862.

From **Dalby** [B3], heart of the rich pastoral land of the Condamine, it is 60 km north to the **Bunya Mountains National Park** (via Kaimkillenbun and Yamsion, though the route south from Kingaroy is an easier drive). The park, set aside in 1908, contains the last significant stand of bunya

GAZETTEER

QLD

RISOTTO WITH ROCKMELON

All sorts of melons are grown in the Chinchilla district, as well as grapes, vegetables and grains. The town's name is from the Aboriginal word for the cypress pines that also grow here, 'jinchilla'.

125 g butter
1 small onion, finely chopped
500 g arborio rice
1 glass dry white wine
8 cups chicken stock
salt and pepper to taste
a few drops tabasco sauce
1 small ripe rockmelon, peeled, seeded and finely diced
30 g parmesan cheese, grated

Melt half the butter in a large, heavy-based pan. Add the onion and cook over moderate heat for 3–5 minutes, until the onion is soft. Add rice and stir over heat to coat for a few minutes. Add the wine and cook until it is absorbed. Keep chicken stock handy in a saucepan over a low heat and add a cup at a time, stirring until all is absorbed into rice before adding more. Keep cooking and adding stock until a creamy consistency is obtained and the rice is cooked. Add salt and pepper and tabasco to taste. Melt the other half of the butter in a small pan and add the rockmelon. Toss over flame to heat through. Add melon and parmesan to risotto, keeping a little in reserve for decoration. Serves 4–6.

Ann Wilshire, CHINCHILLA

pine in Queensland, after decades of logging. You can still find scars on the surface of the pines where Aborigines cut footholds so they could clamber up the trees to get the sweet bunya pine nuts, which are produced in cones the size of a football. Each cone holds around 60–90 nuts (very large ones up to 120). It is estimated that some of the bunya pines are more than 500 years old.

At Durong South [A3] is

the Manar Tourist Park, which has over 140 km of 4WD tracks, including some rock-hopping tracks. There are also separate areas for trail, trial and BMX bikes, fishing, swimming and 10 hectares of mown camping ground. The Burrandowan Races are held on the second Saturday in May. They have been running for 80 years having begun in 1922. The day ends with a pitfire barbecue and entertainment.

Glenmorgan's [B1] Myall Park

Botanic Gardens, the life work of David Gordon AM (and home to the Grevillea 'Robyn Gordon'), was established in 1941 and covers 132 ha. It has Queensland's oldest collection of Australian semi-arid flora, including many endangered species. Drive, walk or cycle the 4 km garden circuit, open from 10 am to 3pm each day.

Goomeri [A4], at the junction of the

Burnett and Wide Bay Highways, is home to Booubyjan Homestead, one of the oldest slab-constructed homesteads in Queensland. It was built in 1848 and has been in the Lawless family ever since. It's open to the public, but visitors are asked to call ahead: 07 4168 6262.

WILD LIME JAM AND CORDIAL

Wild limes, also known as lime bush, desert lemon, desert lime and native cumquat, grow prolifically around the Condamine region, becoming ripe in November. *Eremocitrus glauca* is a true citrus that originally grew in inland arid areas of Queensland, New South Wales and South Australia. Traditional use is thought to have been as a mouth freshener. Priscilla Mundell, who runs a farm B&B at Nelgai, 16 km west of Condamine, has found other ways to put them to excellent use.

WILD LIME JAM

Cut wild limes into halves or quarters and barely cover with water. Soak overnight and then boil until soft. Measure fruit mixture and add same quantity of sugar. Stir over heat without boiling until sugar is dissolved. Bring to boil, boil uncovered without stirring until jam jells when tested. Pour into hot sterilised jars; seal when cold.

WILD LIME CORDIAL

Squeeze limes to make desired quantity of juice. Boil 1 cup of sugar to 1 litre of wild lime juice for 10 minutes to make a concentrate and then bottle in sterilised containers. This form will keep for years. For a less-potent juice concentrate mix 1 cup of juice to 1–2 cups of sugar and 2 cups of boiling water. Stir until sugar is dissolved and then bottle. Use as cordial and keep in fridge. This makes a deliciously refreshing summer drink on its own or with gin!

Priscilla Mundell,
CONDAMINE

DON'T MISS: Goomeri holds a Pumpkin Festival on the last weekend in May each year. The annual challenge is the Great Australian Pumpkin Roll, down Policeman's Hill—the aim is to roll your pumpkin the greatest distance.

Goondiwindi [D2] hosts the Hell of

the West Triathlon on the first weekend in February. It was also the home of one of Australia's most famous and beloved racehorses, Gunsynd.

The sawmill in # Grandchester [C4]

began production in 1945, and still uses a steam engine manufactured in 1911. The owner fires the steam engine with sawdust. The burning sawdust heats the water to make the steam to drive the engine that cuts the timber, producing sawdust that heats the water … and so on.

In the grounds of # Gympie's [A4]

Gold and Mining Museum is Andrew Fisher's House. Fisher was Australia's first Labor Minister for Trade and Customs. He later became Prime Minister—the first from Queensland. He was elected Prime Minister three times in the years leading up to World War I. About 20 km south of Gympie in the **Amamoor Creek State Forest Park** each August the Toyota National Country Music Muster is held.

Inglewood's [D3] olive growing

industry has replaced its tobacco industry. Each year in March, at the peak of the olive harvest, is the Outback Olive Festival, with olive oil tasting and judging, cooking demonstrations and a Blessing of the Olives ceremony. Inglewood aims to become Australia's olive capital. Locals also claim to produce some of the best honey in the country.

Ipswich [C4] is home to

Walter Burley Griffin's Incinerator, which has been turned into a theatre. It is in Queens Park. While Burley Griffin is most famous for his design of Canberra, he also designed municipal incinerators, a few of which still survive in towns such as Leeton and Griffith in New South Wales (one in Willoughby, Sydney, is classified by the National Trust).

Jimbour [B3] was originally a pastoral

property, from which Ludwig Leichhardt set out in 1844 on his journey to reach Port Essington on the north coast of what was to become the Northern Territory. He was establishing a route to drove livestock between the east coast and the north. Jimbour House, built in 1874–76, was powered by gas produced from coal mined on the property and also had Queensland's first windmill, which supplied water to the home's reticulated system.

The # Jondaryan [C3] Woolshed

lies just outside the town of the same name. Here you'll find steam engines and horses working to thrash grain, grind wheat and do all the other things required on big remote sheep and grain properties at the beginning of the 20th century.

Kenilworth's [A4]

Kev Franzi Movie Museum on Eumundi Road opens for groups of more than 15 (find out when the next group is booked in and tag along with them—they can take up to 60 people). It has a range of old movie cameras and projectors, and the 'show' consists of extracts from movies dating from the silent era to the present: 07 5446 0341.

GAZETTEER

QLD

Kilcoy's [B4] major attraction is a statue

of a very well endowed male yowie, the second such statue to take pride of place in Yowie Park on Hope Street (the first statue's male credentials were castrated by the town's vandals). As Australia's equivalent to the Himalayan Yeti or America's Big Foot, and also apparently part of Aboriginal Dreaming stories, the shire's tourist brochure reports

SMOKED BUNYA NUT LAMB WITH CAESAR SALAD

For thousands of years Aboriginal people from neighbouring areas gathered in the Bunya Mountains when the bunya nuts were ripening to feast on the sweet flesh. These days you can buy the nuts in select delicatessens, especially in the region.

empty bunya nut shells
1kg lamb striploin
FOR SALAD
25 g cooked bunya nuts, chopped
1 bacon rasher, chopped and fried
6 slices smoked lamb
cos lettuce
10 g parmesan cheese, flaked
croutons
anchovy fillets (optional)
Caesar dressing (egg, oil, vinegar)

Place bunya nut shells in a wok on low heat. Place meat, cut in half, on top of shells on a wire rack. Cover with a lid and smoke for approximately 45 minutes, depending on how you like your lamb. If the pan gets too hot, just turn off for a while. Toss all salad ingredients together with the dressing and serve.

Rex Parsons, BUNYA MOUNTAINS

official statistics of more than 3,000 sightings throughout Australia between 1975 and 1979. The last reported sighting in Kilcoy was in December 1979, when two Brisbane schoolboys described the beast as being about 3 m tall with a 'kangaroo appearance' and covered in chocolate-coloured hair. About 20 km south of Kilcoy, also accessible through **Esk** on the Brisbane Valley Highway, is **Somerset Dam**, a popular venue for water sports and fishing.

About 18 km from # Killarney [D4]

is **Carr's Lookout**, overlooking the start of Australia's longest river system. Here are the upper reaches of the Condamine, which eventually flows into the Darling, in turn flowing into the Murray, which eventually reaches the sea in South Australia.

Kingaroy [A3] is not only the peanut

capital of Australia, it is the bean capital as well. More than half of Australia's navy beans are grown in the district. The Bjelke-Petersen property Bethany is open to groups by appointment—07 4162 7046—first left, south past the airport.

DON'T MISS:

Kingaroy's Peanut Festival is held on different dates each year. Call 07 4162 3199 for details.

At the # Kogan [B2]

Emu Farm on the Condamine Highway from June to October you can see eggs being artificially incubated and emu chicks being reared.

Laidley's [C4]
Das Neumann Haus was constructed in 1893 by Hermann Haumann, a violin maker. It now houses a museum of local history. The suspension bridge at the **Narda Lagoon Nature Reserve** spans 80 m and is one of the longest cable suspension bridges in Australia. The Laidley Pioneer Village site is the former camping ground of the teamsters using the old road from Ipswich to Drayton (now part of Toowoomba) and is also the site of the original township of Laidley. It is open the last Saturday of each month.

The Laidley area also hosts skydiving and ballooning operations. The Laidley Valley is said to be the seventh most fertile valley in the world, and Laidley celebrates the fact with

a three-day Spring Festival beginning on the second Thursday of September. Nearby, the Lockyer Valley supports 318 identified bird species.

About 20 km north of # Miles [B2]
underground munitions bunkers, part of RAAF Kowguran during World War II, have been converted to self-contained motel units, a tea room, souvenir shop and memorabilia display, all now part of Possum Park. Train carriages of the same era have been converted to cabins. Miles also boasts an innovative library, art gallery and social history space called Dogwood Crossing @ Miles. Part of the Queensland Heritage Trails Network, the project encourages visitors and locals to share their stories.

HOT 'N' SPICY CORNED SILVERSIDE FRITTERS

QLD

Gympie is South-east Queensland's gold town, first discovered here in 1867 by James Nash, who gave the town its first name of Nashville (Gympie is from an Aboriginal word for a stinging nettle tree of the area). Corned silverside was a favourite of the early settlers as the salted meat kept so well.

- **1/2 kg corned silverside**
- **2 tbsp cider vinegar**
- **dash chilli sauce**
- **pinch ginger powder**
- **1 onion, finely chopped**
- **1/2 cup grated tasty cheese**
- **1 dsp French mustard**
- **1 x 270 g can Golden Circle corn and peas**
- **3 eggs, beaten**
- **3–4 tbsp self-raising flour**

Place meat in a large saucepan with enough water to cover. Add vinegar, chilli sauce and ginger. Simmer for approximately 1–1½ hours, until tender. Cool in cooking water. When cool, dice meat finely. To make fritters, place all ingredients in a bowl, adding flour last. Mix well. Place spoonfuls onto a hot greased frying pan and cook on one side for 3–4 minutes. Turn over and continue cooking until golden brown. Serves 4.

Dot Crane, THE PALMS

INGLEWOOD FOR OLIVES

Inglewood is aiming to become Australia's olive capital, with olives replacing tobacco as the area's main crop. But olives and olive oil are only just starting to take off in Australian cookery, so the good people at Viva have a few suggestions.

VIVA SUNDAY ROAST

4 lamb racks, each with 3–4 cutlets
1 large slice white bread, crusts removed
4 large sprigs parsley
3/4 cup pitted Viva ripe olives
1/2 tsp crushed garlic
1/4 cup Viva Early Harvest Extra Virgin Olive Oil
salt and pepper

BACON AND EGG OPEN-FACE PIES

2 sheets puff pastry
2 tbsp Viva Early Harvest Extra Virgin Olive Oil
2 rashers bacon, rind removed and cut into strips
2 Roma tomatoes, quartered lengthways
4 eggs
salt and cracked black pepper
sprinkle of fresh or dried thyme
1/3 cup chopped Viva black or green olives
chopped parsley or chives

Note: Early harvest olives have a stronger flavour and produce a green oil with a fruity aroma, good for salad dressings and marinades. Late harvest olives are picked when fully ripe, with a golden oil and a more mellow flavour, suitable for cooking, frying and baking.

Preheat oven to 200°C. Push a sharp knife through the centre of each lamb rack to make a cavity. In a food processor finely chop the bread, parsley, pitted olives, garlic and oil. Press filling into the cavities of lamb. Brush racks with oil and season with salt and pepper. Roast for about 20 minutes (still pinkish) or until cooked to your taste. Remove from the oven and rest lamb for 5 minutes before carving. Serves 4.

Preheat oven to 220°C . Brush 4 individual pie tins or flans with oil and line with puff pastry. Brush pastry with oil and place in the refrigerator. Half cook the bacon and tomatoes in a heavy pan moistened with oil. Place bacon and 2 pieces of tomato in each pie shell and break an egg into each. Season with salt, pepper and thyme and scatter on the olives. Bake for about 15 minutes or until the pastry is golden and the egg firm. Sprinkle with parsley or chives and serve. Serves 4.

Both recipes are from Viva, South Australia, using INGLEWOOD olives

East of **Millmerran** [C3] is **Yandilla**'s All Saints Anglican Church, the Millmerran Shire's oldest building and almost certainly the second-oldest church in Queensland. It was consecrated by Bishop Webber in 1887 and for many years was used as a private chapel for the Gore family and the Yandilla Station workers.

Moonie [C2] became Australia's first commercial oilfield in 1961. Production began in 1964 with the oil piped 306 km to Brisbane.

Moreton Island's [B5] tree-covered Mt Tempest is reputed to be the highest coastal sand dune in the world. A huge blowout on the bayside of the dune is visible on a clear day from Brisbane's Mt Coot-tha 50 km away. Much of the island remains wilderness national park with roads suitable for 4WD vehicles only.

At **Murgon** [A3] the fossil of what may well be the world's oldest known songbird was found. The songbirds of south-east Queensland are estimated to have lived 54 million years ago.

GAZETTEER

Nambour [A4], the administrative heart of the Maroochy Shire, is a far cry, though only a stone's throw, from the resorts and beaches of the Sunshine Coast. The sugar cane burnoff and harvest, leading up to the crushing season that begins in June, sends palls of black smoke skyward. The sugar growers also still use some interesting examples of steam train technology. Australia's only ginger factory, and the world's largest, is at **Yandina**, 9 km north.

Nanango [A3] celebrates its pioneer history with a collection of murals throughout the town. Nearby is the Seven Mile Gold Field. While it never grew to the status of Gympie, some quantities of gold were found

and can still be found. The tourist office issues permits for camping and fossicking (07 4171 6871). There are also guided tours of the Tarong Power Station from Tuesday to Friday at 2 pm. Coal was found by chance by a gang of road builders in 1939, leading to the discovery of the Tarong Basin, a coal deposit that stretches 50 km in length and 10 km wide. Its total yield is estimated at 1.15 billion tonnes.

Nerang [C5] is the gateway to **Lamington National Park** in the Gold Coast hinterland. The park, declared in 1915, was named after then Governor of Queensland Lord Lamington, who also gave his name to one of Australia's culinary icons. The road up to Hinze Dam, south-west of Nerang, is known as the Hinze Memorial Raceway—the then Minister of Roads had it built and apparently enjoyed driving it. If you get to a local football game at nearby **Labrador**, try one of Shep's pies, made by the local Sheppard family and only sold through the footy clubs.

In the town of **Nobby** [C3], about midway between Toowoomba and Warwick (west of the New England Highway), is Rudds Pub. Author Steele Rudd, aka Arthur Hoey Davis, wrote three of his Dad 'n' Dave stories on his selection north-east of Nobby. Another famous Nobby native is Sister Elizabeth Kenny, who pioneered radical, and successful, polio treatments. She is buried in Nobby cemetery. **Clifton**, just south of Nobby, is a town whose

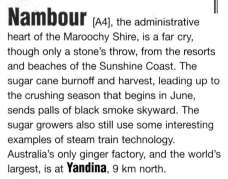

QLD

elders took a pragmatic approach to their need for a new church and their lack of money. The town's first publican, James Mowen, had died leaving a substantial sum for a grand memorial for his own grave. The town fathers used that money for the church, disinterring Mowen's remains from where he lay waiting for his memorial and moving them to the new church.

Noosa

Noosa [A5] is actually four very different locations combined. Aside from the restaurants and apartments of trendy Hastings Street, there are worthwhile walks through the national park extending from Noosa Heads township to the sea, as well as the sleepy fishing village of Noosaville upriver, and the suburban shopping shemozzle that is Noosa Junction. The Noosa Jazz Festival is on each September—phone 07 5449 9189 for details.

North of Noosa (inland through **Tewantin**) is another great beach drive for four-wheel-drivers. The **Great Sandy National Park** takes in most of the coast and coastal heath and wetlands from the north bank of the Noosa River almost to the small seaside village of **Rainbow Beach**. Play it safe though and don't try to drive across the front of the rocky outcrops that extend into the sea—quite a few 4WD vehicles have come to an untimely end caught by a quick wave.

To get to **North Stradbroke** Island [C5] (aka Straddie) take one of the regular car ferries from Cleveland or Redland Bay in Brisbane's south. The island offers 4WD owners great beach driving

and fishing. Cleveland's Grandview Hotel in North Street was built by Commissioner Francis Bigge in 1851, and was previously known as 'Bigge's Folly'. Recently restored, its glorious verandahs make the most of the sea breezes off Brisbane's Moreton Bay.

Oakey

Oakey's [B3] moment of glory came with the birth of the brilliant horse Bernborough at Rosalie Plains in 1939. For the first four years of his life Bernborough was restricted to racing in the local area (because of a Queensland Turf Club ban), and he became something of a legend on the tracks around Toowoomba. In 1945 well-known Sydney restaurateur Azzalin Romano bought him for 2,600 guineas. Over the next 18 months, trained by Harry Plant and ridden by a young Athol Mulley, Bernborough became a national hero. Carrying horrendous weights—he won the Doomben Cup carrying 10 stone 11 pounds (68.5 kg) and the Doomben 10,000 carrying 10 stone 5 pounds (65.8 kg)—he won 15 consecutive races in three states between 1945 and 1946 over virtually any distance. A few kilometres up the road at Jondaryan a life-size bronze horse stands outside the Civic Precinct in his honour. The $13 million Museum of Australian Army Flying is located north of town, at the Oakey army air base. The displays range from old uniforms to aircraft. There is a replica of a Bristol box kite as well as every aircraft flown by the army. These include the Sioux helicopter, the Link Trainer, and an old Spitfire.

Items in the **Pittsworth** [C3] and District Historical Society Folk Museum include a chantilly lace wrap once owned by Florence Nightingale, a love letter written by Governor Bligh's mother, an outdoor display of carts and farm equipment, and memorabilia connected with Arthur Postle, who was proclaimed 'the fastest man in the world' in 1906, when he won the 220 yards World Championship Cup.

The Majestic Theatre in **Pomona**'s [A4] Factory Street is Australia's longest-running cinema, showing its first moving picture in

1921. It was built as a multi-purpose entertainment hall for Mrs Osborne, the licensee of the Railway Hotel, which stood in the same street. It claims to be the only remaining authentic silent movie theatre in the world and its pipe organ is the only one remaining in a Queensland cinema.

DON'T MISS: Each year, over the fourth weekend in July, mountain runners worldwide come to Pomona for the famous King of the Mountain foot race up Mt Cooroora, a 439 m volcanic plug.

Near **Proston** (49 km west) [A3] is Boondooma Homestead, built around 1850. When the building was being restored it was discovered that it had been built to metric specifications by a German stonemason, probably the first metric building in Queensland. You can inspect the old homestead—call 07 4168 0159.

Redcliffe's [B5] Seabrae Hotel on Marine Parade is a beautifully restored 1950s hotel with an enormous

KINGAROY NAVY BEAN DUCK SOUP

Navy beans were introduced to the Kingaroy region in 1941, in order to grow a large enough crop to sustain the defence forces during World War II. It now produces more than half of Australia's navy beans.

200 g navy beans, soaked overnight in water
1 small duck, roasted
1¹/₂ ltr duck stock
1 carrot, cut in half
1 medium onion, cut in half
50 g ham or bacon, cut in half
bouquet garni of your choice
salt and pepper to taste

Remove meat from duck, cut into thin strips and reserve. Make stock by boiling duck bones for 1 hour, uncovered in 2 ltrs of water with a little carrot, onion, celery, bay leaves, salt and pepper, then strain. Place drained navy beans in a large saucepan, add the duck stock, bring to the boil and skim. Add remaining ingredients and cook until beans are very tender, approx. 1 hour. Remove the vegetables, ham and bouquet garni. Blend soup until smooth. Reheat and ladle into bowls topped with strips of duck.
Serves 6–8

Rex Parsons, BUNYA MOUNTAINS

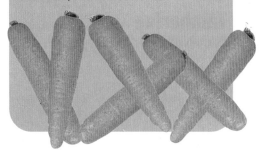

QLD

collection of 1950s memorabilia. The first European children to be born in Queensland were delivered in 1824 in Redcliffe.

Rosewood's

[C4] St Brigid's Catholic Church in Matthews Street claims to be the largest wooden Catholic church in the Southern Hemisphere. Of particular interest are the pressed metal ceiling, the altar—which, although made of wood, has been painted to look like marble—and the stained-glass windows of the three saints: St Brigid, St Agnes and St Philomena.

Stanthorpe

[D3] once recorded -14.6°C, the lowest temperature ever recorded in the Sunshine State, and snow has fallen here on plenty of occasions. The area was one of the first in Queensland to tackle wine making. To the north-west of the town on the New England Highway are the soldier settlements established after World War I. They were named after famous World War I battlefields and so, as the old railway signs at the Stanthorpe Museum on High Street indicate, there were once railway sidings at Amiens, Messines, Bapaume, Passchendaele, Bullecourt, Pozières and Fleurbaix.

Tamborine

Mountain's [C5] National Parks are made up of seven small parks. One, Witches Falls, was the first in Queensland, gazetted in 1908. Thunderbird Park, on Tamborine Mountain, between Tamborine Village and North Tamborine, has Australia's largest amethyst collection.

Tara

[B2] offers a unique 18-hole golf course where the putting areas (the greens) are of sand. It is also home to the Western Downs Championship Sheep Dog Trials at Easter. Visitors travel from all over the country and overseas for the Maranoa Super Shears Shearing Competition in August, with the Trans Tasman Challenge one of the major highlights. Phone 07 4665 3244 for details.

The Texas

[D3] Whyalla Feedlot is the largest cattle feedlot in the Southern Hemisphere. Texas is also home to the Southern Hemisphere's largest ostrich farm—it has 11,000 birds. The town was named for the US state after a dispute between the original settlers and a claim jumper showed all the elements of a border war.

Toowoomba

[C3], which used to be called The Swamp, is now justifiably famous for its parks and gardens. One, the Laurel Bank Park, has a special scented garden for the blind. The Cobb & Co. Museum at 27 Lindsay Street is part of the Queensland Museum and has one of the best collections of horse-drawn vehicles in Australia, including the company's last official courier coach and a landau. The museum is open 10 am to 4 pm daily (07 4639 1971). The area just west of Toowoomba boasts dozens of studs and has produced some of Australia's finest racehorse champions. In 2005 Toowoomba will host the World Shearing Titles.

FAMILY FAVOURITES

GRANDMA'S BANANA TEACAKE

The hinterland of the Sunshine Coast supports a wide variety of produce, from sugarcane to tropical fruit. Bananas are a popular addition to cakes and muffins. This teacake recipe has been in the Fisher family for at least four generations (and is a great way of using up overripe bananas).

1/2 cup sugar	1 tsp cinnamon
1/2 cup butter	1/2 cup milk
1 egg	3 large or 5 small
1 cup self-raising	ripe bananas,
flour	mashed
1/2 tsp salt	
1/2 tsp mixed spice	

Preheat oven to 180˚C. Grease or line a 20 cm round tin. Cream butter and sugar until light and fluffy, add egg and beat well. Fold in flour, salt, spices, together with milk, to form a firm batter. Spread half batter across prepared tin, gently easing some up the sides. Add a layer of banana and top with remaining batter. Bake for approx. 40 minutes (or until browned on top). Serve warm with cream as a dessert or cold cut into slices.

Nev Fisher, MALENY

QLD

LAMINGTONS

Lamington National Park, declared in 1915, was named after then Governor of Queensland Lord Lamington, who also loaned his name to one of Australia's culinary icons.

BUTTER CAKE	ICING
250 g butter	3–4 tbsp boiling
1 cup caster sugar	water
4 eggs	30 g butter
3 cups self-raising	2 tbsp cocoa
flour	2 cups icing sugar
2/3 cup milk	2 1/3 cups desiccated
1 tsp vanilla	coconut
essence	

Preheat oven to 180°C and line a squarish tin with baking paper. Make the cake 2 days before. In a bowl, cream butter and sugar until light and fluffy. Add eggs one at a time, beating well after each addition. Fold in flour alternately with milk. Stir in vanilla. Pour mixture into cake tin and bake for 30–35 minutes, or until cooked. When cool, cut into cubes. To make icing, in a bowl, pour boiling water over butter to melt, then add cocoa and mix. Add icing sugar and beat well. Stand the bowl of icing over a bowl of hot water. Using a long-pronged fork to hold the squares of cake, dip each in the icing mixture and roll in desiccated coconut. Place on wire cooling rack to allow icing to set.

Chole Beaumont, NERANG

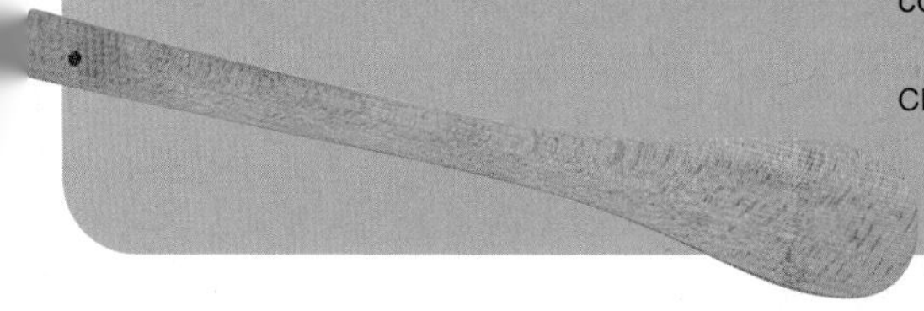

RASPBERRY DACQUOISE

Just south of Stanthorpe in the Granite Belt wine region is Fletcher, where Bob and Una Gray work Rumbala Estate Vineyards. They also grow luscious raspberries.

60 g hazelnuts, ground
175 g caster sugar
1 tbsp cornflour
4 large egg whites
pinch of cream of tartar
¹/₄ tsp vinegar
2 cups cream, chilled
100 g fresh raspberries
200 g almonds, flaked and toasted
icing sugar, for serving

Preheat oven to 180°C and prepare baking trays with three 20 cm discs drawn onto baking paper. In a bowl, combine ground hazelnut, cornflour and half the caster sugar. In another bowl, beat egg whites and cream of tartar until firm peaks form. Gradually add remaining caster sugar, then add vinegar and continue beating until mixture is stiff. Gently fold into hazelnut mixture. Prepare a piping bag with a plain nozzle. Fill bag with the meringue mixture and pipe three 20 cm discs onto baking paper. Bake in oven until dry, 25–30 minutes. In a bowl, beat chilled cream until thick. Fold raspberries into ³/₄ of cream and cover 2 meringue bases with this. Put these on top of each other and place third disc on top. Use remaining whipped cream to coat sides of cake and press roasted flaked almonds into sides. When ready to serve, sift icing sugar over top of dacquoise. Serves 4–6.

Una Gray, FLETCHER

Wandoan
[A1] has one of the biggest windmills in Queensland. The history of the town began with the Juandah Station in 1853. Its name was changed to Wandoan in 1927 to avoid confusion with the town of Jundah. The railway reached Wandoan in 1914, and there it stopped. A lack of funds prevented its continuance to the intended terminus at Taroom.

Warwick
[C4] is renowned for its horse and cattle studs, fine wool, grain, rose gardens and bucking broncos. In fact rodeos have been held here since 1929. An egg-throwing incident at Warwick caused the establishment of Australia's federal police force. In 1917, Prime Minister Billy Hughes did a whistle-stop tour of the nation to talk about the referendum question on conscription. At Warwick a protester threw an egg at Hughes and it knocked his hat off. When the local police did nothing, Hughes was irritated enough to establish a federal police force to uphold the laws of the Commonwealth. Minerals and gems are found nearby at **Goomburra** and **Dalrymple Creek**.

DON'T MISS: The Warwick Town Hall in Palmerin Street, with its large elegant clock tower, can claim to be one of the oldest municipal buildings in Queensland. It was built in 1888 of local sandstone, prompting the local newspaper, the *Warwick Argus* to pontificate: 'The comely edifice has been completed and a monument to the shrewdness and foresight of those aldermen who saw further that the 'morrow now stands where once a humpy reared its unpretentious head.' Around the corner in Fitzroy Street among other prominent buildings is the Warwick East State School, built in 1862, making it one of the oldest schools in Queensland and one of the few in Australia with that many years in service.

DON'T MISS: Warwick hosts an International Rock Swapping Festival every Easter. The Warwick Rodeo is held on the last weekend in October—call 07 4661 9060 for details.

Westmar's [C1] name is an abbreviation of the Western Maranoa transport company, whose fuel depot was the foundation for the town. It grew in the mid-1950s as a stopover for long-distance travellers.

Woodford [B4] is home to Elvis Parsley's Grapelands. Owner Nick Comino developed the idea about eight years ago to combine his love of Elvis, his singing talent and his fruit shop, and

all three have been growing ever since. The fruit is 'fit for the King' and Nick will transform into his alter ego, Elvis Parsley, on request. He is known as the King of Salad, the Singing Salad Seller and the King of Rock and Roughage. Shows in the fruit shop can be booked for groups for $2 a person. Grapelands is located at 87 Archer Street (07 5496 1309), and is open Monday to Friday, 8 am to 5 pm and Saturday 8 am to

QLD

CHICKEN AND GOAT'S CHEESE PARCELS WITH WHITE WINE CREAM AND CHIVE SAUCE

Tamborine is home to one of Queensland's newest boutique wineries, Albert River Wines, located at historic Tamborine House, which was built around 1858. The Albert River is at the property's western boundary. One of Brisbane's historic buildings, Auchenflower House, was moved to the property in 1998, to house the cellar door sales area, ballroom and restaurant.

PARCELS	SAUCE
4 chicken breasts	**100 ml chardonnay**
200 g goat's cheese	**1 clove garlic, crushed**
1 roasted red capsicum, cut into 4	**1 cup chicken stock**
	1 cup cream
salt and pepper	**2 tbsp chopped chives**
1–2 tbsp oil	

Place chicken breasts between cling wrap and flatten with a meat mallet until 5 mm thick, then season lightly. Place a quarter of the goat's cheese in centre of each breast with a piece of capsicum on top. Roll up to form parcels and secure with toothpicks. Heat oil in a pan, add breasts, seam side down, and cook 3–5 minutes until lightly browned, turn over and cook a further 3–5 minutes. Turn heat to low, cover and cook for a further 5 minutes. Remove chicken and keep warm in a low oven. Turn heat up, add garlic and sauté for 30 seconds, then pour in wine and deglaze pan. Allow to reduce to half, then add chicken stock and cream and allow to reduce to sauce consistency. To finish add chives and adjust seasoning. Place chicken onto serving plates, coat with sauce and serve with vegetables of choice. Serves 4.

Michael Penboss, Albert River Wines, TAMBORINE

DROVING DELIGHTS

Yarraman was opened up for pastoral settlers in the late 19th century. A sawmill opened in 1912. Earlier, in the mid-1800s, it was the site of a dinner camp for stockmen from nearby Cooyar and Taromeo stations, who were often marvellous improvisors, as these two recipes attest.

SETTLER'S TEA LOAF

3/4 cup caster sugar
1 cup sultanas (or any dried fruit)
1 cup hot brewed black tea
2 cups self-raising flour

Preheat oven to 180°C and grease a loaf pan (11 x 21 cm) and line with baking paper. Put sugar, fruit and tea in a bowl and let stand for 15 minutes. Add flour and mix together. Pour into loaf pan and bake for approx. 45 minutes, or until cooked.

TOMATO SOUP CAKE (no eggs)

2 cups plain flour
pinch salt
1 tsp mixed spice
1 cup mixed dried fruit
1 x 250 g can of tomato soup
  (Rosella works best)
125 g butter
1 tsp baking powder
1 cup sugar
1 tsp bicarbonate of soda

Sift dry ingredients, add fruit and mix well. Melt butter and add soup. Stir well. Pour into dry ingredients and mix well. Bake in moderate oven (180°C) for 1 hour.

John Carey,
GOOMBUNGEE

12 noon. The Woodford Folk Festival takes place from 27 December to 1 January each year. For details call 07 5496 1066.

Yarraman [B3] is where the New
England Highway either begins or ends. At any rate it runs into the junction of the D'Aguilar and Burnett Highways and stops. Or starts. To the south on the New England is **Cooyar**, which has one of the smallest national parks in Queensland. The 12 ha Palms National Park lies 6 km from the town.

From Yuleba [A1] the last Cobb &
Co coach service in Australia departed for Surat to the south in 1924. A mural at Yuleba commemorates the run. The route can be retraced but it's a dry-weather road only. Check with the Bendemere Shire office in town beforehand. At Yuleba, you might even spot Jersey the cow taking cover under the shade of an umbrella.

Diary of Events

Town	Event	Date	Contact
Beenleigh	Cane Festival	May	0404 807 715
Caboolture	Medieval Tournament	June	07 5495 1652
Chinchilla	Melon Festival	14–16 Feb 2003 (biennial)	07 4662 7056
Coolum	Wildflower Show	August	07 5441 5747
Coominya	Grape and Watermelon Festival	January	07 3221 8411
Durong South	Burrandowan Races	May, 2nd Saturday	07 4164 3184
Goomeri	Pumpkin Festival	May, last Sunday	07 4168 1925
Goondiwindi	Hell of the West Triathlon	February	0412 717 929
Gympie	National Country Music Muster	August	07 5482 2099
	Ginger Flower Festival	January	07 5446 7100
Inglewood	Outback Olive Festival	March	07 4667 4152
Kingaroy	Peanut Festival	TBA	07 4162 3199
Laidley	Ripcord Skydivers Valentine Boogie	13–14 Feb 2004	07 3399 3552
	Spring Festival	mid-September	07 5465 7642
Maroochydore	Gold Rush Festival	October	07 5482 1077
	Sunshine Coast Winter Bowls Carnival	July–August	07 5443 2191
	Sunshine Coast Wineries Festival	August, last weekend	07 5478 5558
Noosa	Jazz Festival	September	07 5443 9189
	Nude Olympics	February	07 3200 1658
	Long Weekend	June, last week	07 5442 7244
Pomona	King of the Mountain Foot Race	July, 4th weekend	07 5485 4125
Stanthorpe	Apple and Grape Harvest Festival	March 2004 (biennial)	07 4681 2057
Tara	Western Downs Championship Sheep Dog Trials	March	07 4622 8653
	Festival of Culture and Western Downs Camel Races	August (TBA)	07 4665 3244
	Maranoa Super Shears Shearing Competition	August	07 4665 3244
Warwick	Rodeo	October, last weekend	07 4661 9060
Woodford	Woodford Folk Festival	27 Dec–1 Jan	07 5496 1066

QLD

From the pristine sands of Fraser Island, north to the fertile district of Proserpine and west to the gemfields of Emerald, the Central East offers a wealth of travelling experience.

get off the beaten track

discover

the central east

The **Anakie** [C1] gemfield area is the world's largest known source of sapphires. Gemfest is in August (second weekend). The Star of Queensland, the world's finest black star sapphire, was discovered here in 1935.

Banana [C2] is the namesake town in the shire of Banana, which was named after a light dun coloured bullock whose tongue hung out like a ripe banana when working hard. He was part of Mr Moses Wafer's team in the 1850s. Banana was trained as a decoy to make life easier for the stockmen who had to round up wild and difficult animals. The shire was named after the bull in 1880. You won't find bananas growing here but you can stop for a drink at the Banana store and read some of the memorabilia.

In **Bargara** [D3] you can see stone walls built by the Kanakas, on Bargara Road, near the western edge of town, and near the road between Bargara and Mon Repos. Kanakas were young Melanesians who were taken from their homes, by force or by deception, and brought to Queensland (and to Fiji) to work on the canefields—the practice was known as 'blackbirding'. The **Mon Repos Environmental Park**, just north of Bargara, has the largest concentration of nesting marine turtles on the eastern Australian mainland and is one of the two largest loggerhead turtle rookeries in the South Pacific Ocean region.

BUNDY MUFFINS

In Bundaberg the entire sugar production process takes place, from growing to milling, refining, research and distilling. Molasses is a milling by-product piped from the Millaquin Mill to the Bundaberg Distilling Company next door to become the famous Bundaberg Rum.

- 350 g self-raising flour
- 100 g Bundaberg brown sugar
- 1 healthy pinch bicarbonate of soda
- 100 g walnuts, chopped
- 100 g dark choc bits
- 2 ripe Cavendish bananas, mashed
- 2 eggs, lightly beaten
- 250 ml low-fat cultured buttermilk
- 50 ml Bundaberg golden syrup
- 70 ml light vegetable oil
- 60 ml Bundaberg Rum Royal Liqueur

Preheat oven to 220°C. Place flour in a large bowl and mix through sugar, bicarbonate of soda, nuts and choc bits. In a second bowl mix the bananas and eggs together and then add buttermilk, oil, golden syrup and rum. Add bananas to flour mixture and gently mix until just combined. Spoon into a lightly greased non-stick muffin tray (third-cup size, approx. 80 ml). Bake for approx. 15 minutes or until golden brown. Remove from oven and stand muffins on cake tray to cool. Makes 12.

Stephanie Hunt, BUNDABERG

At **Biggenden** [D3] is Chowey Bridge, a concrete arched railway bridge that is one of only two of this style of bridge ever built in Australia. It was opened in 1905.

QLD

Biloela

Biloela [C2] has a museum of primary industry named The Silo. About 16 km to the south-east is Mt Scoria, whose basalt columns ring like a xylophone and echo across the valley when hit with metal objects.

Blackwater

Blackwater [C1] mine is one of several massive open-cut coal mines of the region that conduct tours. For details phone 07 4986 0666. Other tours are at Peak Downs and Blair Athol mines.

Bundaberg

Bundaberg [D2] is the birthplace of pioneer aviator Bert Hinkler, the first man to fly solo from England to Australia, in 1928. It

was here, watching the local ibis, he became fascinated with flight. When his former English residence was threatened with demolition in 1982 Bundaberg locals, along with members of the British, Australian and Dutch naval forces and British Aerospace, had the house dismantled, shipped to Bundaberg and reassembled on Mt Perry Road, North Bundaberg. It is open to the public. 'Our Glad'—singer Gladys Moncrieff—was also born here in 1892. If you think you are passing fields of spuds, you are. The soils and mild climate of the region around Bundaberg (and Gatton in South-east Queensland) are perfect for the high-quality potatoes that Smith's uses in their chips.

Capella

Capella's [C1] Pioneer Village complex is the current home of the Peak Downs homestead, built in 1869 of pitsawn timber, mainly local spotted gum, in a drop-slab construction (no nails were used in the walls), the largest of its type in Australia. The roof is comprised of 60,000 shingles. After lying empty for 30 years and suffering much termite damage, the homestead was moved

the 30 km to Capella in 1988, with thousands of hours of volunteer time ploughed into its restoration.

Childers

The **Childers** [D3] Pharmaceutical Museum (also the Tourist Information Office) in Churchill Street was built in 1894 and retains much of the charm of the late 19th century. There are cedar shop fittings, old leather-bound prescription books, mortars and pestles that are works of art, and a 1906 cash register.

Clermont

Clermont [B1] is the site of the second-worst flood in Australia's history in terms of loss of life. On the night of 28 December 1916 cyclonic waters rushed through the town, sweeping houses away, forcing people to clamber up trees and drowning at least 65 people. At the town's entrance is a

large concrete 'tree' with a white mark far up its trunk, indicating the height of those flood-waters. The Blair Athol mine, 20 km to the north-west, has the world's biggest seam of high-grade steaming coal.

Collinsville

The area around **Collinsville** [A1] was first opened up as a grazing run in 1861. Later gold mines were operated and coal deposits were discovered. The name Collinsville was given to the area in 1921. Several murals in the main street depict the early days of settlement. Every year there is the Bowen River Rodeo on the Queen's Birthday weekend in June.

Eidsvold

Eidsvold's [D2] Alice Maslens Hitching Rail was erected in 1980 for an old woman who still brought her horse and sulky to town. First settled in 1848,

Eidsvold Station, and the town, were named after Eidsvoll, where Norway's constitution was signed in 1814. Queensland's first game of golf was played at the station. The slab-constructed Knockbreak Homestead in the Eidsvold Historical Complex was built in the 1850s and contains a lot of Eidsvold's history, including the George Shafer collection, Queensland's largest collection of rocks and gems.

Don't go to **Emerald** [C1] looking for emeralds. The name came from the brilliant colour of the new grass that grew with heavy rain after fire. Emerald also has a wonderful 'gingerbread' railway station.

Sapphire, on the other hand, about 50 km to the west, produces about one-third of the world's yellow, blue and green sapphires, including the world's largest. The blue sapphire, at 2,303 carats, was carved into a bust of Abraham Lincoln (bringing it down to 1,318 carats) and is now kept at the White House, Washington DC. And you'll find no rubies in **Rubyvale**, about 8 km north of Sapphire—just black sapphires.

Emerald's Big Easel, featuring a copy of one of Van Gogh's sunflower paintings, was completed in 1999 by Canadian artist Cameron Cross. It is the largest painting on an easel in Australia, one of seven to be erected around the world.

GAZETTEER

QLD

REDCLAW CRAYFISH AND SALSA

1¹/₂ kg fresh Queensland redclaw crayfish
1 lime or lemon, chopped
1 cup white wine
mixed lettuce and blanched asparagus, to serve

MANGO (OR PAWPAW) SALSA
1 cup diced mango or pawpaw
1 small avocado, diced
¹/₂ red capsicum, finely diced
1 spring onion, finely sliced
1 tbsp each of finely chopped fresh coriander and mint
1 chilli, finely chopped (optional)

DRESSING
2 tsp fresh ginger, grated
1 tbsp white wine vinegar
juice of 1 lime
1 clove garlic, crushed
cracked pepper

The popularity of redclaw farming has grown in the past 15 years in Central Queensland. Moderately large freshwater crays, redclaw live in waters up to 5 m deep. Regulations apply about catching them in the wild.

Chill the crayfish in the freezer for one hour. Bring a large pot of water to the boil, add the chopped lime or lemon and wine and drop in the crayfish. Bring back to the boil and cook for 3 minutes. Immediately remove crayfish from the water and plunge into a salted ice slurry (a combination of salt, water and ice in the proportion of ¹/₂ cup salt to 4 ltr ice water). Remove crayfish head, crack shell open and remove flesh. In a bowl, mix all salsa ingredients together. In another bowl, combine all dressing ingredients. Arrange lettuce and asparagus on a platter, place cray meat in centre and spoon salsa around side. Drizzle both with dressing. Serves 2–4.

Glen Burfitt, CHILDERS

Emu Park's [C2] Singing Ship sculpture sings almost constantly because of the on-shore breezes—and its concealed organ pipes. The sculpture, on a headland overlooking Keppel Bay, was designed by Mrs CM Westmoreland, who won a local competition to commemorate the 200th anniversary of Cook's claiming of Australia. It represents the sails, mast and rigging of the *Endeavour*. All the islands and landmarks in Keppel Bay that Cook named are visible from it.

Fraser Island [D3] is the world's largest sand island. The sand dunes reach a height of 240 m and are estimated to rise up from 600 m below the sea. It is one of the few places in the world where rainforest grows on pure sand. Today Fraser Island is a very popular destination for holidaymakers, especially recreational anglers who come here to cast their lines into the surf for tailor, swallowtail dart, bream, tarwhine, whiting, flathead and trevally. Fraser Island is also a Mecca for four-wheel-drivers and the beach drive north from the ferry at Inskip Point is one of the best in the world. Don't feed the dingoes—they become a nuisance and the only way to control them is to shoot them. Eliza Fraser, who was shipwrecked on the island in 1836, returned to England, where she published a book of her adventures, somewhat discredited since, that told of her 'barbarous treatment' at the hands of the resident Badjalla people, who had assisted her and some of the crew members to survive.

DON'T MISS: The 'perched' lakes that nestle among the dunes, Eli Creek and the 1935 *Maheno* wreck about halfway up the eastern coast. **Hervey Bay**, in the lee of Fraser Island, provides access to some of the best fishing grounds on the Queensland coast. These days it is almost more famous for whale watching. From early August to mid-October, southern humpback whales that calved in warm northern waters make an annual stopover in this protected bay.

Gayndah [D3] claims to be the oldest town in Queensland (as opposed to older cities such as Brisbane and Ipswich).

Beyond the Council Chambers, at the end of town, is the old schoolhouse, which is reputedly the state's oldest continuously operating schoolhouse (since 1863). Mellors Drapery Store, at 28 Capper Street, is one of the few buildings in Australia that still uses a 'flying fox' to deal with transactions. The flying fox was a device much used until the 1950s—the cash clerk was located on a mezzanine floor above the counters. Money was placed into small containers that were propelled up wires to the clerk, who counted out the change and sent it whizzing back.

Gin Gin's [D3] claim to fame is the Boolboonda Tunnel, the largest unsupported tunnel in the southern hemisphere. It was burrowed through rock in 1883–84 as part of the railway line laid from North Bundaberg to Mt Perry to open up the mineral and agricultural resources in the area. Gin Gin was also home to Queensland's only real bushranger, the 'Wild Scotchman' James McPherson, who held up the Royal Mail on several occasions—then wrote to the local newspaper disputing its reports of his misdeeds. East of Gin Gin (27 km, on the Bundaberg Road) are the 35

GOLDEN SPUR BEEF STEAKS

Eidsvold calls itself the beef capital of the Burnett. Eidsvold Station, after which the town is named, was one of the first studs to introduce Santa Gertrudis cattle into Australia. Eidsvold also has a highly successful citrus industry.

6–8 steaks
MARINADE
4 cloves garlic, crushed
1/4 cup port
1/4 tsp black pepper, powder
1/2 tsp black peppercorns, lightly crushed
1/2 tsp thyme, chopped
1/2 tsp basil, chopped
macadamia oil

The night before cooking, put garlic and port in a bowl. Next day strain well and add to the garlic, the peppers, herbs and enough macadamia oil to make a paste. Brush over the steaks. Place on hot barbecue plate, sear both sides and cook to your liking. Serve with Golden Spur Salsa, potatoes wrapped individually in foil and cooked in the coals, barbecued onion rings and asparagus spears. Serves 8.

GOLDEN SPUR SALSA
1 orange, peeled and diced into small cubes
1 red onion, chopped
fresh mint, finely chopped
1 tbsp cider vinegar
freshly ground black pepper
Place all ingredients in a bowl. Toss to combine.

ONION RINGS
1 kg white onions, sliced into 1 cm rings
1 tbsp each olive and macadamia oil
fresh thyme sprigs
salt and freshly ground black pepper
Toss onions with oil, thyme, salt and pepper. Spread out onions on barbecue plate. Reduce heat, cook for 20 minutes, turning often. Add extra oil if needed.

BARBECUED ASPARAGUS SPEARS
500 g asparagus spears
1 tbsp olive oil
salt and freshly ground black pepper
100 g fetta cheese
Trim woody ends off asparagus spears. Toss in oil, salt and pepper. Place on oiled barbecue plate. Cook for 4 minutes, turning a few times. Arrange on plate, crumble fetta over.

Peter Webster, EIDSVOLD

QLD

Mystery Craters, so called because, even though they're 25 million years old, no one knows quite how or why these peculiar geological formations came into being.

Gladstone [C2] is home to the

world's largest alumina plant and Queensland's largest port. In 1983 it became the first Queensland port to handle over 20 million tonnes of cargo—most of it coal and alumina—and in 2000 it handled 50 million tonnes. It is the largest multi-commodity port in Queensland and is capable of providing a safe port for ships of more than 220,000 deadweight tonnes. The alumina plant at Parsons Point processes more than 8 million tonnes of bauxite from Weipa each year. A 1949 cyclone was very selective in Gladstone. It wiped out all the churches and left all the pubs untouched.

VEGETABLE PIE

On Melinee Leather's cattle property Boolboonda they grow a lot of their own vegetables, often more than they can use. Melinee created this recipe to use up some of those vegetables.

1 packet frozen puff pastry sheets	1/4 cup sundried tomatoes, chopped
1 eggplant, sliced thinly	1/2 cup sliced mushrooms
olive oil	1/2 cup grated tasty cheese
2 carrots, sliced	
2 zucchini, sliced	1/2 cup grated parmesan cheese
1 sweet potato, sliced	
1 bunch silverbeet, chopped	250 g fresh ricotta cheese
1 cup shredded cabbage	2 garlic cloves, crushed
	1 egg yolk, beaten

Preheat oven to 200°C. Line a springform pan with puff pastry sheets. Fry eggplant slices in a pan with a little olive oil. Steam all remaining vegetables until just cooked. Layer vegetables, tomatoes, mushrooms, cheeses and garlic in the pan. Drizzle with a little olive oil. Cover pie with puff pastry and brush with a little egg yolk. Bake for about 45 minutes or until golden brown. Delicious served with a garden salad and a bottle of verdelho. Serves 4–6.

Melinee Leather,
GIN GIN

The people of **Injune** [D1] suggest four possible reasons for the town's name: that Leichhardt passed through it in June; that it was named by the Railway Department after the Parish of Injune; that this was the interpretation of an indistinct word on an 1864 map of Queensland; or that it is derived from the Aboriginal 'ingon' for sugar glider. Injune has Australia's smallest courthouse and bushranger James Kenniff's grave is on a private property in the area. Injune is also the gateway to the famous Carnarvon Gorge.

Mackay [A1] is the sugar capital of
Australia, producing about one-third of the nation's sugar harvest. The Mackay Bulk Sugar Terminal at Mackay Harbour is the largest in the world, capable of holding over 700,000 tonnes.

In **Maryborough**'s [D3] Bond Store Museum on Wharf Street is the Time Gun. It was traditionally fired on Thursdays at 1 pm, but is now fired only on special occasions. The gun was a gift to the city from Queensland Premier John Douglas in 1877. It had been found on the Torres Strait island of Mabuiag (most likely a relic of a Dutch East India Company vessel during the 17th century) and was presented in response to the criticism that the town had no clock. Maryborough was from early times an important industrial and commercial centre and has some impressive colonial architecture, including the fully preserved Brennan & Geraghty's Store, 64 Lennox Street. In the 1970s the town became a battleground as locals divided over the issue of logging and sandmining on nearby Fraser Island.

Around **Mirani** [A1] there still exists a rare opportunity to see platypus in the wild. A popular spot is at Broken River in **Eungella National Park**, 36 km west of the town. A viewing platform has been constructed and platypus can often be spotted at dawn or at dusk.

Just 2 km south of **Monto** [D2] is the Bonnie View Collection, which includes more than 1,000 dolls. A little further south is **Mulgildie**, whose residents have passed down for generations the story that the lagoon 4 km out of town was once the home of a bunyip.

Mount Morgan's [C2] mining

activity has turned what was once a large mountain into one of the largest artificial holes on Earth. It is over 2.5 km long and more than 300 m deep. Enormous quantities of gold and copper were dug from this ironstone mountain for over a century (until 1981). The railway from the coast had to travel up a gradient of 1:16.5 at the Razorback outside the town, so a special ABT rack locomotive (Australia's first) was purchased and a toothed rack rail was built between the normal rails to give the trains extra traction going up and down the hill. A portion of this toothed line is displayed on the median strip in front of the museum in Morgan Street.

Mundubbera [D2] is situated on

the Burnett River and claims to be the Citrus Capital of Queensland, a fact it reinforces with its Big Mandarin (known sometimes as

the Enormous Ellendale). The Mundubbera area produces about one-third of Queensland's citrus fruit. It boasts one of the largest citrus orchards in the southern hemisphere, the Golden Mile Orchard, named because the trees were planted in mile-long rows. There is a lungfish display at the Tourist Information Centre in Bicentennial Park on Durong Road. The lungfish (Neoceratodus forsteri) is only found in the Burnett and Mary Rivers (apart from in the Amazon). A bizarre living fossil, it cannot breathe in water, nor survive away from it. It

can, however, stay underwater for a long time, coming to the surface to gulp air into its lung-like sac. In a creekbed in the Auburn River National Park, 40 km south-west of Mundubbera on the Hawkwood Road, are two pink granite boulders, 'dinosaur eggs' that have been worn smooth from being rolled around when the creek is running. The area is often in drought so they are usually visible, though not easy to spot.

At **Nebo** [B1] the 1800s photographic works of John Henry Mills take pride of place at the Pioneer Tracks of Queensland Gallery. In May Nebo has the Memorial Graham Stuart Rodeo honouring the founding member of the Bushman's Carnival Association begun in 1952.

Proserpine [A1] hosts

the annual Lions Harvest Festival usually held each spring—call 07 4945 1336 for details. The area is also home to the Proserpine rock wallaby, discovered in 1976 and recognised as a separate species in 1982. It is related to the rare yellow-footed rock wallaby of

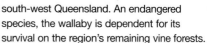

south-west Queensland. An endangered species, the wallaby is dependent for its survival on the region's remaining vine forests.

Rockhampton [C2] is the beef

capital of Australia with more 'official' statues of bulls (six) than any other city in Australia. It also has the 14 m Capricorn Spire, marking the Tropic of Capricorn, in Curtis Park. Only 23 km north (on the Bruce Highway) are the Capricorn Caves, the oldest tourist attraction in Queensland. John Olsen, a Norwegian migrant, discovered the 16 caves in 1882, opening them to the public two years later. Formed from an ancient coral reef 380 million

QLD

years ago, they are the only privately owned caves in Australia. You can book them for weddings— call 07 4934 2883 for further information.

IRISH STEW

People travelling through Springsure are often told the story of how the town was named by an Irish teamster, as a 'camp of sure springs', to be sure.

6–8 mutton chump or forequarter chops (or lamb)	1 large onion, sliced in wedges
4 large potatoes, peeled and quartered	sprig of fresh rosemary, chopped
2 large carrots, sliced	salt and pepper to taste
2 stalks celery, sliced	3–4 cups water
	1 tbsp plain flour

Preheat oven to 200°C. Trim excess fat from chops and place in bottom of large flame-proof casserole dish, season with rosemary, salt and pepper, add layers of vegetables with extra rosemary, salt and pepper. Add enough water to just cover. Cover with lid and cook for 1¹/₂–2 hours. Skim off any excess fat (it's best to chill the stew and lift off fat, then reheat stew). Blend flour with a little water to make a smooth paste and dribble hot stew stock into paste, then add slowly to stew, stirring constantly to thicken. Serves 4–6.

Val Davies, BRISBANE

Near **Rolleston** [C1] is the **Nuga Nuga National Park** and Lake Nuga Nuga, believed to be the home of the male and female Rainbow Serpent (Mundagarri). The myth said that if they were disturbed and left, the lake would dry up. The lake is a birdwatcher's paradise.

The **Sarina** [A1] Distillery, opened in 1927, is one of the biggest distilleries in Australia. It processes molasses from the area's sugar mills. It is a considerable operation with a world-first plant design, producing more than 50 million litres of ethanol a year for use in products as varied as paint and pharmaceuticals both in and outside Australia.

DON'T MISS: On the May Day long weekend Sarina hosts the Queensland Mud Trials in which competitors race standard cars, buggies and bombs on a mud track. Racing in mud is just one of the attractions.

At **Seventeen Seventy** [C3] Captain Cook made his second landing on Australian soil, on 24 May 1770 (his first had been at Botany Bay). This occasion is commemorated by the Captain Cook Memorial at nearby Round Hill Head. The seas off Seventeen Seventy and Round Hill Head provide excellent fishing, especially for Spanish and school mackerel, red emperor and coral trout. The estuaries hold good stocks of mangrove jack plus the odd barramundi and mud crab. **Agnes Water** has the east coast's most northerly surfing beach. It's not great surf but it's the last chance at a wave before the reef further north flattens out the water. Turn off the Bruce Highway at Miriam Vale (a third of the 57 km is unsealed) to reach Seventeen Seventy and Agnes Water just to the south.

Springsure [C1],

an old pioneer town, was named for the permanent springs in the creeks and gullies at the time of settlement. The remark, 'To be sure, it's a camp of sure springs,' was made by an Irish teamster and the name stuck.

The **Taroom** [D2] area's first European visitor was Ludwig Leichhardt, who not only passed through but carved his initials on a coolibah tree that now stands in the middle of the main street. On his dubious and ill-fated expedition from Jimbour to Port Essington, on Australia's far northern coast, Leichhardt carved LL 44 (Ludwig Leichhardt 1844). The bark has since grown over the marking. Today all that is left is a very healthy, if unmarked, tree.

Theodore [D2]

started life as Castle Creek and ended up, by its own choice, being named after one of Australia's most controversial politicians, EG 'Red Ted' Theodore (Premier of Queensland 1919–25 and Treasurer and Deputy Prime Minister 1929–30). The Theodore Co-operative Hotel Motel on The Boulevarde, which is owned by the townsfolk, uses its surplus profits to fund community activities and projects.

DON'T MISS: At Cooee Bay in **Yeppoon** each year (usually in late July or August) there is an all-day Cooeeing Competition during an event called Ozfest, which also includes such all-Australian activities as thong throwing, billy boiling and damper making (dampers are auctioned at the end of the day), to name a few.

GAZETTEER

Diary of Events

Town	Event	Date	Contact
Anakie	Gemfest	August, 2nd weekend	07 4985 4795
Childers	Multicultural Festival	July	07 4152 2333
Collinsville	Bowen River Rodeo	June, Queen's Birthday weekend	07 4785 5887
Gayndah	Orange Festival	June 2003 (biennial)	07 4161 1242 or 07 4161 1569
Mackay	Festival of Arts	July	07 4952 2677
Monto	Dairy Festival	June, Queen's Birthday weekend	07 4152 2333
Nebo	Memorial Graham Stuart Rodeo	May	07 4950 5440
Proserpine	Lions Harvest Festival	Sept/Nov	07 4945 1336
Sarina	Qld Mud Trials	May Day weekend	07 4956 2251
Yeppoon	Yeppoon Lions Tropical Pinefest	Sept/Oct	07 4939 5746
	Ozfest	TBA	07 4933 6052

The lush tropical vegetation and bustling holiday towns of Queensland's far north contrasts vividly with the vast distances of the gulf.

get off the beaten track

travel
the tropical north

Atherton's [D4] Chinese Joss House,

on Herberton Road, is a temple to Hou Wang Miau, commander of the bodyguard to Emperor Ti Ping, the last emperor of the Sung Dynasty around 1280 AD. The large Chinese population of Atherton planned the temple for 10 years. Completed in 1903, it is a mixture of traditional Chinese architecture and local corrugated iron. The ornate interior, with its subtle pink shading and cedar lining, is truly remarkable. The building is next to the town's Information Centre and is part of the National Heritage Trail. Also at Atherton is an imaginative mineralogical museum, the Crystal Caves, at 69 Main Street.

Visitors put on helmets with torches attached and pass through the museum's tunnels and passages, which are highlighted by special filtered lights. There are 700 mineral specimens to be viewed. **Lake Tinaroo**,

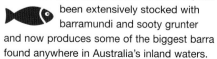

north-east of Atherton on the Tablelands, has been extensively stocked with barramundi and sooty grunter and now produces some of the biggest barra found anywhere in Australia's inland waters.

Ayr [E5] has Australia's

finest collection of butterflies and beetles, in the House of Australian Nature, in Wilmington Street.

The Babinda [D4] State Hotel was

built in 1917 by a state government that claimed it was encouraging controlled drinking and stamping out sly grog shops. The town has the record for being the wettest in Australia, with an estimated average annual rainfall of 4,616 mm. **The Boulders**, 7 km west of town, are a series of large

TOMATO PRAWN CUPS

Bowen is known Australia-wide for its tomatoes, and doesn't have a bad handle on prawns either. This recipe is one some readers will remember from the 1960s—a colourful and tasty addition to any buffet table.

6 medium tomatoes	1/2 red capsicum, finely sliced
1 cup cooked rice	1 cup cooked medium-size prawns, peeled and deveined
1 tbsp lemon juice	
1 tbsp parsley, finely chopped	
1/2 cup egg mayonnaise	salt and pepper cucumber slices extra virgin olive oil
1 stick celery, finely sliced	

Cut top off tomatoes and scoop out flesh. Reserve 6 prawns and mix rice, lemon juice, parsley, mayonnaise, celery, capsicum and remaining prawns together, season to taste with salt and pepper. Fill tomato shells with mixture and top each with an extra prawn. Serve each tomato on a ring of cucumber slices drizzled with a little extra virgin olive oil. Serves 6.

Glenda Beverley, BOWEN

boulders in the river that have been worn smooth by tropical rains. Since 1959 several people (mostly young men) have drowned in this beautiful but deceptive stretch of water, held under by powerful currents.

Bamaga [A3] is the most northerly

town in Australia. Possession Island, just off the coast, is where Captain Cook formally took possession of the east coast of Australia in 1770. The town was formed when the people of Saibai Island, under their leader Bamaga Ginau, moved to the mainland in 1947. Bamaga is a popular stepping-off point for recreational anglers, who flock to these fish-rich northern waters every year in search of barramundi, big Spanish mackerel, queenfish and other tropical species. Its twin town, **Seisia**, is the ferry departure point for nearby **Thursday Island**.

Bowen
[E5] has 19 mural sites depicting its early history, most commissioned by the Bowen Shire Festival of Murals Society, and most painted by well-known Queensland artists, though two are by Ken Done. Bowen's North Australia Hotel got its liquor licence in 1862. It has the longest continuous licence in north Queensland, if not the state. Bowen also gets a great deal of sunlight—eight hours a day, year round, on average.

Between remote **Burketown** [D1] and **Sweers Island** one of the world's most exotic and interesting meteorological phenomena takes place. The Morning Glory is a spectacular propagating cloud that often appears near dawn as one or more rapidly advancing, rather formidable tubular formations that extend from horizon to horizon—often more than 1,000 km long. They usually occur in the sparsely populated southern margin of the Gulf of Carpentaria from September through November. In Burketown on the Normanton Road there is an artesian bore that has been running since 1897. The minerals in the water have built up so that now it looks more like a piece of modern sculpture than a tap to an underground supply of hot water.

Redlynch, in **Cairns** [D4], is famous in the literary life of Australia. Novelist Xavier Herbert, who wrote the mammoth *Poor Fellow My Country*, lived here for 38 years. The book, published in 1975, is still Australia's longest novel. Herbert lived opposite the railway station and wrote the tale in a shed behind the house.

Cairns is famous as an embarkation port for anglers keen to fish the productive waters of the northern Great Barrier Reef, particularly for the giant black marlin that come here in late September, October and November to spawn. In the dry season the water over the Barron Falls in

Barron Gorge National Park (about 15 km north-west of Cairns) reduces to a trickle. However, just before the tourist train arrives at Barron Falls Station someone opens one of the floodgates and, quite miraculously, the falls begin to fall. This is a phenomenon worth watching as you pass by on your way to Kuranda by car. Just north of Cairns is the **Tjapukai Aboriginal Cultural Park**. Tjapukai began in 1987 as a small dance-theatre company. They feature in the 1997 *Guiness Book of Records* as the longest running show in Australia. The park offers a broad range of cultural and educational experiences from dance, theatre and art to boomerang throwing and didgeridoo playing. Call 07 4042 9900 for more information.

Camooweal
[E1] is linked to Mount Isa by a road known to the locals as 'Tojo's Highway'. It was built during World War II with American funds. Check out the old-time Freckleton's general store in Camooweal, where it feels as if nothing much has changed since the 1930s.

GAZETTEER

GREEN MANGO CHUTNEY WITH GINGER AND DATES

Mangoes are another of Bowen's specialties, and when there are plenty of them ripening at the same time a recipe that uses them up in bulk deserves a gold star. This one makes a superb chutney, nicely spicy.

25 green mangoes, skinned and sliced
1/2 cup salt
1 1/2 bottles (750 g size) malt vinegar
2 kg sugar
500 g dates, seeded and chopped
1/4 cup green ginger, grated
1/4 cup garlic, chopped
250 g sultanas

Place mangoes in a large bowl, sprinkle with salt and stand overnight. Rinse and drain mangoes, place in a large saucepan with malt vinegar and sugar and stir over heat without boiling until sugar is dissolved. Add remaining ingredients, bring to boil and simmer, uncovered, for about 3 hours, or until mixture is thick. Stir occasionally. Pour into hot sterilised jars. Seal when cold.

Glenda Beverley, BOWEN

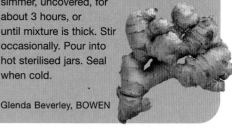

QLD

Cape Tribulation's [C4]

rainforest boasts some extremely ancient plant families including the flowering *Idiospermum australiense* and the *Angiopteris evecta*, one of the world's largest ferns, whose fronds grow up to 7 m long.

Cape York [A3] is the northernmost

tip of Australia's mainland, reached by a well-used 4WD track that for much of the way follows the old overland telegraph line. It's a route full of adventure and some of the most pristine rivers and surrounding bush you'll find on the Australian mainland.

On the Cardwell [D4] beachfront

there is a monument that reads: 'In memory of Walter Jervoise Scott, one of the pioneers of the station known as the Valley of Lagoons.' The cattle station, which is still working, is beyond the mountains of the Ingham hinterland. The monument was sent out from England after his death in 1890, but the road to the Valley of Lagoons was too hazardous and difficult, so the family and the teamsters decided that, while Scott was indeed buried at the Valley of Lagoons, the headstone would remain on the coast.

The Charters Towers

[E4] central financial district is at the intersection of Mosman and Gill Streets. It was here that the town's Stock Exchange came into operation. Built in 1887–88 as a shopping arcade, 'The Royal Arcade' became the Charters Towers Stock Exchange in 1890. Today it houses the National Trust and a few specialist shops. St Columba's Bell Tower (1887) at St Columba's Catholic Church has been designed to look like a mine poppet head.

GAZETTEER

Cooktown

[C4] once had 65 licensed premises. It was the site of the first white 'settlement' in Australia when Captain James

Cook, having struck the Great Barrier Reef north of Cape Tribulation, struggled up the coast and beached the barque *Endeavour* on the shores of the Endeavour River. Cook and his crew were to stay on the river's edge from 17 June to 4 August 1770. There are a number of Cook monuments in the town: a cairn where he beached the *Endeavour*, a smaller monument a few metres away, a Bicentennial statue of the good Captain in a nearby park, and a huge civic monument further down the road. The James Cook Museum also has artefacts from the *Endeavour*, including one of the cannons jettisoned from the vessel when it ran aground on Endeavour Reef, and an anchor.

DON'T MISS: The Cooktown Discovery Festival is held each year on the Queen's Birthday Weekend and highlights include the re-enactment of Captain James Cook's landing here in 1770.

Gordonvale

[D4], a sugar town in the Mulgrave Valley, has the rather dubious privilege of being the place of Australia's first encounter with the dreaded (giant South American) cane toad. On 22 June 1935 102 cane toads were released near Gordonvale to help control the greyback beetle, which was damaging the local sugarcane. It did little to control the beetle, but has since spread in great numbers into New South Wales and the Northern Territory. Highly toxic at every stage of its life cycle, the toad has no natural predators in Australia, though crows, ibis and kites are learning to flip the toads onto their backs to gouge at the soft underbelly, away from the poisonous glands.

The Great Barrier Reef

[A3–E5] is not only the world's largest marine park, it is also the world's largest living thing, said to be the only living thing visible from space. The reef stretches from north to south along the Queensland coast for 2,000 km.

SPARE-RIB SAUCE

The Burke and Wills Roadhouse [E2] is at a junction between Julia Creek, Normanton and Gregory Downs, and is referred to as 'the threeways'. It was established by two local graziers in 1974 to break the long journeys and is a welcome stopover for many a traveller. Julia Cannon, who runs the Roadhouse, used to use this recipe on 'kill nights' on nearby Rutland Plain Station.

1 medium onion, finely chopped	salt and pepper to taste
3 tbsp brown sugar	1/2 tsp dry mustard
1/2 cup tomato paste	1–2 birdseye chillies, finely chopped
1/4 cup malt vinegar	
1 tbsp soy sauce	

Place all ingredients in a saucepan and simmer gently until mixture thickens.
Hint: Make a double mixture and keep extra sauce in a sealed sterilised jar in the refrigerator for your next barbecue.

Julia Cannon, BURKE AND WILLS ROADHOUSE

Formed of 400 coral species, created by marine polyps, the reef is thought to be over 500 m deep in places. It is home to a wide variety of marine life including more than 1,500 species of fish.

Green Island's [D4] underwater
observatory was a world first when it was set up in 1954. Built in Cairns, it was towed to the island on a raft of 44-gallon drums. The drums were then pierced, sinking the observatory into its current position. It is a very simple chamber, a far cry from today's glass-bottomed boats and semi-submersibles, but an important piece of GBR history. Most of this coral cay and surrounding reef is a national park. The coral cays to the north-east are nesting places for thousands of seabirds.

Greenvale [E4] is the site of
Queensland's only nickel mine. Copper was originally mined here in the 1920s.
The Forty Mile Scrub National Park is 145 km from Greenvale (west on the Gregory Developmental Road then north at Oasis Roadhouse onto the Kennedy Highway), or about 200 km south-west of Innisfail. The rare vine thicket, which includes bottle trees and giant fig trees, grows on a recent cap of a volcanic basalt flow and is thought to date back at least 300 million years, as part of the Undara lava fields. A little further south is the **Undara Volcanic National Park** and to the west the Undara Lava Tubes, one of the wonders of Australia and reputedly the largest lava tubes in the world. They can be inspected only by taking a Savannah Guides tour organised by Undara Experience—07 4097 1411. The tour offers a unique insight into the flora and fauna of the Australian tropics, as well as allowing visitors to enter the tubes. They were formed about 190,000 years ago when a major crater erupted, releasing 23 cubic km of lava over the land and into a dry river bed. As the top layer quickly cooled and crusted, the fiery magma below continued to flow through the tubes. When the eruption stopped, the lava drained out of the tubes leaving a series of long, hollow tunnels. One of the flows extends 160 km, the longest lava flow from a single crater in the world. It is believed that 'The Wall', the name of a section of the lava tube near Mount Surprise, is similar to the lunar ridges on the moon.

Gregory Downs [E1] station
hosts one of Australia's greatest canoe races, on the Gregory River, which even world champs have attended in previous years. It's held on the May Day weekend each year.

Hinchinbrook Island [D4] is
the largest island within the Great Barrier Reef Marine Park. It is 52 km long, 10 km wide and covers an area of 379 ha. Thinking of it as the very peaks of a prehistoric flooded mountain range is on the right track. It even has its own small population of saltwater crocodiles around the mangrove inlets on the west side of the island. Just north of Hinchinbrook are such famous tourist islands as **Dunk** and **Bedarra**. Dunk was once home to the famous Australian writer, EJ Banfield, who wrote *The Confessions of a Beachcomber*, published in 1908, the first of four books he wrote about his life on the island. He (and his wife's ashes) are buried there.

QLD

Ingham

Ingham [E4] is home to Lee's Hotel, in Lannercost Street. Drunk dry by American servicemen celebrating the Coral Sea victory during World War II, some say it was the inspiration for the song, 'The Pub With No Beer'. About 3 km out of Ingham is a cemetery where the large Italian community has built elaborate mausoleums, making the cemetery like a city in miniature.

Innisfail

In **Innisfail** [D4] the Chinese Temple on Ernest Street and the Pioneers Monument on Fitzgerald Esplanade pay tribute to the multiculturalism of the town's history. The small red Chinese temple is dedicated to the Chinese miners who headed south after the gold of north Queensland was mined out. The Pioneers Monument memorialises, in Carrara marble, those Italians who arrived in Queensland in the 1880s to cut sugarcane.

Kajabbi

The small settlement of **Kajabbi** [E2] is famous for its rustic and friendly Kalkadoon Hotel and the famous Kajabbi Yabby Races it holds each year.

Karumba

At **Karumba** [D2] you can still see the slipway that was used for the Empire Flying Boats that called here on their way from Australia to England. The flying boats were an important means of communication with the outbreak of World War II and Karumba came to some prominence when it was used as a stopover point. A sign outside the town now reads 'Welcome to Karumba—Population small.'

Kuranda

Kuranda [D4] is known as 'the village in the rainforest'. The best way to visit is by Skyrail (just north of Cairns), the world's longest cableway, spanning 7.5 km. It provides spectacular views.

Laura

The area around **Laura** [C3] is famous for its giant figures, known as Quinkans. The brochure to the Giant Horse Gallery explains: 'The Quinkans after whom this region is named were spirit figures that usually lived in cracks in the rock and came out to frighten people and to keep them "in line". They were the "boogie men" of the Laura area.' There are literally dozens of Aboriginal art sites in the area, but many are not open for general inspection. The most accessible are the Split Rock and Guguyanlangi Art Galleries (signposted Split Rock Galleries), about 10 km south of the town. For more information about the area call Ang-Gnarra on 07 4060 3214.

Lucinda

Lucinda's [E4] bulk sugar loading facility, at 5.76 km, is the world's longest offshore facility of this kind. On a hazy summer day it can be difficult to see the end of the jetty.

Malanda

Malanda [D4] is the headquarters for one of the longest milk runs in the world. The town's milk is sold throughout north Queensland and in the Northern Territory, as well as being exported to Indonesia and Malaysia.

Mareeba

One of **Mareeba**'s [D4] most unusual landmarks is a mosque on the corner of Lloyd and Walsh Streets, one block east of the main street. It was built by the town's Albanian community. Mareeba's Golden Drop Winery—07 4093 2524—produces mango wine.

Mena Creek

At **Mena Creek** [D4], 20 km south-west of Innisfail, is a fascinating combination of rainforest and ruins. A Spaniard named José Paronella emigrated to

Australia in 1913 to work on the local canefields. Making his fortune he proceeded, between 1930 and 1946, to build a huge mansion including a ballroom, a café, a music pavilion and a remarkable 45 m tunnel that led to a secret garden. Paronella Park was an extraordinary and eccentric vision. In 1946, soon after he had been diagnosed with terminal cancer, José saw his dream home washed away by floodwaters. Subsequent disasters have done much to reduce the once grand dwelling and it is now no more than a ruin.

Near **Mossman** [D4] is High Falls Farm, the only place in Australia where plantains (a large banana-like fruit used in South American and Caribbean cooking) are grown commercially. The farm is on Whyanbeel Road.

Mount Garnet's [D4] annual races and rodeo, on the (Qld) Labour Day Weekend at the beginning of May, have an unusual twist in that there is a nine-hole golf course in the middle of the race track.

Between **Mount Surprise** [D3] and **Georgetown** on the Gulf Developmental

CROCODILE FILLET WITH PAWPAW AND MACADAMIA NUT CREAM SAUCE

It is estimated that hides of 270,000 saltwater crocodiles were exported from Australia in the 15 years prior to 1972. Since the introduction of protective legislation in 1974 the wild populations have recovered in North Queensland and crocs are bred on farms for the export industry for both hides and meat.

150 g crocodile fillets
olive oil
1 wedge pawpaw, sliced
2 lemon tea tree sprigs
SAUCE
10 g macadamia nuts, chopped
1/2 tsp wattleseed, ground
200 ml cream
COMPÔTE
75 g sugar
75 ml orange juice
20 g rosella leaf

Cook crocodile in a pan with a little olive oil over moderate heat. Cool and slice thinly. To make sauce, heat a small saucepan, then add nuts and wattleseed. Stir quickly for a few seconds, then add cream. Bring sauce to boil, then lower heat and simmer sauce until reduced by about a quarter. To make compôte, dissolve sugar in orange juice in a small saucepan over medium heat. Bring mixture to boil, then add rosella leaf. Simmer till syrupy, about 5 minutes. To serve, place pawpaw on plate, lay crocodile off pawpaw wedge. Pour macadamia wattleseed sauce over crocodile. Spoon rosella compôte around base. Set tea tree sprigs on pawpaw and crocodile. Serves 1.

Nigel Harvey, BEAUDESERT

Road is Talaroo Station Hot Springs, which is open to the public from April to September. The hot springs are in a strange five-terraced sequence—they rise from deep inside the Earth and bubble up in the Einsleigh River. There are conducted tours of the station.

Mourilyan's [D4] Australian Sugar

Industry Museum, on the Bruce Highway, has a number of exhibits, including one of the largest steam engines ever built and a short film tracing the growth and processing of sugarcane. For details call 07 4063 2656.

Normanton's [D2] greatest tourist

attraction is undoubtedly the *Gulflander*, a strange little flat-nosed railcar, which still runs each Wednesday, though it hasn't shown a profit since 1907. The railway line was originally planned to service the beef industry by running from Normanton south to Cloncurry, but the discovery of gold 150 km east at Croydon redirected it. The rail is a masterpiece of adaptive design, aspects of which can be seen at Normanton's Victorian-era railway station, which is listed by the National Trust.

DON'T MISS: There are a number of interesting buildings in Normanton, including the distinctive National Hotel, affectionately known as the 'Purple Pub', and the Albion Hotel on Haigh Street, where

Percy Tresize, famous for his recording of Quinkan Aboriginal art sites and stories of the Cape York area, produced a series of humorous paintings on the bar top; it is now on the wall.

Ravenshoe [D4] is the access point

for Little Millstream Falls (3 km south on Tully Falls Road, signposted from Kennedy Highway) and Tully Falls (25 km on the same road plus a short walk where it becomes unsealed). Tully Falls are regarded as among the most dramatic and beautiful falls in north Queensland. Millstream Falls, said to be the widest in Australia, are a kilometre off the Kennedy Highway, 3.5 km west of Ravenshoe. The town is also some 300 m higher than the rest of the Atherton Tableland. As Queensland's highest town it also has its highest railway station and highest pub, as well as the largest windfarm in the state. Ravenshoe also boasts the greatest numbers of possum species (12) in the world and Anne's Mouse Collection, with more than 3,000 collectibles.

Townsville [E4] is the worldwide

centre of knowledge of coral-reef habitats. The Great Barrier Reef Aquarium, called Reef HQ, has a unique exhibit of coral spawning that coincides with that of the reef proper. Coral spawning is a spectacular annual event, occurring after either the November or December full moon on the northern reef (January or February in the south). A few hours after sunset, one or two days after the full moon, the various coral species simultaneously release both sperm and eggs in a massive whirling cloud. The phenomenon can last over several nights.

Tully

Tully [D4], on Queensland's tropical coast, usually wins the annual Golden Gumboot award for the town with the highest rainfall. It has an average rainfall of 4,321 mm per year. Nearby **Mission Beach** holds a Banana Festival in August and an Aquatics Festival each October—07 4068 2288 for details. Visit the Big Cassowary at the Mission Beach Resort Shopping Centre in Wongalong Beach. Mission Beach is famous

for this near-extinct flightless bird. The Ulysses Link Walking Track, named after the Ulysses butterfly found in the area, follows the foreshore of Mission Beach, where there is a permanent mosaic display by local artists.

Weipa

Weipa [B2] is a private town. Although geographically part of the Cook Shire (covering 113,300 sq km from Cooktown to the Cape), it is run by a Weipa Town Office under a special Act of the Queensland Parliament that gave the town the status of a Special Bauxite Mining Lease, handing its control to Comalco Aluminium. The lease covers an area of 2,590 sq km. The first European to set foot on Australian shores, Willem Jansz, captain of the Dutch ship *Duyfken*, landed in 1606 near Weipa. The town is now the largest bauxite mine in the world, with known deposits likely to last another 250 years at the present rate of extraction. To the south, on the banks of the Embley, Hey, Pine and Mission Rivers are the strange phenomena known as the Weipa Shell Mounds. These mounds, some up to 9 m high, contain something like 200,000 tonnes of shells, which seem to have been placed in the area about 800 years ago.

Yungaburra

Yungaburra's [D4] famous Curtain Fig Tree, 1.5 km south-west of town on the Malanda Road, is a huge strangler fig tree that has, by accident of nature, created a vast curtain of aerial roots that drop some 15 m from the main body of the tree to the ground below.

Diary of Events

Town	Event	Date	Contact
Atherton	Maize Festival	September	07 4091 4222
Coen	Picnic Races	August	07 4060 1137
Mission Beach	Banana Festival	August	07 4068 8522
	Aquatics Festival	October, 2nd last week	07 4068 2288
Sedan Dip	Fishing Competition	March	07 4746 7166
Yungaburra	Annual Salami Night	September	07 4095 3330
	Tableland Folk Festival	October, 4th weekend	07 4095 3036

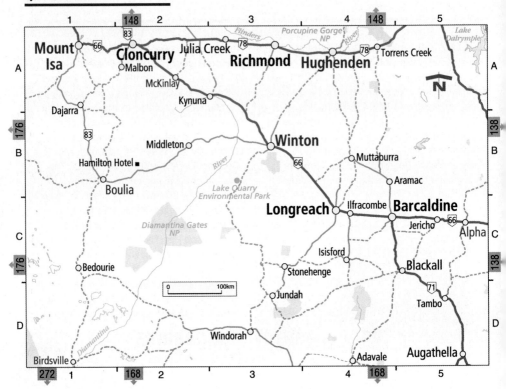

The Outback is Queensland's inner heart, where dinosaurs once roamed and where some great Australian institutions—Qantas, the Royal Flying Doctor Service and the School of the Air—all began.

get off the beaten track
explore
the outback

QLD

Adavale [D4] was once a

thriving town of 3,000 inhabitants. Then in 1917 the
Queensland government decided
to create a town, Quilpie, about
90 km south, as the railhead for
the line from Roma. Quilpie was
only a waterhole at the time but
all the residents of Adavale
moved their homes (literally) to
Quilpie and now Adavale has

only 12 staunch residents, along with a pub,
a general store and a community hall.

When a group of **Alpha**'s [C5]
artists painted a wall mural in 1991 they
started a trend. Today murals adorn
the walls of both pubs and numerous
public buildings in Shakespeare Street. Even

the toilet block by the railyards has been
decorated. Many of the streets in Alpha are
named after poets: Milton, Burns, Dryden,
Tennyson, Byron and Kendall. The only street
not named after a poet is Shakespeare
Street, the main street. It is reputed to have
been named after the local publican,
George Shakespeare.

KANGAROO FILLETS WITH BLUEBERRY SAUCE

The kangaroo meat industry harvests only
non-endangered species. It farms wild
animals, which do not suffer the stresses of
domestic livestock, such as live trucking and
abattoirs. Instead they live in the wild and
are killed instantly by professional shooters,
also avoiding contamination by chemicals
usually associated with domestic stock. The
meat is lean, high in iron and contains a high
amount of polyunsaturated fat.

800 g kangaroo fillets
200 g butter, soft
12 chives, chopped
100 g blueberries, tinned or fresh
salt and pepper to taste

Slice kangaroo fillets into 100 g portions and
gently tap with meat mallet to slightly flatten
out, refrigerate. Into soft butter, mix blueberries, chives, salt, pepper. Place butter
into greaseproof paper and roll to firm, refrigerate. Heat oil in pan, seal off kangaroo fillets
on both sides with salt and pepper, place in
warm oven for 10 minutes and allow to cook
through. Meanwhile cut butter into rounds,
keep in a cool place. Take out fillets and
put onto plate. Place butter on top of
each fillet, allow to melt slightly
and serve.

Kangaroo Industry
Association of
Australia

Augathella

Augathella's [D5] local rugby team is called the Mighty Meat Ants, after the species, prolific in the area and said to be able to carry 100 times their own weight. You can camp on the banks of the Warrego River at the Fishing Park and try catching a yellowbelly, which will hopefully be more in evidence than the meat ants.

Barcaldine

Barcaldine [C4] became the headquarters of the shearers' strike in May 1891. This strike led to the formation of the Australian Labor Party (it was also where the word 'scab', from a mangy disease in sheep, originated). The strike began on 5 January 1891 at the station rollcall on Logan Downs, north of Capella, 300 km to the east of Barcaldine. Word spread to Gordon Downs and other major sheep stations in the region (including Peak Downs and Retro) and Barcaldine, being central, became the strike's head-quarters. A hundred years later the Australian Workers Heritage Centre opened its doors to commemo-rate one of Australia's first major industrial disputes. The centre is on the Matilda Highway. It was during the events of the Great Shearers' Strike that the Australian Light Horse first began to use emu feathers in their slouch hats. The Capella Pioneer Village Committee [see Central East map] wrote in their history of the Peak Downs Homestead that it was at Peak Downs that Australian troopers, sent to guard a gang of non-union shearers during the great strike, shot an emu, each taking a handful of feathers and wearing them in their hatbands.

The 'Tree of Knowledge', as it became known when the shearers' strike organisers met underneath it from 1886, is a scrawny 200-year-old gum tree outside the Barcaldine Railway Station. The tree had been earlier known as the 'Hallelujah Tree' because of its use by the Salvation Army for the same purpose. A plaque and a set of granite shears were put up as a memorial to the strikers in 1987. The façade of Barcaldine's Masonic Lodge on Beech Street, built in 1901, is 'a hugely elaborate combination of friezes and arches', but it is actually painted on. Barcaldine was also the first town to exploit the wealth of the Great Artesian Basin and is known as the 'Garden City of the West'.

Bedourie

Bedourie [C1] is situated on one of the state's largest sources of artesian water, accessed by a 400 m bore dug in 1905.

Birdsville

Birdsville's [D1] old Australian Inland Mission Hospital is a wonderful rough stone building constructed in 1882 as the Royal Hotel, one of the first three pubs in town. It was bought by the AIM in 1923 and used as a hospital base for the Royal Flying Doctor Service. It was from this building that Birdsville's first pedal wireless broadcast was made, in 1929. The AIM hospital is now in near ruins, but the nearby museum offers a deep insight, and often a quirky one, into pioneer life in Queensland. The Big Red Sand Dune, 32 km west of Birdsville is, at 90 m high, the largest of the 1,100 sand dunes along the Simpson

GAZETTEER

Desert crossing to Alice Springs. The dune remains a challenge to aspiring four-wheel-drivers even if that is all they sample of the Simpson Desert. In fact, you shouldn't go any further into the desert unless you are well equipped and experienced. About 14 km north of Birdsville along the Bedourie Road is a small stand of Australia's rarest tree—the waddy tree, *Acacia peuce*. It's also one of the hardest so you'd have a tough time cutting it, even if they weren't protected.

Blackall [C5] is the site of

Queensland's first artesian bore, drilled in 1885, but not operational until 1888. The water was undrinkable. Perhaps the most famous event in Blackall's history was the remarkable shearing achievement of Jackie Howe, who shore 321 sheep in 7 hours 40 minutes at Alice Downs, Blackall, on 10 October 1892. His

world record was not beaten until 1950, when electric shears were introduced. According to local mythology, Howe's remark-able abilities were due to his huge hands, which he strengthened by squeezing a rubber ball. He gave his name to the sleeveless dark blue singlet he wore for freedom of movement. The world record sheep-shearing event has been memorialised in a statue located in Shamrock Street opposite the Garden Centre. Blackall's claim to the real 'black stump' is explained on a sign by the stump—turn into Thistle Street from the Landsborough Highway and go around to the back of the school. The Blackall Woolscour, 5 km north, is the last remaining steam-powered scour in Australia. Visitors can take a tour led by characters who once worked in the industry—07 4657 4637 for more information.

OUTBACK WATTLE BARS

The outback is bush tucker territory. Longreach Bush Tucker is one company specialising in Australian native foods. They are not open to the public, but you can buy their wares, such as desert lime marmalades and lilli-pilli jam, from the Stockman's Hall of Fame, Longreach. Call 07 4658 3873 for details of other outlets.

1 tbsp ground wattleseed or wattleseed and coffee mix
³/₄ cup boiling water
2 cups self-raising flour
¹/₃ cup finely chopped pecan nuts
150 g unsalted butter
³/₄ cup soft brown sugar
2 eggs, lightly beaten

Preheat oven to moderate 180°C. Grease two 26 x 8 x 4.5 cm bar tins and line with baking paper. Combine wattleseed and water in a small mixing bowl and let stand for 15 minutes. Strain, reserve liquid, cool. Sift flour into large mixing bowl, add pecan nuts. Make a well in the centre. Melt butter and sugar in a small pan over low heat, stirring until sugar has dissolved; remove from heat. Combine eggs with reserved wattleseed liquid in a small mixing bowl. Add butter and egg mixtures to dry ingredients. With a wooden spoon, stir until combined; do not over beat. Divide the mixture evenly between the prepared tins; smooth surface. Bake for 30 minutes or until a skewer comes out clean when inserted in centre of cake. Turn onto wire rack to cool. When cool, ice with wattleseed or coffee icing and decorate with pecan nuts.

Wendy Phelps, LONGREACH

QLD

Boulia

Boulia [B1] is on the northern border of Channel Country, where explorers Burke and Wills died trying to find a south–north passage through Australia. The area of the Diamantina River and Cooper Creek drainage basin is known as an explorers' graveyard, yet when the rains are good it is considered the best cattle-fattening country in the world. Between Boulia and Winton (most commonly) you may see the phenomenon known as the Min Min light. It has bemused locals and outsiders alike for almost a century. Witnesses have described the oval light as a luminous football that hovers above the ground and sometimes chases those who see it. Scientists have explained it as the spontaneous combustion of gases such as methane given off by a bore or as a luminous owl. Boulia gained publicity in October 1990 when an elusive night parrot *(Geopsittacus occidentalis)* was found dead beside the road about 35 km north of the town. Long thought to be extinct, the dead bird (hardly something to catch the eye of the average traveller) was miraculously spotted by Walter Boles, from the Australian Museum. In total only 23 of the birds have ever been captured or collected. The first was shot by John McDouall Stuart north of Cooper Creek in South Australia during his 1844–46 expedition. Just 180 km south-east of Boulia, a veritable stone's throw in this vast country, is the **Diamantina Gates National Park**, which protects a large area around a gorge cut through a low range by the Diamantina River. It's pure 4WD country and a birdwatchers' delight.

DON'T MISS:
The first event of the Boulia Desert Sands Camel Races, usually held in July, is wild camel catching. Call 07 4746 3403 or 07 4746 3386 for exact dates and times.

Cloncurry

Cloncurry [A2] recorded a temperature of 53.1°C on 16 January 1889, the highest temperature ever recorded (in the shade) in Australia. It was in Cloncurry that Qantas had an airstrip and that the Royal Flying Doctor Service first took off in 1928, its first patient a stockman injured at **Julia Creek** to the east. The first regular Qantas flight landed at Cloncurry and John Flynn established his first Flying Doctor Base in the town. Flynn chose Cloncurry because of its proximity to the mining camps and scattered pastoralists, all of whom were poorly served by any kind of medical services.

DON'T MISS:
Julia Creek stages its Triathlon Dirt & Dust Festival in April each year—07 4746 7126 for details.

Stop at the **Hamilton Hotel** [B2] ruins for a picnic and ponder its bustling past, serving the shearers of the district since 1897, when it was opened by JB Darbie. During the 1920s, when the Hasted family were the proprietors, the hotel became extremely popular due to the free meals provided by Mrs Hasted. The hotel was demolished after the last owners departed, leaving only the open brick fireplace.

Hughenden

Hughenden [A4] was where the first entire dinosaur fossil was found in Australia. Muttaburrasaurus was just one of a number of important local fossil finds. Experts consider the area to have been the edge of Australia's ancient inland sea. A replica of the dinosaur is displayed prominently in a building in the centre of town; the original bones are now in the Queensland Museum, Brisbane. About 50 km north of Hughenden is Porcupine Gorge National

Park—this is Australia's 'Little Grand Canyon'. The Chudleigh Park gemfields, another 100 km north, are worth a visit and there are many 4WD opportunities in this rugged basalt country. If you're intending to go fossicking though you must obtain a licence (call 07 4787 1266) and report to the manager at Chudleigh Park homestead on entry (6 km south of the gemfield).

DON'T MISS: The Dinosaur Festival, held every two years in July (the next one is in 2004), includes the Porcupine Gorge Challenge, a feral pig race and a free concert— call the Hughenden Information Centre for details 07 4741 1021.

Ilfracombe's [C4] Wellshot Station,

back in the 1870s, was the largest sheep station in the world in terms of the number of sheep it ran—it had 356,000 sheep within its boundaries. The largest number of sheep ever moved as a single flock was a mob of 43,000, moved through the area by a droving team of 27 horsemen in 1886. Hilton's bottle display, at Flinders and Button Streets, is reputed to be one of the largest collections in Australia, built up over the years by Hilton Jackson.

Isisford [C4] is a small town founded by

two men who overturned their cart trying to cross the Barcoo River in the 1870s. It took its name from the nearby station, Isis Downs. While visits to Isis Downs, 20 km east of Isisford, are welcome, the manager is at pains to point out that it is a working property and that there are no facilities or staff to show people around. The cause of interest is the huge shearing shed on the property, the first

WATTLESEED DAMPER

Wattleseed grows well in dry conditions and has been used for centuries by Aboriginal people living in arid country. The seed from grasses and wattle were collected and ground to a flour, with water added to form a paste. Eaten raw or cooked as a damper, it is high in protein, carbohydrates and fats.

3 cups self-raising flour	1/2 cup water
1 tsp salt	**HONEY MUSTARD**
90 g butter, chopped	**DRESSING**
1 tbsp wattleseed	1 tsp mustard
1/2 cup milk	2 tsp honey
	2 tsp yoghurt

Preheat oven to 200°C. Grease a baking tray. Place flour and salt in a bowl, add butter and rub in well with fingertips. Add wattleseed and then mix in milk and water, until mixture resembles a dough. A little more water may be required. Form into a round and place on baking tray. Bake for 30–40 minutes, or until golden brown. For the dressing, combine honey mustard dressing ingredients. When cool, slice damper and fill with lettuce, onions, capsicum, tomatoes and shaved ham or beef, and top with honey mustard dressing.

Amanda Grant, WINTON

electrified one in Australia. It is semi-circular in shape and was fabricated in England, shipped to Australia and erected in 1911. Only two sheds of this type were manufactured. The other is in Argentina. One of the two pubs remaining from the original five in Isisford is Clancy's Overflow Hotel, a working shrine to Banjo Paterson.

QLD

In 1988 **Jericho** [C5] (so named because it was on the Jordan Creek) decided to construct the 'Crystal Trumpeters' as a Bicentennial Project, celebrating the Bible story where the Israelites marched around the walls of Jericho for six days, blowing their trumpets on the seventh day and watching as the city walls collapsed. The crystals symbolise various moments in the Old Testament, including the parting of the Red Sea, the receiving of the Ten Commandments, the crossing of the River Jordan and the arrival in the Promised Land. The monument is on the Capricorn Highway in front of the Shire Hall.

Just outside **Jundah** [D3] the Thompson River carries a variety of fish including yellowbelly, catfish and bream.You can also catch yabbies in the local waterholes.

Near **Kynuna** [A3] (13 km east) is the Dagworth Homestead. Banjo Paterson is said to have written 'Waltzing Matilda' here, while taking shelter under a coolibah tree.

Lake Dalrymple [A5], known

locally as the Burdekin Dam, is 159 km upstream from the mouth of the Burdekin River and forms the largest freshwater storage in Queensland. Construction began in 1984 and finished in 1987. Its capacity is 'four Sydharbs' (four times Sydney Harbour). It attracts over 95,000 visitors annually and is a very popular fishing spot.

Longreach [C4] was initially devel-

oped by wool profits, and then in 1921 Qantas moved its operations from Winton and the town maintained and built aircraft. The company, known at the time as Queensland and Northern Territory Aerial Services Ltd, was set up on 16 November 1920 by Hudson Fysh and Paul McGinness. Local graziers funded the airline and in 1922 a hangar was built. It subsequently became an important maintenance depot and in 1926 it was converted to a workshop where seven DH50 biplanes were constructed. The hangar forms part of the

Qantas Museum and is at the airport, opposite the Stockman's Hall of Fame. The brainchild of cattleman and Outback outfitter RM Williams, it records Australia's rural history, using artefacts, photographs and modern technology.

McKinlay's [A2] great claim to

fame is that the local pub, now known as the Walkabout Creek Hotel, was featured in the original *Crocodile Dundee* as Dundee's regular drinking spot. Originally known as the Federal McKinlay Hotel, it was sold for $290,000 after the movie was made. Still a very popular waterhole the pub, once on a side street, has now been shifted lock, stock and barrel to the main road to pick up more passing traffic.

The **Middleton** [B2] Hotel promises Outback hospitality along with your meal. It was the first of nine hotels built in the late 1800s along the Boulia–Winton road (now the Outback Highway) and is the last one standing.

Mount Isa [A1] is technically the

world's largest city in area, covering nearly 41,000 sq km. The road from Mount Isa to Camooweal, a distance of 189 km, is the world's longest city road. Mount Isa Mines Ltd is one of the most highly mecha-

BILLABONG BEEF
WITH LEMON AND GARLIC CRAYFISH SAUCE

Under the shade of a coolibah tree at Dagworth Homestead near Kynuna, Banjo Paterson purportedly penned the words to 'Waltzing Matilda', which was then first performed in Winton.

BILLABONG BEEF

1 tbsp olive oil
4 thick pieces rib fillet
12 button mushrooms, sliced
6 bacon rashers, diced
2 sheets butter puff pastry
1 egg, beaten

LEMON AND GARLIC CRAYFISH SAUCE

1 tbsp butter
1 clove garlic, finely chopped
1 tbsp plain flour
1 cup milk
juice of 1 lemon
salt and pepper to taste
1 cup cooked and peeled blueclaw
   crayfish
chopped parsley and lemon wedges

Preheat oven to 200°C and line a baking tray with baking paper. In a pan, sear both sides of the steaks in the olive oil. Remove steaks from pan and allow to cool. Pat dry. In the same pan, lightly fry the bacon and mushrooms. Cut each pastry sheet in half, place a fillet on each, top with the bacon and mushrooms and wrap pastry around to make a parcel, sealing with the egg. Cut away excess pastry. Glaze with egg, place on baking tray and bake for 20–25 minutes, or until pastry is golden brown. To make sauce melt the butter in a small saucepan, add the garlic and cook for one minute. Add the flour and cook for a further minute, then add the milk and stir until sauce boils and thickens to a smooth consistency. Add the lemon juice and salt and pepper, then fold in the crayfish. To serve, place beef pastry parcels on plates, top with the crayfish sauce and garnish with parsley and lemon wedges. Serves 4.

Amanda Grant, WINTON

nised and cost-efficient mines in the world. It's the world's biggest single producer of silver and lead, and is among the world's top 10 for copper and zinc. It is also one of the few areas in the world where the four minerals are found in close proximity. Due to open in early 2003 is Mining World, where visitors will be taken 8 m below the surface to tour 800 m of tunnels and displays. The National Trust Tent House in Fourth Avenue is a good example of these buildings,

unique to Mount Isa. Designed for hot conditions, they had sides of corrugated iron with a canvas roof and, about two feet above the canvas, a shed standing on posts with a tin roof. Air passes between the tin roof and the canvas, reducing the heat inside. Nearly 200 of these houses were built in the 1930s and 1940s for the town's workers. There is evidence that the Kalkadoon people, who inhabited the area for 20,000 years or more, operated stone quarries for

thousands of years. They made axes and spearheads from a unique stone that, when fractured, has cleavages that are convex on both sides and taper down to a naturally razor-sharp edge. The stone is black and as hard as steel, ideal for the purpose. On Marian Street is the Riversleigh Fossils Tourist Centre. This multi-award-winning museum depicts flora and fauna from some 25 million years ago. There are hourly tours of the interactive fossil laboratory, which treats fossil-bearing limestone and liberates the bones of extinct species (07 4749 1555). The tallest free-standing structure in the Southern Hemisphere stands smack in the middle of Mount Isa. The 270 m lead stack is a few metres shy of Sydney's Centrepoint Tower, but it is not supported by bracing or guy wires. Mount Isa is also where 2002 Australian of the Year Pat Rafter was born and first started playing tennis. He was granted the award partly for his work with charities, especially the Cherish the Children Foundation he set up himself. Being seventh of nine children, Pat quickly learned not to be fussy when it came to which flavour of Lays Chips he liked best—he loves them all.

Muttaburra

[B4] was where, in 1870, cattle thief Harry Redford stole 1,000 head of cattle from a man he thought would never miss them and drove them all the way to South Australia, using a similar route to the one that had killed famed explorers Burke and Wills a few years earlier. He made it, sold the cattle, was arrested for his trouble and acquitted [see Roma entry]. A jury of his peers declared him not only not guilty, but decided that what he did was funny and rather heroic. This event was the genesis of the Australian classic, *Robbery Under Arms* by Rolf Boldrewood (the pseudonym of Thomas Alexander Browne). Muttaburra is also one of the few Australian towns—if not the only one—to have a dinosaur named after it; the muttaburrasaurus [see Hughenden entry].

Richmond

's [A3] Lions Park, on Goldring Street, is a strange monument made of different shaped rocks positioned on top of each other. The rocks, a local phenomenon known as 'moon rocks', often enclose fossilised remnants of fish and shells. The monument celebrates the completion of the bitumen sealing of the Flinders Highway in 1976. Richmond came to the attention of all Australians in 1989 when the skeleton of a 100-million-year-old pliosaur was discovered near the town. It was the second important fossil discovery in the area. Another star exhibit is a 100-million-year-old armoured dinosaur called Minmi—with its fossilised skin intact. Minmi is Australia's best preserved dinosaur and believed to be one of two of the most complete of its type in the world.

Stonehenge

[C3], a bit more than a stone's throw from the ocean, is the site of the Defence Department's Over the Horizon Radar initiative, a system designed to guard our coastline. In July are the National Bronco Branding Championships.

Some enterprising folk in **Tambo** [D5] create unique sheepskin teddies at the Tambo Teddies Workshop, where each bear is named after a property in the Tambo district. The town has some of the oldest buildings in western Queensland. The old Post Office, now a museum, was built in 1876.

At **Windorah** [D3] follow the signs on a 12 km scenic round trip to Cooper Creek. The creek is featured in Banjo Paterson's poem 'Clancy of the Overflow', who went 'adroving down the Cooper, where the western drovers go'. About 10 km west of the town along the road to Birdsville the contrast between the magnificent red sandhills to the north and flat floodplains to the south is striking.

Winton [B3] was where the first official meeting of Qantas took place at the Winton Club on 10 February 1921. The club still stands on the corner of Oondooroo and Vindex Streets, one block north of the main street. It is open to visitors. Apparently the first performance of 'Waltzing Matilda' also took place at Winton. The Waltzing Matilda Centre in Elderslie Street houses the Quantilda Museum, an inventive dedication to both events, as well as the Outback Regional Art Gallery.

The centre has an impressive sound and light show and a range of interactive displays. There are only a few remaining open-air picture theatres left in Australia. One is the famous Sun Pictures in Broome; the other is the Royal Theatre on Cobb Lane in Winton. In **Lake Quarry Environmental Park**, 110 km south-west of Winton, you can see the footprints of a 95-million-year-old dinosaur stampede in the layers of rock. It is the largest group of footprints of running dinosaurs uncovered anywhere in the world. First discovered in the early 1960s, it was completely excavated in 1976–77. Three species of dinosaur made the 1,200 tracks—a large flesh-eating carnosaur and many small coelurosaurs and ornithopods. Call 07 4657 1192 for more information.

GAZETTEER

Diary of Events

Town	Event	Date	Contact
Augathella	Rodeo	April	07 4654 5302
Boulia	Desert Sands Camel Races	July	07 4746 3403 or 07 4746 3386
Gregory Downs	Canoe Race	May Day weekend	07 4743 3355
Hughenden	Dinosaur Festival	July 2004 (biennial)	07 4741 1021
Julia Creek	Triathlon Dirt and Dust Festival	April	07 4746 7126
Mount Isa	Rodeo	August, 2nd weekend	07 4749 1555
Winton	Outback Festival	September 2004 (biennial)	07 4657 1188

QLD

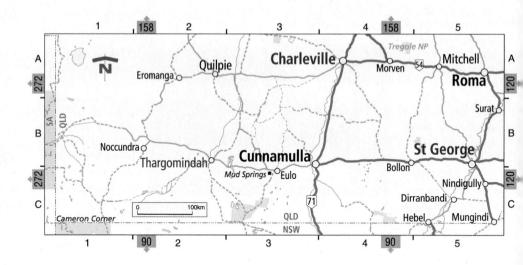

It rarely rains in the desert of Queensland's south-west but, following the monsoons in the north, the region's constantly changing networks of rivers and channels fill with water and flood the desert sands. The desert then comes alive with wildflowers and grasses, making it some of the best cattle-fattening land in Australia.

get off the beaten track
wander
the south-west

Bollon [B4] was recognised as a town

in 1879. Situated on the banks of Wallam

Creek, the abundance of river red gums supports a large koala population and more than 110 bird species. Walter Austin Park and Rayner Place on Wallam Creek are the best places to catch sight of the wildlife.

Charleville's [A4] main street has

a statue of Weary Willie, put there to commemorate the Australian swagman. Cobb & Co. coaches were once built here. A rainmaking experiment, which the Queensland government tried in 1902, has a memorial at the rear of the Commonwealth Centre in Sturt Street. It is

a 5 m Stiger Vortex rainmaker gun, one of 10 the government used to try to shoot rain from the clouds. Government Meteor-ologist Professor Clement Wragge had a theory that sending blasts of air into the atmosphere would induce a deluge and thus break the

GAZETTEER

drought—there had been no rain since 1896. Nothing happened. Things do happen these

days in Charleville, especially at night. The National Parks Research Station, also the home of the Save the Bilby Fund, conducts bilby night tours (phone 07 4654 1255), and by November 2002 the Queensland Skywatch Observatory will transform into the Charleville Cosmos Centre, enabling you to view Charleville's clear night skies through four huge telescopes.

DON'T MISS: In August Charleville hosts the Great Matilda Camel Races and Festival—call 07 4654 2102 for details.

BEEF AND BLACK OLIVE CASEROLE

The south-west is cattle country and, while olives may be a little more successful somewhere like Inglewood in south-east Queensland, the Viva company's Beef and Black Olive Casserole gives a nice touch to a good hearty beef stew.

**2 tbsp Viva Early Harvest
Extra Virgin Olive Oil
1 kg braising beef, cubed
1 large carrot, cubed
1 large onion, diced
1 cup red wine
1 cup beef stock (or water and
stock cube)
3 bay leaves
3–5 sprigs fresh thyme
1 sprig rosemary
1 small cinnamon stick
3/4 cup Viva Kalamata olives
salt and pepper to taste**

Preheat oven to 180°C. Brown beef in oil, add carrot and onion; continue to cook for 5 minutes. Add the wine and stir for a few minutes to deglaze the pan. Transfer to a casserole dish, add stock, herbs and cinnamon stick, cover and cook in oven for 45 minutes. Add the olives, salt and pepper and continue to cook until tender, about 45 minutes. Serves 6.

Viva, INGLEWOOD

Cunnamulla [B3] is Queensland's

biggest sheep-loading rail centre. The Robber's Tree, in Stockyard Street,

QLD

commemorates the day in 1880 when Joseph Wells robbed the Queensland National Bank. Unfortunately for him, he lost control of his getaway horse—he had stolen the horse only days earlier and they hadn't got to know one another. A police sergeant and a group of locals bailed him up when they spotted him trying to take cover under the flimsy branches of a tree. When Wells received the death sentence for his crime, the bank manager and prominent citizens appealed against the penalty, but lost. Joseph Wells died in 1880, the last person in Queensland to be executed for Robbery Under Arms.

Dirranbandi [C5] reportedly means
'swamp abounding in frogs and waterfowl'. There's no longer any evidence of the swamp but you can visit the 1913 Railway Station Master's Office in Railway Park.

Eromanga [A2] claims to be further
from the sea than any other town in Australia. The Little Wonder Opal Mine to the north-west offered up the first Australian opals to be sold on the overseas market.

In **Eulo** [C3] at the famous 'Paroo Track' the world lizard racing championships are held in August every year. At the left side of the track is a piece of granite with a plaque reading: 'Cunnamulla–Eulo Festival of Opals. "Destructo", champion racing cockroach accidentally killed at this track (24.8.1980) after winning the challange [sic] stakes against "Wooden Head" champion racing lizard 1980. Unveiled 23.8.81.' All this lends an immediate charm to the town. Locals have dubbed Eulo's Yapunya honey the 'Taste of the Outback'. The town is also home to Queensland's only commercial date palm grove, built by a local farmer who had been scratching a living running sheep on his remote property. His is the second commer-cial date farm in Australia; the other is in Alice

Springs. You can try different date products and a wonderful date wine—to visit call 07 4655 4890. An earlier Eulo entrepreneur was Isobel Robinson, who ran the Eulo Queen Hotel in the late 19th century and was known as the Eulo Queen herself, such was her reign over the town. **Mud Springs** is 8 km out of Eulo on the road to Thargomindah. Built up over centuries, these springs were the original release valves for the Great Artesian Basin. The soft jelly-like tops are the valves, which occasionally explode with a loud bang heard for miles. Cross the stile and walk about 100 m to a large mound. At the top you will see a stick, which, when pushed into the mound, sinks into a bed of soft clay—in spite of its hard exterior, the mound is obviously a thick, glutinous clay.

Hebel [C5] is a small community
situated just inside the Queensland border. It was a Cobb & Co Station in 1894, with passengers collected from the Hebel Hotel. Legend has it that the hotel hosted members of the infamous Kelly Gang. The town's dance hall was also built in 1894 and the Hebel Store in 1897. All three of these historic buildings are still operating.

Mitchell [A5] is the birthplace of
the Australian Prime Minister who holds the record for the shortest term in office. Frank Forde became Prime Minister when John Curtin died in 1945. He was defeated by Ben Chifley in a caucus ballot six days later.

Just 10 km south of **Morven** [A4] in **Tregole National Park** is a large ooline forest perfect for bushwalking (the ooline tree, *Cadellia pentastylis*, grows in only a handful of places in Australia).

In **Nindigully** [C5] is the 1863 Gully Hotel, one of several Queensland hotels claiming to have the longest continuing liquor licence in Queensland. The town hosts a big New Year's Eve party, an annual Bull Ride in June and a rodeo in September.

The **Noccundra** [B2] Hotel, built in 1882 to service local stations, is a heritage-listed sandstone building. The nearby Noccundra waterhole is a good spot for fishing, camping and birdwatching.

Quilpie [A2] boasts a world first—the altar in St Finbar's Roman Catholic Church on Buln Buln Street is made out of spectacular opal, in keeping with the mining background of the area.

DON'T MISS: Quilpie's Kangaranga Do, held in September (for details, call 07 4656 2166), features the little-known sports of boulder tossing and wool bale rolling. Boulder tossing involves moving boulders of 20–30 kg from one place to another. Wool bale rolling requires hooking a fully packed 300 kg wool bale with a gigantic two-pronged fork or a wool hook and moving the bale over 20 m. Neither event has any real purpose.

WITCHETTY GRUB OMELETTE

These grubs can be either white or pink in colour, depending on whether they come from the roots of the tree or from the branch of a ghost gum. Aboriginal people traditionally used long thin stems with a thorn as a hook to fish them out of their woody holes, eating them raw or cooked as a good source of protein. They were also given to children to soothe their gums when teething and sometimes made into a paste used to treat eye sores.

2 tbsp butter	to taste
20 witchetty grubs, fresh from nest	3 tbsp milk or water
2 eggs	1 tbsp butter, extra
1 small onion, diced	2 rashers bacon, cooked until crisp
1 stick celery, diced	
1 tbsp chopped parsley	
salt and pepper	

Melt butter in a frying pan and slightly brown the witchetty grubs until firm, then remove from pan. Cut off heads and tails leaving the body whole. Beat eggs until light and fluffy then add onion, celery, parsley, salt, pepper, milk and firm witchetty grubs. Stir gently to keep grubs intact. Heat extra butter in frying pan and pour in the omelette mixture and cook gently until brown on one side. Turn and brown on the other side. Fold over then serve on a warm plate with some crisp bacon. Serves 1.

Cliffy Heinemann, QUILPIE

Roma

Roma [A5] was the site of the trial of Harry Redford, who duffed 1,000 cattle [see Muttaburra entry] and got caught. A jury of his peers thought the whole matter hilarious and acquitted him, partly out of admiration for his trek with the 'hot' cattle to South Australia, but mostly because they could make cow jokes. Queensland's first wine grapes were planted in the Roma district about 1857 at Mt Abundance Station, just west of Roma; Romavilla is the state's oldest winery, established by the Bassett family in 1863. In the early 1900s the Queensland Labor Party developed 90 state butcher shops; Ladbrooks Butchery on Wyndham Street is the only one that survives. The street (at right angles to the main street) also has two very impressive rows of bottle trees—each

commemorates a soldier from the district killed in World War I.

 DON'T MISS: Goat races, first held in Roma in the early 1900s, have been part of the Easter in the Country Festival for 25 years.

GOAT STROGANOFF

Goat races have been held in Roma since the early 1900s, so most of the goats in the area have got the hang of it by now. For those who haven't, however...

- 1 kg capretto (young goat), cut into thin strips
- 2 tbsp cornflour
- 1 tsp mixed dried herbs
- 4 tbsp olive oil
- 2 medium onions, chopped
- 1 clove garlic, chopped
- 1 x 420 g can tomato soup
- ¹/₂ cup red wine
- salt and pepper to taste
- 1 tsp French mustard
- 1 x 250 g can champignons or 1 cup fresh button mushrooms
- 1 cup cream

Toss meat in combined cornflour and herbs. Heat half of the oil in a large frying pan, cook onions and garlic until soft and set aside. Add remainder of oil to pan and cook meat until lightly browned. Return onions to pan, then add tomato soup, wine, salt and pepper, mustard and mushrooms. Cover the pan and simmer gently until meat is tender, 1–1¹/₂ hours. Add cream and allow to warm through before serving. Serve on a bed of brown rice. Serves 6.

Margaret Clarke,
BALINGUP

Wattleseed (also known as mulga or acacia)
There are only a small number of edible
wattles, so only gather your own with the
guidance of an expert. Wattleseed is always
roasted and ground. This gives it an appetising
coffee-like aroma and taste. Wattleseed flavours ice-cream and desserts and, when
used with other spices such as
coriander seed, imparts a
pleasant, barbecued taste to
meats, especially full-flavoured
seafood such as salmon and tuna.

St George [B5] is the inland fishing

capital of Queensland, the Balonne River
yielding Murray cod and
yellowbelly. An ancient rock
well, hand-carved by Aborigines and
thought to be thousands of years old, lies
37 km east of town. The plaque beside the
Balonne River on the western side of the
town explains how the town got its name:
'At this spot on St George's Day—April 23,
1846—Sir Thomas Mitchell crossed
the Balonne and established
a camp calling the crossing
St Georges Bridge. This was the
GAZETTEER origin of the town St George.'
The town is also home to Rosehill
Aviaries, the largest privately owned aviary
in Australia. It has more than 600 birds in
more than 80 aviaries. There
are also many other species
of Australian animal.

Thargomindah's [B2] artesian

bore, 2 km out of town on the Noccundra
Road, was drilled in 1891. By 1893,
having drilled to a depth of 795 m,
the water came to the surface, the
town then successfully attempting a unique
experiment. The pressure of the bore water
was used to drive a generator that supplied
the town's electricity. This was Australia's
first hydro-electricity scheme, and the
Bulletin magazine put Thargomindah right
up there with London and Paris, calling it
one of the three great centres of
electricity in the world. The system
operated until 1951 and the bore still
provides the town's water supply. The GAZETTEER
water reaches the surface at 84°C. In
1908, when the local Methodist church
was sheeted with cane grass, the local
goats ate the church's walls, leaving only
the roof and the front door intact.

Diary of Events

Town	Event	Date	Contact
Charleville	Great Matilda Camel Races and Festival	August	07 4654 2102
Eromanga	Camp Draft and Rodeo	April	07 4656 1133
Eulo	World Lizard Racing Championships	late Aug–early Sept	07 4655 2481
Quilpie	Kangaranga Do	September	07 4656 2166
	Quilpie Show	September	07 4656 1133
Roma	Picnic Races	March	07 4622 1416
Yowah	Opal Festival	July	1800 247 966

Snack with Snaith on the road.

Pack up the back of the car with Snaith clear plastic bins and go see Australia.

The see-through plastic bins are perfect for storing food for picnics, clothing and camping equipment you need to find fast. The bins are strong and durable, chemical and water resistant with 'clip lock' lids.

They are convenient, secure and portable and come in two ranges, 'HURO' clear, and 'Classique Collection' tint blue. Available at selected supermarkets, hardware and department stores.

Classique Collection
Superior Designed Products

SNAITH INDUSTRIES PTY LTD
32 Queen Street, Revesby NSW 2212
Ph: 02 9772 1211 Email: office@snaith.com.au

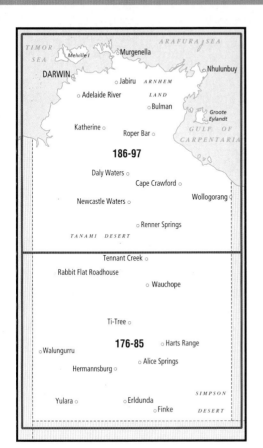

It is in the Northern Territory that the great Australian contrasts are most evident. In the Top End, the capital of Darwin shares the tropical climate with ancient rainforest remnants and the majestic rock formations of Kakadu National Park. The lush Top End adjoins the harsh desert environment of the Red Centre where sits the most famous of all Australian icons, Uluru (Ayers Rock) and the neighbouring Kata Tjuta (the Olgas).

NT

northern territory

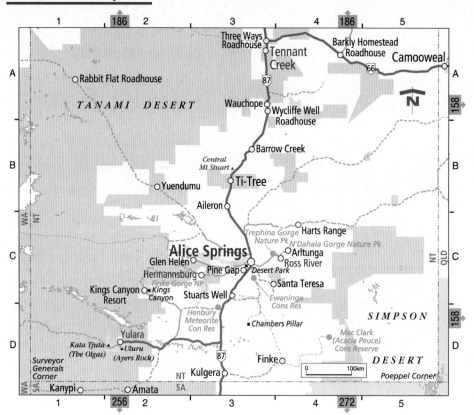

The Red Centre is the site of Australia's most famous landmark, Uluru. Surrounding it is a vast red desert and the major Outback town of Alice Springs, which balances its early pioneering history with its current status as a major tourist centre.

get off the beaten track

roam
the red centre

Aileron's [B3] roadhouse on the Stuart Highway features a selection of historic photographs on the walls. It also boasts a collection of original paintings by renowned Aboriginal artist Albert Namatjira.

The **Alice Springs** [C3] repeater station, built in 1872, marks the site of the

first European settlement in Central Australia. The station closed its telegraphic operations in 1932, when it became for a time a home for Aboriginal children. Now an important heritage site, it is open for inspection for a small fee. (The Telegraph Station Historical Reserve is just north of Alice Springs.) The station, largely built of local stone, includes the postmaster's residence, an observatory and storeroom, the telegraph room and barracks, and the original blacksmith's forge. One of Australia's newest walking tracks opened in April 2002. The **Larapinta Trail**, built by Aboriginal workers from Arrernte Council and Tjuwanpa Outstation Resource Centre, extends for 250 km, taking trekkers from the Telegraph Station west to Mount Sonder in the MacDonnell Ranges.

Adelaide House in Todd Mall, designed and built by John Flynn, was the first Alice Springs Hospital. The idea for a hospital was originally suggested by Sister Finlayson, who arrived in the Centre in 1915 and was horrified to find that seriously sick patients had to be transferred by cart or wagon to Oodnadatta, more than 600 km away. Built between 1920 and 1926, the hospital employed a unique cooling system that combined air tunnels with wet hessian—making the whole hospital a kind of huge Coolgardie safe. The walls are nearly 45 cm thick. Around the back is the stone **Radio Hut** where Alfred Traeger (the South Australian inventor who devised the famous pedal wireless, powered by turning a pair of

NT

KANGAROO MEDALLIONS WITH MARMALADE GLAZE

Tip for travellers: If you hear the phrase, 'He's got kangaroos loose in the top paddock,' don't offer to run out and help round them up. This is Australian slang inferring that a person is intellectually inadequate.

4 kangaroo fillet steaks,
** or 8 if small, trimmed**
cracked pepper
olive oil
1 cup white wine
2 tbsp marmalade
1 tbsp wholegrain mustard

Season steaks well with pepper and quickly cook in a hot pan with a little olive oil until browned on both sides. Allow to rest in a warm place while preparing sauce. Deglaze pan with wine, add marmalade and mustard and reduce to about half to concentrate flavours. Pour glaze over meat and serve with potato mash and wilted spinach. Serves 4.

Janet Todd, TERRITORY TRAVELLER

bicycle pedals) and John Flynn made their first field radio transmission in 1926. It was also the site of the first field radio telegram transmission in Australia. Today Adelaide House has an interesting photographic display of the early history of the Centre.

Alice's **Araluen Art Centre**, worth a visit in itself for the beautiful stained glass work, hosts a Beanie Competition and Festival. Hand-made beanies have long been valued in Central Australia as a necessity of crisp, cold winter nights. Every year in the last week of June beanie enthusiasts gather to admire the latest handiworks, giving the Centre a national (if

RED CENTRE EMERGENCY CRAB SOUP

This is a delicious and easy recipe, ideal for campers or caravan travellers.

- **1 x 410 g tin tomato soup**
- **1 x 210 g tin crab meat, drained**
- **1/2 tsp dried marjoram leaves, or herb of choice**
- **salt and pepper to taste**
- **1/4 cup cream, optional**

Prepare soup according to directions on tin using milk, not water, as the liquid. When heated through add crab meat and marjoram. Add salt and pepper and swirl through cream, if desired, and serve. Serves 3–4.

Janet Todd, TERRITORY TRAVELLER

not international) reputation for the production of quirky beanies.

The **Aviation Museum**, on the corner of Larapinta and Memorial Drive, holds what remains of the *Kookaburra*, a light plane that went down in the desert while searching for Charles Kingsford Smith in 1929. The famous aviator was on the first leg of a round-the-world flight in his plane, the *Southern Cross*, flying from Sydney to London, when he hit bad weather on the Kimberley coast and was forced to land. While he waited near fresh water, two associates flew in the *Kookaburra* from Sydney to look for him. They hit trouble over the Tanami Desert and made an emergency landing but, without food and very little water, they died within three days. When Kingsford Smith was rescued and returned to civilisation looking none the worse for wear, sceptics believed the whole thing had been a publicity stunt.

DON'T MISS: South of Alice (11 km south of Heavitree Gap on Petrick Road) is **Chateau Hornsby**, Central Australia's only winery. Because of the heat, the grapes ripen early. As a result, this is where Australia's first grapes are picked every year and where, therefore, Australia's vintage begins. Enjoy a jazz combo with the locals on a Sunday lunchtime in cooler months or evenings in summer. The winery also hosts concerts, festivals and bush dances. Spinifex Balloons takes passengers for a ride in a hot-air balloon, finishing with breakfast at the winery each day.

The **Desert Park**, 7 km west of Alice Springs on Larapinta Drive, is the world's first bio park, a re-creation of three of Australia's desert habitats and of the evolution of the indigenous people and the native plant and animal species that have adapted themselves

to it. It illustrates the dry desert; desert with minimal water; and mostly dry desert (subject to flash flooding). It was designed for environmental research, education and conservation, particularly of the flora and fauna that face extinction. On the way there, stop off at the **Reverend John Flynn Memorial** (2 km closer to town). Having established the Inland Mission and the Royal Flying Doctor Service, Flynn died in 1951 and is buried at the foothills of Mt Gillen. His grave was marked by one of the Devils Marbles, from near Wauchope. When the Marble was moved it upset the Aboriginal custodians so greatly that it has since been returned to its original place. The Arrernte people, from the Alice Springs area, have replaced it with a sacred stone of their own.

In the **Old Pioneer Cemetery** in Alice Springs there is a dramatic gravestone depicting a wizened old miner panning for gold. This is the grave of Harold Lasseter, a quixotic adventurer who believed he had found vast reefs of gold in Central Australia. During the Depression he persuaded people to fund an expedition there, but it went seriously wrong and he died in what is now the Petermann Aboriginal Land Trust, south-west of Alice Springs (beyond Uluru). His body was found by Aboriginal trackers and buried nearby. It was exhumed and interred in the Alice Springs cemetery in 1958. The graveyard is also the final resting place of distinguished Aboriginal painter Albert Namatjira, who died in the Alice Springs Hospital in 1959.

Panorama Guth, in Hartley Street, is a 360-degree painting 6 m high and 60 m in

Alice Springs' hot, dry climate is ideal for growing dates. In fact date palms date back to the days when the Afghan cameleers apparently introduced them. The best place to sample the local product is at Bruce Cotterill and Liz Martin's Date Gardens, 74 Palm Circuit. Here you can tuck into 'Datevonshire Teas'. Try your luck with date scones, muffins, rum and date chocolate ice-creams and more.

diameter, featuring many of the sights of Central Australia. Dutch-born Artist Henk Guth got the idea for the painting from an 1880 seascape in The Hague, Holland. It is a circular painting on canvas to be viewed from a platform, giving the impression of a lookout. Foundations for Guth's painting were laid in 1973 and the completed canvas, consisting of 33 pieces of Irish linen held together with aluminium strips, was hung in 1975.

DON'T MISS: In September Alice Springs hosts the internationally famous Henley-on-Todd Regatta. A 'boat race' for bottomless boats whose crews carry their boats as they run along the dry bed of the Todd River, this is an amusing desert diversion—except when, as has happened twice recently, it is cancelled because of flooding. The town also hosts the annual Camel Cup in July—and it really is a race for camels. Call 08 8952 5800 for futher details. Also featured is a game called 'pocamelo' or camel polo.

NT

Arltunga

[C4] was officially Central Australia's first town, born out of the gold rush of 1887. Today you can visit the Historical Reserve to see the remains of the mines, old miners' camps and stone buildings. The 'loneliest pub in the scrub', Arltunga Hotel, offers a real 'back-of-beyond' experience. The road is only sealed for the first 76 km.

Barrow Creek

[B3] was named after a preacher, John Henry Barrow, who had the temerity to refuse booze to explorer John McDouall Stuart, who worked up a thirst while trying to open up a route from Adelaide to Darwin. The scarce local water was almost undrinkable. You can visit the Telegraph Station and read up on some of the harrowing events of the laying of the line between Adelaide and Darwin.

Central Mount Stuart

[B3] is a small hill generally considered to be the geographical centre of Australia, an opinion first promulgated by Stuart himself. He named it after his old friend and expedition leader Sturt, and the 'a' was added later to honour Stuart himself. It is a few kilometres off the Stuart Highway in the Central Mount Stuart Historical Reserve, on the edge of the Tanami Desert. In 1988, less romantically, but perhaps more accurately, the Royal Geographical Society of Australasia set out to confirm the geographical centre of Australia. According to the Society, it is 126 km east of **Kulgera**, near the South Australian border. The place was named Lambert Centre, after Bruce Lambert, a surveyor and the first head of the National Mapping Council.

The Ewaninga

[C3] Rock Carvings Reserve contains some of the most interesting and impressive Aboriginal rock carvings in the Northern Territory. It is not known how old the engravings are but they are heavily weathered, suggesting that they are many thousands of years old. The most common markings are abstract designs of circles, spirals and wavy lines.

Finke

[D4] Desert Race brings thousands of competitors and spectators to this small community on the Old Ghan railway line. It started in 1976 when a group of local motorbike riders challenged each other to race from Alice Springs to Finke and back. After the success of the initial ride, the Finke Desert Race was born and it has been held annually on the Queen's Birthday weekend in June ever since. Originally only bikes competed but, as its popularity increased, cars and off-road buggies were introduced. **The Finke Gorge National Park** contains the world's only naturally occurring red cabbage palms, in the Palm Valley oasis. A 4WD route (for the very experienced only) leads through the eastern section of the park and follows the Finke River south to a major permanent waterhole named Boggy Hole. The road beyond this point is impassable. East of Finke is the **Mac Clark Conservation Reserve**. On the edge of the Simpson Desert near Old Andado Station, it is 340 km by 4WD road south-east of Alice Springs (impassable after heavy rain). The reserve protects an extremely rare tree, the *Acacia peuce* (waddywood). In dry years this tree may not grow at all, waiting for a shower to allow it to add a millimetre or so to its height, which can eventually reach 17 m. Its wood is so hard it won't take nails. The trees stand away from each other, and other plants. Access is by private property, so be sure to leave roads and gates as you find them.

GAZETTEER

REDGUM SMOKED BARRAMUNDI

Kuniya Restaurant at Ayers Rock Resort provides visitors to the Red Centre an opportunity to experience the tastes of traditional Australian ingredients in a sophisticated environment. This barramundi dish is served on smashed pink-eye potatoes with a wild thyme and caviar emulsion sauce.

- **4 barramundi fillets, approx. 200 g each, trimmed**
- **500 g pink-eye potatoes, peeled and cut into pieces**
- **2 tbsp lemon juice**
- **4–5 tbsp olive oil**
- **1 tbsp wild thyme, chopped**
- **salt and pepper to taste**
- **1 coriander root, finely chopped**
- **2 garlic cloves, chopped**
- **1 red onion, sliced**
- **1 cup white wine**
- **1 cup fish stock**
- **1 cup fresh cream**
- **4 tbsp fresh salmon roe**
- **1 tbsp chives, chopped**

Lay fish fillets onto an oiled wire rack. Place redgum sawdust in base of an oven tray with rack and fish on top. Cover tray firmly with foil and place directly over a burning flame for 2 minutes. (A wok with sawdust in the base also works.) Remove from flame, stand for 1 hour then refrigerate. Boil potatoes until tender. Drain and half mash, adding lemon juice, olive oil, thyme, salt and pepper. Sweat off coriander root, garlic and onion in a little olive oil until soft. Deglaze pan with wine, reduce until syrupy. Add stock and cream, reduce until thick. Add salmon roe and blend in food processor. Strain and check seasoning. Pan-fry barramundi. To serve, top 2 tbsp potatoes with barramundi fillet. Spoon sauce over. Garnish with chopped chives. Serves 4.

Kaniya Restaurant, AYERS ROCK RESORT
Barra pic courtesy Discover Barra Safaris, Darwin

The spectacular **Glen Helen** [C3] Gorge was formed from quartzite when sandstone was deposited in the area some 500 million years ago. As it subsequently tilted and uplifted, the Finke River slowly eroded its way through the mountain range to shape the gorge. Nearby is the acclaimed Glen Helen Resort, nestling in the West MacDonnell Ranges.

The **Harts Range** [C4] Bush Weekend, held on the Picnic Day long weekend in August, includes a ute competition, various sports events and a bull-tail throwing competition, which involves throwing a bull's tail (apparently minus the bull but still quite heavy).

Hermannsburg [C3]

Aboriginal community was once a mission station and one of the first settlements built by Europeans for the indigenous community. Albert Namatjira, the first Aboriginal painter to be recognised internationally, was born in Hermannsburg in 1902 and lived there for several years. There is a memorial to him on Larapinta Drive. The

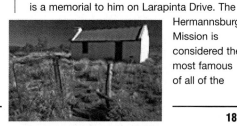

Hermannsburg Mission is considered the most famous of all the

CHAR-GRILLED KANGAROO

Kangaroo meat is now a staple on the Outback travellers' circuit, with many hotels and restaurants serving a multitude of gourmet variations. In this recipe the fillet is either char-grilled or pan-fried and served with a beetroot and turnip mash.

4 kangaroo fillets, trimmed (reserve trimmings)	1 carrot, finely chopped
3 medium beetroot, peeled	2 sticks celery, chopped
1 large pontiac potato, peeled and cut into pieces	2 cloves garlic, crushed
2 medium turnips, peeled and cut into pieces	1 tbsp tomato paste
olive oil	1 cup beef stock
1 onion, finely chopped	300 ml red wine
	salt and pepper to taste
	squeeze of lemon juice

Grill or pan-fry roo fillet to medium rare, keep warm in a low oven. Boil beetroot, potato and turnips until tender. Drain and mash with a little olive oil until smooth. Add salt and pepper if required. To make sauce, brown kangaroo trimmings with a little olive oil, add vegetables and tomato paste and cook for 10 minutes. Add stock and wine and reduce till thick. Add salt and pepper if needed, strain and add lemon juice. To serve, place mash in middle of plates with roo on top. Drizzle with sauce. Serves 4. Note: Substitute kangaroo fillets with beef if desired.

Hotel Novotel, DARWIN

religious missions. It was established in 1877 when two Lutheran missionaries from Germany made an overland trek from the Barossa Valley. From 1896, galvanised iron, stones from the nearby Finke River, mulga logs and lime-rendered sandstone were used to build a series of buildings—these are now classified by the National Trust and are open for viewing. The church is now a museum.

Kings Canyon [C2], within

Watarrka National Park, north of Uluru, is

Australia's deepest gorge, its walls rising 270 m. It's a 4WD to Kings Canyon from Alice Springs by the western route—along the Mereenie Loop Road (a permit is required, as some sections go through Aboriginal land). A conventional vehicle is fine via the Stuart Highway. You can also take a helicopter flight over the canyon, which provides an unequalled view of its attractions.

Pine Gap [C3] is a top secret

underground base located just south-west of Alice Springs (from the air Pine Gap's distinctive above-ground domes are quite visible). It is entirely financed by the US government. Although it is officially known as the Joint Defense Space Research Facility, very few people know what goes on there, including Australian Members of Parliament. The only Australians who are allowed to visit are executives on the National Security Committee and the base employees (many purportedly recruited through Australian newspaper ads for 'radio technicians'). Is it a satellite spy base or a centre for research on extra-terrestrials? It's anyone's guess.

Rabbit Flat [A1] features on most

maps of Australia, not because it is a major urban centre—it usually has a population of three or four—but because there is nothing else in the area to put on the map. Rabbit Flat Roadhouse, which is only open from Friday to Monday (7 am–9 pm), has the almost certainly deserved reputation of being the most isolated pub in Australia. It is on the Tanami Track, a dirt road of dubious quality that crosses the Tanami Desert from Alice Springs to Halls Creek in Western Australia. The first 145 km is sealed but, as nearly 1,000 km are not, conditions can vary, especially west of Yuendumu. In summer the road may be closed due to rain. Always be well provisioned as services are extremely limited. Once you're off the tar and in the desert, the only other stops along the way, apart from Rabbit Flat, are the Yuendumu Aboriginal community and the Tilmouth Wells Roadhouse.

Near **Ross River** [C4] is **N'Dhala Gorge Nature Park**, containing some of Australia's oldest Aboriginal engravings, said to be 30,000 years old. Access to the gorge is strictly 4WD. The drive to Ross River from Alice Springs along the Ross Highway provides

spectacular scenery, with the East MacDonnell Ranges rising up on both sides of the road. Ross River Homestead provides simple accommodation and a restaurant, and features a small museum of relics. North of Ross River, in the **Trephina Gorge Nature Park**, lives Australia's rare black-flanked rock wallaby.

Santa Teresa [C4] started out as a

Catholic mission in 1953. It is an Eastern Arrernte community of about 500 people who have retained their traditional language and culture. Their colourful artworks on silk, terracotta, wood and paper can be seen (and purchased) at the Kerringke Arts Centre.

Stuarts Well [C3] is home to

Camels Australia (formerly Camel Outback Safaris). It is a holdover from the early history of Central Australia, and a kind of memorial to the 'Afghan' (many of them in fact from Pakistan) camel drivers who helped open up the wilderness with their camels. The farm is set in 3.6 ha of natural bushland at the foot of the James Ranges and offers camel rides and longer safaris for those

prepared to brave the swaying back of a camel. It's as close as most tourists will come to experiencing what early exploration of the area was really like. You can even take a camel to **Rainbow Valley**, a sandstone bluff named for the colours highlighted in the rocks at sunset. (If you don't want the camel ride, ask at Jim's Place at Stuarts Well for directions to the unmarked track.) Another 55 km south of Stuarts Well is **Henbury Meteorite Conservation Reserve**. It is the site of 12 meteorite craters that have left depressions in the ground. There is a clearly signposted track around the craters, the largest of which

is 180 m across and about 15 m deep. Scientists estimate that a meteorite made up of iron and nickel crashed into the area several thousand years ago. Each chunk would have been the size of a fuel drum, and the size of the craters will give you a good idea of the violence of the impacts. South-west of Stuarts Well, off the highway is **Chambers Pillar Historical Reserve**, on the edge of the Simpson Desert. Access is by 4WD vehicle only but it is worth it—there is a spectacular red and yellow 50 m sandstone outcrop here that was a vital landmark. The pillar has many engravings made by early explorers, including John Ross, who led the second expedition to cross the country in 1870. Alfred Giles followed two years later. Being old graffiti, these carvings are much valued. Should you contribute your own, modern equivalent you will face a substantial fine. Some miscreants have allegedly been tracked by the evidence of their own markings. It is a magical

place at sunset and dawn. There is a designated campground but it is essential to bring your own water and firewood.

Tennant Creek's [A3] Roman

Catholic Church of Christ the King (turn left off Paterson Street at Windley Street), was once the longest Catholic church in the world. In 1934 when Tennant Creek was declared a town, the church, which was built at Pine Creek in 1906, followed the movement of miners from Pine Creek to new diggings at Tennant Creek. At one point during the move the trucks were spread out along the track with one bogged and overturned at Daly Waters. The front door of the church was in Tennant Creek, the back door was in Pine

Creek and the side walls were scattered for several kilometres along the creek. The Church of Christ the King, in fact, was spread over an area of about 2,000 km. It was the first church to be built between Alice Springs and Katherine, and its unique use of telegraph poles, corrugated iron, Caneite and Masonite make it a rare, if eccentric and somewhat makeshift, example of early Australian architecture. Australia's last gold rush took place at Tennant Creek in the 1930s, with the town growing up around the diggings. The **Nobles Nob** mine, 16 km east of Tennant Creek, was once the Southern Hemisphere's largest open-cut pit and yielded some of the richest ore ever recovered. A recently opened mine continues Tennant Creek's gold mining heritage. One of the greatest of Tennant Creek's mines was Peko Mines, which became Peko Wallsend, then North Broken Hill Peko. Peko was the name of a local dog.

DON'T MISS: Nearby, the wonderfully named Kraut Downs Station (3.5 km south on the Stuart Highway) offers all sorts of Outback experiences including bush medicine, bush tucker (such as witchetty grubs), damper cooking and whip cracking. The station got its name when its German owner good-humouredly decided to adopt the graffiti locals had painted on the fence.

Three Ways Roadhouse

[A3] is a place desperately short of good press. Its only attraction, a monument to the Reverend John Flynn, the man who made the flying doctor a reality, is commonly considered one of the ugliest memorials in the universe.

Just north of **Wauchope** [A3] (about 10 km) are the Devils Marbles, a group of huge 1,700-million-year-old granite boulders precariously balanced one on the other. They form part of an Aboriginal sacred site.

Wycliffe Well [A3] boasts what is

alleged to be the largest selection of foreign beers in Australia. There are reputed to be 300 to choose from, as well as the pub's own home brew. This may explain why it also has the reputation as the UFO capital of the Northern Territory (the pub has a display of press clippings of reported sightings).

The **Yuendumu** [B2] Festival, a major celebration of sports and culture, is held over the August Picnic Day long weekend. While you're there you might bump into the stars of *Bush Mechanics*, an occasional but popular video broadcast on the ABC. Yuendumu's Walpiri Media Association and the Central Australian Aboriginal Media Association produced the program.

Yulara [D2] is a tourist resort 25 km from

Uluru (Ayers Rock), designed to blend in with the environment, including being powered by the sun. Uluru–Kata Tjuta National Park's 1,260 sq km is jointly run by Anangu, the local Aboriginal people, and Environment Australia. Within the park are two of Australia's most extraordinary landmarks, Kata Tjuta and Uluru. It is World Heritage listed for both its natural and cultural values. Uluru itself is perhaps Australia's most readily identifiable landmark. It is a 600-million-year-old bornhardt—a dome-shaped or rounded rock or rock outcrop generally found in the tropics—but it is far from being the biggest rock in existence. It measures 9.4 km around and 348 m high. The traditional owners of Uluru, the Pitjantjatjara and Yankunytjatjara people, request that you don't climb Uluru. What visitors call the 'climb' is the traditional route taken by ancestral Mala men on their arrival at Uluru and is therefore of great spiritual significance. Anangu also feel a huge sense of responsibility for looking after visitors on their land and feel a great sadness when a person dies or is hurt in a fall. **Kata Tjuta** (the Olgas) is linked to the Rock and the Yulara resort by a tarred road. Walking in the red stone gorges of Kata Tjuta can be very rewarding.

DON'T MISS: In the early evening, the Sunset Viewing Area facing Uluru fills with tourists admiring the colour changes that may play over the rock face, depending on the light. It's an unforgettable experience.

Diary of Events

Town	Event	Date	Contact
Alice Springs	Henley-on-Todd Regatta	September	08 8592 3040
	Camel Cup	July, 2nd Saturday	08 8952 5800
Araluen Centre	Beanie Festival	June, last week	08 8592 2615
Finke	Desert Race	June, Queen's Birthday weekend	08 8592 8886 or 0419 866 938
Yuendumu	Sports and Culture Festival	August	08 8951 6211

NT

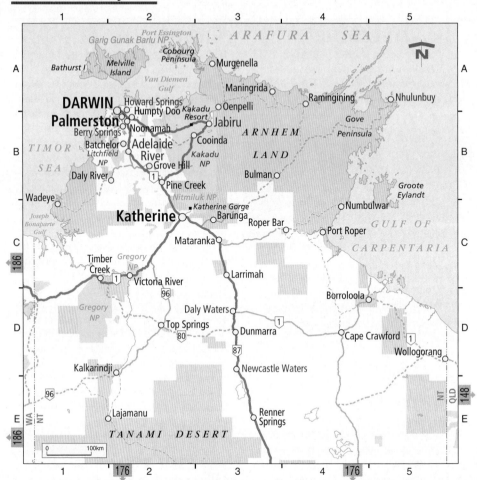

The Northern Territory's Top End is an adventure in itself, with vast untamed country, gorgeous waterfalls and unique plants and animals.

get off the beaten track

tour the top end

Adelaide River [B2] during

World War II was a major military centre for 80,000 Australian and US troops. The War Cemetery north of the town is the only one on Australian soil. In it rest the

bodies of 432 servicemen and 63 civilians, all of them killed during Japanese bombing raids. At that time there were 60 airfields and 35 hospitals on the Stuart Highway between Daly Waters and Darwin. More than 100,000 US servicemen were stationed along here. The Adelaide River

Races, in the third week of June, give a great taste of a Territory race day. Adelaide River's other main attraction is 60 km away but worth the effort if you want the opportunity to watch crocodiles being fed. Some of them are reputedly 6 m long. Call 08 8988 8144 for cruise

details. Further downstream, near its mouth, the Adelaide River offers excellent fishing for barramundi, black jewfish and delicious mud crabs. What many people don't know is that before the last big rise in sea levels, the Adelaide River continued its winding way 100 km further north-west, across what is now Beagle Gulf, and that the drowned valley of this ancient river today forms the Apsley Strait, dividing Bathurst and Melville Islands.

In Arnhem Land [B3–4], the

world's oldest evidence of the use of axes with ground-stone heads was found, along with the earliest evidence of Aboriginal occu-pation of northern Australia. Apart from a few mission stations and early (failed) attempts at pastoralism, white settlement in Arnhem Land was not permitted until the 1970s, when mining for bauxite was allowed by the federal government, with royalty payments to the traditional owners. The nation's third-largest bauxite mine is on the Gove Peninsula. Eastern Arnhem Land is one of the traditional centres of bark painting. Western Arnhem Land is the centre for rock art, most styles of

NT

MT BORRADAILE ART

The spectacularly scenic region of **Arnhem Land** geographically includes Kakadu National Park, which is visited by thousands of people each year and is renowned worldwide for its natural and cultural wonders. However, east of the park, there is an even wilder side of Arnhem Land. Known for more than a century as one of Australia's last frontiers (as it still is), Arnhem Land is Aboriginal country and apart from one town,

Nhulunbuy, visitors need special permission from the Aboriginal owners to enter the region. Call the Northern Land Council's toll-free number, 1800 645 299, or check the website: **www.nlc.org.au**, where there is a section called 'Visiting Aboriginal Land'. Here you can obtain the regional phone numbers or download a permit application form. People travelling together require only a single permit, issued to the nominated driver, with all passengers' names listed (each person will also have to sign the permit and agree to the conditions). It is a real privilege, though, to travel through this land, so respect for those conditions is paramount.

which can also be found in Kakadu National Park, such as at Nourlangie Rock. Some sites are thought to date back 60,000 years and longer, and can be seen via organised safari tours. Rock artists recorded evidence of earlier overseas visitors, the Macassans (from Ujung Pandang on what is now Sulawesi), and of the first European sailing ships.

Barunga's [C3] annual

sporting and cultural festival attracts hundreds of visitors every June on the Queen's Birthday weekend. At the festival in 1988, Australia's bicentennial year, then Prime Minister Bob Hawke received a painting, representing both Central Australian and Top End art styles, in which was set a proposed treaty between Aboriginal and non-Aboriginal Australians, the Barunga Statement. Barunga is in Jawoyn land and its residents include Mangarrar, Mora, Myilly, Ngarrbun and Rambarrnga people. The main languages spoken are Kriol and Jawoyn. Kriol (so called because it shares a hybrid structure with the Caribbean Creole) is a type of Aboriginal English but with variations depending on the language group of the speaker. It is spoken mainly in the Top End.

Batchelor [B2] used to be the main

town for the Rum Jungle uranium mine, which began mining in the 1950s and closed in 1963. This was the first time in Australia that uranium had been found and mined. The scar left by the open-cut mining process is now an artificial lake, after much rehabilitation. Rum Jungle got its name from some mishap involving teamsters taking rum to the miners at Pine Creek. They got bogged when crossing the east branch of the Finniss River and had no alternative but to polish off the rum. Take a look at the scale replica of a German castle in the town. From here you can take a bitumen road into the main area of Litchfield National Park.

Bathurst Island [A1] and

Melville Island together make up the Tiwi Islands, home of the Tiwi people, famous for their distinctive art including the Pukumani burial poles. The only way to see the Tiwi Islands is on an organised tour, allowing you to experience the traditional Tiwi culture by visiting the community arts and craft centres and a Tiwi burial site. The Tiwi people are also famous for their love of football (having produced such footy greats as Maurice Rioli), which started when a bag of rags was given to a boy on Bathurst Island in the 1930s. The Tiwi Island Football League organises games between Bathurst Island, Milikapiti and Pirlangimpi (Garden Point).

The Berry Springs [B2]

Territory Wildlife Park is a much-praised park showing the animals of Northern Australia in natural settings. Next door is Berry Springs Nature Park, which has a small thermal waterfall and pools for swimming.

GAZETTEER

Borroloola [D3] was once a hotspot
for bootleg booze—rum was smuggled in
from Thursday Island and sold to cattle
drovers working the Queensland–Kimberley
run. The town, situated just above
the normal flood level of the
McArthur River, is also the stepping-
off point for the Gulf Track, a 4WD route that
heads across the Gulf to Burketown and
Normanton in Queensland.

Bulman [B3] is an Aboriginal
community in Arnhem Land on the Mainoru
Road. Attractions include fishing, exploring
Weemol Station and enjoying
a soak in Weemol hot
springs. To visit, obtain a permit or join a tour.
The best months to visit are May to
November. Wongalara Safaris offers fishing
and walking tours of the nearby Wilton River.
For the adventurous, the company also runs
overnight canoeing trips down the Mainoru
and Wilton Rivers where you can camp under
the stars and have a go at catching your own
barramundi for dinner.

The Cape Crawford [D4]
roadhouse is called Heartbreak Hotel. From
here travellers go on to explore the
Bukalara Rock Formations and the Lost
City, a collection of sandstone turrets, domes
and arches formed by water seeping through
cracks in the sandstone. This is an important
Aboriginal ceremonial site only accessible by
helicopter and visitors must go with a guide.
From the hotel you can head north to **Roper
Bar**, via a 4WD route that passes
Nathan River homestead, soon to
be a conservation park protecting
an impressive display of Lost City type formations. The route also crosses a number of
rivers that make it impassable in the Wet.

Cooinda [B2], in Kakadu National
Park, is the gateway to **Yellow Water**, a large

CREAMY COCONUT AND JACKFRUIT RICE WITH MANGO

The Top End is the place to experience real
tropical fruit. Jackfruit is the world's largest
tree fruit and tastes like banana bubblegum.
It's just one example of the unusual varieties
grown by local farmers. At Bees Creek farm,
30 km south-east of Darwin, Chris Nathanael
grows all manner of odd fruits including
five-cornered carambolas and a cross-bred
'Northern Gold' guava. He suggested using
the highly nutritious green jackfruit for
this recipe.

**1 cup jasmine rice
1 can coconut milk
1/2 cup caster sugar
1 cup water
1/2 cup jackfruit, finely sliced
2 mangoes, peeled and diced
juice of 1 lime
1 tsp palm sugar
1 lime, quartered**

Combine rice, coconut milk,
sugar, water and jackfruit.
Bring to boil, then simmer
on low heat for 20
minutes (or until cooked),
stirring frequently to stop
sticking. Transfer mixture
to a lined 2 cm deep tray.
Cover and chill in fridge. Toss
mangoes with lime juice and
palm sugar. Cut coconut rice into four
squares. Arrange mango on squares with a
wedge of lime. Serves 4.

The Waterhole Restaurant, DARWIN

NT

QUEENFISH WITH LIME, CHILLI AND CORIANDER

After experiencing the fish-feeding frenzy at Larrakeyah you might feel in need of a feed yourself. Ask local suppliers for a queenfish, or 'queenie', as it is popularly called in the Northern Territory, and try this recipe, which is best eaten on the day of the catch.

1 large fresh queenfish, filleted, skinned and cut into thin strips across the fillet
juice of 10 limes
2 cloves garlic, minced
1 cup fresh coriander, chopped
1 tbsp coriander seed, crushed
1/2 cup caster sugar

Mix all ingredients together in a stainless steel bowl. Taste for seasoning and adjust if necessary. Pack together so all fish is covered. Refrigerate for one hour before use. Serve with crisp greens and jasmine rice. Serves 2–3.

The Waterhole Restaurant, DARWIN

billabong that joins with Jim Jim Creek and the South Alligator River. Crocodiles and an abundance of birdlife inhabit the paperbark forests, pandanus, freshwater mangroves and tropical vegetation. Catch a shuttle bus from Gagudju Lodge in Cooinda to Yellow Water to connect with the renowned Yellow Water Cruises. At the turtle-shaped Warradjan Cultural Centre, 1 km south of Cooinda, there are cultural displays and arts and crafts are on sale.

Daly River [B2] Mango Farm has the

perfect camping site under a shade canopy created by a grove of huge 83-year-old mango trees. As well as camping, it provides accom-

modation, boat hire, fishing and bush walks. The property may be closed during the wet season but is accessible by conventional vehicle in the Dry.

Daly Waters [D3] boasts Australia's

oldest international airport. The town, originally built to provide a repeater station for the Overland Telegraph, became a vital refuelling stop during Australia's early aviation history. From its time as a stopover for Qantas flights during the 1930s, Daly Waters graduated to refuelling fighters and bombers en route to the battle zones of South-east Asia during World War II. The airfield was closed in the 1970s, when long-haul flights no longer needed to touch down. On the way into town (the actual town of Daly Waters is 3.5 km west of the Stuart Highway) is the Stuart Tree. This remarkably dead-looking tree has a plaque that reads: 'The explorer John McDouall Stuart is presumed to have carved the initial S on this tree on 23 May 1862 during his successful journey from Adelaide to Darwin 1861–62. Erected by the Northern Territory Forces in 1944.' If you look long and hard you can see a vague 'S' on the eastern side of the tree. Within 10 years of Stuart's exploits the Overland Telegraph line had been put up and Australia was connected to the rest of the world by wire.

DON'T MISS: The Daly Waters Pub was built in 1930 and is now one of the oldest buildings in the Northern Territory. Daly

Waters was a busy crossroads, an important stop for people travelling between north and south and for drovers moving cattle across from the Kimberley to Queensland.

Darwin's [A2] harbourside suburb of

Larrakeyah, with its daily fish-feeding
spectacle, is an essential part of a trip to
the city. Owned and
operated by a former
Chief Minister of the
Territory, Aquascene
Doctors Gully has been
attracting thousands of
visitors for well over
twenty years. For a
modest cost, you can
hand-feed bread to
massive milkfish and
diamond scale mullet

measuring up to a metre in length.
Session times vary with the tides, so
check for current details before you go
(08 8981 7837). **Mindil Beach**, not far from
the centre of Darwin, is the site of the Beer
Can Regatta every August. The racing boats

are made
entirely of beer
cans, which are
in plentiful
supply because
Darwin drinks
more beer per
capita than any
other place in
Australia.
Mindil Beach

Markets are on the 'don't miss' list in the dry
season (around April to September), on
Thursday and Sunday evenings. About
60 stalls offer a wide variety of different foods
including tropical vegetables, herbs, spices,
fruits, ices, steamed mud crab, Arafura
prawns, grilled barra, crocodile, buffalo and

green pawpaw salad.
Hire a table and chair
and tuck in on the
nearby grass.
Phone 08 8981 3454
or 0414 646 543.

Dunmarra [D3] is best known for the

monument to the Overland Telegraph Line—
beside the Stuart Highway 27 km south of
town. It has three poles in the style of the
original line. The plaque reads: 'The northern
and southern parts of this epic overland
telegraph line were finally joined about one
mile west of this spot by RC Paterson,
engineer, at 3.15 pm on Thursday August 22,
1872 thus making possible for the first time
instantaneous telegraph communication
between Australia and Great Britain.' Just
north of the roadhouse the modern
day equivalent of the famous Murranji
stock route heads west in the form of the
Buchanan Highway—a sandy 4WD affair that
leads to **Top Springs** (purely a roadhouse).

Gove [A4], or more correctly

Nhulunbuy, the modern mining town

GAZETTEER

situated on the Gove Peninsula in the
far north-east of Arnhem Land, is
slowly opening its doors to travellers. While
most fly in, a permit can be obtained from
the Northern Land Council to travel
the Central Arnhem Road to the town.
It's a good 4WD trip that's not too difficult
outside the wet season. Nhulunbuy offers
accommodation, some fantastic
beaches and great fishing. Just
40 km south of Nhulunbuy is Gulkula, the site
of the Garma Festival, one of Australia's most
significant indigenous events. Gulkula is
set in a stringybark forest with views
to the Gulf of Carpentaria. Here,
according to Aboriginal lore, the ancestor
Ganbulabula brought the yidaki (didjeridu)
into being among the Gumatj people (from
north-eastern Arnhem Land). Garma is a
celebration of the Yolngu (people of central
and eastern Arnhem Land) cultural inheri-
tance. The festival is designed to celebrate
and share traditional practices of dance,
song, art and ceremony. Events often
continue late into the night and may include

NT

live bands, workshops on fire making and spear throwing. Guests are invited to learn, observe and participate in some of the activities. World Expeditions can arrange your attendance at the festival including permits, camping, meals and airport transfers. Call 1300 720 000 for details.

The bush pub at **Grove Hill** [B2] is so authentic it's listed on the National Estate. Now named the Grove Hill Licensed Heritage Hotel and Museum, it was built in 1934 of corrugated iron in the middle of the goldfields to cater for thirsty prospectors.

Howard Springs [A2], less

than half an hour's drive east of Darwin (about 30 km), is well worth a visit. It's one of the few safe, crocodile-free places to take a freshwater dip close to town, and the rainforest sanctuary makes a wonderful backdrop for hand-feeding the waterhole's 'tame' barramundi (some of them more than 20 kg) and long-necked turtles.

The **Humpty Doo** [A2] Uniting

Church (turn off the Arnhem Highway in Humpty Doo at the sign that says 'Church') is an unusual open-air construction without walls. Nearby is **Fogg Dam**, a waterbird haven originally built to supply a huge irrigation project. Intended to produce large quantities of rice, it failed at least partly because the waterbirds kept eating the seedlings. Now they have the dam all to themselves.

Jabiru [B3] is one of four

major mining centres in the Northern Territory and devoted to servicing the Ranger Uranium Mine. The town was built in 1981 on a 13 sq km lease within Kakadu

National Park, and its services were designed to limit the town's impact on the park itself. It was named after Australia's only native stork. The Gagudju Crocodile Holiday Inn in Jabiru is a 250 m long crocodile-shaped building partly owned by the Gagudju people, whose totem is the crocodile and who approved the design.

Kakadu [B3] National Park is

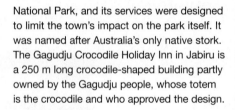

Australia's largest national park, covering 20,000 sq km of the Top End. The park protects one of the most ecologically diverse regions in the country. It has been given a World Heritage listing to protect its magnificent scenery, from the harsh plateau catchment area to the wetlands below, and the enormous variety of plants and animals that thrive there. The rock art of Kakadu produced through at least 50,000 years of Aboriginal presence rivals, and often surpasses, the importance of the paleolithic art sites of France and Spain. The rich mineral reserves in Kakadu have meant there is an ongoing battle between miners and environmentalists

as to whose interests should take precedence. The only mining activity currently taking place is at the Ranger Uranium Mine, but other leases exist at Jabiluka and Koongarra. So avid is the interest in Kakadu that the Ranger Uranium Mine is often described as the most regulated and scrutinised mine in the world. Apart from its many other attractions, Kakadu offers the opportunity to camp out in almost prehistoric wilderness at several sites. The best is probably the camp ground just below Jim Jim Falls, but there are several others (4WD tours out of Darwin will take you there).

WILD RICE PANCAKES FILLED WITH GREEN PAPAYA SALAD

Pick up a papaya (known as pawpaw by most Australians) at Parap Village Market, one of Darwin's longest running markets and a meeting place for locals every Saturday between 7.30 am and 1 pm. Being high in vitamins A, B complex and C, papaya is a great hangover cure and this recipe might provide the perfect kickstart to your day. (You can also buy prepared papaya salad at many of the stalls, prepared to your taste while you wait.)

PANCAKES

1 tbsp olive oil
1 tbsp ginger, grated
1 fresh chilli, finely chopped
6 eggs
3 cups cold water
6 tbsp melted butter
1¹/₂ cups plain flour
¹/₂ teaspoon baking powder
1 cup wild rice, cooked
soy sauce and pepper to taste
fresh coriander, for garnish

GREEN PAPAYA SALAD

1 green papaya, peeled, seeded and finely shredded
1 carrot, finely shredded
1 cup shredded coriander
2 cloves garlic, minced
1 chilli, minced
2 tsp brown sugar
¹/₄ cup fresh coconut, grated
1 tbsp vinegar

For pancakes, sauté ginger and chilli in olive oil, then allow to cool. In a bowl, combine eggs, water and butter with flour and baking powder. Mix to a smooth batter. Combine ginger, chilli and rice with batter and add soy sauce and pepper to season. Precook pancakes and put aside for salad filling. To make salad, combine all ingredients, squeezing together firmly. To serve, lightly reheat pancakes, place on serving plate and half fill with salad. Fold over and serve with fresh coriander. Serves 4–6.

The Waterhole Restaurant, DARWIN

DON'T MISS: The Ubirr rock art gallery offers one of the best displays of Aboriginal rock paintings available to the public anywhere in Australia. It has five art sites on public display, including some of the finest examples of X-ray art in the world. The paintings of barramundi at the main gallery are widely recognised as masterpieces of this style. X-ray art is fascinating

GAZETTEER

because the artist not only paints what he can see from the outside but also depicts what he knows exists on the inside. The gallery includes a painting of a pipe-smoking European whose body is X-rayed through his clothing. Scientific investigation of occupation deposits in this region has yielded some of the oldest evidence of man's presence in Northern Australia, with dates in the order of 23,000 years ago.

Kalkarindji [D2] is 478 km south-west of Katherine along the Buntine Highway. Once called Wave Hill Station, founded in

1883, it is now better known as the place where the Northern Territory land rights movement began (though an unsuccessful petition for land ownership was served by the Yirrkala people in 1963). In 1966 the Gurindji Aborigines who were working on the station, and being paid a pittance, walked off the job and laid claim to the land. They did not achieve their wish until 1975, when Gough Whitlam's Labor government handed over 3,200 sq km of Wave Hill land.

Katherine [C2] was founded at

Knotts Crossing (the town has since been moved), where the Overland Telegraph crossed the river. Springvale Homestead, built in 1878, is the oldest remaining homestead in the Territory. Have a look near the old gallon store, so called because the owners were licensed to sell alcohol by the gallon: a bomb crater is still visible, a reminder of the time in 1942 when a Japanese fighter plane attacked the town, killing one person. The RAAF's 75 Squadron is now based out at the Tindal Air Base, a major tactical fighter base, about 20 km south-east of town. Katherine's Cycad Gardens feature stands of these unimaginably ancient plants, dating back before the time of the dinosaurs. Southern states have flea markets; the Top End has tick markets (fleas don't thrive up here, though ticks do). Open on the first Saturday each month April to December, 5 pm until 8.30 pm, the Tick Markets sell crafts, clothing, food and other

assorted produce and put on live entertainment. **Cutta Cutta Nature Park** is 27 km

  south-east of Katherine; its caves are famous for their orange horseshoe and ghost

bats. The former is now near extinction.

DON'T MISS: Nitmiluk (Cicada Dreaming) National Park was previously called Katherine Gorge. It is an ancient river system cut through sandstone that is some 1,650 million years old. The gorge is a major tourist destination.

The **Larrimah** [C3] Hotel was originally the pub at Birdum (once the terminus of a railway line from Darwin) but was moved to Larrimah in 1952. The Gorrie Airstrip, one of the longest dirt airstrips in Australia and formerly the largest army base in Australia during WWII, is 3 km west along a dirt road.

Litchfield [B1] National Park is

the place to go if you've ever wanted to bathe under a waterfall, in the style of a shipwrecked Hollywood starlet.

GAZETTEER There are several opportunities to indulge in this harmless vice. There are said to be a 'few' crocodiles about ... There's an interesting 4WD trip south from the more tourist areas of the park to the old Blyth Homestead. Push on a little further and you'll get to Sandy Creek Falls, a delightful and quiet swimming spot. If you want to spend longer in 4WD mode continue heading south and you'll reach the bitumen Daly River Road after another 33 km.

Maningrida [A3] is an Aboriginal

community lying on the estuary of the Liverpool River, on the Arnhem Land coast. The Kunibidji people are the traditional land-owners of this country. The name Maningrida is an Anglicised version of Manayingkarirra, which comes from the phrase 'Mane djang karirra', meaning 'the place where the dreaming changed shape'. Maningrida Arts and Culture is one of Australia's largest community-based Aboriginal arts coopera-tives, servicing over 350 artists.

Mataranka [C3] is near the

former site of the 5,062 sq km **Elsey Station**, the subject of Jeannie Gunn's enormously popular semi-autobiographical novel *We of the Never-Never*. A sign on the Stuart Highway, about 10 km south of the town, points to the Elsey Cemetery and National Park located another 5 km to the east. The cemetery contains the remains of Aeneas James Gunn, who died on 16 March 1902 of malarial dysentery, only 13 months after he had moved to the area with his wife, Jeannie, who then returned to live in

Melbourne. Next to his grave is a memorial to Jeannie, which reads 'In loving Memory of the "Little Missus".' She died on 9 June 1961, having outlived her husband by nearly half a century. Mataranka also has what is believed to be the world's largest termite mound (at almost 5 m) and is also the site of a beautiful thermal pool.

Newcastle Waters [D3] is

a large cattle station first established as a repeater station for the Overland Telegraph in 1870 and taken over as a pastoral lease by the early 1880s. The town is now classified on the Heritage Trust of Significant Places for

ROPER RIVER BARRAMUNDI IN WINE SAUCE

Barramundi fishing at Roper Bar was once a well-kept secret by the locals. Today, however, the secret is well and truly out and the area now attracts many visitors who have heard about the legendary barramundi.

6 barramundi fillets
1 cup white wine
2 tbsp lemon juice
2 egg yolks
1 cup cream
1 tbsp chopped parsley
salt and pepper to taste
lemon slices

Poach barramundi fillets in wine and lemon juice over medium heat until tender. Remove fish and keep warm in a low oven (150°C). In a saucepan, heat wine in which fish has been cooked and boil for a further 5 minutes, to reduce. In a bowl, beat egg yolks and cream together. Pour into wine mixture, stirring constantly. Gently heat through, but do not boil. Add parsley, salt and pepper and pour over fish on warmed serving plates. Garnish with lemon slices.
Serves 6.

Maryanne Lewis,
MATARANKA

NT

its historic value. One of the oldest buildings is Jones Store, which sold stores to drovers moving cattle on the historic Murranji, Barkly and north–south stock routes. The Junction Hotel was built in 1930 out of scraps of old windmills by men who owed the publican money, as a form of repayment.

Numbulwar [C4] is an Aboriginal

community of about 1,000 people at the mouth of the Rose River. Traditional crafts are still taught at the local school and are part of everyday life, the women weaving mats and string bags from pandanus leaves and men making fishing spears and didjeridus. Ceremonies are held regularly in the community and, except for sacred men's ceremonies, non-Aboriginal people are welcome to watch. Visitors require a permit from the Northern Land Council. Note: the community is not accessible by road during the wet season— generally October till March.

Also known as Gunbalanya, **Oenpelli** [A3] is an Aboriginal community. Artists from this region are represented in every major collection of Aboriginal artwork. Their work is distinguished by the bold use of black, red, white and yellow. To get a feel for it, visit the Injalak Arts and Crafts Centre. Visitors should either obtain a permit or join a tour group.

Palmerston [B2], one of Australia's

newest cities, was established in 1981 as a satellite to Darwin. In August 2000, when the population reached 23,000, Palmerston was officially declared a city.

Pine Creek's [B2] National Trust

Museum, in the 1873 Pine Creek Repeater Station, has excellent displays about goldmining and the Chinese in the area. There are interesting displays of old bottles, Chinese artefacts and local rocks, including a piece of yellow cake (uranium ore), and some superb

shrimp fossils. Pine Creek is undergoing a resurgence as goldmining has begun again. On the edges of town are giant termite mounds, a feature of the area.

Port Essington [A2], at the tip

of Cobourg Peninsula, was the site of the last of three early attempts at European settlement of what is now the Northern Territory. Victoria settlement began in 1838, with 24 cottages and a hospital established, but the adverse conditions saw the settlement fold in 1849. British scientist Thomas Huxley passed through Victoria just before it closed, recording that Port Essington was 'most wretched, the climate the most unhealthy, the human beings the most uncomfortable and houses in a condition most decayed and rotten'. However, it must have been a welcome sight to the haggard and bedraggled Ludwig Leichhardt, who arrived at the settlement on 17 December 1845, having travelled more than 4,800 km overland from Moreton Bay on the east coast. All that remains today is a collection of more or less fascinating ruins. Access to the **Garig Gunak Barlu** (formerly Gurig) **National Park** is via a long 4WD track that heads north from Jabiru via **Oenpelli** and **Murgenella** (permit required). Camping is allowed near Black Point where a tour of the Victoria settlement can be arranged. There's some great fishing in the area.

At **Ramingining** [A3] you can visit the Bulabula Arts Centre to see the work of many local Aboriginal artists or go further afield by taking a tour with Didgeri Air Art Tours by air and 4WD.

Timber Creek [C1] offers a truly

remote outback experience in one of the last relatively untouched places in the Territory, featuring spectacular red escarpments and semi-arid vegetation.

The **Victoria River** [C2], or 'the Vic', as it's better known to most locals, is one of the very best places in the Top End to try your luck at catching a seriously big barramundi. Every year, barra over 20 kg are hauled from this broad, muddy river, mostly by boat anglers trolling brightly hued, deep-diving lures with colourful names such as 'Elton John', 'The Terminator' and 'Priscilla'. West of here you have the opportunity to experience some really wild country by following the Bullita stock route. This 4WD track takes you through the western portion of the **Gregory National Park**, which features some of the most spectacular and rugged escarpment country in Australia. Victoria River Downs, south of Victoria River Roadhouse and next to Gregory National Park, was once the largest cattle station in the world. It is now less than half its original size. The Victoria River District is home to some of the most significant Aboriginal cave paintings in Northern Australia. This famous station straddles the Buchanan Highway, which gives access to it via the impressive Jasper Gorge.

Wollogorang [D5] Station is a

place where the elusive 'spirit of the Territory' is most persuasively captured. This is Outback Australia, with all its rough edges, at its most authentic. Wollogorang is a holding of more than 7,000 sq km. It has 80 km of frontage onto the Gulf of Carpentaria and lies across the Queensland–Northern Territory border. It is a working station, running some 20,000 cattle. The cattle are mustered by helicopter— sometimes as many as five in the air at once. The cattle are then taken by road train to Darwin for sale. The station, established in 1883, boasts the longest continuous occupation in the Territory. Wollogorang Roadhouse has a licensed restaurant.

Diary of Events

Town	Event	Date	Contact
Adelaide River	Race Day	June	08 8927 9769
Arnhem Land	Garma Festival	August, last week	08 9192 1325
Barunga	Sports and Culture Festival	June, Queen's Birthday weekend	08 8975 4504
Darwin	Beer Can Regatta	August, 1st Sunday	08 8999 3900
	Mindil Beach Markets	April–Sept, Thurs/Sun nights	08 8981 3454
Katherine	Tick Markets	Saturday, 1st each month	08 8999 3900

NT

ACCOR

WE BUILD SMILES

ibis
ACCOR
hotels

summit
RESTAURANT

SHOWBOATS

MAGISTIC
CRUISES

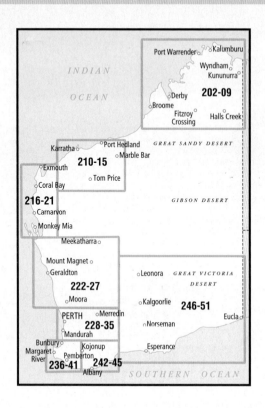

western

Discover the holiday opportunities in Western Australia. There's plenty to see and do, whether you're looking for a coastal or an inland experience.

Be captivated by the mysterious Bungle Bungle formations in the Kimberley, explore ancient gorges in the Pilbara, meet wild dolphins at Monkey Mia, marvel at the colour and variety of 12,000 species of wildflower, discover the charm of the Goldfields, take in the beauty of tall timbers and rugged coastline in the South-west, or visit wineries, the amazing Wave Rock and the eerie Pinnacles.

WA

australia

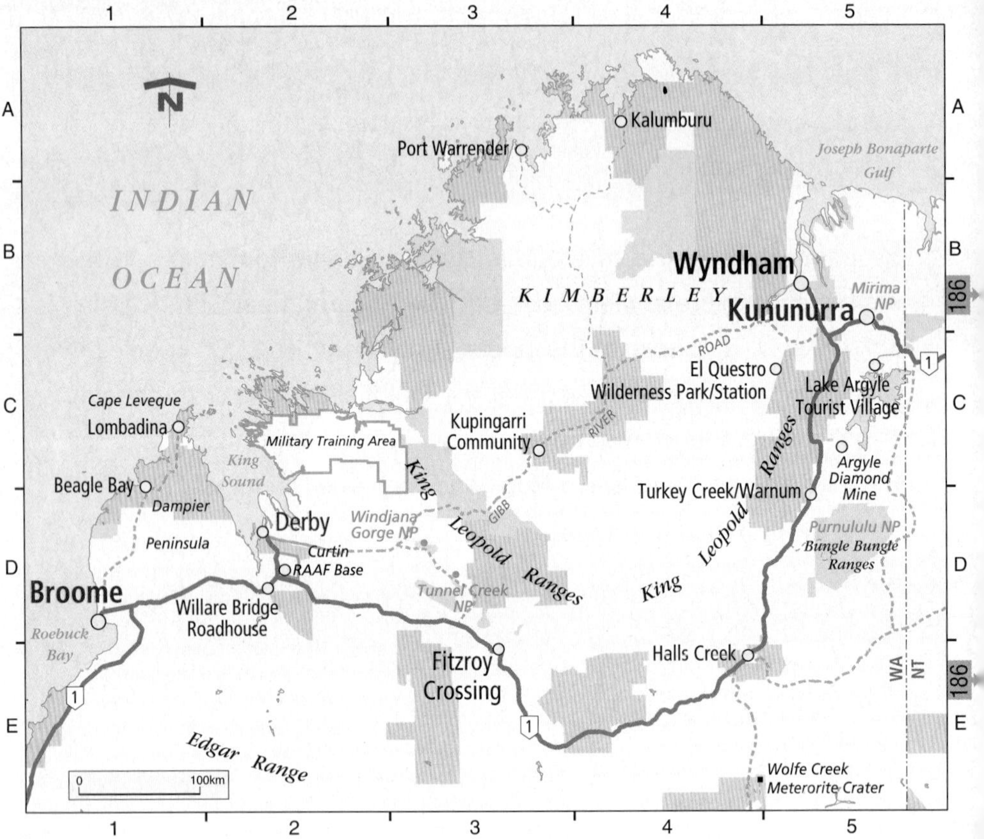

The Kimberley region is considered one of the world's last frontiers, with its spectacular gorges, cattle stations and Aboriginal culture.

get off the beaten track

wander the kimberley

Once **Broome** [D1] was the pearling capital of the world, until the mother-of-pearl industry was almost wiped out by the invention of the plastic button. Cultured pearl farming, from the 1970s onward, revived the pearling industry and tourism has also boomed. North of Broome you can visit **Willie Creek** Pearl Farm and enjoy the pristine pleasures of **Barred Creek** and **Coconut Well** (4WD recommended but not essential).

The Broome Court House was originally built as a cable station and was shipped in prefabricated form from England. The solid metal shutters were designed to resist attack.
The Sun Pictures building in Carnarvon Street in Chinatown was built in 1916—locals consider it the oldest open-air cinema in the world. It showed silent movies until 1933. The cinema still operates, and offers a pleasant and unusual way to spend an evening. Broome has the largest Japanese cemetery in Australia. It dates back to the early pearling days and bears witness to the close ties Japan established with Broome in the early 20th century. The pearl beds were very deep, often more than 27 m. Hundreds of young Japanese divers (as well as Aboriginal, Malay and Filipino divers) died either from the bends or drowning. The first recorded interment in this cemetery is 1890. The cemetery also contains a large stone obelisk to commemorate those who drowned at sea in a 1908 cyclone. There are 710 graves in the cemetery, some with unusual headstones of coloured beach rocks.

FISH SOUP AND RICE

Agnes Pigram used to watch her mum cook fish soup when she was growing up in Broome during the 1930s. Today people hear about fish soup and rice when the Pigram brothers (Agnes's sons) sing about it in 'Feel Like Going Back Home', one of the many memorable songs from the musical *Bran Nue Dae*, written by Jimmy Chi and the band Kuckles … 'Feel like going back home. Right now while the mangoes are ripe. / Frangipanis starting to bloom. And the blue bone are starting to bite. / Hey Mum I can just taste your fish soup and rice. I'm coming back home to you. / Can't hack the pace of the city life. Soon I'll be dreaming of Broome.'

1 large or medium-size fish (blue bone is best, fresh)	1 stalk lemon-grass (fresh)
	2 stalks celery
1 brown onion	salt and pepper to taste
4 cloves garlic	a little flour
a little cooking oil	1 tsp butter
2 tbsp vinegar	water (1–1¹/₂ cups to cover)
soy sauce to taste	
2 ripe tomatoes, chopped	steamed rice to serve

Fillet fish, chop up bones and head, fry onion and garlic in oil until brown. Place the bones and head in a large heavy-based pot. Cut up fillets in chunks and add to pot. Add vinegar, soy sauce, tomatoes, lemongrass, celery, salt and pepper. Cover and steam until fish is almost cooked. Add a little flour sprinkled on top and butter. Cover for a few minutes then add water just to cover the fish. Cover and bring to boil for 5 minutes. Serve with rice.

Agnes Pigram, BROOME

WA

MANGO CHEEKS IN LIME AND VODKA

Locals are always looking for new ways to utilise the abundant supplies of mangoes in the tropical Kimberley region. At the Mango Festival the chefs of Broome find all sorts of ways to transform the mango harvest yields into delicious meals at their annual Cook-Off.

4 mangoes, sliced
250 ml good vodka
100 ml sugar syrup, cooled (50 g sugar
** dissolved in 50 ml boiling water)**
juice of 4 limes
lemon or coconut gelato, for serving

Slice each side of whole mango from top to bottom on both sides of the seed. Take each piece and, using a large spoon, scoop out the cheek from the skin. Then cut into slices. In a bowl, make the marinade by mixing the vodka, sugar syrup and lime juice. Soak sliced mango in the marinade for at least 30 minutes, then serve with lemon or coconut gelato. Serves 4.

Janet Prince,
KIMBERLEY TRAVELLER

Cable Beach is a 22 km stretch of white sand so named because it was the terminus of the underwater telegraph line connecting Broome with Java in Indonesia. Take a camel ride here along the beach at sunset. South of Broome, on **Roebuck Bay** toward **Crab Creek**, is the RAOU Bird Observatory overlooking one of the world's top four non-breeding grounds for migratory Arctic waders. The Indian Ocean waters offshore from Broome and the Pearl Coast are famous for the calibre of recreational angling they offer, from reef fishing for red emperor, coral trout and the like to sport and game angling for mackerel, tuna, sailfish and marlin. In particular, these seas play host to large numbers of sub-adult Indo-Pacific sailfish in the dry season, from about April or May until

late October. The presence of these sailfish, typically weighing 12–30 kg, means there are several very popular catch-and-release fishing tournaments based in Broome during this period. To see one of Broome's natural wonders, head south from the town along Port Drive and turn west onto a dirt road just before the BP fuel depot. The road leads to **Gantheaume Point**, or Minyirr, where the distinctive red soil of the region (known as 'pindan') meets the white sand of the beach and the impossibly blue sea. The interplay of these three colours is one of the most dramatic sights anywhere in Australia. At the tip of Gantheaume Point are 120-million-year-old dinosaur footprints, which you can see at extremely low tide. At other times you can look at concrete castings of the footprints, conveniently placed at the top of the cliff.

GAZETTE

DON'T MISS: In August, apart from Broome's well-publicised Shinju Matsuri (Festival of the Pearl), there's also the Obon Festival, a Japanese Buddhist welcoming of the dead. In November Broome celebrates the Mango Festival (taking care of the glut of more than 40 varieties of mango grown in the district). There's a Mardi Gras, tastings and the Great Chefs of Broome Mango Cook-Off.

The Dampier Peninsula [D1]

north of Broome is worth a trip in itself, but you will probably need a 4WD vehicle, or you can charter a light plane. Don't miss out on visiting the church at **Beagle Bay** Aboriginal Community. It is a real work of art, made from pearl shell and other local shells. **Lombadina** also has a church of architectural note, built of corrugated iron outside, supported by bush timber, and lined with paperbark. You can

also stay at the Lombadina community but bookings are essential. **Cape Leveque** is as far as you can go—the Kooljaman Resort, run by the local Bardi Aboriginal people, offers accommodation and camping, plus great reef walking at low tide (but watch out for the speed of the incoming tide).

Derby [D2] is on the shores of King Sound,

which has the world's second-largest tidal range (after the Bay of Fundy, in Canada). The tides vary up to 12 m. It is part of Australia's largest shire, covering 102,706 sq km. The first European known to have set foot on West Australian soil was William Dampier, who arrived on board the *Cygnet* in 1688. He was not impressed with what he saw: '... no Trees that bore Fruit or Berries, ... no sort of Animal nor any Track of Beast ... neither is the Sea very plentifully stored with Fish'. Derby's Boab festival is the longest running festival in Western Australia. It began in 1960 and has

grown to a month-long event in July each year. Highlights include an art exhibition by the local Aboriginal community of Mowanjum, a mud football tournament and a Mardi Gras parade. Contact the Visitor Centre on 08 9191 1426 for details.

The **Gibb River Road** runs for 670 km from Derby to the Great Northern Highway between Kununurra and Wyndham. It is mostly dirt and is impassable in the Wet, but provides unequalled access to the wonders of the Kimberley when it's dry.

DON'T MISS: On the outskirts of town, 7 km south on the Derby Highway, are the Boab Prison Tree and Myall's Bore. The huge boab tree was used as a lock-up for Aboriginal prisoners in the 1890s. It was the last

GAZETTEER

stopover point for patrols returning to Derby. Capable of holding a number of prisoners, it has an entrance about 1 m wide and 2 m high. Myall's Bore was originally sunk in 1912 to a depth of 322 m, and yielded a daily water flow of 315,000 ltr. Beside the bore stands a 120 m cattle trough, built in about 1920 and reputed to be the longest in the Southern Hemisphere. It is claimed that when the trough was in use 1,000 head of cattle could be watered at one time. The bore was capped in 1980.

WA

El Questro [C5] is a working,

400,000 ha cattle ranch that also operates several levels of accommodation for visitors keen to sample the Outback life, enjoy the visual splendour of the Kimberley and perhaps cast a line for barramundi in the deep, rocky gorges of the Chamberlain and Salmond Rivers. Owned and operated by eccentric expatriate English aristocrat Will Burrell and his wife Celia, El Questro has won numerous tourism awards over the years and is regarded by many as a 'must see' destination in the Kimberley.

Fitzroy Crossing [E3] has the

oldest pub in the Kimberley—the Crossing Inn, near Brooking Creek, established as a shanty inn by Joseph Blythe in the 1890s. Inquire at the tourist bureau about a visit to a cattle station owned and run by the local Yiyili or Ganinyi people for an insight into a very different way of life. Windjana Gorge and Tunnel Creek are 63 km from the main Derby–Fitzroy Crossing Road. This unique formation was created when the waters of the creek cut a 750 m tunnel through the ancient reef. The tunnel is 15 m wide and up to 12 m high, and offers visitors an excellent opportunity to see the ancient 'barrier reef' from an unusual vantage point.

The original town of Halls Creek

[E4] was where Western Australia's first gold rush occurred in 1855. It lasted just three months. Halls Creek got its first airport in 1948, and the town moved west to be closer to it. A memorial in town commemorates a local legend called Russian Jack who, in 1886, put his sick friend into a wheelbarrow and pushed him the 366 km to Wyndham to get medical help. In the Halls Creek graveyard is the tomb of James 'Jimmy' Darcy. A stockman at Ruby Plains Station, 75 km south of Halls Creek, Darcy fell from his horse and was seriously injured while mustering cattle. His friends took him by buggy to Halls Creek, but there was no doctor in the town. Nor was there any help in Derby or Wyndham, where the doctors were not available. The local postmaster, FW Tuckett, telegraphed a Dr Holland in Perth. Darcy was diagnosed as having a ruptured urethra. Holland then directed the reluctant postmaster through an operation using a pocket knife, a razor and a bag of Condy's crystals—without anaesthetic. Complications set in and a doctor had to get to Halls Creek. In the meantime, Darcy's dilemma caught the imagination of the Australian public, who followed the saga with insatiable interest. Dr Holland took a cattle boat from Perth to Derby, then travelled the last 555 km by T-Model Ford, horse and sulky and on foot. He arrived in Halls Creek to find that Darcy had died the day before. It is said that this event inspired the Reverend John Flynn to establish the Royal Flying Doctor Service. A few kilometres out of town, on the Duncan Road, is a sign

to the **China Wall**, 1.5 km off the road. This strange formation, rising from a creek to become a small hill, is a natural feature of white quartz that does look a little like a mini version of the Great Wall of China. The **Bungle Bungle Ranges**, some 53 km along a 4WD track from the Great Northern Highway north of Halls Creek, has some of the most unusual rock formations in the world. They are sandstone domes, rising up to 578 m above sea level, marked with alternating bands of orange rock and greyish-black cyanobacteria. They are protected within **Purnululu National Park**. The stone is very friable and the domes are extremely fragile; they are thought to have formed 350–375 million years ago. The Bungle Bungles are most easily seen from the air, on sightseeing flights from Kununurra or Halls Creek. If you want to get up close you are probably best advised to join a guided tour.

DON'T MISS: Wolfe Creek Crater lies 145 km south of Halls Creek, along a less than perfect dirt road. It is the second-largest crater on Earth (the other being in Arizona) in which meteoric material has been found. It was created when an iron meteorite weighing over 50,000 tonnes slammed into the ground. The crater has a diameter of 880 m and is 60 m deep, although it was probably as deep as 120 m when it was originally formed. From a distance it appears as a low hill, but from the rim the crater is a sight of great symmetry and beauty. Evidence suggests that Wolfe Creek Crater was probably formed about 300,000 years ago.

Kununurra's [B5] Celebrity Tree

Park is a delightful arboretum on the shores of Lake Kununurra, out on the Victoria Highway just west of the town centre. Particularly intriguing is a paperbark gum that, according to some locals, was so disgusted with the sign nailed to its trunk that it actually grew over it, like a melting Salvador Dali watch. Take a cruise through the Everglades, an area of flooded trees close to town—it's a haven for birdlife. Out on the Packsaddle Plain, west of the town on Packsaddle Plain Road, is the centre of zebra rock production. This remarkable stone is found nowhere else on Earth, and

KIMBERLEY ADDICTION

Arno and Neenya Tesling established the first mango orchard in the Kimberley, planting 300 seedlings in 1981, and in 1996 they began marketing Australia's first mango wine, Tesling Mango Wine. The winery is open for tastings and Arno and Neenya will happily take you on a tour of the orchard and share a yarn about the early days of Broome. Here's one of their favourite mango cocktail recipes.

30 ml Tesling's Mango Liqueur
15 ml Midori
1 fresh mango cheek
45 ml pineapple juice
dob of cream

Blend ingredients and drink.

Arno and Neenya Tesling,
Tesling Mango Wines,
Yamashita Road, ROEBUCK

transforms into unique jewellery and ornaments. About 80 km south of Kununurra is the world's largest producing diamond mine, the **Argyle Diamond Mine**. The 1,600 m long Argyle diamond pipe has an annual yield of 30 million carats of mainly industrial diamonds. Among the small number of gem-quality diamonds found here is the famous Argyle pink diamond. When the pipe was discovered in 1979 it was the first time diamonds had been discovered in the rock lamprolite. The mine can only be visited on guided tours from Kununurra, but you can inquire at the tourist information centre.

Mirima (Hidden Valley) National Park, 2 km east of Kununurra, has some fine examples of the art and culture of the local

Miriuwung people, although they are not open to public view. Mirima is known as a mini Bungle Bungles because of its resemblance to the main event further south.

Kalumburu

[A4] is the state's most northerly accessible point, but only via 4WD on one of the toughest dirt roads in Australia. There are just two services on the journey: Drysdale River Homestead and Kalumburu Mission, which is owned by the Aboriginal community. You should obtain a permit before visiting (08 9161 4300), although you can get one upon arrival. Attractions in the area are the trek to **King Edward Gorge** and exceptional fishing. Possible catches include barramundi and bream from King Edward River and spanish mackerel, golden trevally, threadfin salmon, golden trout and cod from the sea. The sunsets are spectacular.

Lake Argyle

Tourist Village [C5] is on the shore of one of the most beautiful artifical lakes in Australia. Dammed as part of the Ord River Scheme, it is also Australia's largest lake, with an area of 980 sq km at normal storage levels. Beyond the village is an excellent lookout from which Lake Argyle can be viewed. Keen fishermen and canoeists can easily launch a small tinnie or canoe here and follow the Ord

River down to Kununurra. Paddling will take a couple of days—a motor will speed things up. There's some wild scenery and good fishing. The same course is followed by the Dam 2 Dam Dinghy Race, which is held each year in June.

Turkey Creek

[D5], officially named **Warnum**, is a tiny settlement owned by the Gidja Aboriginal people and used by visitors as an access point to Purnululu National Park and the Bungle Bungles. The roadhouse is the focal point of the settlement. It supplies fuel and food, operates a camping area and is the departure point for helicopter flights to the Osmond Ranges, Bungle Bungle Massif, Beehive Domes, Horseshoe Valley and the Western Wall (call the roadhouse on 08 9169 1300 for further information). Across the road is the Daiwul Gidja Culture Centre, which showcases local Aboriginal arts and crafts. Gidja paintings are characterised by their use of earth pigments including ochre, oxide, kaolin clay and charcoal, the same palette as for traditional ceremonial body painting.

Near ## Wyndham

[B5], at the Five Rivers Lookout, you can (predictably enough) see five rivers at the one time. They are the Durack, King and Pentecost to the south, the Forrest to the west and the Ord to the north. The lookout is clearly signposted from Wyndham and offers one of the most

Driving during the Wet

From late December, and sometimes even earlier, the Monsoon begins to take effect across the Top End of Australia, sending lashings of tropical storms across the Kimberley. Rivers swell to breaking point and crossings can be hazardous, with washouts and submerged debris. Sometimes you can even get through one crossing to find that the next is impassable. In the meantime the river behind you rises and you can find yourself trapped between the two crossings. During the Wet take great care when travelling the Northern Highway between Kununurra and Broome, and particularly around Fitzroy Crossing, and check with police and traffic authorities for road conditions.

dramatic views anywhere along the Australian coastline. At the entrance to Wyndham Three Mile, you can't help noticing a 20 m concrete crocodile in the middle of the road. This 'tourist attraction' is an interesting example of computer technology put to creative use. Designed and built by sculptor Andrew Hickson and students from the Halls Creek TAFE, it is made from 5.5 km of steel rod, 10 rolls of bird mesh and 6 m³ of concrete. The blueprint for construction was generated from a photograph of a crocodile, which was mapped using 2,400 mathematical coordinates by a computer at Curtin University.

DON'T MISS: One block east of the main street is a wonderful relic of Wyndham's history and a great venue for hot and steamy nights—a classic outback cinema with comfortable deck chairs, a small screen and enclosed projector booth. Films are shown there about once a month.

WA

Diary of Events

Town	Event	Date	Contact
Broome	Shinju Matsuri	Aug/Sept	08 9192 2222
	Obon Festival	Aug/Sept	08 9192 2222
	Mango Festival	November	08 9192 2222
Derby	Boab Festival	July	08 9191 1426
Halls Creek	Fishing Competition	March	08 9168 1177
Kununurra	Dragon Boat Race	June	08 9168 1177
	Mardi Gras	June, 3rd Saturday	0409 691 335
	Agricultural Show	July, last weekend	08 9168 1177
	Races and Race Ball	August, 4th weekend	08 9168 1177
Lake Argyle	Dam 2 Dam Dinghy Race	June	08 9168 1177
Wyndham	Races and Race Ball	August, 3rd weekend	08 9168 1177

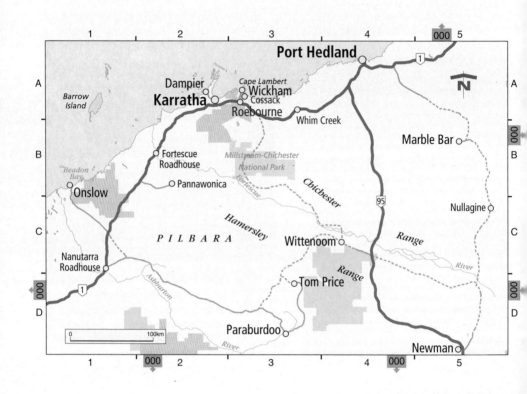

get off the beaten track

explore
the pilbara

Barrow Island [A1] was recorded

on a Dutch East India company map as early as 1628, visited by Abel Tasman in 1644 and explored by Philip Parker King in 1818. King named it after John Barrow, the Under Secretary to the British Admiralty at the time. Despite the fact that the island was declared a nature reserve in 1908, the discovery of oil in the 1950s and the heavy refinery activities that have since ensued caused considerable environmental damage. However, Barrow is still considered to be one of Australia's most biologically important islands supporting 15 species of land mammal, 7 marine mammals, 110 species of bird and 40 reptiles. Many of these are threatened or extinct elsewhere. Natural historian and television personality Harry Butler visits the island regularly to conduct environmental awareness courses for the islanders who live and work there.

The town of Cossack [A3] was originally known as Tien Tsin Harbour, after the ship that brought the first settlers. It was renamed after HMS *Cossack* when the warship visited with the Governor of WA, Sir Frederick Weld, on board. It was the first port in the north-west and a base for the early pearling luggers. Cossack, rather than Broome, is where pearling in the north-west actually began. As ships outgrew Cossack's

Pilbara is one of the oldest geological areas in the world, with a rugged coastline and beautiful inland gorges. The region also has some of the world's largest deposits of iron ore and natural gas.

WA

CHILLI MUD CRAB

Visit Port Hedland from July to October and you might be lucky enough to spot a humpback whale on its annual migration. It's a great place to try some serious fishing for a variety of species off the wharf, from the beach or by charter out to sea. Locals say that if you want to catch a mud crab the best places to try are anywhere near mangroves, particularly around Finucane Island and Six Mile Creek.

12 green mud crab claws
1/3 cup peanut oil
1 cup chilli sauce (the best is Linghams)
1 cup tomato sauce
1/3 cup soy sauce
1 dsp sugar
5 cm piece fresh ginger, peeled and thinly sliced
6 cloves garlic, chopped

Break each crab claw into 3 pieces. Use a hammer to crack the shells, to allow the sauce to penetrate the meat and for easy removal when eating. Fry the claws in the peanut oil in a large covered pan until cooked through (about 5 minutes each side). Keep lid on to cook crab faster. Once cooked, set aside. While the crab is cooking, combine chilli, tomato and soy sauces with sugar in a bowl and set aside. Remove cooked claws from pan. Pour off any excess oil and turn heat to low. Gently fry the ginger and garlic but do not allow to brown. When aromatic, add the sauce mixture and simmer for 5 minutes. Return the claws to the pan and stir the sauce through. Serve with rice. You will need a large bowl of warm water with sliced lemon for hand rinsing. Serves 4–6.

Kate Davies, PORT HEDLAND

port facilities the port was moved to Point Sampson, and Cossack became a ghost town. Most of the town has now been restored, with many fine period buildings and a cemetery with a Japanese section.

 DON'T MISS: At full moon and low tide the Stairway to the Moon (a feature shared with Broome) is visible from Hearson's Cove. As the moon rises, its reflection in the water resembles a golden stairway reaching from the water to the moon.

GAZETTEER

Karratha [A2] and its neighbouring

town of **Dampier** hold their annual fair, the Fe-NaCl-NG Festival (pronounced Fee-nackling and comprising the chemical symbols for the materials that provide the

region's wealth—iron, salt and natural gas) in August. Call 08 9144 4600 for details. You can also walk Karratha's 3.5 km Aboriginal Jaburara Heritage Trail (which starts behind the tourist centre on Karratha Road and takes in Aboriginal carvings, old quarries, grindstones and shell middens) or inspect Dampier's port facilities. Karratha is a thriving

town of around 10,000 people. It's quite a 'new' town—mapped out in 1968 on a site originally known as White Gum Creek. About 130 of Karratha's inhabitants work on the nearby Dampier solar saltfield, where salt is produced by solar evaporation of seawater. It's one of the most advanced and efficient saltfields in the world, and Dampier Salt is the world's biggest producer of seaborne salt and exports

to Asia, the Middle East, Africa and the USA. Salt is used by chemical industries in the production of plastics, glass and soaps, and is used in other industrial applications such as petroleum drilling, water conditioning, tanning, textiles and dyeing. But, of course, food wouldn't taste the same without it. In the past people went to war over salt. In Roman times the army received salt as part of their pay, called 'salarium argentum' and from this comes our 'salary' today.

Marble Bar [B5] is known as the

hottest town in Australia, a distinction recorded by the *Guinness Book of Records* and one well founded. For 161 consecutive days to 20 April 1924 the temperature in the town did not drop below 100°F (37.8°C), and for 113 of those days it was above 38.4°C. This is the longest hot spell ever recorded in Australia, a record that stands after nearly 80 years. Since records have been kept for the town, the temperature has never dropped below 0°C. Marble Bar was named somewhat inaccurately, after a unique bar of jasper (a highly coloured cryptocrys-talline variety of quartz) that crosses the Coongan River about 5 km west of town. It is clearly signposted off General Street beyond the government buildings.

Newman [D5] was settled between

1967 and 1969, when the Australian-controlled Mount Newman mining company commissioned Bechtel Pacific Corporation to develop what became Australia's most productive iron ore mine. The largest single open-cut iron ore mine in the world, constructed in semi-desert, was named Mt Whaleback after the hill from which it was built. Newman was constructed alongside the longest privately owned railway in the Southern Hemisphere, which covers more than 426 km from Newman to Port Hedland. The track gangs drank nearly 1,000 litres of beer for every kilometre of track they laid. In June 2001 the present mine operators, BHP Billiton, broke their own world record (previously set in 1996) for the heaviest single train on this track, with a 7.35 km long, 682-car train weighing 100,000 tonnes. Mt Whaleback currently produces 30 million tonnes of ore every year. A standard fully loaded ore truck weighs 250 tonnes, more than a Boeing 747. You can arrange with the tourist office to visit the mine (08 9175 2888). Check out the panoramic views from Radio Hill lookout. The drive north out of Newman through the **Hamersley** and **Opthalmia Ranges** is one of the most scenic in the state.

Nullagine [C5] sits on the edge of

the **Great Sandy Desert** on the 'Road to Nowhere' (the Rippon Hills Road). Gold was first discovered in the area by NW Cooke in 1886, but the town wasn't gazetted until 1899. In 1902 Nullagine was the site of the first discovery of Australian diamonds. Today the tiny town comprises a pub, a general store, a school, park and police station. The main reason people visit is to fossick at **Beaton's Rockhole and Gorge**, 4 km west of the town. Summer here is scorching so winter is the best time to come.

WA

The harbour at **Onslow** [B1] has been battered so badly by cyclones that in 1925 the town was actually moved. The town's deepwater jetty, originally built to cater for shipments to and from inland sheep stations, caught the fury of yet more cyclones and was eventually closed. Dubbed 'Cyclone City', the town was relocated from the mouth of the Ashburton River up the coast a few kilometres to Beadon Bay, but the year after it was hit by

yet another cyclone, and again in 1934, 1961 and 1964. You can visit the old town ruins 45 km away to see some of the original old stone and concrete buildings including the post office, police station and jail. Houses in present-day Onslow are now fitted with special steel shutters and iron roofs that are cleated on in order to withstand cyclonic winds.

 DON'T MISS: If you are keen on fishing, **Mackerel Island** off Onslow is for you. Snapper, groper, red emperor and Spanish mackerel abound, as do crayfish and oysters. Turtles breed here too.

Pannawonica [B2] was built to
house the families of workers for the Robe River Iron mines. There's not much to see except in September when the town comes alive for the Robe River Rodeo. It's the only event of its kind in the Pilbara region with competitors coming from across the state.

North of **Port Hedland** [A4], the stretch of coast is called 80-Mile Beach. The beach is actually 110 miles (176 km) long. Founded as a pearling port, the town is now dedicated to shipping out the mineral wealth from the Pilbara's mines.

Roebourne [A3] is the oldest
town on Western Australia's north-west coast. It has many substantial **GAZETTEER** buildings, a result of the Pilbara gold rushes of the 1880s, and some of these are now classified by the National Trust. They include the Victoria Hotel, the last of the town's five pubs. About 87 km south of Roebourne is the **Millstream–Chichester National Park**, which includes Chinderwarriner. This pleasant waterhole is

covered by waterlilies and shaded by the indigenous millstream palm, protected by the park. Date palms, supposedly planted in the 1880s by Afghan camel drivers, surround the Millstream homestead, which now houses the park's visitors centre.

Tom Price [D3] is an iron ore town
established in 1965 by Hamersley Iron, and is Western Australia's highest town, at 747 m above sea level. Every second weekend in August, Tom Price hosts the Nameless Festival—named after the nearby mountain of the same (no) name. The town sits on the

fringes of **Karijini National Park**, which is the second largest national park in Western Australia, at some 6,274 sq km. The first European here was explorer Francis Thomas Gregory in 1861, who named the range after his sponsor Edward Hamersley (naming rights are nothing new). Most of the park's attractions are in its northern sector, something of a bushwalker's delight, with a number of marked trails. At **Oxers Lookout** the four gorges of Joffre, Hancock, Red and Weano all join, with a sheer 100 m drop down to the river. **Joffre Falls** is a curved waterfall forming a natural ampitheatre; and Gorge Rim Walk follows the rim of the gorge between Circular Pool Lookout to the **Dales Gorge** car park. Although all the roads are gravel, they are suitable for cars and caravans. The Visitor Centre in the park might interest architecture buffs. It is designed to represent a goanna, symbolic to local Aboriginal people. The high weathered steel walls represent the gorges that are the main feature of the park. The materials and structure of the building are designed to withstand the frequent fires in the area. Call to check opening times on 08 9189 8121.

Don't pass **Whim Creek** [A3] without stopping at the pub. Local lore has it that if you pass the pub and don't stop, your car will break down before you reach your final destination. The pub used to have a fireman's pole from the bedroom to the bar to allow for quick service at any time of the day or night and, although it has been affected by a number of cyclones over the years, it still remains a unique experience.

 DON'T MISS: Not so much a hot spot as a hot time is the annual Black Rock Stakes Wheelbarrow Race, over 110 km from Whim Creek to Port Hedland. Every June teams take turns pushing their barrows, loaded with 11 kg of iron ore, to raise money for charity.

GAZETTEER

Near **Wickham** [A3] is **Cape Lambert**, which has an iron ore loading facility claimed to be one of the longest and highest open ocean wharves in Australia, standing 14 m high.

Wittenoom [C4] is almost a ghost town—the shops have been boarded up and the school has closed. You would think that it is ideally located for people wishing to visit the beautiful Wittenoom Gorge, but it's actually not a place many people will want to stay, having been named 'The Valley of Death'. The town was originally built when Lang Hancock began mining blue asbestos in Wittenoon Gorge in 1943. The mine was closed in 1966. Today we are all aware of problems associated with asbestos tailings; and this is clearly highlighted by signs around the town— 'Danger: Asbestos Tailings Risk Area. Inhaling asbestos fibres may cause cancer.'

WA

Diary of Events

Town	Event	Date	Contact
Karratha	Fe-NcCl-NG Festival	August	08 9144 2344
Pannawonica	Robe River Rodeo	September	08 9184 1222
Tom Price	Nameless Festival	August, 2nd weekend	08 9189 1029
Whim Creek	Black Rock Stakes Wheelbarrow Race	June	08 9176 4914

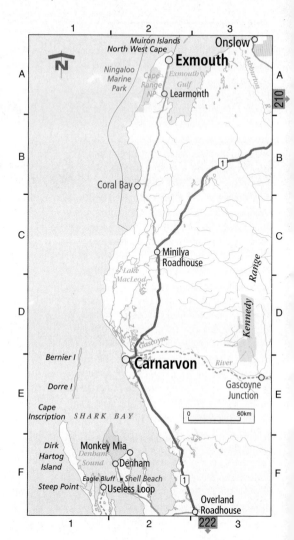

Gascoyne, or the Outback Coast, is a beautiful and ecologically diverse region stretching from Exmouth to Shark Bay . Cliffs and ancient gorges, clear blue seas and abundant wildlife are among the natural features.

get off the beaten track

roam
the gascoyne

Carnarvon's [E2] roads, built in the

1880s, were made 40 m wide to allow a camel train to turn full circle. These teams brought the wool from Carnarvon's sheep stations, some of the largest in Australia, to the port. Author Nene Gare, who lived in Robinson Street in the 1950s, wrote of the streets' origins in her novel *Green Gold:* 'The wide main streets were made to take a double team of camels pulling twelve-foot-high drays shod with big iron wheels. There had to be room for the Afghan drivers to make a U-turn, with the result that today there is parking space in the middle of the road as well as on either side.' The Gascoyne

Transport Company (renamed the Gascoyne Trading Company in 1935) began here in 1924 when two young go-ahead pilots, Charles Kingsford Smith and Keith Anderson, chucked in their jobs with West Australian Airways (the first airline established in the British Commonwealth). They purchased a truck and set up in opposition to Mick Stroud, who had started a one-truck haulage company from Carnarvon when motorised transport began and it became obvious the days of the camel teams were numbered. Kingsford Smith and Anderson did not do as well on the ground as they did in the air, however. They sold out to Stroud just two years later and returned to the skies, where flooded rivers and harsh terrain would not bother them. The 180 m **Bibbawarah Trough** near the Bibbawarah artesian bore, 16 km north of Carnarvon, is believed to be the longest in the Southern Hemisphere.

MANGO MOUSSE

Gascoyne's primary produce is mainly fuelled by the Gascoyne River, where a collection of waterholes and the underground water supply is recharged each wet season. The horticulture industry takes advantage of the climate, producing out-of-season fruits to be exported to Asia and the Middle East. Mangoes are second only to bananas as the major fruit yields in this tropical region.

3 whole eggs
1 egg yolk
40 g caster sugar
grated rind of 1 orange
2 ripe mangoes, puréed
juice of 1 orange, strained
2 tbsp lemon juice, strained
1 sachet Davis Gelatine (10 g)
300 ml thickened cream

Place the whole eggs and egg yolk in a large bowl. Add caster sugar and whisk until pale, thick and creamy. In another bowl, stir orange rind into mango purée and gradually add this to egg mixture. Place orange and lemon juice in a small bowl, sprinkle gelatine over the surface and stir gently to ensure that all grains are covered. Leave to soak for 10 minutes. In another bowl, beat cream to mousse consistency. Using a metal spoon, fold half the cream into the mango mixture. Stand the bowl with gelatine in a pan of gently simmering water and warm until gelatine liquefies and clears. Pour gelatine into the mango mixture, gently stirring all the time to combine thoroughly. Pour mixture into a 2 ltr shallow serving dish or 4 serving glasses and refrigerate overnight covered with cling wrap. Serves 4.

Danielle Hill, CARNARVON

WA

DON'T MISS: Join a tour in town to visit the museum in the pedestal of the big dish at the Carnarvon Space Tracking Station. Artefacts relating to the lunar landing are exhibited, including the hand prints of the astronauts who visited the station.

CYCLONE BANANA CAKE

Being close to the Tropic of Capricorn, Carnarvon is blessed with a virtually endless summer but is also prone to cyclones. The banks of the Gascoyne River provide lush green market gardens and banana plantations, the traditional crop of the region. If a particularly fierce cyclone hits, the banks of the river have been known to break and the waters wash away the essential topsoils. After one such cyclone bananas that had been ripped from the trees were in desperate need of eating, and so this recipe was born.

- **125 g butter or margarine**
- **125 g caster sugar**
- **2 eggs**
- **6 small or 4 medium ripe bananas, mashed**
- **2 cups self-raising flour**
- **1 tsp bicarbonate of soda**
- **1 tbsp milk**

Preheat oven to 180°C and line 2 x 20 cm x 10 cm bar tins with baking paper. In a bowl, cream the butter and sugar until light and fluffy. Add eggs and mashed bananas and beat to combine. In a cup, mix together bicarbonate of soda and milk. Fold in the flour and the milk mixture alternately, until well combined. Place equal portions into each pan and bake for 30–35 minutes. Serve either iced with flavoured icing or as buttered slices.

Agnes O'Grady, MANLY

Coral Bay 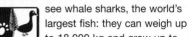 [B2] is the best place from which to reach **Ningaloo Marine Park**, which stretches 14 km out to sea. This is the largest fringing coral reef in Australia and is 250 km long. Between March and June it is the best place to see whale sharks, the world's largest fish: they can weigh up to 18,000 kg and grow up to 18 m long. You can even snorkel with them. Ningaloo is also the place to watch humpback whales on their way from their Antarctic feeding grounds to breeding grounds on the north-west shelf.

Denham 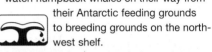 [F2] is Australia's most westerly town. The only major human habitation west of the town is at **Useless Loop**, a vast salt mine that is visible across the Freycinet Estuary from Denham. There are several buildings in town, including a church constructed from blocks cut from compacted and fossilised shell 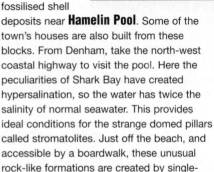 deposits near **Hamelin Pool**. Some of the town's houses are also built from these blocks. From Denham, take the north-west coastal highway to visit the pool. Here the peculiarities of Shark Bay have created hypersalination, so the water has twice the salinity of normal seawater. This provides ideal conditions for the strange domed pillars called stromatolites. Just off the beach, and accessible by a boardwalk, these unusual rock-like formations are created by single-celled organisms known as cyanobacteria.

They grow at a rate of less than 1 mm a year and are called 'living fossils' because they are among the very oldest forms of life on the planet. Cyanobacteria produced the oxygen that made life on Earth possible. The old telegraph station at Hamelin is now an

eclectic museum with displays ranging from the ancient (a stromatolite in a tank) to the risqué (a photograph of a naked telegraph linesman, high on a ladder, repairing the wire). It also has a vast collection of several hundred telecommunications insulators including some dating from 1884, when the station was built.

Dirk Hartog Island [F1] has

an old post to which Dirk Hartog nailed an inscribed pewter plate when he landed in 1616. The plate, after which **Cape Inscription** is named, is now held at the Rijksmuseum in The Netherlands. The island is a fantastic fishing destination, too. Its rugged, rocky cliffs and beaches provide superb opportunities for land-based anglers wishing to do battle with big tailor, pink snapper, mackerel, trevally and the delicious baldchin groper. Boat anglers can head a short distance offshore and add Spanish mackerel, tuna, cobia and even sailfish to this list.

There is a well-appointed lodge on the island (part of the homestead of an operating sheep station); 4WD vehicles can be brought across from the mainland on the lodge's barge.

Exmouth's

[A2] streets were named after the 23 Australians who died during Operation Rimau, an unsuccessful attack by Australian commando unit Z-force on Japanese shipping in waters around Singapore during World War II. Exmouth was officially created as a town in 1967, when the Harold E Holt Base, a major naval communications station, was established. The station, 6 km north of town at **North West Cape**, is a restricted area, but tours can be arranged through the Exmouth Visitors Centre. The base has 13 radio towers, each higher than the Empire State Building, which monitor the movements of US warships in the Indian Ocean and the western Pacific—this is probably Australia's most vulnerable point in the unlikely event of nuclear war. **Cape Range National Park**, south-west of town, takes in much of North West Cape and offers magical camping along the coast, plus the impressive sight of Yardie Creek. This deep creek is cut off from the ocean by a sandbar and is nestled below dramatic cliffs. It can only be accessed by 4WD, but not at all after cyclones or heavy rain. In 1875, a few years before settlement of the Gascoyne began, the Croatian barque *Stefano* struck Black Rock just off this rugged coastline. Seven of the 17 on board died that night; the rest made a gruelling trek south to find a settlement. Over the next month they struggled across inhospitable country, suffering near-starvation and

WA

cyclonic weather until there were only two survivors. They spent the next six months being nursed back to health by a local Aboriginal tribe before being picked up by the cutter *Jessie*, captained by Charles Tuckey, an ancestor of Wilson Tuckey, who became the Honourable Member for O'Connor.

Near Gascoyne Junction

[E3] keep a weather eye out for wedgetail eagles. They can be slow to take off, especially if they've had a big meal, and their wingspan can reach nearly 2.5 m. **Mt Augustus** (or Burringurrah), about 200 km due north-east of Gascoyne Junction, is the largest monocline or 'monadnock' in the world. Although more than twice as big as Uluru (Ayers Rock), standing 858 m above the surrounding plain, it is not as impressive because it is partly overgrown by vegetation. The central ridge is almost 8 km long. The rock of the mountain itself is estimated at 1,000 million years old; the granite beneath it may be 1,650 million years old. Climbing Mt Augustus takes at least six hours. The rock changes colour constantly, from bright red through shades of green to blue and then to orange and gold at sunset.

Learmonth

[A2] Solar Observatory is one of the six solar velocity imagers worldwide in the Global Oscillation Network Group, which provides nearly continuous observation of the Sun's oscillations, or pulsation. It is jointly operated by the Australian government and the US Air Force.

Minilya Roadhouse

[C2] earns a place on the map, as it is roughly halfway between Carnarvon and Coral Bay and the last stop for fuel. If you get there late it's probably best to stay over—the road to Coral Bay is treacherous at night because cows wander onto the road and are invisible in the pitch black. Even the locals avoid driving after dark.

Monkey Mia

[F2] was a sleepy little town with few permanent residents until the early 1960s, when a small group of five adult female dolphins and two male calves

came to meet swimmers in the shallow waters near shore and allowed themselves to be touched and hand-fed. Now Monkey Mia attracts tourists and marine biology students from all over the world. A dolphin information centre was opened in the early 1990s and the hand-feeding has been restricted to prevent the dolphins becoming dependent.

Shark Bay

[E1] was the site of one of the first known European landings on the Australian mainland (Willem Janszoon in the *Duyfken* beat everyone to the punch by landing at Weipa in Queensland in 1606). Dutch navigator Dirk Hartog landed at the bay's entrance in 1616 on the island later named after him. Shark Bay was also the site of Australia's first foray into the pearling industry in the 1870s. The bay's proliferation of marine life, from turtles and dugongs to whales and sharks, is due largely to the seagrass that pollinates underwater and grows over 4,000 sq m of the bay. In 1991 Shark Bay was included on the World Heritage List.

When he arrived in Shark Bay, William Dampier noted the unique shells of the area. On 7 August 1699 he wrote: 'The shore was lined thick with many other sorts of very strange and beautiful Shells, for variety of Colour and Shape, most finely spotted with Red, Black, or Yellow, &c: such as I have not seen any where but at this place.' Shark Bay is famous in fishing circles for its stocks of big pink snapper, mulloway and various other species. Sadly, pink snapper numbers here declined dramatically through the late 1980s to mid-1990s, but Fisheries WA established a series of strict catch controls and closures that have allowed the snapper population to rebuild. Other features in the bay include **Eagle Bluff**, about 20 km south of Denham, where a substantial population of dugong lives. They can be seen in summer when they come close to the shore to feed on the seagrass.

Shark Bay has the reputation of being home to the world's largest population of these harmless marine mammals. **Steep Point**, the most westerly point of the Australian mainland, can be reached from near here, via a rough, sandy 4WD track that winds among the dunes to these sheer cliffs. Steep

Point is one of the most famous rock- or land-based fishing locations in all of Australia if not the world. The sky is literally the limit for rockhoppers fishing from this rugged and isolated headland. Marlin, sailfish and giant tiger sharks are regularly hooked from the shore here. The land-based specialists who target game and sport fish from these high rocks use float-suspended live and dead baits and various lures and even saltwater flies. One of the most productive and exciting techniques is to drift whole or live garfish and long tom baits suspended beneath helium-filled balloons. The baits dance and skip across the sea as the prevailing easterlies carry these rigs hundreds of metres. You need a cliff gaff to land fish from the high ledges and it goes without saying that these are potentially dangerous rock platforms and rockhoppers need to exercise extreme caution.

DON'T MISS: Shell Beach, near Eagle Bluff, is one of only two beaches in the world made up of non-fossilised shells. The entire beach consists of millions upon millions of tiny coquina shells and at low tide it is possible to walk 100 m into the bay, treading on a seemingly endless surface of shells all the way.

Diary of Events

Town	Event	Date	Contact
Carnarvon	Gascoyne Expo	May	08 9941 1146
	Fishing Competition	May/June	08 9941 1146
	Bowling Carnival	June	08 9941 1146
Gascoyne Junction	Junction Races	September	08 9941 1146

WA

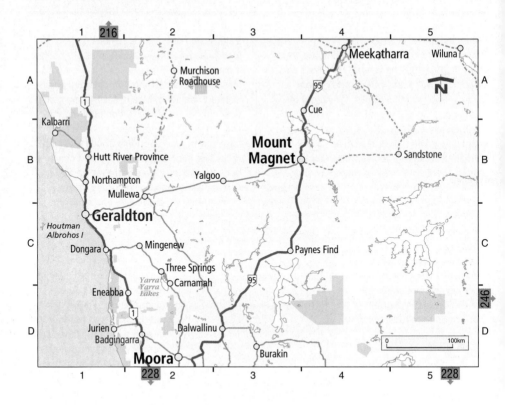

Western Australia's Mid-west is home to the world's finest collection of flowering plants. The spring blooming is regarded as the finest explosion of wildflower colour in the world.

get off the beaten track
travel the mid-west

Badgingarra

[D2] is awash with wildflowers in spring. A good way to view them is on one of the nature trails at Waddi Emu and Wildflower Farm, a medicinal herb farm and resort. Located 2 km off the Brand Highway and on 480 ha of wildflower country, the farm grows and harvests wildflowers and raises emus for commercial use.

Burakin

[D3] has recently earned the epithet 'earthquake capital of Australia' due to an extraordinary series of quakes, known as an earthquake swarm. A swarm is characterised by numerous earthquakes with similar magnitudes; there is often no clear main event. On Christmas Day in 2001 there were two earthquakes of about 3.5 on the Richter scale. The town recorded more than 10,000 earthquakes and tremors in the eight months from 28 September 2001. The largest measured just over 5 on the Richter scale.

Carnamah

[C2] has two giant murals. 'The Rover's Rest' on the walls of the Reynolds Store in Yarra Street measures 16 x 4.5 m and took 46 volunteers 442 hours

to complete. The mural 'Sale-o' on the wall of the Wesfarmers shed in Robertson Street shows a sheep sale. It's the only way to see a sheep sale in Carnamah as the yards have been demolished. Just west of Carnamah are the **Yarra Yarra Lakes**, a salt lake system with water that ranges in colour from salty pink in summer to a deep blue in winter.

DON'T MISS: The Carnamah Rodeo is held each year on 15 September (call 08 9954 5040 for details).

In the small town of **Cue** [A4] the Masonic Hall in Dowley Street is the most unusual among several interesting buildings in town.

The plaque outside says it all: 'Built in 1899 of timber and galvanised iron with a pressed tin interior, this unusual building is said to be the largest corrugated iron structure in the Southern Hemisphere. The lodge itself was consecrated on 21 April 1897 and brethren often travelled from as far away as Big Bell to attend the monthly meetings.

DON'T MISS: North of Cue (48 km) and more than 300 km from the sea, a mysterious Aboriginal depiction of a white, square-rigged sailing ship with two masts and square portholes graces **Walga Rock**. The painting has not been dated accurately, but it is almost certainly hundreds of years old.

Dalwallinu

[D3], long known as the biggest wheat producer in the state, is now gaining new fame with the most diverse concentration of acacia species in the world.

The fishing village of **Dongara** [C1] was the birthplace of Western Australia's longest-serving Premier, Sir David Brand, who held the position from 1959 to 1971. Among the 17 sites on the town's heritage walk is the Anglican Rectory and Church, which were built in about 1882 from limestone hewn from local quarries. The church pews, which are still in use today,

WA

were made from ballast collected from the beach next to the Church. More recyling is in evidence at Russ Cottage, a typical yeoman's cottage with a unique feature—the kitchen floor is made from the hard-packed material from scores of anthills. The main street is lined with Moreton Bay fig trees that were planted in 1906 by the Road Board at a cost of 16 shillings and 4 pence. At the southern end of the town at Leander Point is a Fisherman's Memorial and Lookout, constructed in 1869 as a guide for shipping. The Blessing of the Fleet is held at Dongara Port Denison at the start of the rock lobster season in November each year.

Eneabba

[D2] is famous for two things: welding rods and wildflowers. Not only is it one of the prime destinations for flower viewing in the spring, it also has 80 per cent of the world's rutile, the mineral used to manufacture welding rods.

The **Geraldton** [C1] Maritime Museum is devoted to ships that sank off the West Australian coast during the 17th and 18th centuries. The museum has remnants taken from the wrecks of the *Batavia*, which sank off the Abrolhos Islands in 1629; the *Zuytdorp*, wrecked near Kalbarri in 1712; and the *Zeewijk*, which struck a reef near the southern Abrolhos Islands in 1727. The lighthouse at Point Moore, built in 1878,

is the only all-steel lighthouse in Western Australia. It stands 34 m high and can be seen 26 km out to sea, but is not accessible for sightseeing. A small submarine on display on Marine Terrace, built for a local fishing group, was intended to test the feasibility of a fishery for green crayfish, but was never put into action.

DON'T MISS: St Francis Xavier Cathedral is widely regarded as the architectural masterpiece of priest-architect Monsignor John Hawes, and the most original and unusual cathedral in Australia. Built between 1916 and 1938, it is an eclectic Byzantine-style building.

Houtman Abrolhos Islands

[C1] is a chain of islands 60 km off the coast. In the early 17th century a Dutch merchant ship from Batavia came to grief on one of the islands. The captain set off in an open boat back to the city of Batavia, now Jakarta, for help. Meanwhile, members of the crew mutinied and began a massacre. On the captain's return all but two of the mutineers were captured and hanged, the first executions under a European legal system to take place on Australian soil. The remaining two were left to fend for themselves on the mainland near the mouth of the Murchison River. They were never seen again.

Hutt River Province

[B1] was the scene for a highly eccentric episode in Australian history: 'Prince Leonard' renamed his wheat farm the Hutt River Province, declared himself a prince and his wife Shirley a princess, seceded from Australia and Western Australia and, as a nice little earner, started printing his own stamps and currency. Of course none of his grandiose

ambitions had any validity, but he did attract an inordinate amount of publicity and simultaneously created a major tourist attraction.

Just south of **Kalbarri** [B1], on Red Bluff Road, is **Rainbow Jungle**, a rainforest bird park in a dry setting that might have been built as a set for a *Star Wars* film. Inside its stone walls you will find several species of endangered parrot. There's fantastic fishing on offer at the famous Blue Holes, Chinaman's Rock, Red Bluff, Frustration Rock, Oyster Reef and Waikarri Beach.

In **Meekatharra** [A4] Shire, you might get a surprise when you drive across what seem like cattle grids (or you would if you hadn't read this). The 'grids' are actually neatly painted white lines, designed to fool the

cattle into thinking they are proper cattle grids. That they apparently work speaks volumes about the intelligence of the local cows.

Mingenew [C2] has the distinction of being the largest inland receiving point for grain in Australia. It also boasts the country's largest (man-made) sheaf of wheat, erected in the centre of town.

Moora [D2] is the nearest town to the Berkshire Valley Folk Museum, a heritage farm with a homestead (1847), stables (1867),

SAVOURY MUFFINS

Travelling around the Mid-west of Western Australia can mean long hours in the car taking in the beautiful wildflower colours, so make sure you stock up on treats. One local recommended this recipe for muffins, which provide a hearty travelling snack.

1 cup self-raising flour
1 cup grated tasty cheese
1 cup milk

VARIATIONS
2 tbsp chopped parsley and/or
2 rashers of bacon, chopped and fried
**   with 1/2 chopped onion and/or**
130 g can creamed corn

Preheat oven to 200°C and grease large muffin tins. Place flour and cheese in a bowl and add milk and optional ingredients. Mix together lightly and spoon into muffin tins. Bake in oven for 15 minutes, or until golden brown. Makes 6–8.

Yvonne Launer,
CARNAMAH

shearing shed (1869), barn, manager's cottage (1856) and bridge (1869). The estate was built in the mid-1800s by James Clinch, a poor Berkshire farmhand who made good in the colonies. This was his attempt to reproduce a Berkshire farm, down to the finest detail, in the dry wheatlands of Western Australia. The locals claim that the two-arched bridge near the entrance to the village was the first of its kind to be built in Western Australia.

TRAVELLING DIPPAS

Doritos® Dippas are one of the biggest-selling snackfoods in Australia. These 100% white corn chips are delicious dunked into salsa or guacamole. Prepare and chill these recipes overnight before heading off for the day's journey.

SPICY GUACAMOLE
3 medium avocados
1 small onion, finely chopped
2 tbsp lemon juice
2 tbsp Doritos® Hot Salsa
1 medium tomato, peeled, seeded and
finely chopped
2 tbsp sour cream
1 tbsp chopped coriander
salt to taste

Place ingredients together in bowl and mash with fork. Mix in sour cream and lemon juice. Stir in remaining ingredients. Chill and serve with Doritos® Dippas Corn Chips.

SEVEN-LAYER DIP
Doritos® Mexicana Bean Salsa Dip
guacamole
sour cream
chopped tomatoes
chopped black olives
shredded cheddar cheese
chopped green onions

In a serving bowl layer the above ingredients in order. Chill and serve with Doritos® Dippas Corn Chips.

The Smith's Snackfood Company Ltd

Mullewa 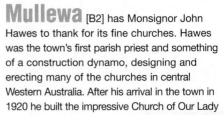 [B2] has Monsignor John Hawes to thank for its fine churches. Hawes was the town's first parish priest and something of a construction dynamo, designing and erecting many of the churches in central Western Australia. After his arrival in the town in 1920 he built the impressive Church of Our Lady St Carmel and the Holy Apostles St Peter and St Paul, which is Romanesque in style. Next door is the rectory, where he lived. It is open to the public and now houses a museum of his memorabilia.

 DON'T MISS: Mullewa's Wildflower Show on the last weekend of August is said to provide one of the best mass displays of wildflowers in Western Australia.

Murchison [A2] is the only shire in Australia that has no townsite. The sole business in this 43,800 sq km shire is the Murchison Roadhouse and Caravan Park. All roads are dirt. The total population of the shire is 160 people.

Sandstone's [B5] London Bridge—up the track from the State Battery—is the town's most interesting natural phenomenon, one of the spectacular sandstone breakaways in the area. It is nearly 800 m long and 10 m high at the centre. In the early 1900s carts would pass both across it and through it. The bridge is now regarded as too dangerous to walk on. East of Sandstone (166 km) is the Brewery, a specially constructed cave used to store beer.

GAZETTEE

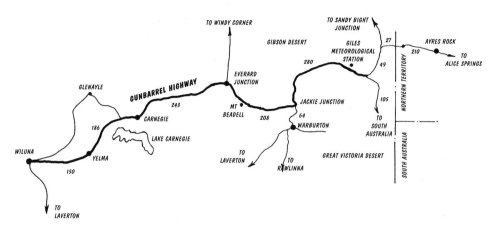

Three Springs [C2]

is dominated by massive wheat silos. Open-cut talc mines on the eastern edge of town supply the cosmetics and hygiene industries. The town is also in the heart of wildflower country.

Wiluna [A5]

is the western end of the famous Gunbarrel Highway and the beginning of the Canning Stock Route to Halls Creek, one of the best and toughest 4WD trips in Australia.

Yalgoo [B3]

has one of the most interesting and unusual of the church buildings constructed by famous West Australian architect–priest Monsignor John Hawes. In 1920 Hawes designed the wood and stone Dominican Chapel of St Hyacinth for the Dominican Sisters, and subsequently helped build it. The work calloused his hands so badly that he feared he might tear his silk vestments.

WA

Diary of Events

Town	Event	Date	Contact
Dongara	Larry Lobster Festival	September	08 9927 2186
Geraldton	Australian Speed Shearing Competition	August	0428 231 401
	Sunshine Festival	Sept/Oct	08 9956 6663
	Dragon Boat Classic	October	08 9964 1664
Mullewa	Agricultural Show	Aug/Sept	08 9961 4544
	Wildflower Show	August, last weekend	08 9961 1680

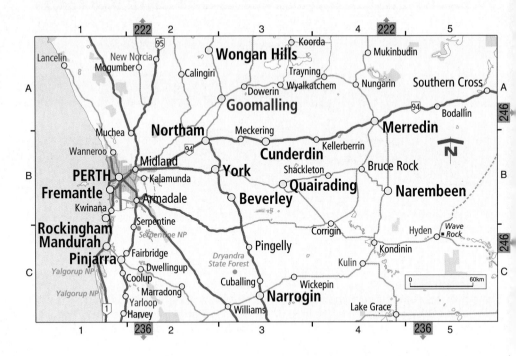

Bordered on the north-west by the Indian Ocean, Heartlands is known for its fresh rock lobsters, fantastic fishing and world-class windsurfing. Inland are rich farmlands and ancient jarrah forests.

get off the beaten track

head

to the heartlands

The major attraction in **Beverley** [B3] is the Aeronautical Museum, built to honour local inventor Selby Ford, who, with his cousin Tom Shackles, built a biplane called the *Silver Centenary*. The two men designed the plane in chalk on the garage floor and then spent two years building it. It first flew

in 1930 and was later taken to Maylands Airfield, where aviatrix Amy Johnson flew it. The centrepiece of the museum is the plane, which was never licensed because there were no blueprints (it's hard taking a garage floor to the licensing board). The Wheat Sheaf Inn was left isolated when the town moved closer to the railway station. It is now the Dead Finish Museum. Avondale Vintage Ploughing Day is held every year in Beverley at the Avondale Discovery Farm on the second Saturday in July. Visitors can participate in the traditional ploughing of the fields and see the Clydesdales at work.

 DON'T MISS: Visit the banks of the Avon River on the second Sunday in September when the Beverley Duck Race is on. Decorated plastic ducks vie for the honours down the river. There's a separate category for Best Dressed Duck and you can bet on your favourite with the Honest Bookies of Beverley.

Coolup [C1] Campdraft is the largest annual campdraft in Western Australia and a fantastic weekend of yarning, dancing under the stars and some serious campdrafting, with competitors travelling from all over the state to attend. It's held in November each year.

Corrigin [C4] is an unassuming little wheat-belt town with a fascinating and bizarre dog cemetery 7 km out of town

on the Brooktown Highway. Loving owners have placed quite elaborate headstones over the remains of their faithful four-legged companions, dedicated to 'Dusty', 'Rover' and 'Spot'.

Cuballing [C3] is east of **Dryandra State Forest**, one of the largest remaining areas of natural woodland in the West Australian wheat belt and a popular spot for birdwatchers. The forest now functions partly as an educational resource, giving some idea of what the wheat belt was like before it was cleared.

West of **Cunderdin** [B3] is the tiny settlement of **Meckering**. At 10.59 am on 14 October 1968 Meckering was struck by an earthquake measuring 6.8 on the Richter scale. It is regarded as the worst in Australia's history, splitting the countryside with a deep gash that can still be seen. It's marked by a sign, 'Earthquake Fault Line', about 4 km west of town on the Great Eastern Highway. Photographs of the earthquake are displayed in the Cunderdin Museum.

Dowerin's [A3] major claim to fame is its annual Field Days for agricultural machinery, held on the last Tuesday and

Wednesday of August. One of the largest events of its type in the Southern Hemisphere, it attracts more than 400 companies and crowds of up to 50,000 people.

Dwellingup's [C2] big attraction is

its steam trains, on either the Hotham Valley Tourist Railway to Pinjarra or the Etmilyn Forest Tramway. It was one of several towns burnt down in 1961—but the only one rebuilt.

Fairbridge [C1] is a fascinating

settlement, established in 1912 by Kingsley Fairbridge. It was intended as a farm school for educating orphans and poverty-stricken children of the British Empire. The houses nestle among stands of trees and all bear the names of famous Britons, such as Clive, Shakespeare, Nightingale, Exeter, Evelyn, Raleigh and Hudson. The setting is particularly pretty and things appear unchanged since the days of the orphanage. It operates now as a youth and environmental education and training centre, and still supports young people considered to be at risk.

The # Goomalling [A3] horizon

is dominated by four giant grain domes, the only ones of their kind in the Southern Hemisphere. Grain is usually held in flat or cell-type constructions, but these unique domes are better suited to the earthquake-prone geography. The town's one-teacher schoolhouse, built in the 1930s, is now Goomalling Museum, and the school room has been restored to its original state. It's a typical example of the schools that serviced the state's remote towns between 1900 and 1940. There's also a display of rare windmills. As the habitat of the Koomal possum, the town seems aptly named: Goomalling is an Aboriginal word meaning 'place of many possums'.

Harvey [C1] has the Moo

Shoppe with the largest range of cow giftware in the state, and Western Australia's own 20 m Big Orange. South of Harvey is the 'Big Tree', reputedly the largest jarrah in existence. Drive about 25 km south along the Mornington Road and follow the signs to the Big Tree.

Hyden's [C5] granite outcrops include

the spectacular Wave Rock, which is 2,700 million years old. At 14 m high and 110 m long it looks very much like a petrified breaking wave. The shape has been greatly highlighted by vertical streaks caused by chemical deposits that have been washed down the face of the wave by rain. The water, charged with carbonate and iron hydroxide, creates the varying greys, rusty reds and lighter sandy shades, giving an impression of the rolling sea.

Koorda [A3] is a typical wheat-belt

town which, in a bid to differentiate itself from all the other wheat-belt towns, promotes itself as 'corn dolly country'. The English custom of plaiting straw was brought to the area by Frank Lodge, who arrived in 1911 and continued plaiting until his death in 1962. In 1982 the local show took up the idea and instituted Australia's first (and presumably only) Corn Dolly Festival, held in September each year (call 08 9684 1219 for details).

Kulin

Kulin [C4] hosts the Kulin Bush Races every year on the first weekend in October at the base of the great Jilakin rock. It also boasts the Tin Horse Highway, leading from the town to the Jilakin Race Track. The roadside is dotted with a collection of around 30 horses made (from drums and bits and pieces from farm workshops) by farmers along the road east of Kulin. Not to be outdone, the people west of Kulin put together the West Kulin Whoppa. This is a giant horse made from a 28,000 ltr fuel tank; the legs are four 44 gallon drums and the head is made of two 60 ltr oil drums. It stands 7 m tall and 10 m long.

Lancelin

Lancelin [A1] is one of the world's top windsurfing spots. It's also home to the largest area of mobile sand dunes in the Southern Hemisphere, which cover more than 400 ha. The pristine 5,000-year-old sand dunes are shifting in a constant cycle and can reach heights of up to 50 m. They are among the few dunes in the world that flow to the water's edge. To see them you can join the world's largest 4WD tour coach, the Desert Storm. The vehicle is the brainchild of Glenn Doyle, a former professional international speedway rider. It was adapted from a 32-seat American school bus, equipped with specialised military running gear and tyres identical to those used

STRAWBERRY AND CUCUMBER SALAD

Strawberry Fields, just outside Wanneroo, produces some 100 tonnes of strawberries each year. They suggest that chicken, prawns, scallops or fish combine well with the flavours of this recipe. For a touch of difference, toss a cup of cooked bite-size pieces of your choice through the salad.

1 large burpless cucumber	1 tbsp finely chopped fresh mint
1 punnet strawberries	ground pepper
¼ cup olive oil	
1 tbsp orange juice	
2 tbsp lemon juice	

Rinse cucumber, cut into quarters lengthwise and remove seeds. Slice in finger-width sticks about 2 cm long. Combine all ingredients for the dressing in small airtight container and shake well. Marinate the cucumber sticks in the dressing for about 1 hour. Add strawberries and gently toss through to ensure strawberries are well coated with dressing. Garnish with extra chopped mint.

Sandra Langlands,
Strawberry Fields,
WANNEROO

WA

on American Monster Trucks. Tours run 7 days a week and offer sand boarding along the way (08 9655 2550).

Mandurah [C1] is a fast-growing

cosmopolitan centre famous for the delicious blue manna (swimmer) crabs that can be found in the Peel Inlet and Harvey Estuary in their hundreds of thousands. The peak crab-catching season is between late October and April. The town stages a large and colourful Crab Festival on the last weekend of February, with a range of cultural displays and a crab cook-off. Heading down the coast, **Yalgorup National Park** is one of only three sites in Western Australia where stromatolites are found. Ancient

formations made of microorganisms that trap sediment particles in layers, they are one of the first known life forms on Earth. The park also protects stands of tuart trees, eucalypts native to south-west Australia.

Merredin [A4] Railway Museum

is considered one of the finest railway museums in Australia, and is housed in the restored station building (1895). It has every piece of railway memorabilia imaginable as well as an 1897 locomotive that once hauled the Kalgoorlie Express. On Easter Saturday, 1999, Merredin won the title of 'Home of the World's Longest Road Train' and the right to be named in the *Guiness Book of Records*, a feat designed to raise funds and promote the

SPAGHETTI ALLA CIOCIARA

Fremantle is a town with a long history of accepting migrants from all over the world, the Italians being no exception. Fremantle, being a port town, was popular with Italian immigrants. The first Italian consulate was to be set up by Royal Consul Leopoldo Zunini in Albany in 1905 but when he arrived there he discovered that Albany was no longer the principal port of Western Australia. He travelled all over the state and pursued his passion for furthering Italian settlement in Australia.

 150 g smoked bacon, cut into
   small cubes
 1/3 cup good olive oil
 500 g tomatoes, peeled and chopped
 salt and pepper to taste
 oregano to taste
 chilli pepper to taste
 4 egg yolks
 1 bunch parsley, finely chopped
 500 g spaghetti, cooked al dente
 70 g pecorino cheese, grated

In a saucepan, cook the bacon with the oil until the bacon is transparent. Add the tomatoes and cook over a fairly high heat for a few minutes. Add salt and pepper, oregano and chilli and continue cooking for about 15 minutes, until the sauce thickens. A moment before removing the saucepan from the heat, add the four egg yolks. Mix them quickly, keeping the heat very low. Finish off by stirring the chopped parsley through. Add the sauce to the pasta and serve in large bowls, sprinkled with the pecorino. Serves 4.

Caroline Simpson, FREMANTLE

community. In the centre of town a stand of merritt trees is preserved as a reminder how the town got its name—from the Aborginal word 'merritt-in' meaning 'place of the merritt trees'. The trees were considered ideal material for making spears.

Midland

[B2] is the largest town in the Swan Valley and a base for touring the valley's vineyards, many of which trace their beginnings back to the early days of European settlement. Others were established later by Italian and Croatian immigrants. For information on the 41 wineries and 4 breweries in the Swan Valley visit the information centre in the town of Guildford at 111 James Street (a 10–15 minute drive south-west of Midland along the Great Northern Highway) or call them on 08 9379 9420. Time your visit for the Spring in the Valley wine, food and music festival, which is hosted at various wineries in the Swan Valley on the second weekend in October (call 08 9250 4400 for details).

Mogumber

[A2] was the site of the Moore River mission camp, Western Australia's main destination for Aboriginal children who were removed from their families from the 1930s on. The original chapel, an isolation ward and jail building are the only remaining buildings of the former site and inspired the set recreated for the film *Rabbit Proof Fence*. Director Phillip Noyce began his research for the film by visiting the former mission, now the Mogumber Aboriginal Settlement, with the story's author, Doris Pilkington Garimara. The settlement is run as a community centre and farm.

At ## Narembeen
[B4] the Hall Damara farm has the largest genetic pool of Damara sheep outside of Africa with 30,000 Damara breeding ewes. Damara sheep have a strong body, muscular shape and spiral horns. Their meat is considered especially tender and tasty.

GAZETTEER

New Norcia

[A2] was founded as a mission in 1846 by two Benedictine monks, Dom Rosendo Salvado and Dom Joseph Serra. Their original vision was to create a largely self-sufficient village based on agriculture. However, after the decimation of the local indigenous people by introduced diseases in the 1860s, Salvado concentrated on providing education for indigenous children brought to New Norcia from all over the state. With the arrival of Dom Fulgentius Torres in 1901, there was a change of direction and New Norcia became more like a traditional monastic settlement. Torres established the mission as a centre of ecclesiastical art and culture. The library holds a great number of rare books, one volume dating back to 1508. There is a fine museum, with what is considered to be one of the greatest collections of religious art in Australia. On the wall of the Abbey Church is a painting of the Mother of Good Counsel, allegedly the cause of the first miracle to occur at the settlement. The New Flour Mill, reputedly the oldest working flour mill in the state, was built in 1879. It is still operational and flour from the mill is used to produce the bread baked in the monastery's ovens. The Old Flour Mill over the road dates from the 1850s, and is the oldest surviving building in New Norcia.

The Avon River in ## Northam
[B2] is home to some unusual white swans; as the state emblem is a black swan, these white ones are quite a novelty. They were brought to Northam from England around 1900, and have thrived on the river ever since. This is the only place in Australia where these large birds have found a natural breeding ground. The

suspension bridge that crosses the river near the Fitzgerald Street Bridge is, according to the locals, the longest pedestrian suspension bridge in the Southern Hemisphere.

WA

Nungarin [A4] is host to the Wheatbelt Markets on the first Sunday of every month (except January and February)—the biggest country markets in Western Australia, with a huge variety of stalls lined up along the main street of the town from 10 am to 2 pm. Also at Nungarin is the Heritage Machinery and Army Museum, which has an extensive collection of army vehicles, uniforms, equipment, agricultural machinery, a doll collection and even a matchbox car and truck collection. The museum is located in the only intact army building remaining in the town and reflects Nungarin's role as the Army Depot and Workshop, set up after the outbreak of World War II to support the army if Japan invaded.

Pingelly's [C3] main attraction is the Old Court House Museum, on the corner of Pasture and Parade Streets, which contains the usual folk museum memorabilia plus a wonderful idiosyncrasy—an amusing rock that swings outside the museum and which, we are assured, you should not miss.

Pinjarra [C1] is one of the oldest towns

in Western Australia, and has a number of picturesque old buildings on the banks of the Murray River. Cooper's Mill on **Culeenup Island** was the first in the region.

Rockingham [B1] has a recent addition to its industrial landscape—a huge wheat terminal. With a capacity approaching one million tonnes, it is reputedly the largest wheat storage and shipping complex in the world.

 DON'T MISS: For information about the Rockingham Rodeo, including dates, call 0408 863 331.

Serpentine [B2], best known for the waterfall that cascades over a sheer granite rock face, is also important for two rare species of tree—the Darling Range ghost gum and the salmon white gum.

The bank at # Shackleton [B4] claims to be Australia's smallest bank. Since it measures only 3 m x 4 m, few are likely to dispute the claim.

Southern Cross [A5] was the site of the first gold rush in Western Australia. A man named Glass found the gold while cleaning out a granite-bottomed pond. Streets are named after the stars and constellations. The town marks the end of the wheat-belt and the beginning of the goldfields to the east.

Wanneroo [B1] is home to Strawberry Fields, about 10 km north of town on Wanneroo Road, where around 100 tonnes of strawberries are harvested each year for domestic and overseas markets. They sell strawberries, port, liqueurs, sparkling wines, apple cider and honey mead, all homemade from their crops.

GAZETTEE

The highlight of # Wickepin [C3] is Albert Facey's house, which still contains the original Facey family furniture. He walked out of this house during the Depression, and it offers a glimpse of the rugged lifestyle of the small wheat-belt farmer in the early 1930s. The success of Facey's autobiography, *A Fortunate Life* (1981), is a remarkable event in recent Australian publishing history. He vividly describes the area around Wickepin in his book, and anyone familiar with it will find the AB Facey Heritage Trail well worth following.

In **Williams** [C3] a very unusual underground tank was constructed by convicts in the 1880s, with a capacity of 4,500 ltr. It is near the river on the Albany side of town.

In **Wyalkatchem** [A3] one of the original bulk wheat bins now serves as a museum housing a wide range of farm machinery.

Yarloop [C1] is an historical timber town that has preserved some of the old workshops from the days of horse and steam power. The Yarloop Heritage Trail is a 2.5 km walk starting outside the Replica Store at the Yarloop Workshops and taking in the Mill Cottages in McDowell Street, which date from the 1890s, the Old Wooden Pub, St Joseph's Catholic Church, the mill doctor's residence, the hospital, single men's quarters, boarding house and finally the Yarloop Mill Workshops.

GAZETTEER

The **York** [B2] Motor Museum has reputedly the largest display of vintage cars in Australia. It is a working museum and many of the cars participate in rallies, displays and other events. One exhibit is a Renault from the first series of cars ever built by the company, in 1901. The museum also has one of the famous 4.5 ltr 'Blower' Bentleys, possibly the most sought-after Bentley of all, despite the fact that this model never won a major race and did not finish a single long-distance event. Western Australia's biggest jazz festival is held in York annually on the Queen's Birthday weekend.

DON'T MISS: The Festival of Motoring, a century of vehicles in action, is held every year in July (call 08 9641 1301 for dates).

Diary of Events

Town	Event	Date	Contact
Armadale	Springtime Tulip Festival	October	08 9497 3543
Avon River	Duck Race	September, 2nd Sunday	08 9646 1200
Beverley	Avondale Vintage Ploughing Day	July, 2nd Saturday	08 9646 1004
	Duck Race	September, 2nd Saturday	08 9646 1555
Brookton	Old Time Motor Show	March 2004, biennial	08 9642 1017
Coolup	Campdraft	November	08 9531 1827
Dowerin	Field Days	August	08 9361 1021
Fremantle	Festival	November	08 9431 7878
Koorda	Corn Dolly Festival	September	08 9684 1219
Kulin	Bush Races	October, 1st weekend	08 9880 4017
Mandurah	Mandurah Crab Festival	February, last weekend	08 3483 1111
Merredin	Regional Wildflower Display	September	08 9041 1202
Rockingham	Rodeo	TBC	0408 863 331
Swan Valley	Spring in the Valley	October	08 9379 9420
York	Jazz Festival	Queen's Birthday weekend	08 9641 1301
	Festival of Motoring	July	08 9641 1301

WA

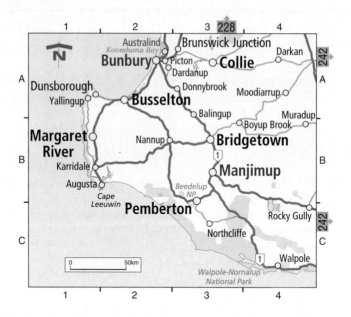

S tretching south from Busselton through Margaret River to Augusta, the South-west offers a range of activities including underground caves, whale-watching cruises, diving tours, canoe tours, bush tucker and some of the world's most famous surfing beaches. Beyond are magnificent forests, such as the Valley of the Giants in the Walpole–Nornalup National Park.

get off the beaten track

savour the south-west

South of **Augusta** [B1], off the rocky headland of **Cape Leeuwin** at Australia's most south-westerly point, two great oceans meet. You can see the juncture of the Indian and Southern Oceans from the headland or you can climb the limestone tower, reaching 56 m above mean tide level, for a better look. The walk up to the 1896 lighthouse is dotted with wildflowers, and the view out over the point is one of the great experiences on the West Australian coast. The lighthouse is the tallest in Western Australia and is still operational. Nearby is a thoroughly calcified waterwheel, locked in place by the calcium carbonate in its own water supply.

Australind's [A2] St Nicholas' Church is reputed to be the smallest in Western Australia. It is only 3.6 m wide and 8.2 m long, and was originally built in 1848 as a workman's cottage. The church is always open. It was

bought by the Church of England in 1915. The name of the town comes from 'Australia' and 'India', because it was originally intended that the region should breed horses for the Indian Army. Unfortunately, the Australind settlement failed because of the poor soils.

In **Balingup** [A3], at Birdwood Park Fruit Winery, you can enjoy wine made from—you guessed it—local fruit. Nearby, in **Donnybrook**, the Old Goldfields Orchard and Tearooms produces cider from its own apples.

Near **Boyup Brook** [B3] there is an intriguing sight—a huge grapevine, which residents believe to be the largest in Australia, possibly the world. The current owner's grandmother is said to have brought a piece of grapevine back from Bridgetown as a switch for flicking the horses pulling her sulky. She planted it and, more than 100 years later, it has grown into a huge plant. To view this remarkable vine, ask at the Boyup Brook Tourist Centre at the corner of Bridge and Able Streets. The vine is on private property and not always accessible.

JILL AND MARJORIE'S FLORENTINES

Jill and Marjorie ran a B & B for seven years in Bridgetown and, although they have now retired, their renowned Florentines are fondly remembered by locals, who say they were very cheering on a crisp morning or, for that matter, at any time.

1 cup sultanas
2 cups cornflakes
1 cup unsalted, roasted peanuts
1/4 cup red glacé cherries, chopped
1/4 cup flaked almonds
2/3 cup condensed milk
300 g dark chocolate, melted

Preheat oven to 180°C and line a baking tray with baking paper. Combine sultanas, cornflakes, peanuts, cherries, almonds and condensed milk in a bowl. Mix well so that it all sticks together. Place heaped tablespoons of mixture on the tray, leaving about 5 cm between them. Bake for about 10 minutes, or until lightly browned. Cool on tray, then remove to wire rack. Spread base of each biscuit with melted chocolate. Make lines with a fork on chocolate as it is just about to set. Once chocolate is firm, store biscuits in airtight containers in the fridge.

Marjorie and Jill, BRIDGETOWN

WA

Bridgetown
[B3] hosts the Blackwood Marathon Relay on the last Saturday in October. This is an unusual relay in that it incorporates horseriding. Competitors run 2 km, canoe 7.3 km and swim 1 km, then ride a horse for 16 km and a bicycle for 20 km.

Brunswick Junction
[A3] is graced with a life-size statue of a Friesian cow, erected by the Lions Club as a tribute to the area's dairy industry.

Bunbury
[A2] was known as Port Leschenault until renamed by Lieutenant Governor Sir James Stirling, after Lieutenant Henry William St Pierre Bunbury, who developed the difficult inland route from Pinjarra to Bunbury. St Mark's Anglican Church in nearby **Picton** is the second-oldest church in Western Australia. It was built in 1842 by the newly arrived Reverend John Ramsden Wollaston with the help of his sons. He used pit-sawn timber, wattle-and-daub construction, and cloth soaked in linseed oil for the windows. The building was extensively restored in 1969. A bell salvaged from the wreck of the *North American* still tolls in the church's belfry. As well as being a port, Bunbury is a centre for the woodchip industry. The site of what is now the Albany Bowling Green is reportedly where potatoes were first grown in Western Australia around 1827. By the end of the century it was clear that yields were better down south and in the 1920s and 1930s irrigation saw an upsurge in production in the area around Bunbury and Dardanup. Today Smith's contracts local farmers to grow pototoes for their quality crisps.

DON'T MISS: The Dolphin Discovery Centre on **Koombana Bay** has an interaction zone down on the beach where wild dolphins drop in more or less regularly. You can stand, swim or snorkel with them in pleasant and generally uncrowded conditions.

GAZETTEER

Busselton
[A2] has quite a few claims to fame, including one of the longest jetties in the world. The jetty, originally built of jarrah, is one of the most distinctive constructions in Busselton. After various extensions it is now nearly 2 km long, but

it was closed to shipping in 1972. It was damaged by a cyclone in 1978 and is now used only by anglers and holidaymakers. The jetty makes for a fine, easy dive and is the best jetty dive in Western Australia. Just offshore from **Dunsborough** (20 km west of Busselton) is one of the best wreck dives in Australia. HMAS *Swan*, a once proud warship, is now an artificial reef. In the town of Busselton the pretty St Mary's Church of England, built in 1844–45, is said to be the oldest stone church in Western Australia. Across the street in Victoria Square is the steam train *Ballarat*, the oldest train in Western Australia. It was built in Victoria in 1871 and was used to haul timber.

Collie
[A3], situated among beautiful jarrah forests, serves Western Australia's only developed coal field. All Saints Anglican Church was built between 1915 and 1928, thanks to a generous English benefactor who never saw the building she paid for. Local lore has it that when the first bishop of Bunbury went to England to drum up funding for his struggling parish, Nora Noyes decided to stump up the cost of a new church in honour of her late husband Colonel Arthur Walter Noyes. As both she and her husband shared an interest in coal mining, she insisted that the church be built in a coal mining town—hence the choice of Collie. According to her wishes it was built in early Italian style, with no east-facing window because of the hot sun. The Tourist Coal Mine, next to the Tourist Information Centre, is a replica of an underground coal mine with tours to show how it all works. Call the Tourist Information Office for times 08 9734 2051.

At **Dardanup** [A2] is the small settlement of Gnomesville. It is inhabited by a whimsical collection of garden gnomes. Visitors are encouraged to send a gnome from their home town back to Gnomesville.

Around **Manjimup** [B3] and Pemberton you'll find the world-famous jarrah and karri trees, which grow up to 45 m and 90 m high respectively. The karri is the world's third-tallest tree species—one felled in Brockman was said to be 104 m. Dotted throughout the jarrah and karri forests is a network of Tree Towers, built by the Forests Department in the late 1940s as fire lookouts. To keep costs down the department simply constructed platforms in the tallest trees, rather than build free-standing towers. To the south of Manjimup, on the South Western Highway, is the Diamond Tree Lookout. This vantage point, for those brave enough to climb up, is 51 m above ground. Out of Manjimup on Graphite Road are 'The Four Aces', a row of four awe-inspiring karri trees around 300 years old. A sign at the site informs us that 'Karri is one of the largest living things on our planet. One tree can weigh over 200 tonnes, grow to 90 metres in height, use 170 litres of water a day, produce 1 kg of honey per season, take nine people holding hands to span its girth, and do it all for 400 years.' Nearby are the remnants of One Tree Bridge, which started as an enormous karri tree felled to span the 25 m river as the base for a bridge. The superstructure was hewn from nearby jarrah trees. The old bridge began to sag and was removed by a work gang, who pulled it onto the west bank in 1971 and faithfully rebuilt the 17 m section you can see there now. It's not just trees you will find here; the region's soils are perfect for potatoes. From the late 1940s the combination of spring planting, sprinkler irrigation and increased fertilising led to a major breakthrough in yields. In 1973 Smith's began the potato crisping industry in the area that today supplies local and export markets.

WA

At Margaret River [B1] you are spoilt for choice. You can shop for superb craftwork in timber or pottery, sample unusual cheeses, climb down into a fossil-filled cave, visit a marron (the west's version of the yabby) farm or one of the many wineries, surf, windsurf or sip a cappuccino at Prevelly Beach. When you've indulged sufficiently you can repent in the stunning, rammed-earth St Thomas Moore Catholic Church, or at the Greek chapel of St John the Theologian at Prevelly Park. The chapel commemorates the Australian, New Zealand and British troops who died in Greece in World War II. Mammoth Cave, 21 km south-west of Margaret River, features the fossilised remains of prehistoric animals and majestically shaped rock formations. The

Leeuwin–Naturaliste National Park

stretches along the coast (starting 30 km west of Busselton) and offers the keen angler, diver and surfer some of the best coastline in Australia. Hamelin Bay and Cosy Corner are just two magical places in the area. The park also boasts some of the world's best caves. Calgardup Cave is spectacular due to reflections from the water covering the floor of its three chambers. Giants Cave is 800 m long. The caves are unlit and self-guided, so take a torch. Margaret River has gone from a sleepy farming backwater enjoyed by a few surfers to an internationally acclaimed wine district in just three decades. Western Australia's wine industry focused almost entirely on the Swan Valley for over a century, but the balance shifted dramatically to the Margaret River from the 1970s. The first plantings were in 1967 (Vasse Felix) and the area quickly achieved widespread recognition for premium quality wines. The strongly maritime-influenced climate of the Margaret River produces wines of very distinctive styles—bracing crisp, herbaceous sauvignon blanc and semillon (frequently blended); contrastingly soft and creamy chardonnay; and cabernet sauvignon that somehow manages to simultaneously display bright cherry fruit and a sinewy, almost gravelly structure. This wine-producing region excites winelovers the world over.

One of Nannup's [B2] local 'legends' is that there may still be thylacines (Tasmanian tigers) in the area. There have been reported sightings over the years and

Deer farming in Western Australia

The first deer introduced into Australia were Indian chital deer, imported in 1803. After it was established that they could sucessfully breed in the wild five further species were introduced. Deer farming started in Western Australia in 1979 from a stock of animals from the eastern states of New South Wales and Victoria. Today there are more than 74 registered deer farms in the state, most in the high-producing lands of the South-west. A popular item on the menu of many Margaret River winery restaurants, venison is a local delicacy.

Tips for cooking venison

Because of its low-fat characteristics venison must not be overcooked. To pan fry or grill steaks, cut 2–2½ cm thick, brush with olive oil, sear in hot pan and cook for 45 seconds to 2 minutes each side. For thin steaks cut 1 cm thick, sear in hot pan, cook for 30 seconds each side. Serve pantried or grilled steaks with your choice of sauce, including mushroom, cream and any sauce made from berry fruits.

fossils in the caves to the west have shown that this was once a thylacine habitat.

Pemberton's

[B3] most popular tourist attraction is the Gloucester Tree, with its fire lookout 61 m above ground. You can climb to the top via a hair-raising 153-rung ladder, made of bolts hammered into the tree. For a less fraught experience visit the nearby **Beedelup National Park**. Follow the trail along to the beautiful Beedelup Falls, which takes in the Loom Cascades and the swing bridge at the foot of the falls.

Just west of **Walpole** [C4] in the **Walpole–Nornalup National Park** is the Valley of the Giants—a grove of tingle trees (huge eucalypts unique to the area) that is part of nearly 160 sq km of wilderness. The tingle trees can be viewed from the Tree Top Walk, a suspended track built 38 m above ground that runs for about 600 m through the treetops. The Nornalup and

Walpole estuaries and their various feeder streams provide a near pristine habitat for many forms of aquatic life and are a magnet for recreational anglers fishing for black and silver bream, trevally (called 'skippy' in this part of the world), herring and a dozen other species of table fish.

Just before **Yallingup** [A1] on Caves Road is the turnoff to Yallingup Cave, accidentally discovered in 1899 by Edward Dawson while searching for missing horses. The limestone cave is notable for the impressive colours of its interior, formed by the iron and manganese present in the rock. Early visitors took a two-hour horse and buggy ride along a dirt road from Busselton just to see it.

WA

Diary of Events

Town	Event	Date	Contact
Bridgetown	Blackwood Marathon Relay	October, last Saturday	08 9761 1555
Busselton	Wildflower Exhibition	September	08 9752 3935
	Agricultural Show	November, 1st weekend	08 9754 2241
Margaret River	*Sunday Times* Margaret River		
	Wine Region Festival	November	08 9483 1111
Nannup	Nannup Music Festival	March, Labour Day weekend	08 9483 1111
	Flower and Garden Festival	August, throughout	08 9483 1111

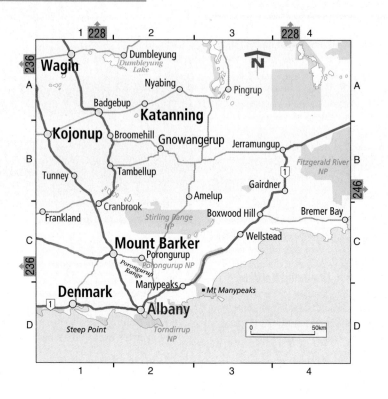

The Great Southern region's scenery varies from sweeping rural plains with wheat, sheep, cattle, fruit and wine grapes, to a coastline with rugged cliffs and headlands, gently curving bays and pristine beaches.

get off the beaten track

groove into
the great southern

Albany [D2] was the first town in

Western Australia, pre-dating Perth by two-and-a-half years. Cheyne's Beach Whaling Station in Albany was Australia's last when it closed in 1978 and now houses the world's largest whaling museum. The coastline around Albany had been sighted by Europeans as early as 1627, when Dutchman Pieter Nuyts sailed across the Great Australian Bight on the *Gulden Zeepard*. It was allegedly on the basis of maps drawn by Nuyts that Jonathan Swift, when writing *Gulliver's Travels*, located the land of the Houyhnhnms, on an island just south of the present site of Albany. With extraordinary prescience, Swift had Gulliver land on the coastline, eat oysters and be chased by Aborigines. This claim is disputed by South Australians who believe the whole scenario belongs to the islands off Ceduna. The Church of St John the Evangelist (1848) claims to be the first church consecrated in Western Australia. It is a fine

example of the severe, square Anglo-Saxon style commonplace in rural England. Patrick Taylor's Cottage is one of the few early Albany buildings still surviving. It is a wattle-and-daub house, probably constructed as early as 1832, now a folk museum. The highlight of Stirling Terrace is the gracious Old Post Office (1869–70), recognised as the oldest post office in Western Australia and now part of the University of Western Australia. Just South of Albany is **Torndirrup National Park**, which has spectacular coastal rock formations. The landscape here is particularly dramatic in spring when heathlands of wildflowers give way to steep sandy slopes and dunes, massive granite outcrops and sheer cliffs.

Isolated # Bremer Bay [C4] township

is one of the two main access points for conventional vehicles into the huge **Fitzgerald River National Park** [see also Hopetoun, in Goldfields and Nullarbor]. This is the only habitat in the world supporting the prickly frilled royal hakea and the delicate pink quaalup bell plant species. At Point Ann a whale-watching platform is the best place to spot Southern Right and Humpback Whales when they visit annually between July and November. Also within the national park is Quaalup Homestead, which includes a small stone cottage built in 1858 by early settler John Wellstead. The Wellstead Estuary is popular for all types of watersports. Bremer Bay itself offers both stillwater and ocean beach fishing.

Cranbrook [C1] is known as the

Gateway to the Stirlings. Together with the town of **Amelup** it is a jumping-off point for **Stirling Range National Park**. The highlight is Bluff Knoll, the highest peak in the south-west of Western Australia at 1,095 m above sea level. The main face of the bluff forms one of the most impressive cliffs on the Australian mainland. The local Qaaniyan and Koreng Aboriginals called Bluff Knoll Pualaar Miial (great, many-faced hill) because the rocks on the bluff resemble faces. The park has 1,500 species of flora (more than in the entire British Isles); 87 of these are found nowhere else on Earth. The best time to visit is late spring and early summer (October to December) when the park is ablaze with wildflowers. At **Frankland**, you can visit Alkoomi Wines, one of the largest vineyards in the south-west of Western Australia and producer of Alkoomi cabernet sauvignon, regarded as one of the best reds in the state. The vineyards are 11 km west of Frankland at 225 Lower Stirling Terrace and are open daily (08 9855 2229).

GAZETTEER

WA

DUTCH MEAT CROQUETTES

Pleun and Hennie Hitzert migrated to Australia in 1980 and decided to build a real Dutch windmill in the Stirling Ranges. In June 1997 the Lily Windmill, an authentic, 16th-century design, brick 'ground sail' mill, turned her sails for the first time. It's one of the largest traditional windmills built in Australia, standing five storeys high. The Lily Windmill is currently a restaurant and wine cellar.

5 tbsp butter	salt and pepper
4 tbsp plain flour	to taste
1 cup stock	$1/2$ tsp nutmeg
500 g cooked veal	1 egg, separated
of gravy beef,	1 tbsp cold water
minced finely	4 tbsp dry fine
$1/2$ onion, finely	breadcrumbs
chopped	oil

Melt butter in a saucepan, add flour and stir over a low heat until dark brown in colour. Add stock gradually, stirring the mixture continually to obtain a smooth thick sauce. Simmer, stirring for 10 minutes. Remove from heat, add the meat, onion, salt, pepper and nutmeg. Add egg yolk, stir to combine and pour mixture onto a flat dish and wait until it is cold. Divide into 8–10 portions and shape into croquettes. Beat egg white with water. Roll each croquette through egg white, then through breadcrumbs. Deep fry in hot oil until golden brown.

Hennie Hitzert, STIRLING RANGES

Denmark [D1] is not named after

the country of Hamlet but after naval surgeon Dr Alexander Denmark, a friend and colleague of the West Australian colony's surgeon–superintendent who explored this coast. **Dumbleyung Lake** is the largest natural body of inland water in Western Australia, at approximately 13 km by 6.5 km. On New Year's Eve 1964, Donald Campbell set the world water speed record here. He drove his boat *Bluebird* across the lake at the remarkable speed of 444.66 km/h (276.3 mph), making him the world's fastest man on both land and water.

Gnowangerup's [B2]

annual highlight is the stud merino field day, reflecting the community's history of sheep farming. The steam tractor in the main street was brought out from England in 1889.

Katanning [A2] is one of Australia's

most multicultural rural towns, with a significant population of Malay Muslims who came to the area in the early 1970s from Christmas Island. It is another town of 'firsts'—the first electric power plant in the state and therefore its first electric street lights (even before Perth), the first free lending library and one of the first inland swimming pools.

Kojonup [B1] was little more than a

freshwater spring until 1837 when local Aboriginal people showed it to Alfred Hillman. He reported the finding back to Governor Stirling who decided to establish a military outpost there. By 1845 it had grown to support a military barracks, built on the site of the spring. Today, the barracks still stands on its original site and houses the Kojonup Pioneer Museum. A four-room stone structure, the barracks is one of the oldest buildings in Western Australia. The old railway station is the tourist centre and reflects the early colonial architecture, using natural materials such as stone and mud. Time your visit to coincide with the annual Wildflower Festival.

Manypeaks [D2] is named after

Mt Manypeaks about 10 km south of the town, which is little more than a rural outpost on the road to Bremer Bay. The mountain is 562 m high and was sighted by Captain Matthew Flinders in January 1802 while surveying the south coast region in his ship *Investigator*. In his journal Flinders wrote: 'There are a number of small peaks upon the top of this ridge, which induced me to give it the name Mount Manypeak.' Access to the mountain is restricted due to environmental concerns.

Pingrup [A3] has joined the long

list of Australian towns with Big Things, with the World's Largest Handpiece (the electric clippers used for shearing sheep). Made of sheet metal, the giant handpiece promotes the town's annual shearing

competition. It stands in the main street outside the town's old wheat containers, which have been converted into a venue for the competition.

South-west of **Porongorup** [C2] is the Porongorup Range, composed of granite dated at about 1,100 million years old and thought to be a melted portion of the Australian continental plate. The **Porongorup National Park** has many unusual natural rock formations, such as

the Balancing Rock and the Tree in the Rock. It is also home to 76 orchid species, including the beautiful slipper orchid, hich blooms each December. The name Porongorup is a corruption of the Aboriginal word 'purringorep'. St Werburgh's Chapel, 12 km south-west of **Mount Barker**, is a small mud-walled chapel built privately in 1872. Its hand-wrought iron chancel screen and altar rails were made on the property. It is just one of just 32 religious buildings in the world dedicated to St Werburgh who was Abbess of

Ely until her death around AD 700. On the outskirts of Mount Barker on Pearce Road is the world's only

complete collection of all 76 banksia species, at Banksia Farm. Guided tours are available (call 08 9851 1163).

Wagin [A1] has one of the largest

historical villages in Western Australia. It consists of 22 buildings and its main street appears as in colonial times. It also features what is allegedly the Southern Hemisphere's biggest statue of a ram.

Diary of Events

Town	Event	Date	Contact
Albany	Wildflower Festival	September	08 9844 4545
Cranbrook	Wildflower Display	Sept–Oct	08 9826 1008
Gnowangerup	Merino Field Day	Aug/Sept	08 9824 1257
Kojonup	Wildflower Festival	Sept/Oct	08 9831 0500
Mount Barker	Wildflower Festival	Sept–Oct	08 9851 1163
Pingrup	Shearing Competition	March	08 9820 1031
Porongorup	Wildflower Display	October	08 9853 1153
Walpole	Native Orchid Show	Sept–Oct	08 9840 1111

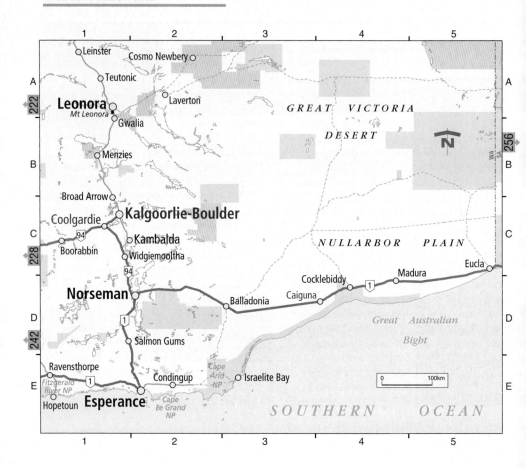

get off the beaten track

trek the goldfields to the nullarbor

The highway from **Balladonia** [D3] to Caiguna includes the longest stretch of straight, tarred road anywhere in the world: 146.7 km without a bend, but beware—the speed limit is still 110 km/h. Balladonia's greatest claim to fame dates back to 1979, when the Skylab satellite hit the ground nearby. Some of those parts are now on display in Esperance.

Caiguna

[D4] Blowhole is 5 km west of Caiguna along the Eyre Highway and clearly signposted. On the Nullarbor, blowholes are formed when the limestone bedrock is eroded by weather or chemical processes to form a vent. The limestone bedrock prevented the burial of early British explorer Edward John Eyre, who was brutally murdered in April 1841 by two members of his expedition. Almost 40 years later locals organised a successful search for his remains and today you can visit his memorial 20 km south of the town.

Cocklebiddy

[D4] Cave, north-west of the Eyre Highway at Cocklebiddy (ask at the roadhouse for directions), is one of the longest underwater caves in the world. In 1983 a French team of speleologists set an underground record here when they made the longest cave dive in the world. For the fit and adventurous, and for those with a good torch, a walking track leads deep under-ground to the water's edge. Allow plenty of

time for this walk and expect to crawl and climb down, and up, ladders. The cave is open at all times but leave the diving to the

experts. The Eyre Bird Observatory, at the end of a 4WD track signposted from the highway east of Cocklebiddy, must be one of the most isolated birdwatches around. It contains the old Eyre Telegraph Station, built in 1897 and now both the Post Office Museum and the warden's centre for the observatory. Since its inception, the observatory has identified about 260 different species, including Major Mitchell parrots, red-necked stints and ruddy turnstones that have migrated over 10,000 km from the icy wastes of Siberia. The observatory holds a complete set of books telling the story of the Earth and its history. The books were donated by Harold Anderson, an eccentric American who decided that the Nullarbor was the best place to sit out the nuclear holocaust he was expecting. He collected all the books he wanted to survive and shipped them to the observatory. Shortly afterward he was mugged in the US, and died before he could join his books.

Coolgardie

's [C1] magnificent Warden's Court Building was reputed to be

the largest building in Western Australia outside Perth when it was built in 1898. It now houses the town's museum. Besides gold, Coolgardie gave the world the Coolgardie safe, a wire mesh box on a wooden frame, with hessian sides kept damp with dripping water. The safe was hung in the

A DESERT MENU

KANGAROO RISSOLES

Populations of the western grey kangaroo, which are found in abundance in the south of Western Australia, are carefully managed. Clearing the land for settlement and agricultural purposes has caused kangaroo populations to search the surrounding pastures for food, causing damage to local farmer's crops. As a child, in the first half of last century, Reva Best lived on the Nullarbor and used to go roo shooting and quandong (wild peach) collecting with her father. This recipe comes from those times, frequently served with a quandong pie to follow.

1 leg kangaroo
3 large potatoes, peeled
3 large onions, peeled
2 carrots
1 large piece pumpkin, peeled
1 parsnip and 1 turnip if available, peeled
2 eggs, beaten
1 cup fresh breadcrumbs
salt and pepper to taste
1 tbsp mixed herbs
flour
oil or dripping for frying

Mince together the kangaroo, and all vegetables. Add the eggs, breadcrumbs, salt, pepper and mixed herbs. Form into rissoles, roll in flour and shallow fry in the oil or dripping until cooked on both sides. Serve with mashed spuds, beans, pumpkin and gravy.

QUANDONG PIE

Collect about half a kerosene tin of quandongs (loose-skin type). Remove flesh from kernel and wash well (or brush grub droppings from underside) and place in large pot with a cup or so of water and a cup or so of sugar (more or less to taste). Cover and gently simmer until cooked, stirring often. Meanwhile, make pastry or use packaged shortcrust pastry and line a pie dish. Fill with fruit, draining back juice. Cover with pastry, brush with milk and sprinkle with sugar. Cook in a moderate oven until pastry is golden and crisp. Serve with custard or cream.

Reva Best,
HERVEY BAY

 breeze to keep provisions cool and free from flies. As late as 1990, major gold finds were still being made by lone prospectors—the Happy New Year Nugget, found in December 1990, weighed 3 kg. Coolgardie Goldfields Water Supply Scheme was an engineering achievement unrivalled anywhere in the world when it was constructed in 1903. Eight steam-driven pumping stations sent water from the Helena River along 566 km of steel pipeline, supplying 23,000 kilolitres of water daily to the goldfields. Nowhere else could boast so much water being pumped so far.

 DON'T MISS: An exhibition in the old Coolgardie Railway Station (1896) tells the story of the famous Modesta Varischetti rescue. In 1907 a sudden rain storm trapped Varischetti

GAZETTE

underground for nine days while fellow miners rushed to bail out the mine and divers desperately attempted to reach him where he was caught, inside an air pocket in the maze of mine tunnels. The drama, and Varischetti's climactic rescue, captured world attention.

Esperance [E2] is the second

windiest place in Western Australia, after Cape Leeuwin (which lies exposed to the full force of both the Indian and Southern Oceans). The reliability of the strong winds made **Ten Mile Lagoon**, 16 km west of Esperance, perfect for Australia's first commercial wind farm, which now generates 30 per cent of the town's energy on windy days. A second wind farm is located at nearby **Nine Mile Beach**. North of Esperance, more than one million hectares of scrubland was transformed into rich agricultural land when minute amounts of trace elements were added to the deficient soil in the 1950s and 1960s. Further east (about 50 km) is **Cape Arid National Park**, with its old telegraph station and fine beaches. You can drive here in a normal car if you drive with care, but a 4WD is handy—any further north along the beach is real 4WD territory.

DON'T MISS: Whistling Rock in **Cape Le Grand National Park** does whistle in certain wind conditions. It is 60 km south-east from town and is well signposted.

Eucla [C5] has moved. The

original 19th-century town is all but buried now under shifting sands; the new town was built about 5 km away on higher ground. A rabbit plague in the 1890s caused the dunes to destabilise. Cats were thought to be the solution to the rabbit problem and a shipment was brought from Adelaide. Unfortunately they only created another plague—feral cats. The old telegraph station is one of the most photographed sites in Australia, despite the fact that it is no more than a few old stone walls slowly disappearing under mountainous white sand dunes on the edge of the Great Australian Bight. The town's location, near the state border, was no accident. Allegedly, messages would arrive in one part of the telegraph station, be carried across to a wall (representing the state boundary), passed through a pigeon hole, then sent on their way by the telegraphist on the other side of the wall. The location was also suitable because it was possible to build a supply jetty, the only place for hundreds of kilometres either way where boats could moor. The ruins of the jetty can still be seen.

DON'T MISS: The cliffs to the east and west of Eucla form one of the longest stretches of uninterrupted cliff face in the world. The combined length of the Bunda and Baxter cliffs, which rise between 40 m and 90 m above the Great Australian Bight, totals 375 km.

Gwalia [B1] is a

goldmining town. The first manager of the Sons of Gwalia mine on the Sons of Gwalia gold reef was Herbert Hoover, later to become chief engineer for the Chinese Imperial Bureau of Mines. In 1929 he changed his resumé completely by becoming the 31st President of the United States. The Sons of Gwalia was the second largest gold mine in Western Australia. Gwalia

WA

was also the site of the state's first tramway, and the first government-owned hotel. Established in 1903 in an attempt to stamp out the sly grog trade, it caused the state's first known beer strike. In March 1919, 50 residents vowed not to return to the hotel unless the glasses were cleaned better and the manager was fired. They kept it up until September. The pub is still there, and the glasses are, reputedly, clean. Gwalia Market Day is held each year on the first weekend in August and includes a billy cart race, a bush dance on the Saturday night and a rock drilling competition.

Hopetoun

[E1] is one of the two main access points for the **Fitzgerald River National Park**. While the park covers only 0.1 per cent of Western Australia's land surface, more than 20 per cent of its plant

species are found there. The graceful weeping gum (*Eucalyptus sepulcralis*) grows only on quartzite in the park. Its given name means 'of the tomb', as this forlorn-looking species was thought to be ideal for cemeteries. The park is also a particularly eerie place, with long vistas overlooking the Southern Ocean. You might even see seals and dolphins playing in the waves. Fishing along the coast and in the river inlets is also popular, salmon being one of the species caught regularly.

Kalgoorlie–Boulder

[C1] is the site of the most recent and most significant gold rush in Australia's history, in 1893. 'The Golden Mile' is thought to be the richest gold-bearing area in the world. Saint Barbara's Festival in December celebrates

the importance of mining to the goldfields community and honours St Barbara, the Patron Saint of Miners. The British Arms Hotel at 22 Outridge Terrace (next to the Museum of the Goldfields) has the dubious distinction of being the narrowest hotel in Australia—only 3.2 m wide.

DON'T MISS: A short distance along Outridge Terrace beyond the pub is a tree planted on the spot (as far as can be determined) where Paddy Hannan found the gold that sparked the 1893 goldrush.

Leinster

[A1] is an isolated nickel mining town with a surprising attraction—an old drive-in theatre that was reopened in 1996 and now screens films once a month. The drive-in is at the end of Worrung Road, on the left when heading into town on the main road.

The Leonora

[A1] countryside is so flat that a popular local diversion is to climb **Mt Leonora** at sunset to watch the shadow of the mountain speed across the countryside. The town was the biggest settlement in the area after being founded as a gold-mining town in 1896. Today it is a railhead for copper and nickel. The first electric trains in Western Australia operated here but they are long gone.

Madura [D4] is a road stop along the
Nullarbor Plain, established here in complete isolation in 1876 as a pastoral homestead. It was well known for breeding horses, producing polo and cavalry horses for the British Imperial Indian Army. Today there is a roadhouse with a shop, a motel, swimming pool, restaurant and camping facitilies (call 08 9039 3464 for details). About 2 km west of Madura, heading north along the Eyre Highway, is a lookout with scenic views of the Madura Pass and Roe Plains. These landforms are estimated to be at least 10 million years old and were the result of changing sea levels caused by the advance and retreat of the ice ages.

Menzies [B1] proudly unveiled its
town hall clock on 31 December 1999. The tower had been blank-faced for nearly a century awaiting its clock, which allegedly sank with the ship bringing it from England. Recent research, however, suggests that the clock may never have actually been ordered. Sandalwood is still harvested near Menzies; it remains high in value because no synthetic alternative exists.

Norseman [D2] is named after the
horse that stumbled over a large gold nugget, which in turn led to its owner's discovery of a huge gold reef—the horse deserves its statue in the main street. Norseman's quartz reef is the richest in Australia. **Dundas Rocks**, 22 km south, are around 500 million years old. The Dundas Hills, the remains of a vast range of folded mountains, are said to be 3,000 million years old, placing them among the world's oldest.

Just west of # Ravensthorpe [E1]
is a boulder with a plaque that marks the West Australian standard time meridian.

It's at the first rest bay along the road. Ravensthorpe has a wildflower show in the first two weeks in September that features over 700 local species.

Widgiemooltha's [C1]
Roadhouse is justly famous for its staggering 'truckie's brekky'—2 sausages, 2 eggs, 2 slices of bacon and 2 pieces of toast, grilled tomato plus your choice of beans or spaghetti.

WA

Diary of Events

Town	Event	Date	Contact
Esperance	Wildflower Show	September	08 9071 2443
Gwalia	Market Day	August, 1st weekend	08 9037 7210
Kalgoorlie	The Croc Festival	Jul/Aug/Sept	08 9820 0700
	Spring Festival	October, 3rd Saturday	08 9021 5858
Ravensthorpe	Wildflower Show	September	08 9838 1277

in search of the perfect wave

Mathew Hooker has surfed in Peru, Mexico, Morocco, California, France, Portugal, Spain, Indonesia and New Zealand, as well as just about every break around Australia, in search of the perfect wave …

Australia is one of the world's most desired surfing destinations. Its coastline is so vast and diverse that, unlike any other country, it can offer the chance to ride perfect waves at any given time. Surfers, driven by their eternal quest to ride perfect waves, frequently leave girlfriends (and boyfriends) and jobs to follow the classic Australian tradition of the 'surf-ari.'

If one were to embark on a surfari in search of the perfect wave, you'd start on the Gold Coast, Australia's surfing mecca. In summer, you can share fun waves with crowds so dense that you can forget about the risk of sharks, and of riding the perfect wave. Perhaps resolve, instead, to enjoy watching some of the world's best surfers dominate one of the world's most competitive arenas.

A short, pleasant drive across the border can see you revelling in some of New South Wales' best waves. Lennox Heads, Angourie and Byron Bay once offered an escape from the flourishing crowds of Sydney and Brisbane. Now, however, they're all well populated with city escapees living 'alternative' lifestyles.

Victoria has a strong surfing community that provides a stable base to global surf company giants Rip Curl and Quiksilver. Bell's Beach, one of the world's first surfing recreation reserves and home to the world's longest-running surf competition, consistently provides perfect waves and even stepped in on the silver screen as the final challenge for *Point Break*'s archetypal philosopher-surfer Bodhi.

Across the channel in Tasmania there is Shipsterns, the most awesome right-breaking wave in the Southern Ocean. Though it's one spot where you would want to leave your surfboard at home. Just watching this giant tube can require a change of underpants. Remaining a local secret for years, it was first exposed in the mainstream surfing media when Australia's most accomplished tow-in team went searching for the island continent's gnarliest wave.

Cactus, on the 'Anxious Coast' of South Australia, is another spot where you'd want to leave you're surfboard behind, that is unless you don't mind sharing waves with large white pointer sharks (the local record is 1,208 kg).

Red Bluff, in Western Australia, is the country's most remote wave, sandwiched between the harsh Western Desert and the indomitable Southern Ocean. Its remoteness is an especially poignant fact to remember if in need of urgent medical attention.

A word of warning: If you're a novice surfer, stick to the well-populated, patrolled beaches. Australia's wild coastline can quickly turn the crystalline dreams of the uninitiated into a waking nightmare.

Photographer: Jason Eadie; Story by Mathew Hooker

Parker's Tomato & Basil.
Not your ordinary 97% fat free pretzel.

Also available in Italian Herb and Cracked Pepper.

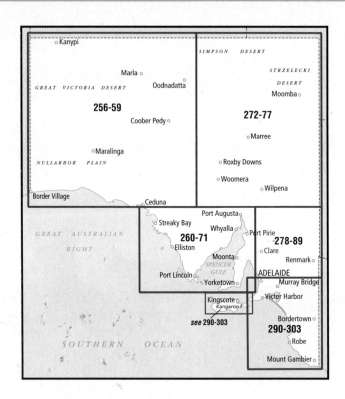

south a

South Australia is a state of contrasts and surprises. The state is a gateway to the Australian Outback and to a dazzling array of unique tourism experiences, including its world-renowned wine regions.

While it is Australia's driest state, with two-thirds of its area given over to desert, the desert eventually yields to lush green hills and valleys, including Australia's most famous wine-growing region, the Barossa Valley. With a Mediterranean climate, 3,700 km of coastline and an area of 984,377 sq km, South Australia can lay claim to some of the best seafood and fresh produce in the world, an unpolluted environment and natural wonders that are second to none.

SA

ıstralia

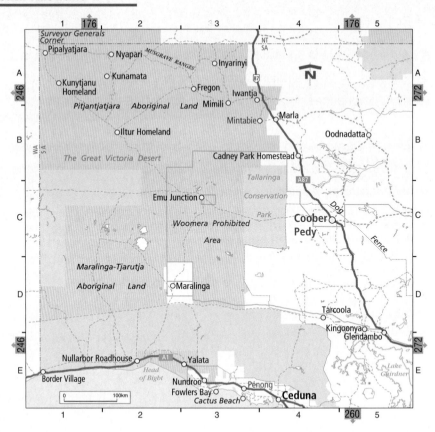

The Nullarbor Plain is the world's largest single slab of limestone, at around 250,000 sq km. Though named because 'nulla arbor' is Latin for 'no trees', there is some vegetation. To the north is the Great Victoria Desert, stretching to the Musgrave Ranges and, beyond, Uluru.

get off the beaten track
span the nullarbor and the desert

The Border Village [E1] area has

two lookouts offering truly awe-inspiring cliff-top views. If you're brave enough (standing 100 m above the Southern Ocean), it is quite common to see seals on the rocks below and to hear their distinctive barking. **The Great Australian Bight** is the largest indentation in the Australian coastline. The Bunda and Baxter Cliffs on the edge of the Nullarbor Plain are said to be the longest cliff line in the world, at 375 km.

Off Ceduna [E4] is where the characters

of Lilliput live, if map references in *Gulliver's Travels* are taken literally. Jonathan Swift wrote that Lemuel Gulliver was shipwrecked in the vicinity of 30°S latitude. Swift's Islands, Lilliput and Blefuscu, are said to be St Francis and St Peter Islands, off Ceduna. This is subject to some dispute. Albany in Western Australia makes similar claims but without the map references. The Ceduna Radioastronomy Observatory, operated by the University of Tasmania, maps compact radio sources in the southern sky at high resolution and studies a range of astrophysical problems. Sea-dune-ah Tours can arrange tours of the observatory. Situated on Murat Bay, Ceduna offers good catches of garfish, snook, tommy ruff, squid and delicious blue swimmer crab.

DON'T MISS: Ceduna's Oyster Festival celebrates the sea's bounty in October.

Coober Pedy [C4] is an

Aboriginal phrase for 'hole in the ground', which is how pretty much everyone lives to escape the heat. About 95 per cent of the world's opals are mined in Australia, well over half of them in Coober Pedy. Anyone with a prospecting permit can strike it rich by either sinking a shaft or 'noodling', sorting through the piles of waste other hopefuls have left. The Big Winch at Coober Pedy has the largest opal fossil in the world on display. Possibly the

GAZETTEER

largest opal in the world, the Olympic Australis, was found here in 1956. One of the highlights of Coober Pedy is a visit to the underground house of Crocodile Harry, aka Arvid Von Blumentals, a Latvian baron forced to leave his country after WWII. He claims to have worked as a crocodile hunter in northern Australia before coming to Coober Pedy to fossick for opals in about 1975. Crocodile Harry's underground house featured

WILD PEACH (QUANDONG) CHUTNEY

Nita Brook says it's best to cook quandongs shortly after picking or store them in the freezer, because they sweat in the heat and mould quickly. She should know; they grow like wildfire around Penong. Nita sells her chutney at the Penong Woolshed, which dates back to 1860 and now houses a museum.

3 kg quandongs, halved, stoned, washed in hot water and drained
1¹/₂ kg green apples, peeled and cut in quarters
5 cups brown vinegar
2¹/₂ cups water
¹/₂ tsp cayenne pepper
30 g cloves
45 g ground ginger
1 tsp salt
1 tsp allspice
750 g sugar

Mince together the quandongs and apples. Place in large saucepan with remaining ingredients and stir over heat without boiling until sugar is dissolved. Bring to boil and simmer, stirring occasionally, for 3 hours. Pour into hot sterilised jars, seal when cold.

Nita Brook, PENONG

SA

in *Mad Max: Beyond Thunderdome*, and before they left the crew created a sculpture out of metallic trash, dubbed the

KANGAROO TAIL SOUP

Reva Best now lives in Queensland at Hervey Bay and experiments with camp-oven cooking, but was brought up on the Nullarbor. In those days there was no electricity or refrigeration and the family of five cooked on a wood stove and ate by kerosene lamps. A traditional Christmas dinner was roast bush turkey (bustard) with pickled wombat (cured by Aunt Best). Reva writes: 'While out roo shooting or collecting firewood it was a thrill to come across a quandong tree loaded with ripe fruit. We'd pick it by the bucketful for Mum to make quandong jam, and on those nights it was kangaroo tail soup or rissoles and quandong pie for dinner (though I never could, and still can't, bring myself to eat roo meat).'

1 kangaroo tail washed and cut into pieces	4 cloves
	salt and pepper to taste
1 carrot, diced	1 tbsp tomato sauce
1 turnip, diced	
3 small onions, diced	2 ltr water or stock

Blanch kangaroo tail in boiling water, drain and place in a large saucepan. Add remaining ingredients. Boil gently for 3–4 hours. When cold, remove excess fat from surface, reheat and serve. (Oxtail is a good substitute.)

Reva Best, HERVEY BAY

Orchestra, that rattles in the breeze. At the eastern end of Coober Pedy is the famous Underground Catacomb Anglican Church, a unique expression of the materials and activities of the local area. The altar is made like a winch, and both the crucifix and lectern are made out of mulga wood. Behind the altar are two air vents. At the local golf course there is not a blade of grass on the fairways and the greens are oiled sand. In Coober Pedy's 'Boot Hill' cemetery lies Carl Bratz, buried in a galvanised iron coffin (he was a conservationist) with a beer keg as a headstone (he was also a sociable man).

About 130 km south-west of Coober Pedy is **Commonwealth Hill**, once Australia's largest sheep station—running up to 70,000 sheep in an area of more than 10,000 sq km—and now within the **Woomera Prohibited Area** (WPA). The WPA is a huge area of 127,000 sq km (about 13 per cent of the state) once used for the processing of uranium ore and still considered contaminated. The land is owned by the South Australian government and Aboriginal communities, with some very small areas belonging to the Commonwealth.

DON'T MISS: The Coober Pedy Opal Festival has a cabaret, street parade, races, dancing and fireworks.

Near **Fowlers Bay** [E3] Beach there is a prominent monument that recalls the occasion in 1802 when Matthew Flinders and party, slowly circumnavigating Australia in the *Investigator*, came ashore, becoming the first recorded Europeans to step onto South Australian soil. At Fowler's Bay you can explore the shifting sand dunes and fish from the jetty or from nearby Scott's Beach and Mexican Hat.

Kingoonya [D5], before the highway

was moved, was a thriving centre. It now has only one general store.

The Maralinga [D2] nuclear tests were

carried out between 1952 and 1963 as a joint venture of the British and Australian governments. The *Maralinga Tjarutja Land Rights Act 1984 (SA)* returned 76,000 sq km of the far north to its traditional Aboriginal owners.

The Mintabie [B3] Opal Field, on the

eastern edge of the Great Victoria Desert, has a 9-hole golf course called the Mintabie Swan Lake Golf Club. Most events are played at dusk due to the heat, and keen members are supplied with luminous golf balls.

East of the Nullarbor Roadhouse

[E2] on the coast is **Head of Bight** (pick up a permit there as you'll be on Aboriginal land), the best place to watch southern right whales mate, between May and October. North of the roadhouse is one of the Nullarbor's impressive caves, Murrawijinie, the only one with general public access. The Eyre Highway runs south of the plain and mainly along the coast. The first bicycle crossing of the Nullarbor Plain was in 1896; the first car crossing in 1912.

Oodnadatta [B5] was once the

Central Australian railhead from where the camel trains ferried freight to the scattered communities of the Outback. The track from Oodnadatta to Alice Springs carried the famous *Ghan* train, named for the Afghan camel traders. Flooding forced the removal of the track to higher ground in the 1970s.

A section of the line remains, and the station is now a museum. You'll find it hard to miss the pink roadhouse run by Adam and Lynnie Plate. The couple were attracted to Oodnadatta's mix of Afghan, European and Aboriginal cultures and decided to settle here. Their choice of colour has turned the roadhouse into a landmark for travellers. The Oodnadatta Track between Marla and Marree, to the east, follows an ancient Aboriginal trade route along a line of freshwater springs.

Just south of Penong [E3] is

Cactus Beach, famous worldwide for big waves and great surfing. Especially popular are three powerful breaks, Cactus, Castle and Caves, which test board riders' ability to dodge the white pointer sharks that also favour the waters. If you are of surfing ilk you'll be welcome at the small jumbled camping ground. South of town is a pleasant coastal drive along good dirt roads. Penong is the first 'real' town as you come from Western Australia—the other names on the map are roadhouses. You can buy cheap diesel here. The Penong Woolshed was established well before there was a town. It was built of local stone and the building has been put to a variety of uses. As well as housing shearers during the season it has subsequently been a post office, church, hall, library and the first school, in 1893. It now houses a historical museum and sells arts and crafts.

Just 7 km east of Yalata [E3] the Dingo

Fence crosses the highway. It is 6,000 km long and runs from the cliffs of Bight to Jimbour in south-east Queensland, passing through Coober Pedy on the way.

SA

Diary of Events

Town	Event	Date	Contact
Ceduna	Oyster Festival	October	08 8625 2780
Coober Pedy	Opal Festival	Easter	0417 833 982

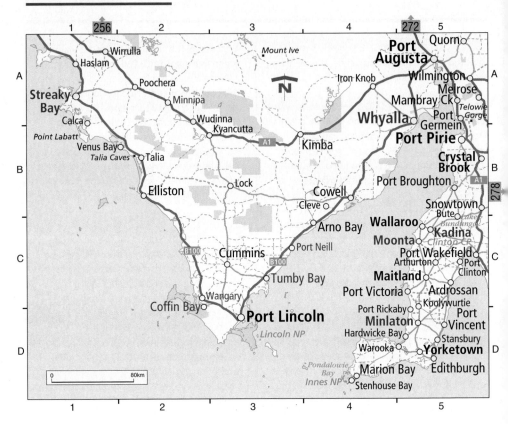

get off the beaten track

discover

the eyre

and **yorke peninsulas**

Ardrossan

[C5], one of the largest ports on Yorke Peninsula, has the Ardrossan and District Historical Museum. The building is where the stump-jump plough was invented in 1876. A working model of the plough is on display in the park beside East Terrace.

Arno Bay

[C4] has a Welcome Wall, made by a local resident, that is 29 m long by 1 m high. It's made of local stone and features a life-size concrete dolphin. Arno Bay is also a good spot for diving, surfing and fishing, from boat, jetty, beach or even the creek. **Redbanks**, 6 km north of Arno Bay is an area of auburn cliffs that drop off to a beach cove with rock pools dotted along the water's edge, and a great place to catch King George whiting or a huge red snapper. For surfing, the most consistent spot in the area is Sandies, a reef about 20 m straight out from the boulders on a beach about 2 km north of Redbanks. There's a signposted turnoff; then follow a small corrugated road up to the beach (4WD is recommended).

At **Bute** [C5], named after Bute Island in the Firth of Clyde in Scotland, there's a bromeliad nursery, claimed to be the only nursery exclusively devoted to bromeliads in the state. Group tours are available by appointment (call 08 8826 2020).

Near **Calca** [A1] on the road from **Point Labatt** back to the Flinders Highway, are the fascinating granite outcrops known as Murphy's Haystacks. It is difficult to see the outcrops from the road—to visit them, ask for specific directions in Streaky Bay or Calca. The

ROAST DUCK

This recipe comes from Mrs Fay Story of Tumby Bay, whose husband Ross has been exhibiting show poultry since 1946, when he was eight years old. He has been twice awarded the champion waterfowl of the Adelaide Royal Show for his white mammoth Muscovy ducks. Buyers come from all over Australia to purchase his birds and, naturally, the Story family eats quite a few of them. They recommend this hot roast duck recipe.

1 large duck
shredded fresh breadcrumbs
mixed herbs
fresh parsley
1 large onion, finely chopped
1 potato, finely chopped
2 eggs, well beaten
4 or 5 bacon strips

Remove all of the bird's inner parts and wash thoroughly. To prepare seasoning, combine shredded breadcrumbs, mixed herbs, parsley, onion, potato and eggs. Mix all together and stuff into the bird, not too tight, as seasoning swells during the cooking process. Tie off the opening or secure with a skewer. Drape bacon strips across the bird, cover with foil, and bake for at least one hour at 200°C. Lower heat to 180°C, remove foil and bake duck until skin is crisp and brown. Serve with hot assorted vegetables of choice and gravy.

Fay Story, TUMBY BAY

'haystacks' are a series of dramatically weathered granite outcrops possibly as much as 1,500 million years old. They were named for two reasons: they look like old-fashioned haystacks, and they stand on Murphy's property. Point Labatt has the only permanent mainland colony of Australian sea lions, with an estimated population of 35–50. To add to the appeal of the area, there is a whale watch between June and October.

At **Cleve**'s [B4] Yeldulknie weir and reservoir, the wheelhouse, completed in 1912, is heritage listed. Overlooking Cleve, the surrounding farms and the Spencer Gulf

GOLDEN SYRUP DUMPLINGS

After finishing off Mrs Story's Roast Duck you can try her favourite family dessert. Ross Story not only exhibits poultry but also set up the first ever Rent-a-Duck business. The ducks are cheap to hire and they work without complaint, removing garden snails and providing a novelty family pet, as well as eggs. Mr Story came up with the idea to keep his show birds occupied and fed.

DUMPLINGS	SYRUP
1 cup self-raising flour	1¼ cups water
pinch of salt	1 tbsp golden syrup
1 tbsp butter	½ cup sugar
1 egg, beaten	1 tbsp butter
milk, to mix	

To make syrup, bring all ingredients to the boil in a saucepan. To make the dumplings, rub butter into flour, add the egg and enough milk to form a light dough. Break the dough into pieces the size of a walnut and drop them into the boiling syrup mixture. Cover the saucepan and cook gently for about 15 minutes. Serve with hot syrup and custard, cream or ice-cream. Makes about 12.

Fay Story, TUMBY BAY

is Ticklebelly Hill, used during World War I as an aeroplane spotting point. There has been much speculation over the years as to the origin of the name, with even a competition aimed at outing the truth. The most popular suggestion is that young lads took their girlfriends to the park area up on the hill. The National Trust have erected a cairn there as a reminder of the hill's war history, alongside cement footings from the original bunkers. In 2000 a 7 m cross was erected to commemorate the new millennium and dedicated to the Christian faith of the early pioneers.

The sprawling **Coffin Bay** National Park [C2] has fabulous protected beaches within the confines of the bay, while the more dramatic unprotected western coastline displays fantastic limestone shapes. There's also some hard four-wheel-driving along a couple of the beaches here.

Cowell [B4] is the site of one of the world's biggest jade deposits, with 115 separate jade outcrops over 10 sq km known as the Cowell Jade Province. The deposit is recognised as containing about 80,000 tonnes, which means that it represents about 90 per cent of the world's known jade reserves (this excludes China, for which figures are not available, and which presumably has considerably more jade). In the decade to 1987 more than 1,500 tonnes of jade had been extracted, of which 40 per cent was either dark green or black. Cowell is also in the process of developing an oyster industry. On the corner of Main and High Streets, opposite the Commercial Hotel, is a rather grandiose 'black stump' weighing 2,060 kg. A plaque explains that a large stump was placed between two hotels as a New Year prank in 1972 so that both could claim to be the best 'this side of the black stump'. Then somebody stole it. This larger, heavier version was later placed in its stead. Cowell was the first Australian home of May

Gibbs, the author of *Snugglepot and Cuddlepie*, after she emigrated to Australia with her family. She lived in a house on the Cowell–Cleve Road in 1881, now marked by a large old tree and a granite stone with a brass plaque.

The **Cummins** [C3] World Championship Kalamazoo Classic is held on the first weekend in April, the only kalamazoo race to be held in Australia. Kalamazoos are the hand-operated railcars (trikes) used by rail workers. A record time of 38.59 seconds over 300 m was set in 2001. The Big Heave Competition—pushing a flat-top, 1.5 tonne railway cart as far as possible—and the Dog Spike Driving Competition celebrate the town's railway heritage.

Off **Edithburgh** [D5], on the heel of the Yorke Peninsula, is Investigator Strait where, in 1909, the steamship *Clan Ranald* sank in heavy seas, with the loss of its 30 crew members. You can take a tour of nearby **Troubridge Island**, and even stay in the lighthouse keeper's cottage.

On the road from **Elliston** [B2] to the coast (40 km out of town) are the Talia Caves. These 'caves' would be more accurately described as large eroded cavities in the cliff face, created by

the action of wind and water on what are essentially compacted sand dunes. One such cavity is 'The Tub', a collapsed limestone crater into which visitors can climb. On the scenic drive from Elliston to Anxious Bay is a spot called Blackfellows where there are some of the best surfing waves in Australia. Take the last turnoff before the road heads up to the lookout.

Haslam [A1] still has, on the edge of town, the corrugated iron tank constructed by the South Australian government in 1917 to collect rainwater for the town's supply. It can hold a quarter of a million gallons (more than four million litres). Now it is used only by the fire services and private tanks.

Iron Knob [A4] is known as the birthplace of the Australian steel industry. Since the mine began operating in 1899, 150 million tonnes of iron ore have been extracted. You can take a mine tour in your own car accompanied by a guide. They leave from the local tourist office. For details call 08 8646 2129.

Kadina [C5], the Yorke Peninsula's largest town, was a bleak and desolate place until Walter Hughes, a former ship owner and opium trader, leased land there in the 1850s. He suspected that there was copper in the area, a hunch that proved correct, with rich deposits discovered. Hughes Chimney, on the foreshore, is the last tangible remnant of the town's golden era of copper. It was built in 1861 from 300,000 bricks and stands 36.5 m high. The presence of copper attracted large numbers of Cornish miners to the area. Kadina and the nearby towns of Wallaroo

SA

and Moonta are collectively known as 'Little Cornwall'. By 1875 there were 20,000 people in the district, most of them of Cornish origin. You can buy and sell coins at the Banking & Currency Museum, an old bank building in Graves Street.

 DON'T MISS:
The Kernewek Lowender is a Cornish festival held in odd-numbered years on the Adelaide Cup long weekend in May. It is held in Kadina in conjunction with Moonta and Wallaroo. Promoted as 'the world's largest Cornish Festival', Kernewek Lowender is a powerful reminder of the impact of Cornish people on the whole area. There are dances (the Furry Dance), craft displays, Cornish folksingers and pastie-making competitions.

In **Kimba** [B3] is the Sturt Desert Pea Shoppe, one of the few commercial outlets selling the plant and its seeds. The Kimba and Gawler Ranges Historical Museum is said to be one of the best of its kind in the state, being comprised of a series of buildings that give a realistic impression of life in pioneer days, including a reconstruction of the original home of the Haskett family, the first pioneers to grow wheat in the area. The reconstruction used the original materials of the home built by Sam Haskett in 1908. Call 08 8627 2349 for more information. On the outskirts of Kimba is White's Knob, an ironstone conglomerate outcrop on Tola Road. There's a good view over the town and surrounding countryside. The Big Galah in front of the Halfway Across Australia Gem Shop on the Eyre Highway at Kimba stands 8 m high. The slang phrase 'you

big galah' (meaning you're a bit of a dill) came from the fact that galahs fly south in the winter, a very foolish thing to do in the Southern Hemisphere.

Near **Kyancutta** [B3] is Corrobinnie Hill, a unique granite outcrop. You can also visit **Pinkawillinie Conservation Park**, which contains 10 per cent of the mallee woodlands remaining from pre-colonisation days. Both places are only accessible by 4WD.

Maitland [C5] was named in 1872 for Lady Jean Maitland, the wife of the first Lord of Kilkerran, Scotland, who is thought to have had a family connection with Governor Fergusson, then Governor of South Australia. The town overlooks Spencer Gulf and the Yorke Valley. The National Trust Museum has an interesting German heritage section because of the number of Germans who settled in the area, particularly at **Kilkerran**.

Marion Bay [D4] was originally a gypsum port. It was named after a shipwreck south of Troubridge Shoal in 1851. There's a safe swimming beach on one side of the town and a surf beach on the other. Beach anglers come here for the autumn mullet run.

Melrose [A5] is the oldest town in the Flinders Ranges. As it was the most northerly outpost of the South Australian colony, in the 1850s it became headquarters of one of the world's largest police districts, spanning the continent from Spencer Gulf north to the Arafura Sea. Bluey Blundstone's Blacksmith Shop was built in 1863 and has been authentically restored and fully equipped with tools and machinery of the era.

 # Minlaton's [D5] major attraction is the Captain Harry

GAZETTEER

BAKED NANNYGAI WITH LEMONGRASS PESTO

The nannygai is a fish sometimes given the nickname 'nanny goat' by anglers but is usually marketed commercially as redfish. There are several different species, with the swallow-tail nannygai of South Australia being the most significant. The Marion Bay Tavern, at the tip of the Yorke Peninsula, serves a delicious baked nannygai, but if you're in the area ask the locals about the best places to catch your own. Their slightly moist white flesh is deliciously sweet and combines beautifully with these herbs and flavours.

1 x 5 kg nannygai, cleaned and scaled
1 clove garlic
salt and pepper to taste
1/2 bunch parsley
1/2 bunch coriander
10 sticks lemongrass, finely chopped
approx. 1/2 cup olive oil
75 g cashews, roasted
drizzle of lemon juice
1 medium tomato per person
small bunch assorted young salad
leaves, rocket and baby spinach

Preheat oven to 180°C and grease a baking tray. Using a sharp knife, make diagonal slits into nannygai flesh through to the bone. To make pesto, in a food processor, blend garlic with a pinch of salt and pepper, then add herbs and lemongrass. Blend until smooth and drizzle in olive oil to form a paste. Season, then add cashews: blend quickly if you prefer them chunky, longer if you want them finer. Add lemon juice to taste. Rub pesto over fish and place on baking tray in oven. Bake until the flesh pulls easily away from the bone at the thickest part near the head (about 20 minutes per kg). Cut tomatoes in half, brush with olive oil, season with salt and pepper. Place on separate oven tray to cook for 20 minutes. To serve, place fish whole on a platter, with the tomatoes placed on either side. Serve young salad leaves, rocket and baby spinach on individual plates. Serves 6.

Tristan Reynolds and Nigel Rich,
Marion Bay Tavern,
MARION BAY

SA

Butler Memorial, which houses the extraordinary Red Devil aircraft. This plane is the only one of its type still in existence. Captain Harry Butler purchased the plane from the British government, shipping it to South Australia in 1919 and flying it on 6 August from Adelaide to Minlaton, where he lived. This was the first flight across sea in the Southern Hemisphere by any plane. Captain Butler then flew the Red Devil for joy rides, barnstorming and peace loan promotion. It had been designed by the British government with great urgency in 1916 to meet the pressing need for a fast, single-seat fighter aeroplane with the greatest possible firepower. It had a speed of 209 km/h. Minlaton also calls itself the Barley Capital of the World. The barley is used chiefly for beer making.

Minnipa [A2], on the Eyre

Highway, is surrounded by rocks that are worth a visit. Just 2 km north is Yarwondutta Rock, which has attracted geologists from around the world for its joint fractures, active tafoni (a granite boulder hollowed out underneath), waves and platforms. Another 10 km north is Pildappa Rock, which rivals Western Australia's Wave Rock in length and height. The deep gnamma holes (depressions that are natural reservoirs) ensure a permanent water supply. From Pildappa Rock you can continue north on relatively good roads but through remote country to **Mt Ive**, a sheep station that caters for passing adventurous travellers. From here you can get to **Lake Gairdner** [see Flinders Ranges and Outback map] where in March every year or so (depending on whether the lake is wet or dry) members of Dry Lakes Racers Australia gather from all over the world to test their nerve and their cars on the flat, dry saltbed. Efforts to break the Australian land speed record still take place on this lake. Call 03 5472 2853 for details.

Moonta [C5] is one of the three towns

(along with Kadina and Wallaroo) that make up Yorke Peninsula's 'Copper Triangle'. Copper was discovered at Moonta in 1861. According to a 1914 history of the Moonta mine, 'The Moonta Company was the first mining company in Australia to pay over £1,000,000 in dividends.' By 1917 the value of the district's copper mining exceeded that of all other mining in the state since its inception in 1836. The remains of the Hughes Engine Pumping House (1865) are on the main road toward **Arthurton**. It once removed water from the likes of the 768 m Taylor's Shaft. Moonta Mines Wesley Methodist Church (1865) shows how deeply Methodism characterised the mining community, particularly the Cornish and the Welsh. It has a huge gallery and a truly beautiful pipe organ. It is said that literally everyone went to church (its capacity is 1,250 people), and that the mine captains sat up the back and made note of any worker not present. The local Masonic hall is the oldest built by the Freemasons in Australia, located in Blanche Terrace and built in 1875. Recent changes regarding the secrecy of Freemasons mean that if you can organise it (and the effort is worthwhile) you can go inside and inspect the unusual ritual regalia.

DON'T MISS: The highlight of any visit to the copper triangle is the opportunity to go down into a mine. A very well-organised tour of the remnants of the Wheal Hughes Mine has made this possible. Purchase tickets at the Moonta Railway Station Information Office. A people mover takes you into the open-cut section to the entrance of the tunnel. From there you head down into the darkness.

At Port Augusta [A5], off the

Stuart Highway, is the Australian Arid Lands Botanic Garden. It showcases a range of arid zone environments within an area of just 200 ha. The Wadlata Outback Centre has exhibi-

tions about the Outback's origins, history and development.

North of **Port Clinton** [C5] is the **Clinton Conservation Park**, an area of 1,854 ha at the head of Gulf St Vincent, stretching around almost to Port Wakefield.

The park features mangroves and tidal mud flats that are a haven for migratory wading birds.

The jetty at **Port Germein** [A5] was once the longest in the Southern Hemisphere. It reaches more than 1,500 m out to meet deep water—the 2,500 m wharf at Cape Lambert (near Wickham) in Western Australia beats it by a kilometre. However, it is still the longest wooden jetty.

Port Lincoln [D3] was once

considered, by Colonel William Light, a possible capital for the state of South Australia due to its popularity with Kangaroo Island sealers and Port Jackson whalers who hunted and fished in the Southern Ocean. The town was passed over because Colonel Light could not find a fresh water supply. It is now the base for Australia's largest tuna fleet and tuna-farming industry, and home to Australia's biggest population, per capita, of millionaires, thanks to tuna.

DON'T MISS: The Tunarama Festival, held every Australia Day weekend, features the World Championship Tuna Toss.

Dangerous Reef is off the coast from Port Lincoln and is where black-faced cormorants breed. They are one of the few exclusively marine cormorants in Australia. Dangerous Reef is well known in fishing and diving circles as the home base for a number of very large white pointer sharks and, at certain times of the year, charter operators will take you out to see the sharks, but for a minimum three days. Constantia Furniture, on the outskirts of Port Lincoln, is one of only six companies in the world to be made a fully accredited member of the International Guild of Craftsmen. Constantia created the Australian Federal Parliament table, which is made of Queensland grey box timber, with 90 veneered layers of Honduran mahogany. It weighs two tonnes and cost $2 million. For a guided tour of the Constantia workroom call 08 8682 3977 or 08 8682 6120 (after hours). The Axel Stenross Maritime Museum has a collection of early maritime photographs and artefacts of the windjammer era. The Seahorse Farm is South Australia's only seahorse breeding facility. Tours can be booked through the Port Lincoln Visitor Centre 08 8683 3544.

DON'T MISS: Watch dolphins frolicking in the waves and whales swimming by from May through September, while you sip a glass of wine at the Boston Bay Winery. The vineyard is 6 km north of Port Lincoln and overlooks the beautiful Boston Bay.

The **Whaler's Way** is a privately owned coastal drive south from Port Lincoln. You'll need a key (in exchange for a small deposit) and a permit (a little more) from the local visitors' information centre. The journey is along some of the most spectacular coastline in the country. For four-wheel-drivers wanting to

SA

SALMON MORNAY

The clean waters of the Southern Ocean provide the perfect habitat for large, healthy salmon. A near-shore species, salmon like bays, estuaries, harbours and rocky shorelines and are found all along Australia's south coast.

4 large potatoes, cooked and mashed
large can of salmon, drained, or
**   4–6 fillets of fresh steamed salmon**
1/2 cup white sauce
1/2 cup cooked peas
2–3 eggs, hard boiled and sliced
1/2 cup fresh breadcrumbs
1 cup of cheddar cheese, grated

Preheat oven to 180°C and grease a casserole dish. Place a layer of mashed potatoes on the bottom. Stir salmon into white sauce and pour over potatoes. Add a layer of peas and cover with eggs. Add fresh breadcrumbs and cover with cheese. Brown in the oven for 30 minutes. Serves 4–6.

Fay Story, TUMBY BAY

test their mettle, the coastal dunes from Wanna Beach around Sleaford Bay is a fantastic sand drive. **Lincoln National Park**, with its 4WD tracks, impressive headlands and fine beaches, takes up the foot of the peninsula.

Near the jetty in **Port Neill** [C3], in front of the Port Neill Hotel, is an anchor unveiled 100 years to the day after the shipwreck, on 20 January 1880, of the *Lady Kinnaird*. She left Port Pirie for England with a cargo of 8,400 bags of wheat. That night she struck bad weather and sank off Cape Burr, near Port Neill. A large whiting stands at the entrance to Port

GAZETTEER

Neill, commissioned by the Local Progress Association and made by the local kids.

Port Pirie [B5] is the site of the
world's largest lead smelting and refining plant. A short distance inland is the rearing bulk of the Southern Flinders Ranges, with a couple of conservation parks tucked in along its flanks. **Telowie Gorge** offers camping and enjoyable bushwalking.

Port Rickaby [D5] serves an area
called Koolywurtie, established in 1876. The jetty, built in 1879, started off at 123 m in length; by 1949 it had been lengthened three times, finally making it to 250 m. Wind-jammers left here for the voyage via Cape Horn to Europe, transporting bagged grain. The last one to depart from here was the *Passat* in June 1949.

Port Victoria [C5] was once the
main port for sailing ships that carried grain to overseas markets. The last of these commercial sailing ships left for England in

1949. From this small coastal town head south just a short distance back from the beach on a 4WD track that can lead all the way to the even smaller holiday village of **Hardwicke Bay**. There are some good fishing spots and a couple of pleasant camping areas along this seldom visited coast.

The **Port Vincent** [D5] Walking Trail takes you through native scrub in the Water Reserve, on the town's northern boundary. There are around 40 species of native vegetation.

Port Wakefield's [C5] town and
river were named after an ex-convict who became a coloniser and planner. Edward Gibbon Wakefield served time in Newgate Gaol in Great Britain, for abducting a school-

girl heiress. The town was established to ship copper from the Burra Burra mines to Adelaide. Today, the local wharf is an excellent spot for recreational fishing and the town has a delightful seafaring atmosphere.

Quorn [A5]

is one end of the Pichi Richi railway line—it runs to Port Augusta. The railway is one of the oldest intact rail systems still operating (from March to December) in the world. **Warrens Gorge**, just north of Quorn, is worth a trip. While a normal car can do it, a 4WD is more suitable. There's pleasant camping and enjoyable walking within and around the gorge.

From # Snowtown [B5]

there is a fine lookout across **Lake Bumbunga**, a very substantial salt lake.

Just 5 km south of # Stansbury [D5]

is Kleine's Point Quarry, South Australia's largest limestone quarry. Stansbury itself once had the best oyster beds in the state. There are daily shop and shed sales at Southern Yorke Oysters opposite the water tower on Brentwood Road.

South of # Streaky Bay [A1]

named by Matthew Flinders once he saw the seaweed in the water, is a very pleasant coastal drive to places such as Smooth Pool, High Cliffs, Speeds Point, the Granites and the Dreadnoughts, where you can take

your choice of fishing, surfing, diving or just watching the ocean. About 20 km north of Streaky Bay is **Perlubie Beach**, famous on the Eyre Peninsula for its unique New Year's Day Race Meeting. The race is a 1,600 m event along the beach at low tide and has been run since 1913. The jockeys' pockets are apparently filled with sand to get them up to correct handicap weight. Between race meetings the stands and saddling enclosures, all weathered by the sea, stand forlornly on the beach.

At the entrance to # Tumby Bay

[C3] stands the Tumby Bay Tin Man, armed and ready with a fishing line. The locals are prone to hang all sorts of objects off the end of his line, so don't be confused about what you might be fishing for. The waters off Tumby Bay are home to some of the biggest and most prolific King George whiting in Australia—these delicious fish are a major drawcard for anglers. The rich fishing grounds of Spencer Gulf also have an excellent reputation for crabs, oysters and crayfish. Tumby Bay was the site of the first—and probably only—Rent-a-Duck scheme, when local poulterer Ross Story discovered the efficacy of ducks as snail removers and leased a few of his White Indian Runners to local gardeners. Catch a boat from Tumby Bay to the **Sir Joseph Banks Conservation Park** for a spot of dolphin, sea lion and bird watching.

DON'T MISS: The Koppio Smithy Museum, 30 km from Tumby Bay, is home to an unusual exhibit—the Bob Dobbins

Barbed Wire and Fencing Collection. It also displays pioneer artefacts and antiques (call 08 8684 4243).

Needle Eye Lookout at **Venus Bay** [B2] is a great place for spotting southern right whales from June to October. South of Venus Bay, about 10 minutes by car, is Mount Camel Beach where there is excellent surf fishing.

Wallaroo [C5] was the first Copper

Triangle town to be surveyed and was the export port for the ore—it is now the main port for wheat and barley exports. The 'big stack', a copper smelter chimney, still stands. The Heritage & Nautical Museum has the story of the square-rigger and a display about Caroline Charlton, who wrote the words of 'Song of Australia'.

Wangary's [C2] Old Hotel, built in

1871, is one of the very few pubs in Australia actually to boast to the passerby 'No Beds—No Beer'. Now a general store, it hasn't had a liquor licence since 1933. Its great moment came when someone found an old horse carriage being used by the hotel's chooks in a shed out the back. Closer investigation found the motto 'Crede Biron' on the carriage, and it was discovered that its original owner had been the famous English poet Lord Byron. The carriage disappeared while plans were being made to restore it. Only 10 km from Wangary is Farm Beach, which has a truly fascinating and bizarre collection of tractors. On the weekends and during holidays the beach and foreshore are crowded with anglers who use

old tractors to get their boats over the mountains of seaweed washed up on the beach. The result is a parking area for up to 50 tractors, all of them ancient and rusty. At the south end, just near the main launching point, there is a rough dirt road leading to the beach where the invasion scenes in the movie *Gallipoli* were filmed. This section of the coastline is now named Gallipoli Beach.

Every two years **Warooka** [D5] holds a black-tie event with a difference. Locals put on their finest for the Party on the Peesey, which takes place in a marquee on a dried salt pan. Call 08 8854 5005 for details.

DON'T MISS: Flaherty's Beach Sandbar Golf Classic is held annually in February or March, with competitors dodging the tide on two 6-hole courses.

Whyalla [A5] is the largest provincial

city in South Australia and was once a centre of iron ore mining and heavy industry. The largest ship ever built in Australia, a bulk carrier called the *Clutha Capricorn*, was launched from the Whyalla shipyards in 1972. At the northern entrance to the city stands the 650 tonne corvette *Whyalla*, the first ship to be built at Whyalla, launched in 1941. She was a minesweeper and anti-submarine vessel, then surveyed the previously unknown coast

of Papua New Guinea. She was attacked by the Japanese, was grounded on a coral reef and collided with a whale. After the war she was renamed the *Rip*, and operated pile lights at Melbourne's Port Phillip Bay. Since 1987 she has been standing 2 km from the ocean, the largest permanently landlocked ship in Australia. The National Trust Mount

Laura Homestead Museum is an old homestead in the heart of suburbia. Outside is Whyalla's original wood and corrugated iron lock-up, the only known example of a portable jail in South Australia. Whyalla waters are home to the largest snapper in Australia, and each year massive specimens, in excess of 14 kg, are landed here. The annual snapper fishing competition, held every Easter weekend, draws around 800 keen boat anglers from all over the state, as well as from neighbouring Victoria. For those who love diving, it's worth visiting between the months of May and August when hundreds of thousands of giant cuttlefish come to the small area around Black Point and Point Lowly to spawn.

In the **Wudinna** [A2] district, Turtle Rock is one of the whalebacks, or inselbergs, for which the upper Eyre Peninsula is famous. They are called whalebacks for obvious reasons but, like clouds, you can see whatever shapes you can imagine. The result is a landscape littered with oversized rock animals. Turtle Rock is estimated to be between 1,800

and 2,400 million years old. Mt Wudinna Rock, 10 km north-east of the town, is the second-largest granite outcrop in the Southern Hemisphere (the biggest is Bald Rock in New South Wales) and stands 260 m above the plains.

Yorketown [D5], the main commercial and administrative town at the southern end of the Yorke Peninsula, was once called Weaners Flat, after the meadows nearby where lambs were weaned. It was later proposed that the town be renamed Salt Lake City because of the salt pans in the area. It became Yorketown (perhaps no one could agree). Heading south-west from Yorketown you reach **Stenhouse Bay** and the beautiful **Innes National Park**, which has some spectacular coastal scenery and great surfing, attracting board riders from around the world. Within the park is Inneston, an historic mining town managed as an historic site by the Department for Environment, Heritage and Aboriginal Affairs. If you get this far, head north to **Pondalowie Bay**, a real gem with protected swimming, great surf and stunning scenery. **Bublacowie** Military Museum at Bublacowie campsite, on the Minlaton–Yorketown road, has photographs, written documents, medals and other memorabilia to do with the Australian Defence Forces. It's only open on Sundays (for information call 08 8853 4379).

SA

Diary of Events

Town	Event	Date	Contact
Cummins	World Championship Kalamazoo Classic	April	08 8676 2106
Kadina	Kernewek Lowender	May	08 8825 1891
Mt Ive	Dry Lake Racers Australia	March	03 5472 2853
Perlubie Beach	Race Day	New Year's Day	08 8626 1126
Port Lincoln	Tunarama Festival	Australia Day Weekend	08 8683 3544
Whyalla	Annual Snapper Fishing Competition	Easter Weekend	08 8645 7900

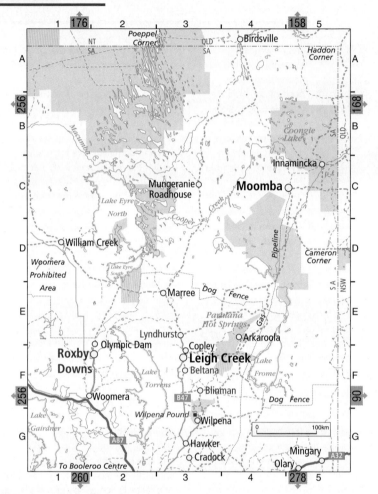

get off the beaten track

roam

the flinders ranges

and the outback

Arkaroola

Arkaroola [E4] is the personal vision of the late Dr Reg Sprigg, who purchased the 610 sq km property in 1968 and slowly converted it into a wildlife sanctuary, complete with a lodge. It is probably the most isolated self-supporting village in Australia. Some of the rocks are estimated to be older than 1,000 million years, and the area includes the only crystal quartz mountain in the world. The only access to the mountain is via the Ridge Top Tour (ask at the Arkaroola reception centre for details). The Arkaroola Astronomical Observatory houses two substantial telescopes, with tours and viewings on nights when the sky is clear (a common phenomenon in the desert). The 360 mm computer-operated telescope offers excellent viewing of other galaxies and distant planets. There are plenty of 4WD opportunities around Arkaroola, with the Echo Camp Backtrack being one of the best for experienced drivers. **Paralana Hot Springs**, 27 km north of Arkaroola, are the last vestige of active volcanism in Australia. The evidence of this is water at near boiling point flowing from the ground.

Beltana

Beltana [F3] was the first Afghan settlement in Australia. Once a ghost town, it is now restored as a time capsule of the 19th century. It was here that Thomas Elder and Robert Barr Smith, cofounders of the Elder Smith Company, built a camel stud in 1866. The Smith of Dunesk Mission at Beltana was a legacy of Lady Henrietta Smith of Scotland, who requested that proceeds from the rental of her land in South Australia be used for the benefit of local Aborigines. By 1893 the asset had a value of £3,000, and the Reverend Robert Mitchell, anticipating Flynn of the Inland by more than 20 years, set up an Inland Mission at Beltana in 1895. One of the great legends of Beltana tells of a local baker in the 1880s who believed someone was raiding his woodpile, into which he inserted a stick of dynamite to catch the thief—it blew up one night demolishing the bakery. The remains of the bakery were uncovered in 1995 and it has subsequently been rebuilt. The town is now a state heritage area. The Mount Hack Public Access Route (PAR) gives four-wheel-drivers an opportunity to travel east from Beltana into the Flinders Ranges and to the ruins of Sliding Rock, one of the best relics of mining in the ranges—well worth exploring.

Blinman

Near **Blinman** [F3]—10 km south on the road to Wilpena—are some unusual geological formations, essentially lines of rocks topped with ironstone. They look a little like the Great Wall of China, after which they are named. Blinman is now a thriving town offering self-guided tours of the copper mines.

Booleroo Centre

Booleroo Centre's [G2] people have memorialised their pioneers with a giant rock set in the centre of town. Booleroo's main attraction is an excellent collection of steam and traction engines at the Booleroo Steam and Traction Preservation Society Museum. The museum is open by appointment. Ask at the post office.

 DON'T MISS: In March/April each year Booleroo Centre hosts a rally for lovers of steam power, who all bring their

SA

antique engines and tractors to the town. There are strange items such as the Fowler Steam Ploughing Engine built in 1882 and weighing 26 tonnes.

The town of **Copley** [F3] has its own fishing club, the Copley Desert Ranges Angling Club. It was founded by a fishing fanatic who stocked the

PICKLED OLIVES

Feral olive trees are considered an invasive weed in South Australia and are a target of eradication programs. They grow well in the South Australian climate, which has cool, wet winters and dry summers, similar to the Mediterranean climate, where olives have grown since biblical times. They are prolific throughout the southern Flinders Ranges region.

Rinse olives and slit each olive about three times or crack with a hammer. Prepare brine solution of 1 cup salt to 5 ltr water and soak olives. Change the brine every day for 10–14 days. Make preserving solution at double the strength of soaking solution, 2 cups salt to 5 ltr water. Place olives in sterilised jars and pour over the preserving solution to cover. Add lemon juice, lemon slices, chilli, herbs or garlic, etc if desired. Top jars with olive oil to seal then leave in the dark for a few weeks. If too salty, pour off brine and replace with fresh water 24 hours before eating.

Sue Overell, BEAUDESERT

Retention Dam (which stops the flooding of the Leigh Creek open-cut coal workings) with yellowbelly. They mainly catch carp. **Iga Warta**, between Copley and Arkaroola, is an Aboriginal-owned environmental and cultural centre on Nepabunna Aboriginal Land. It is run by the five sons of Clem Coulthard, the man whose dream it was. Here you can see Dreaming sites and 10,000-year-old paintings, and hear the songs and stories of the Adnyamathanha, or 'hills people'. Call 08 8648 3737 for details.

At **Hawker** [G3] on the corner of Cradock and Wilpena Roads, is Fred Teague's Museum, housed within Hawker Motors service station. The late Fred Teague started the museum in the 1950s to give his customers something to look at while they were waiting for their cars to be repaired. Most of the articles were collected by Fred during his time in the Outback, though there are also some donations. The collection consists of gemstones, minerals, fossils, photographs, antique bottles and memorabilia and is open 7.30 am to 5.30 pm daily. **Yourambulla Caves**, a few kilometres south of Hawker, have rock paintings and some fine views.

In **Innamincka** [C5] there is a monument to explorers Burke and Wills; about 25 km west of the town is Wills' grave, and some 50 km east is the famous 'Dig' tree (over the Queensland border) where supplies were left for the explorers. **Coongie Lake**, about 112 km north-west of Innamincka, is home to what is considered the largest and most varied collection of frogs in central Australia. To visit the lake, which also teems with birdlife and fish, you'll need a 4WD and a Desert Parks Pass for access to the many regional and national parks of northern South Australia.

Leigh Creek [F3] is a coal-mining

town leased by NRG Flinders. At the lookout point there is an old walking dragline known as a Bucyrus Erie 9W. It began service at Leigh Creek in 1951. It has a 49 m boom and a 7 m³ bucket, at the time the largest in Australia.

There is also a huge tyre that achieved a world record of 289,215 km and 17,520 hours in service before it was 'retired'. At **Yalpuna Veri**, south-east of the town, are some of the finest examples of ancient Aboriginal rock paintings. The town's main water supply is **Aroona Dam**, south-west of the town, where you may spot the rare yellow-footed rock wallaby.

Lyndhurst [E3]

sits at the beginning of the famous Strzelecki Track (and at the end of the bitumen), which runs to

the Moomba gas field and on to the old Customs Post at Innamincka. Legendary cattle duffer Harry Redford pioneered the track when he drove 1,000 stolen cattle from Queensland to South Australia in 1870. North of Lyndhurst (5 km) there is a tyre beside the road with the words 'Ochre Cliffs' crudely written on it. A road heads off the main track to the west for a couple of kilometres before reaching a remarkable quarry that is a feast of harsh desert colours—reds, yellows and browns. It was an important site for the local Aborigines and it is believed that ochre quarried here was traded with other Aboriginal groups.

Marree

[E3] sits at the junction of two famous tracks, the Birdsville and the Oodnadatta. Toward the end of the 19th century Marree was a staging post for Afghan traders, who loaded their camel trains here to ferry goods to remote stations in the Outback. North-west of Marree is **Lake Eyre**. When taken together, Lake Eyre North and Lake Eyre South total almost 10,000 sq km. It is Australia's largest natural lake and the world's largest saltpan. At its lowest point the lake is 16 m below sea level, making it the lowest land in Australia. In 1964 Donald Campbell set a world land speed record of 648.72 km/h on the lake in his famous jet-powered *Bluebird*. Scenic flights over the lake are available from several nearby airstrips. While you can fly over the lake

SA

Map labels

TO BEDOURIE
DIAMANTINA RIVER
70
TO BEETOOTA
NORTHERN TERRITORY
BIRDSVILLE
108
29 91
CORDILLO DOWNS
STURTS STONY DESERT
117
QUEENSLAND
BIRDSVILLE TRACK
INNAMINCKA
89
BURKES D16 TREE
45
MOOMBA GAS FIELD
158
115
COOPER CREEK
LAKE GREGORY
TO TIBOOBURRA
TO OODNADATTA
191
L. BLANCHE
211
STRZELECKI TRACK
MARREE
82
NEW SOUTH WALES
78
LYNDHURST
LEIGH Cr
BIRDSVILLE & STRZELECKI TRACKS
TO PORT AUGUSTA

from either Marree or William Creek, a couple of 4WD tracks give access to the lake's shore. One heads north from Marree through Muloorina Station to the south-east of the

KANGAROO TAIL BRAWN

This brawn is a tasty mix of kangaroo tail, ox tongue and rabbit. Kangaroo numbers have steadily increased since the arrival of Europeans and the ongoing development of grasslands and water supply through dams. Numbers are so great that they are considered by many farmers to be pests. Since the introduction of rabbits to Australia for sport shooting in 1859, at first considered a roaring success, their population soon got out of control. Wild rabbits now range from deserts to coastal plains, wherever the soil is suitable for burrowing.

2 medium	salt and pepper
kangaroo tails	to taste
(blue roo is best)	1 tsp allspice
1 rabbit	8 cloves
1 ox tongue	herbs of your
1 onion, cut in half	choice

Soak the kangaroo, rabbit and ox tongue in salt water. Drain and joint all meats. Place in a large saucepan and add onion, salt, pepper, spices and herbs. Cover with water, bring to the boil, cover and simmer until meat leaves the bones (2–3 hours). Strain liquid and reserve. Remove all bones, remove skin from tongue and chop meat into small pieces. Place meat into moulds and pour strained liquid over to just cover. Leave to set before removing from mould. Cut into slices to serve.

Reva Best, HERVEY BAY
(ex-Outback SA)

lake at Level Post Bay, while the other leaves the Oodnadatta Track south of William Creek to Halligan Bay on the west side. Less adventurous souls can visit the shores of Lake Eyre South with a short bumpy diversion off the Oodnadatta Track west of Marree.

The area around **Moomba** [C5] is where natural gas was discovered in 1966. The gas is piped all the way to Adelaide and Sydney. In 2000 oil was also discovered here.

Near **Olary** [G5], on the Barrier Highway, is Radium Hill, which has been abandoned three times in its history as the profitability of mining radioactive ores rose and fell.

At **Roxby Downs** [F2] the water restrictions allow only some of the fairways on the golf course to be kept green. The others are pure sand and players carry small pieces of carpet GAZETTEER from which to play each shot. Olympic Dam at Roxby Downs is the largest multi-mineral ore body in the world. It has attracted some controversy because of the uranium mined here alongside the gold and silver.

William Creek [D1], just off the
Oodnadatta Track, is South Australia's

smallest town but home to the world's largest cattle station. Anna Creek Station, 15 km west of the town, covers 23,888 sq km.

Wilpena Pound [G3], within the Flinders Ranges National Park, is a natural

amphitheatre formed 450 million years ago by massive earth movements. It is accessible only through one narrow gap carved by Wilpena Creek. The resort of Wilpena at its entrance takes its power from one of the largest solar power systems in the Southern Hemisphere. Located off the road to Blinman from Wilpena is the Cazneaux Tree, one of the most famous trees in Australia. Photographed by Harold Cazneaux in 1937 and called 'The Spirit of Endurance', it has been reproduced on calendars and posters all over the world. For four-wheel-drivers there are a number of privately owned self-drive 4WD trips that can be enjoyed around Wilpena. Try the very scenic Arkaba Wonderland trek, the famous Skytrek or the more challenging Mt Samuel 4WD Experience.

DON'T MISS: Wilpena Pound, being a natural amphitheatre, provides a perfect music venue. Wilpena Under the Stars in February each year is a black-tie affair with a three-course meal, bands and a fundraising auction. Call 08 8238 3333 for details.

Woomera [F1] Lions Club's Aircraft

and Missile Park and the Woomera Heritage Centre have a comprehensive display of rocket technology and artefacts from the more recent past. The town was aptly named after the Aboriginal spear-thrower. Outside the building are well-preserved examples of most of the rockets launched at Woomera, including the Black Arrow, a large rocket launched four times between June 1969 and October 1972. The first launch was destroyed almost immediately because it was unstable. The second and third launches were experimental firings. The fourth put a Prospero satellite into orbit—it is still circling Earth. You may be able to arrange a tour of the missile range—ask at the Heritage Centre. The Australian monument, an obelisk at the town's main intersection, depicts a woomera bearing an orbiting satellite in the arc of a dish to represent the Island Lagoon deep space tracking antenna, the first such station outside the United States. Erected in 1960, the 26 m antenna has been part of various projects, including the first successful mission to another planet, the flyby of Venus in December 1962. It ceased operations in December 1972 and the antenna was dismantled and sold for scrap in 1973.

Diary of Events

Town	Event	Date	Contact
Booleroo Centre	Steam Power Rally	March/April	08 8667 2050
Wilpena Pound	Wilpena Under the Stars	February	08 8238 3333

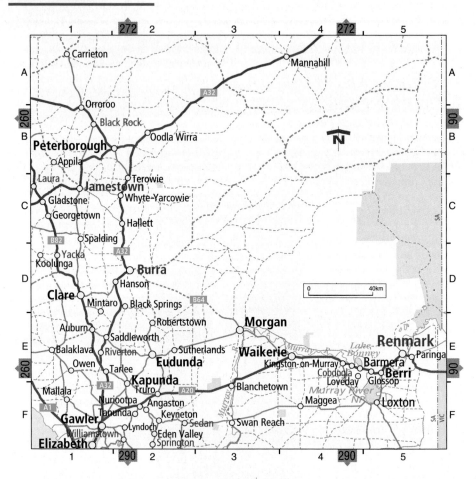

get off the beaten track

drink in

the

riverlands

and wine valleys

Angaston

Angaston [F2] is where the Yalumba Winery, Australia's oldest family winery, was founded by Samuel Smith in 1849. It is also home to Collingrove Homestead, built in 1856 by George Angas and famous for breeding Merino and Lincoln sheep, Durham cattle and Clydesdale horses.

Auburn

Auburn [E1] is where poet CJ Dennis was born in 1876, in the old Auburn Hotel, a metal model of which stands outside the Senior Citizens Club. CJ's father, James Dennis, a retired sea captain, ran the pub from 1864 until 1876. Dennis is famous for the creation of that quintessential Australian innocent, 'the sentimental bloke'. He is commemorated with a birdbath and a drinking fountain. Vincent Street is a heritage street and the 1859 courthouse and police station are now a museum.

The town of **Balaklava** [E1] was surveyed in 1877 and named after a battle against Russian forces in the Crimean War in 1854. In the old days, bullock wagons used to take a break here on their way from the Burra Burra mines to Port Wakefield. South-east of the town is the Rocks Reserve, a unique rock formation carved by the River Wakefield. There's a walking trail through the reserve. The Old Centenary Hall, built by the Church of Christ in 1878, was used as Balaklava's first high school between 1922 and 1928. Situated in May Terrace, it's now

YABBIES AND ALMONDS

About 1 km from Swan Reach on the Loxton Road is the Murray Aquaculture Yabby Farm. The proprietor, David Strutton, conducts group tours (book on 08 8570 2025) where you can get the goods on yabby production and even have a go at catching them for yourself. The Strutton family originally bought the property to grow almonds and today their farm produces more than 130 tonnes of almond kernel per year. The best time to visit is when the almonds are in full bloom in August.

3 tbsp lemon juice
pinch cayenne pepper
1/2 tsp freshly ground black pepper
1 tbsp olive oil
750 g medium, raw yabbies, peeled and deveined
3/4 cup blanched, slivered almonds
4 tbsp butter
1 red capsicum, julienned
2 tbsp chives, finely chopped
2 tbsp parsley, finely chopped
1/2 tsp salt
1 lemon, cut into wedges, for garnish

Combine 2 tbsp of the lemon juice with the peppers and oil, and marinate yabbies in mixture for 15 minutes. Sauté almonds in 2 tbsp of the butter until they turn golden. Add yabbies and capsicum and cook for approx. 3 minutes or until yabbies are just tender. Remove from heat and stir in herbs, salt and remaining lemon juice and butter. Garnish with lemon wedges. Serves 4.

David Strutton,
SWAN REACH

SA

a folk and historic museum open every second and fourth Sunday (call 08 8862 1467 for more information). South Australia is not all wine. Healthy crops and healthy yields are what you will see year round as you explore the state. The Adelaide Plains region, surrounding towns such as Balaklava and Millala, has heavy, black soils, frost-free winters and warm summers, perfect for growing superb potatoes that are much sought after by processors such as Smith's Crisps for their high-quality production.

Barmera [E5], on the shores of **Lake Bonney**, is the country music capital of South Australia. The town is home to Rocky's Country Music Hall of Fame. In the collection is Slim Dusty's hat. A plaque on the lake's edge,

on Queen Elizabeth Drive, records the fact that in 1964 famous English speedster Donald Campbell attempted to break the world water speed record on Lake Bonney. The only man to ever hold both the land and water speed records, Campbell's attempt failed. He did reach 347.5 km/h but the lake was too small and the waves created by the speeding craft too dangerous. He eventually set the land speed record at Lake Eyre in South Australia's Tirari Desert—also in 1964, 648.72 km/h. His last (of seven) world jet-boat water speed records was set at Lake Dumbleyung in Western Australia, also in 1964 (444.7 km/h).

Berri [E5] is home to the largest winery in Australia, probably the largest in the

BRULÉE RICE PUDDING WITH RHUBARB COMPOTE

Rhubarb is botanically a vegetable, though it is eaten like a fruit. It grows best in a temperate climate, Waikerie being the prime growing area in South Australia. Only use the bright red stalks (the green leaves contain an acid that should not be eaten). Simply cut off the leaves and any white root area, then cut the stalk crosswise into 25–50 mm lengths.

1 ltr water
1¹/₂ cups short-grain white rice
pinch salt
3 cups hot milk
1 cup hot pouring cream
1 cup caster sugar
1 tbsp unsalted butter
3 egg yolks
¹/₂ tsp ground cinnamon
¹/₂ tsp vanilla extract
¹/₂ cup caster sugar (extra)
8 sticks rhubarb, lightly poached in a
  sugar syrup

Bring water to the boil, add rice and salt. Cook, stirring occasionally, over low heat for 10–15 minutes until water is absorbed. Add 1 cup of milk and cook, stirring occasionally until the milk is absorbed. Stir in remaining milk, hot cream, sugar, butter, egg yolks, cinnamon and vanilla and cook over the lowest heat, stirring occasionally, for a further 10 minutes until creamy. Spoon into an 8-cup flame-proof dish, cool, cover and refrigerate until cold. Sprinkle sugar over the top and place under hot grill until it caramelises. Serve with rhubarb. Serves 6.

Salopian Inn,
MCLAREN VALE

Southern Hemisphere. Berri Estate Winery opened in 1922 as a cooperative winery and distillery. It's on the Sturt Highway at **Glossop**. South of Berri, tucked into a great bend of the River Murray, is the biggest single section of the **Murray River National Park**. A number of 4WD tracks give access to the park and its camping areas. Visitors can occupy themselves canoeing, fishing and birdwatching.

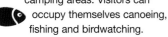

Just beyond **Black Rock** [B1] is Magnetic Hill where, the locals claim, if you park your car at the bottom, switch off the engine and place the gears in neutral, it will roll up the hill. Strange forces indeed.

The site of **Blanchetown** [F3] was surveyed in 1855. It was named by the governor of South Australia, Sir Richard Graves McDonnell, after his wife, Blanche. The hotel here is an example of original pioneer construction. The nails were hand-made and the rafters were shaped with a broad axe. Downriver from Blanchetown is an extraordinary collection of shacks, some of which were built more than 30 years ago out of corrugated iron, fibro and anything else that came to hand. Others are two-storey holiday homes with River Murray frontages.

Burra [D2] was once South

Australia's largest country settlement, and is now one of Australia's best-preserved mining towns. Copper was first discovered in the district in 1845 by two shepherds, William Streair and Thomas Pickett. According to some, the town's name is Hindi for 'big', the area itself so substantial it was initially

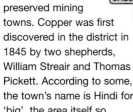

known as 'Burra Burra'. The names of the different parts of the town reflect the various origins of its early settlers: Hampton is laid out like an English village, Redruth was inhabited predominantly by Cornish miners, while Llychwr, next to the smelting works, was named by the mostly Welsh smelters. There is also a section of town called Aberdeen, but the name is thought to be linked to the company that funded the mine's construction. The powder magazine in Burra was built in 1847 and is the oldest mine building in Australia. In 1980 the film *Breaker Morant* was filmed at Burra using Redruth Jail, the oldest provincial prison in South Australia.

The Sevenhill Cellars in **Clare** [D1] is the valley's oldest winery. It was started by Austrian Jesuits in 1851. St Aloysius church has intricate carvings around its front door. These were done by Brother Waldman, who was able to finish the carvings despite going completely blind. Bungaree Station, 12 km north of Clare, was first settled by Europeans when George Hawker chose the site for his station in 1841. It grew to become one of the great South Australian properties, and is now recognised as one of Australia's finest merino studs. It is also a thriving tourist accommodation and function centre.

✋ DON'T MISS:

The Clare Valley Gourmet Weekend on the long weekend in May is the longest running of the region's festivals. Meet some of the winemakers and of course sample the produce. Tastings and other events are listed closer to the date (call 08 8843 0222).

SA

Cobdogla's

GAZETTEER [E4] Irrigation and Steam Museum contains the world's only working Humphrey Pump. These gas-driven pumps were used in early irrigation projects. They operated like a water cannon, with the water being propelled from the river into irrigation channels by an explosion of gas.

Eden Valley

[F2] is Australia's most celebrated region for the growing of riesling grapes, for which the climate and acidic soilds are ideal. The warm days and cool nights promote a long, slow ripening period, producing a crisp, firm flavour. Wander the walking trails of **Kaiser Stuhl Conservation Park** to glimpse great views over the valley. The Heysen Trail passes through the park and into the **Mount Crawford Forest Reserve**.

Eudunda

[E2] was the birthplace of Colin Thiele, author of *Storm Boy* (later made into a film), about a boy's relationship with a pelican. There is a statue of Thiele with a pelican in the park in Kapunda Street, just south of the main street. The statue was unveiled by Thiele himself in 1995.

Gawler

[F1] is South Australia's oldest country town, laid out in 1839 and soon called 'The Colonial Athens', partly because of its many gracious buildings and spacious parks, and partly because it was a cultural centre even in its early days. Roseworthy College, north of Gawler, is Australia's oldest agricultural college. The store called Simply Pine Plus, located on the western side of Murray Street, was once called HB Crosby. Its 'flying fox', a wonderful device that took money from the six counters to an accounts section (on the mezzanine level) where change was provided, is still inside. HB Crosby's store was built in 1886 and the original façade still stands.

Georgetown

[C1] is a small town with a magnificent heritage hotel and general store. It's a pleasant place with beautiful wide streets and parks.

Gladstone

[C1] has South Australia's largest inland grain storage facilities. They are next to Booyoolie Station, where 'bully beef' originated. A meat cannery was established on the station in the 1880s, which supplied Australian troops in the Boer War in South Africa at the turn of the 20th century. Bully is a mispronunciation of Booyoolie, rightfully pronounced 'bowley'.

In Jamestown's [C1]

GAZETTEER cemetery is the grave of two men killed by a rock in an 1878 quarrying accident. The rock has been used as their headstone. A few kilometres south-west of Jamestown is part of the **Heysen Trail**, one of the longest walking tracks in the world. It begins at Cape Jervis, at the tip of the Fleurieu Peninsula, and ends 1,500 km later at Parachilna Gorge in the Flinders Ranges. **Bundaleer Forest**, 5 km south of Jamestown, is the oldest government-planted forest in the Southern Hemisphere. William John Jenkins Curnow opened the first nursery there in the late 1800s. He applied a method he adapted in India of 'tube stock planting', which involved using bamboo shoots from the gardens of Bundaleer Forest. The method is now used worldwide.

CORNISH PASTIES

South of Orroroo, the copper-mining town of Burra is mapped out to reflect the different origins of the early inhabitants of its suburbs. Hampton, for instance, is like an English village, while the suburb of Redruth was settled mainly by Cornish miners, as were several towns on the Yorke Peninsula to the west. Known as Little Cornwall, by 1875 the majority of the district's 20,000 people were Cornish, and the pasties were in demand.

PASTRY
1 1/2 cups lard or dripping
3 cups plain flour
pinch of salt
1 1/2 cups boiling water
2 tbsp soft butter or margarine
1 egg, beaten, for glazing

MEAT FILLING
500 g minced beef (use low-fat mince, finely ground)
1 large potato, peeled and grated
1 medium onion, peeled and finely chopped
1 turnip, peeled and grated
250 g pumpkin, grated
salt and pepper to taste

Preheat oven to 230°C and line a baking tray with baking paper. In a bowl, rub lard or dripping into flour and salt, then mix in the boiling water to form a dough (you may not need all the water). Let dough stand until cold, preferably overnight. Make the meat filling by combining all ingredients in a bowl. Roll out pastry to 0.5 cm thickness and spread with the soft butter or margarine. Fold over and roll out thinly. Cut into large circles (use a saucer) and brush edges with beaten egg. Spoon meat mixture on one half of pastry circles, then fold other half over and seal with a fork. Brush finished pasties with egg glaze and prick with a fork. Bake for about 30 minutes or until golden brown. Note: Frozen puff pastry can be used instead of the pastry recipe. Makes 12.

Margaret Chapman, ORROROO

DON'T MISS: Jamestown holds a Fly-in every three years, when aircraft from all over Australia gather at the Aero Club. The next one will be held in 2003. On the third Thursday of every month the town holds the largest sheep sales north of Adelaide.

Kapunda [F2] is a town of firsts:
Australia's first copper mine opened here in 1844. Australia's first croquet was played in Kapunda 24 years later, and less than a decade later the nation's first bowling green was put down in the town. Buildings in town are decorated with fine examples of iron lace work. The Kapunda copper mine contributed greatly to the economic development of South Australia, which had become bankrupt in 1840. By 1850 the mine was producing 99.5 tonnes of ore per month. The copper

SA

BERRI GOOD RECIPES

Australia's leading producer of fruit juices, nectars and fruit juice drinks, Berri Limited, is located in—you guessed it—the Riverland town of Berri. Berri's canned juices and nectars have absolutely no added preservatives or artificial flavourings and the convenience of a long shelf life. These recipes have been specifically created to be tasty, healthy, quick and easy.

SWEET POTATO AND ORANGE SOUP

1 tbsp butter
2 onions, chopped
2 tsp ground cumin
2 tsp curry powder
375 ml chicken stock
1 cup water
1¹/₂ cups Berri orange juice
1 kg sweet potato, peeled and chopped
cream, for garnish (optional)

Saute onion in butter until transparent. Add cumin and curry powder, cook for 2 minutes. Stir in stock, water, orange juice and sweet potato. Cover, simmer for 15 minutes or until sweet potato is tender. Blend or process soup and garnish with cream if desired. Serves 4.

APRICOT CHICKEN

1¹/₂ kg chicken pieces
seasoned flour, for coating chicken
425 g can Berri apricot nectar
1 pkt French onion soup powder

Preheat oven to 180°C. Roll chicken pieces in flour until well coated. Place in casserole dish. Heat apricot nectar and soup powder in saucepan on high until thickened. Pour over chicken pieces. Cover and bake for 1–1¹/₂ hours. Garnish with chopped nuts and parsley if desired. Serve with rice or noodles. Serves 4.

GRAPEFRUIT AND ORANGE MORNING PICK-ME-UP

425 ml Berri grapefruit juice
1¹/₂ cups Berri unsweetened orange juice
¹/₄ cup Berri lemon squeeze
2 passionfruits
2 tbsp fresh mint, chopped

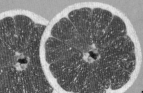

Combine all juices with passion-fruit pulp and mint when ready to serve. Pour over ice into serving glasses. Serves 4.

Berri Limited, BERRI

was 22.5 per cent pure, probably the richest ever found anywhere in the world. At its closure in 1878, ore to the value of more than £1 million had been produced there, with a peak annual production of 4,038 tonnes of copper in 1857.

The small village of **Keyneton** [F2], in scenic eucalypt country, is home to Henschke Wines, established in 1847. The winery has cellar door sales.

Kingston OM [E4] was called the Town of Thurk (after a local station) until 1940, when the name was changed to Kingston OM, meaning 'On Murray', to distinguish it from Kingston SE in the south-east of the state.

The people of **Koolunga** [D1], a small farming community, in 1883 made attempts to capture the legendary bunyip. The creature was supposedly seen near a local waterhole.

The trail must have been cold, for the animal proved as elusive as ever. Bunyip Park and Bunyip River Walk recall the event.

Laura [C1] is where

poet CJ Dennis lived for years. His first poem was published in the *Laura Standard* in 1895. Outside the Dick Biles Gallery is a large copper statue of the poet designed by Dave Griffiths. Dennis's father was licensee of the Beetaloo Reservoir Hotel, 1892–1910. CJ worked as a barman for his father in 1898 but they soon fell out and he went to Broken Hill.

DON'T MISS: Try one of Laura's famous Golden North ice-creams, produced here since the 1920s, at a tasting at the Laura Brewery. The Laura Folk Festival takes place in April (phone 08 8663 2221).

GAZETTEER

Loveday [E4] was the site of one of

Australia's largest internment camps during World War II—at its peak it held 5,380 internees and more than 1,500 Australian military personnel. The camp was self-sufficient and even profitable. Opium poppies were one of the crops grown to supply the forces with morphine. Cobdogla Irrigation

and Steam Museum has information about Loveday, and you can go on a guided tour (for details call 08 8588 7031).

The town of **Loxton** [F5] took off after World War II, when the state government began South Australia's largest soldier settlement scheme, opening up 2,500 ha of irrigated land. The new settlers planted vineyards and orchards and broadened the town's economic base of wool and wheat. Daisy Bates, who devoted her life to Aboriginal causes, lived in a tent for four years in Loxton. A plaque memorialises her at the Pyap Reserve, outside Loxton. A lot of the area's history is reproduced at the Loxton Historical Village on the river. There are 25 buildings fully furnished in period style. A replica of William Loxton's hut is shaded by the 100-year-old pepper tree he planted. The town is now surrounded by huge vineyards.

Around **Lyndoch** [F2] is where the Barossa Valley's first grapes were grown, or so it is claimed. It's a good place to start your exploration of the wineries as there are many nearby with cellar sales and tastings.

The **Mallala** [F1] Uniting Church appears to be out of balance, having only one turret. The church was built in 1909 and the stone was laid by Sir Samuel Way, then Lieutenant-Governor of South Australia.

Mintaro's [D1] Magpie & Stump Hotel

has been licensed since 1851, when it catered for the needs of the itinerant bullock and mule drivers passing through the town. Beyond the pub's baker's oven is a room devoted to the Mintaro Coursing Club, which started in 1884. The last live hare was chased to its doom in 1986. The sport continued with a drag lure until 1997. Between the Magpie &

SA

Stump and the old council chambers are the historic bullock stables. Around the back, on the wall facing the street are huge rings where the bullocks were tied up at night, probably so the drivers had only a short walk to the pubs on either side of the stable. The grand Georgian-style mansion, Martindale Hall, on the road between Mintaro and Manoora, was used in the filming of *Picnic at Hanging Rock*.

Morgan's [E3] Port of Morgan Historic

Museum, in the old railway buildings on the riverfront, has a display including the PW *Mayflower* (1884), South Australia's oldest paddle wheeler.

Nuriootpa [F2], recognised as the

commercial centre of the Barossa Valley, has grapevines seemingly growing everywhere, including down the main street. South of town is Maggie Beer's Farm Shop where you can taste and purchase her gourmet food products, including verjuice (the unfermented acid juice of unripened white grapes).

Orroroo [B1] has

the Yesteryear Costume Gallery, at 50 Main Street, one of the most interesting rural museums in Australia. The range of costumes, some of which are still worn, is impressive.

In # Paringa [E5]

there is yet another black stump—the massive root system and stump of a 600-year-old river red gum—on the Murtho Road. It measures more than 8 m across. Opened on 31 January 1927, the Paringa

Suspension Bridge is one of only four across the River Murray. It still opens when the very occasional large paddle steamer comes through.

Peterborough [B1] was a major

rail centre when Australia's disparate colonies boasted different rail gauges. It was one of the few places in the world that could cater to trains needing narrow, medium and broad gauge tracks. The Steamtown Railway

Preservation Society of Peterborough is now a static museum displaying steam engines and carriages, as well as numerous narrow-gauge freight vehicles (it has ceased operating its locomotives because of public liability insurance costs). The town also has one of Australia's two abattoirs properly licensed to slaughter horses for human con-sumption. St Cecilia's, on Callary Street, was once the home of the diocese's Catholic bishop. It has magnificent stained-glass windows and is open to the public. The Peterborough Gold Battery, constructed in 1897, is still crushing ore after more than a century of use.

GAZETTEER

The # Renmark [E5] Hotel,

opened in 1897, was the first community hotel to be established in the British Empire. It is run by an elected board, distributing profits back into the community. Australia's first cooperative winery was also opened in Renmark in 1916. Harding's Folklore Gallery, located in Murtho Street, is built around a 74 sq m mural, which took 3,000 hours to paint, depicting Australian colonial life. Bredl's Wonder World of Wildlife, on the corner of the Sturt Highway and 28th Street, has a large collection of reptiles including two reticulated pythons measuring more than 6 m, the largest in Australia. More than 200 different species of reptile, including alligators, crocodiles and snakes—taipans, tiger snakes, death adders, rattlesnakes, pythons and boa constrictors—can be seen there.

Riverton's [E1] railway gained

notoriety on 22 March 1921, when a passenger travelling on the *Broken Hill Express* from Adelaide fired a number of shots into the dining room and Percy Brookfield, a Member of Parliament for Broken Hill, was shot and killed when he tried to disarm the gunman. Even though the complex is beautifully restored, if you know where to look you can still see the bullet holes in the walls.

From Robertstown [E2] follow

the signs for 20 km, heading north, to Burra Creek Gorge. There's a walking trail up into the gorge, and swimming, fishing and camping.

Go fly a kite on Sedan [F2] Kite

Day, held in October. The Yookamurra Earth Sanctuary, 24 km north-east of Sedan, covers more than 1,100 ha and is surrounded by the world's longest feral-proof fence (14 km). Native animals once common to the area, such as the bilby, woylie, boodie rat and numbat, are being reintroduced here. Book to visit on 08 8562 5011.

Cast a line at Spalding [C1] on the

Broughton River, one of the state's top trout fishing locations. The river is fed by underground water and has permanent spring-fed pools. Geoff Matters owns a property alongside the river and issues fishing permits (ask at the Spalding Hotel for directions) and in July hosts the fly-fishing National Titles.

Springington [F2] is most

famous for the Herbig Tree, a large, hollow river red gum that Johann Friedrich and Caroline Herbig once called home. Herbig was a tailor turned farmer who arrived in South Australia in 1855. He leased 200 ha from George Angas. Desperately poor, he decided to live in the large, hollow red gum, which was 300–500 years old—it had probably been hollowed out by fire after being struck by lightning. A year after his arrival Herbig married Caroline Rattey, only 18 at the time, at Lyndoch. He took her back to live with him in the tree and it was there that the first two of their 16 children were born. In 1860 Herbig and his family moved out of the tree into a small house, which still stands.

The Swan Reach [F3] Museum

in the old school has photographs of huge floods in 1936 and 20 years later in 1956. On both occasions sandbags proved ineffective and the town was nearly washed away. It is open Wednesdays and Sundays 2–4 pm, Saturdays 10 am–12 midday or by appointment (call 08 8570 2019). The adventurous can try the South Australian Water Canoe Challenge, held in March each year. A canoeing and orienteering event, it's open to anyone over 14 years old. Call 08 8226 7010 for details. For a guided tour of a yabby farm, contact Murray Aquaculture on 08 8570 2025. The farm also grows almonds.

SA

At **Tanunda**'s [F2] centre is der Zeigenhart, or Goat Square, on the corner of John and Maria Streets, which was a meeting place for bartering goods. There are four Lutheran chuches in Tanunda, including the Tabor Lutheran Church with its 26 m spire topped by an orb that holds old church records. At the Keg Factory on St Hallett Road, you can see wine cask and keg construction. At the Barossa Wine and Visitor Centre in Murray Street visitors can drink in the heritage of this famous wine-growing region.

DON'T MISS:

The Barossa Vintage Festival, held every odd-numbered year, was founded in 1947 and is Australia's most famous and longest running celebration of regional wine, food and heritage. It includes more than 100 events: lunches, concerts, dinners, tastings, tours, exhibitions, displays, breakfasts and brunches in the heart of the beautiful Barossa. There's also Barossa Under the Stars in February and a jazz weekend in August. Call 08 8563 0600 for dates. The Barossa was named by Colonel Light after Barrosa (Hill of the Roses) in Spain, where he had fought the French in the Peninsula War in 1811. The spelling mistake was never corrected.

Terowie

Terowie [C2] was the site of an army camp during World War II. General Douglas MacArthur made his speech, 'I came out of Bataan and I shall return,' here and a plaque commemorates this at the railway station. Terowie was once one of the towns where the railway gauge changed and all passengers had to do likewise.

Truro

Truro [F2] was founded in 1850 after the discovery of copper in the area. The town has stone walls instead of the usual fences, a reminder of the settlers' Cornish origins.

Waikerie

Waikerie [E4] started as a communal settlement when the government shipped 200 people there in 1894 in a bid to relieve South Australia's unemployment problem. Despite the town being surrounded by dry mallee scrub, the farming community eventually became Australia's largest citrus-growing area, an oasis in the desert and the site of the world's largest cooperative fruit-packing sheds. The name Waikerie is said to mean 'things that fly', remarkably appropriate for a town that is a major centre for gliding. You can learn to glide or take a joy ride in a glider by contacting the Gliding Club 4 km east of

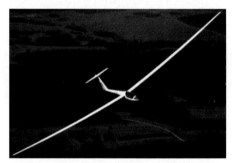

Waikerie on the Sturt Highway. Waikerie hosts the Riverland Rock'n'Roll Festival on the first weekend in May (call 08 8541 2332). The Rotary Cliff-Top Walk stretches east from the Waikerie ferry through to the pumping station, on to the town lookout, then along the picturesque cliff top.

At Whyte–Yarcowie

At **Whyte–Yarcowie** [C2] the Farming through the Ages exhibition on the Barrier Highway has 70 tractors, 20 stationary engines and 10 veteran and vintage cars to see (call 08 8665 3247).

Williamstown

South-west of **Williamstown** [F2] is the Whispering Wall, the huge curved retaining wall of the Barossa Reservoir. The acoustics are such that you can speak in a normal voice and be heard clearly at the other end of the wall,

GAZETTEE

PRAWN SALAD WITH GRAPEFRUIT, HONEY AND CHILLI SAUCE

Festivals in the Barossa and Clare Valleys celebrate local produce as well as wines.

2 carrots, peeled and julienned
2 zucchini, julienned
$1/3$ cup honey
2 tsp Thai sweet chilli sauce
$1/2$ cup white wine
1 cup Berri grapefruit juice
1 tsp grated fresh ginger
2 tsp cornflour
2 tsp water
16 cooked king prawns, shelled and deveined, tails intact

Boil, steam or microwave carrot strips until tender, rinse under cold water and drain. Combine carrot and zucchini in a bowl, cover, chill until ready to serve. Combine honey, chilli sauce, white wine, grapefruit juice and ginger in a small saucepan. Bring to boil, reduce heat and simmer for 2 minutes. Blend cornflour with water, add to sauce and stir constantly until sauce thickens. Divide carrot and zucchini onto 4 plates, top each with 4 prawns and sauce, serve immediately. Serves 4.

Berri Limited, BERRI

140 m away. You'll need a friend at the other end of the wall to get the full effect.

Yacka [D1] has a tiny historical precinct, where the Institute Hall (begun in 1875) is side-by-side with the War Memorial, of fine Carrara marble. The old bank building next door is home to the Yacka Archives, open on the afternoon of the last Sunday of each month or by appointment. Over the road is the old Tilbrook blacksmith shop and further along, in the old butcher's shop, is a craft shop that raises money for the upkeep of the hall; further again is the former hotel, built in 1873.

GAZETTEER

SA

Diary of Events

Town	Event	Date	Contact
Barmera	Supreme Australian Sheepdog Championships	October	08 8588 2559
Clare	Clare Valley Gourmet Weekend	May	08 8842 2131
Jamestown	Fly-in	Oct/Nov 2003 (triennial)	08 8664 1838
Laura	Folk Festival	April	08 8663 2221
Sedan	Kite Day	October	08 8565 2004
Tanunda	Barossa Under the Stars	February	08 8563 0600
	Barossa Vintage Festival	April 2003 (biennial)	08 8563 0600
	Jazz Weekend	August	08 8563 0600
Waikerie	Riverland Rock'n'Roll Festival	May	08 8541 2332

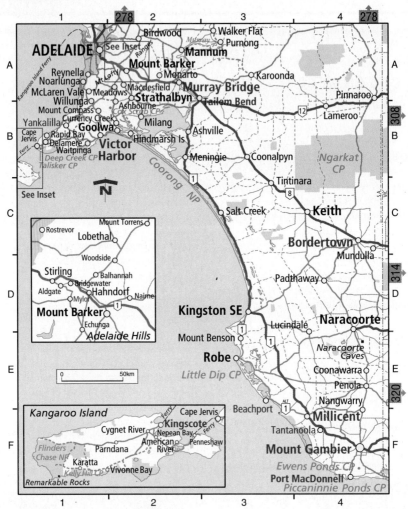

get off the beaten track

cruise
the adelaide hills
to limestone coast

Aldgate [D1] is most famous for the

Aldgate Pump, across from the Aldgate Pump Hotel. The original pump was used to water the horses and bullock teams on their way south to the Echunga goldfields.

American River [F2] is a tidal

estuary on Kangaroo Island from where big game fishermen chase the world's biggest sharks.

Ashbourne [B2] is a tranquil place

with roadside produce stalls. The **Cox Scrub Conservation Park** on the Meadows–Goolwa Road has walking trails and a camping ground and is ideal for birdwatching and photography. It was originally a habitat for the Mount Lofty Southern Ranges emu wren, until the Ash Wednesday bushfires of 1983, but they are currently being reintroduced to the area.

The # Balhannah [D1] Hotel, which

opened in 1850, has a typical Adelaide Hills atmosphere, with open fires in winter and wide, cool verandahs to lounge on in summer.

Beachport [E3] was the south-

east's first whaling station. A lake, the **Pool of Siloam**, is located on the Scenic Drive. It is about as close as Australia gets to the Dead Sea. The pool is fed by underground springs and, with a salinity seven times that of seawater, it is popular for therapeutic purposes. It also means that non-swimmers can float, even lying on their backs reading a book. For keen four-wheel-drivers there are a couple of beach drives nearby that are first class, but they can be tough, so go prepared. **Woakwine Cutting** (a huge trench), 10 km north of Beachport, converted a large area of swamp into farmland. It took local man MB McCourt three years to complete, and is declared locally as 'probably

Australia's biggest engineering feat performed by one person'. There's an observation platform where you can admire the man's tenacity and hard work.

Birdwood [A2] is the home of the

National Motor Museum, Australia's premier collection of motor vehicles and one of the best in the world, with vehicles and motorbikes dating back to 1898. It also has the famous old mail truck in which postman Tom Kruse transported mail from Marree, in the far north-west of the state, to Birdsville in Queensland, along the Birdsville track. Kruse's adventures were superbly captured in the 1952 Venice

SA

award-winning documentary *Back of Beyond*. The film chronicles the ingenuity involved in taking mail and supplies across a desert prone to flooding, being bogged in sand dunes and dealing with breakdowns. The

LOW-FAT JAMBALAYA

There are as many jambalaya recipes as Louisiana bayous, but they are mostly high in fat. This low-fat version is just as tasty.

1 cup sliced low-fat sausage
1 cup chicken breast, in bite-size pieces
2 tbsp vegetable oil
1 1/2 cups chopped onion
1 cup chopped celery
1 cup red pepper
1/2 tsp black pepper
1 tsp each of cayenne, salt, white pepper and thyme
2 tsp oregano
2 bay leaves
2 cloves garlic, minced
2 cups diced tomatoes with juice
1/2 cup tomato purée
5 cups chicken or seafood stock
1/2 cup minced green onion
2 cup uncooked brown rice
12 small peeled prawns, roughly chopped
12 oysters in own liquid, roughly chopped

Preheat oven to 180°C. Sauté sausage and chicken briefly in oil. Add onion, celery and red pepper, and sauté further. Add seasoning, herbs and garlic to taste. Add tomatoes and tomato puree, cook 5 minutes, stirring continuously. Add stock, bring to the boil, stir in green onion, rice and seafood. Bake in a covered flame-proof dish for 1 hour.

Penelope Herbert, ADELAIDE

annual Bay-to-Birdwood Run, with classic and vintage vehicles alternating each year, starts at Glenelg and ends at the museum. It is held on the last weekend in September. As a change of pace Birdwood also features the annual Rock'n'Roll Rendezvous in March—call 08 8568 5006.

Bordertown [C4] is, in fact, 20 km

west of the South Australia–Victoria border, the name being decided upon before the state boundaries were finalised. It is the home of the white kangaroo—not an albino but actually a white-haired western grey.

Former Australian Prime Minister Robert Hawke was born in Farquhar Street, Bordertown, in 1929. The Padthaway Estate winery south of Bordertown, which is in an old woolshed, has the only traditional French champagne press in Australia. On the walls of the woolshed is original shearers' graffiti, including their tips for the Melbourne Cup. Phar Lap was one of them.

GAZET*

At Bridgewater [D1], on Mount

Barker Road, is Petaluma's Bridgewater Mill. This winery is based in an exceptionally beautiful old watermill, whose huge water-wheel was built in 1860.

The drive to Cape Jervis [B1] on

the southern tip of the Fleurieu Peninsula west from Victor Harbor is particularly enjoyable. If you want to camp in a wild natural setting along the way visit the **Deep Creek Conservation Park**, which takes up quite a stretch of coastline. Cape Jervis is also the ferry departure point for Kangaroo Island for further adventuring. What was once a silver and lead mine, from the 1860s to 1925, is now the **Talisker Conservation Park**, where you can explore the mine ruins. Turn onto Range Road north of Cape Jervis on the way to **Delamere**.

The site of Currency Creek

[B2] was once planned to be the capital of South Australia. The Currency Creek Cemetery is the final resting place of many of the early riverboat captains who travelled the Murray in their paddle steamers. The Aboriginal inhabitants also made good use of the Murray and its tributaries, evidenced by the many 'canoe trees', large eucalypts with sections carved from their trunks for building canoes. Visit in April for the Currency Creek Jet Sprint Races, described as rally driving on water, with 13 ft jet boats.

Cygnet River [F2] is a small

township close to the airport and home to Duck Lagoon, a wildlife reserve with superb birdwatching opportunities. Visit Emu Ridge Eucalyptus Distillery, a short drive away, where you will see the traditional manufacturing process of the narrow leaf mallee. Also located in the Cygnet River area is the Gum Creek Marron Farm, with viewing ponds, aquariums and the opportunity to sample marron (yabbies on the east coast).

Echunga [D1] was laid out in

1849 by Jacob Hagen. In 1852 gold was found by William Chapman, leading to Echunga being proclaimed South Australia's first goldfield. Diamonds were discovered in 1859.

Flinders Chase National Park

[F1] on Kangaroo Island has the **Remarkable Rocks**, a collection of granite boulders weathered by the sea into fantastic and unusual shapes. Admirals Arch has also been

carved out of the rocks. A new $7 million visitor's centre is an essential stop for entrance permits and park information.

In Goolwa [B2] the South Australian

Wooden Boat Festival is held biannually (the next one in March 2003), with many events and the opportunity to see boats in action. Call the Signal Point Interpretive Centre on 08 8555 3488.

Hahndorf [D1] is the oldest surviving

German settlement in Australia. On the corner of Balhannah Road and Church Street is St Michael's, the oldest continuing congregation of the Lutheran Church in Australia dating back to 1858. The original German Arms Hotel began trading in 1839. 'The Cedars', the Bavarian-style home of famous Australian painter Hans Heysen, is in Heysen Road, off Ambleside Road. Heysen's studio, complete with very familiar gum trees across the paddocks, is virtually untouched. The house, still owned by the Heysen family, is in pristine condition.

The Hahndorf Museum on Main Street tells the history of the first German migrants to South Australia in 1839.

Karoonda [A3] narrowly missed being hit by a meteorite in 1930—a specimen weighing around 25 kg smashed to the ground 4 km east of town. You can see it at the council offices on Railway Terrace.

DON'T MISS: Get your lips limbered for the Australian Gum Leaf Playing Championships, in Karoonda in April.

Keith [C4] used to be called Mount Monster and the area surrounding it carried the name Ninety Mile Desert until it was changed to the more benign Coonalpyn Downs. In 1949 it was the site of an experiment in soil improvement when the CSIRO corrected soil deficiencies by the addition of minute quantities of metallic elements and minerals. Nearly 300,000 ha of arable land was created within 10 years.

The **Kelly Hill** Conservation Park [F1], off the South Coast Road on Kangaroo Island, is 2,180 ha of coastal heath and hardy mallee. The Hanson Bay Hike winds through the park to the coast from Kelly Hill Caves, thought to be some 120,000 years old. This extensive area of caves, caverns and sinkholes was named after a horse, Kelly, that fell down one of the sinkholes.

Kingscote [F2] was first settled in 1836 and was South Australia's first official European settlement. Eighty years later Australia's first truly Australian export, eucalyptus oil, left the town. You can see the process in operation at the Emu Ridge Eucalyptus Oil Distillery, about 20 km south of town. The colony's first mulberry tree was planted at Reeves Point. It still bears fruit, which the locals still use to make jam. The

Kingscote Cemetery is one of South Australia's oldest. At Hope Cottage (the National Trust Museum), on the hill above Kingscote, the original lantern, lens and operating machinery of the Cape Willoughby lighthouse have been re-erected. The lighthouse, built in 1852, is the oldest in South Australia and was originally on the eastern extremity of the island.

The town of **Kingston SE** [D3] welcomes visitors with Larry the Lobster (actually a crayfish), at the town entrance.

The big lobster is 17 m high, weighs 4 tonnes, and is justified by the fact that Kingston SE is one of Australia's best lobster/cray fishing areas. The Sundial of Human Involvement is located at Maria Creek, next to Apex Park. When it was completed it was one of only eight in the world. No matter which direction you approach Kingston SE from, you cannot miss the sundial and the sculptures. There is an elephant seal and cub, a blue-tongue lizard and a Japanese crab, all carved from large granite rocks. There is a shingle-back lizard behind the Wood Hut craft shop, a mulloway in the town's Lions Park and a kangaroo near the Aboriginal burial ground.

FILLET OF BEEF WITH ROASTED TURNIPS AND ANCHOVY AND RED WINE BUTTER

The McLaren Vale wine district on the Fleurieu Peninsula boasts vineyards and olive and almond groves, as well as a diverse range of regional produce. This rich bounty forms the basis of every item on the menu at the Salopian Inn, in the district's outskirts.

ANCHOVY AND RED WINE BUTTER
1 tsp fresh thyme leaves, chopped
3 cloves garlic, roasted until soft
50 g anchovies, drained of oil
1 tsp honey
1 cup red wine, reduced to 50 ml
200 g unsalted butter
black pepper to taste

TURNIPS
18 baby turnips, trimmed and peeled
50 g unsalted butter
1 tbsp olive oil
1 tbsp sugar
1 cup chicken stock

BEEF
6 fillet steaks, 200 g each
olive oil
salt and pepper to taste
1 tbsp fresh chervil, roughly chopped
1 tbsp flat leaf parsley, roughly chopped

To make anchovy and red wine butter, put thyme, garlic, anchovies, honey and red wine into a food processor and process to form a paste. Put butter (at room temperature) into a mixing bowl and whisk until pale in colour. Add the anchovy mixture and pepper to the butter and fold in until well combined. Place mixture on a large piece of baking paper and roll into a cylinder. Roll the cylinder in aluminium foil and twist both ends until firm, and refrigerate. Preheat oven to 180°C. Prepare the turnips. Heat butter and olive oil in an oven-proof pan, add turnips and cook until lightly browned. Add sugar and stir well, then add stock and finish cooking in oven for 10–15 minutes. The stock should be reduced enough to glaze the turnips. Rub the steaks with olive oil, salt and pepper, and cook evenly on both sides in a hot pan to medium rare. Remove pan and rest in a warm place. To serve, place 3 turnips per person in the centre of a warm plate, top with steaks and then a slice of anchovy butter. Garnish with the roughly chopped chervil and parsley. Serves 6.

Salopian Inn,
MCLAREN
VALE

SA

Just 3 km from **Lameroo** [B4], on the old Yappara Road, is the Byrne Homestead, the first house in the district. It was built in 1898 out of pug and pine and gives an idea of how the early settlers lived. It's not generally open to the public (most people just drive by and take a look).

Any exploration of **Lobethal** [C2] should probably start with the rich Lutheran complex in the town's main street. It includes Australia's first Lutheran Seminary (a small pug wall construction), built in 1842, the oldest surviving Lutheran church (built in an act of extraordinary devotion largely by one man with the help of the local women who carried the bricks for him), and the Lobethal Archives and Historical Museum. Open on weekends, it contains a lot of information about the German settlers. There are also a number of historic graves in the grounds.

 DON'T MISS: Scattered throughout the Adelaide Hills are several conservation parks: **Cleland Conservation Park** and its wildlife park, just below the crest of Mt Lofty and its television towers, is one of the best places to get up close and personal with Australia's cuddly animals. The **Mt Crawford Forest**, from Lobethal to Williamstown, is also worth a visit. **Morialta Conservation Park** surrounds the waterfalls of the same name at the end of Morialta Road in **Rostrevor**. Rock climbers often pit their skills against the sheer rock faces here.

The good people of **Lucindale** [D4] have got their finger on the pulse of what qualities a dog needs to be a good yard dog. You can share this knowledge at the Best Yard Dog Competition in Lucindale, during South East Field Days, the largest field day event in Australia (call 08 8766 0032).

In **Macclesfield** [A2] the riverside willows grew from cuttings of the trees growing near Napoleon's grave on St Helena Island. They miraculously survived being transported to Australia slotted in potatoes. The founders of Macclesfield, the Davenport brothers, are thought to have planted the trees in the 1840s. If you're visiting in November, don't miss the Strawberry Fete (call 08 8388 9414).

McLaren Vale [A1] is an increasingly productive wine growing region, and the annual June Sea and Vines Festival celebrates the fact, as well as its idyllic location.

Mannum [A2] is where Australia's first steam car was built, in 1894. Restored, it now stands in the National Motor Museum in the old Birdwood Flour Mill. The biggest stern paddle steamer in the Southern Hemisphere, the *Murray Princess*, is based in Mannum.

 DON'T MISS: The Big Fishing Competition is in Mannum in February (call 08 8569 1303).

Near **Meadows** [A2] is the Kuitpo Forest, where flocks of yellow-tailed black cockatoos are prolific.

Meningie's [B2] Point Malcolm Lighthouse is Australia's smallest inland lighthouse, established to help guide paddle steamers across Lake Albert and Lake Alexandrina.

Opposite the **Milang** [B2] Historical Railway Museum stands a willow tree planted in 1867 by the Duke of Edinburgh, son of Queen Victoria, who went on a shooting expedition on Lake Alexandrina. The Milang–Goolwa Freshwater Classic is Australia's largest freshwater sailing race. It's held on Lake Alexandrina and the River Murray on the January long weekend.

 # Millicent's [F4] Living History Museum at the Visitor Information Centre boasts a superb collection of horse-drawn vehicles, a 'shipwreck room' and

GAZETTEER

gorgeous gowns, as well as examples of Aboriginal rock art from Ice Age caves of the area. The town itself was built on a limestone ridge exposed when the Millicent flats were drained in the late 1860s. The Millicent Swimming Lake is a large artificial swimming pool complete with a beach on one side. On the corner of Park Terrace and Rendelsham Road, it's open from December to March.

In **Mount Barker**'s [D1] early

days allotments were sold as prospective wheat farms, but the absence of a flour mill deterred settlers. John Dunn was offered free land to establish a mill. He built the first South Australian steam flour mill outside Adelaide in 1844. The mill operated successfully for the next 50 years and helped develop the town. It still stands today. The Mt Barker summit (517 m) provides one of the best views in the Adelaide Hills area. On a clear day it is possible to see Mt Lofty in the north and Lake Alexandrina in the south-east. Take Springs Road from what is now the Adelaide suburb of Mount Barker, named after the mountain.

Mount Benson [E3] is relatively

new to wine growing, the first vines being planted in the area in 1989 and the first vintage produced in 1992. The influence of the Great Southern Ocean, moderating the year-round temperature of the region, is said to produce fruit of a distinctive character.

Mount Compass [B1] holds the

Compass Cup, a cow race and the only one of its kind in the country, in February (08 8556 9115 for details).

There's a choice of fly or bait fishing at the Tooperang Rainbow Trout Farm, Clelands Gully Road, Tooperang, 6 km south of Mount Compass (call 08 8556 9048).

Mount Gambier [F4] itself is an

extinct volcano, while its namesake is now the largest settlement in the south-east of the state. It was the first area in South Australia to be named, in 1800. It is now home to Australia's largest softwood industry and is sited amid the biggest softwood plantation in the Commonwealth. Mount Gambier's most spectacular sight is **Blue Lake**. Each November the lake's waters turn cobalt blue and remain that way for the rest of the summer. The colour change is caused by calcite particles in the water, which absorb all visible light except blue. The water's colour reverts to normal once the warm weather disappears. Mount Gambier boasts a unique Visitor Centre. A fully integrated complex, the Lady Nelson Discovery Centre was built, as a community project, of local coraline limestone and timber, to blend with its surroundings. It starts with a full-size replica of the *Lady Nelson*, the brig in which Lieutenant James Grant first sighted Mount Gambier. It then moves on to the Geology Room (explaining the area's volcanoes and how Blue Lake was formed), then the Cave Walk (displaying local fossils and ancient kangaroo bones), and concludes outside with a sample of the local wetlands crossed by a boardwalk. It is on Jubilee Highway East. Beside the town hall, in Commercial Road, is an ornate and beautiful marble fountain.

SA

Captain Robert Gardiner commissioned it at a cost of £700, donating it to the city in 1884. It is claimed to be the first marble fountain made in South Australia. Captain Gardiner was the grandfather of famous ballet dancer Sir Robert Helpmann, born in Mount Gambier in 1909.

Mount Torrens [C2] was named

after Colonel Robert Torrens, chairman of the Board of Colonisation Commissioners that founded the colony of South Australia in 1836. A tavern was built to serve the teamsters from Mannum and the township was laid out in 1853. Many of its 19th-century buildings still exist.

The **Mundulla** [C4] Hotel served as a store and post office in the 1870s, from 1884 to 1912 as a licensed hotel, and it's now an art and craft museum and restaurant.

Murray Bridge's [A2] St John

the Baptist Pro Cathedral on Mannum Road is the smallest cathedral in Australia. In 1970 the Diocese of the Murray was formed out of the Diocese of Adelaide and, because St John's Church is the mother church of the diocese and holds the Bishop's Cathedra (chair), St John's automatically became a Pro Cathedral. The bridge itself, opened in 1879, was the first to span the Murray River. The roundhouse—strictly speaking it's hexagonal—was built for the overseer during construction and has been restored. It's now used for community functions. You can visit it as part of a group (call 08 8532 3396). Murray Bridge is

also home to one of a dying breed of entertainment venue, a drive-in theatre. To the north-west is the small community of **Monarto**. In 1973 there were plans to turn Monarto into a satellite city housing 250,000 people. The idea was eventually abandoned.

DON'T MISS: In June the Back-to-Back Competition is held in Murray Bridge. A sheep is shorn with hand shears, the wool is then spun and knitted into a garment. The fastest time from sheep to sweater wins. In 2001 they did it in less than six hours. The Spinners & Weavers Guild conducts the competition (phone 08 8532 3289).

Mylor [D1] has the fascinating

Warrawong Earth Sanctuary, founded by passionate environmentalist Dr John Wamsley, who has waged a campaign to protect small Australian mammal species. His passion also includes a hatred of the feral cat, manifested in his 'Davy Crockett' style hat and a large wall mat, both

made out of cat skins. Warrawong Earth Sanctuary has a fence that no cat can climb or get under. There are dawn and dusk guided walks (call 08 8370 9197 to book).

Nairne [D2] is one of South Australia's

oldest settlements and many of its historic buildings have been restored. One of the town's industries is bacon and smallgoods.

The **Nangwarry** [F4] Forestry and Logging Museum delves into the history of logging in the area, with exhibits of chainsaws and other logging equipment, an old fire truck and one of the first crane trucks. It's open 10 am–3.30 pm on Sundays and public holidays, as well as Tuesdays and Thursdays during school holidays, or by appointment (08 8739 7321).

South-east of **Naracoorte** [D4] is the **Naracoorte Caves National Park**. Its fossil caves have delivered up one of the richest collections of Pleistocene fossils in the world. The caves have South Australia's

only World Heritage listing. The Wonambi Fossil Centre features 17 robotic re-creations of the animals fossilised in the caves, allowing visitors to get some idea of what the ancient marsupial lion and giant echidna looked like. Bat Cave is widely recognised as a significant

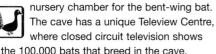

nursery chamber for the bent-wing bat. The cave has a unique Teleview Centre, where closed circuit television shows the 100,000 bats that breed in the cave.

Parndana [F2] hosts the Kangaroo

Island Easter Fair, where you can sample local produce including cheese, wine and seafood. Honey is one of the local specialties. Bees from Liguria in Italy were brought to Kangaroo Island in 1881. You can taste their honey at various farms on the island.

Penneshaw [F2] is home to

Frenchman's Rock. During his exploration of the area in 1803 Nicholas Baudin anchored at Hog Bay, came ashore and scratched an inscription on a rock. It translates to 'Expedition of discovery by Captain Baudin in the *Geographe*, 1803'. The sea and weather damaged it so much that it was

SPICY PUMPKIN SOUP

Beryl Franzese grows her own vegetables at her home on the Fleurieu Peninsula. She developed this recipe to use up her excess supplies of fresh, home-grown pumpkin.

1 dsp butter
1 large onion, chopped
1 tsp curry powder
1 tsp chilli powder
$1/2$ small butternut pumpkin, peeled and chopped
4 medium potatoes, peeled and chopped
500 ml chicken stock
salt and pepper to taste
$1/2$ cup cream

Sauté onions in butter with curry powder and chilli powder until soft. Add potato, pumpkin and stock and simmer, covered, until tender. Allow to cool a little, then blend to a purée. Return to pan, warm through. Stir in salt and pepper and cream. Serve topped with chives and sour cream if desired. Serves 6.

Beryl Franzese, ONKAPARINGA HILLS (via Noarlunga)

removed, a more durable facsimile replacing it. The original is at the Gateway Visitor Information Centre on Howard Drive. It's open weekdays 9 am–5 pm and on weekends and public holidays 10 am–4 pm.

Penola [E4] is the oldest town in the

south-east. Here in 1866 Mother Mary MacKillop established Australia's first school to cater for children regardless of their social and income groupings. Built in 1867, the Woods–MacKillop Schoolhouse, on the corner of Portland and Petticoat Lanes, was the first purpose-built Josephite

SA

Schoolhouse. The town is now a destination for pilgrimages. Yallum Park is a glorious old sandstone house 8 km west of Penola, built between 1878 and 1880 for John Riddoch. From this base Riddoch established his Coonawarra vineyards, planting some 95,000 vines in 1891. If you're here in May, make time for the Penola Festival, which celebrates the literary and artistic heritage of the town (at one time it was the home of Adam Lindsay Gordon) and features a writers' weekend at the local community library as well as dance, theatre and music.

In **Pinnaroo** [A4] the Mallee Tourist

and Heritage Centre houses the DA Wurfel Cereal Collection, a labour of love by a local farmer who became fascinated by grain varieties from a young age. It contains more than 1,300 varieties.

Near **Port MacDonnell** [F4]

is Dingley Dell, home to poet Adam Lindsay Gordon from 1864 to 1867. Gordon reportedly bought the cottage for £150 from its owner, George Randall. The deep ocean waters not far off Port MacDonnell play host to a superb run of albacore and southern bluefin tuna, most years during late April, May and early June. The albacore taken here can weigh up to 30 kg, making them the biggest of their species likely to be encountered in Australian seas, while the bluefin tuna are mostly school fish

in the 15–30 kg range, with the odd larger specimen further out to sea. Some big sharks accompany these fish. Just east of town and reached by a good dirt road are the **Ewens Ponds** and **Piccaninnie Ponds Conservation Parks**. These limestone-fed ponds are crystal clear and have gained worldwide acclaim as a place to dive. You need a permit to snorkel or dive in Piccaninnie, but not for Ewens. This chain of ponds makes for an enjoyable but cool swim and fabulous snorkel or scuba dive.

DON'T MISS: On the beachfront at Port MacDonnell each October locals enjoy Breakfast at Boatlight, when the fishing fleet light up their vessels as they leave port, resembling a floating village. It's reportedly a beautiful sight, for those who don't mind an early start.

Rapid Bay [B1] was where the

Surveyor-General of South Australia, Colonel William Light, first stepped ashore on the mainland. (He had explored Kangaroo Island first in 1836 but was not impressed with the lack of surface water or arable land so moved his exploration to the Rapid Bay area.) The boulder he engraved with his initials has now been incorporated into a beachside monument. Fishing is good off the long jetty here. The leafy sea dragon, an endangered species, has made Rapid Bay its home, attracting many divers to this spot. The Fleurieu Fishin' Fest is held in March every year between Carrickalinga and Rapid Bay (call 08 8558 2999).

The **Reynella** [A1] district's first winery

was established by John Reynell in 1838. He had received vine cuttings from William Macarthur (son of John Macarthur of Elizabeth Farm) in New South Wales. Chateau Reynella produced its first wine in 1842 and therefore makes claims to being the country's oldest winery. There is still evidence of the early history of the vineyard. The cellars date from 1842. Today the winery is called Hardy's Reynella Winery and it is said that its founder, Thomas Hardy, once worked for John Reynell.

Robe's [E3] Obelisk (drive around Boat

Haven and continue west to the headland), built to help shipping, is a prominent landmark. Completed in 1855, the obelisk was built from stone carted to the headland by bullock teams. It was originally painted white, and sailors complained that by the time they could see the obelisk they were already too close to the rocks—which stretch for nearly 2 km from the base of the cliffs. It is now painted red and white. Standing 13 m high and 33 m above sea level, it is visible 15 km from the coast. The Robe Village Fair, held in November, includes a golf tournament and wine barrel rolling competition, as well as fantastic food such as local Robe rock lobster, prime beef and lamb

and Robe spring-water barramundi, and wines from local Mount Benson, Coonawarra and Robe vignerons. A great beach drive south through the **Little Dip**

Conservation Park leads to some good fishing spots. This coast, unprotected from the swells of the southern ocean, is wild and untamed. For the not so adventurous, take the coast road south to the protected bay of **Nora Creina** and historic Beachport. Although it's rough, the road is accessible to conventional vehicles.

At Salt Creek [C3] the Friends of

the Coorong helped develop the Lakes Nature Trail, which skirts Pipeclay Lake. At only 3 km, it's an easy walk across a mallee-covered sand dune to the lake, which is salt. Also at Salt Creek there is a replica of an oil rig. In 1892 a group of entrepreneurs, believing that a compacted vegetable substance (known as 'coorongite') was an indication of oil further down, drilled Australia's first oil well. They were not successful. The Coorong's beaches, dunes and vast estuary system provided settings for memorable scenes in the film *Storm Boy*, and its estuary waters are today a happy hunting ground for recreational anglers in pursuit of bream, mullet, mulloway and Australian salmon.

Historic Stirling [D1], with its tree-

lined streets and cottages, has a distinctly European atmosphere. Its climate is ideal for flower gardens and orchards.

Kick up your heels in Strathalbyn

[A2] for the Glenbarr Gathering, a one-day event in October. There's the kirking (blessing) of the tartan, folk dancing and athletics. Don't forget to pack your kilt—if you're wearing one you can take part in the haggis and wellington boot-tossing. Call 08 8537 0451 for details.

Near Tailem Bend [A3] is Old

Tailem Town, a showcase of early settlement. Having visited Swan Hill village in 1971, Peter Squires, the creator of the town, began collecting buildings from a 240 km radius to

put together in the form of a town of the 1920s–1960s. Construction started in 1982. The buildings include the Wolesey and the Wattleford Methodist Churches (both from

1900), Long Flat Town Hall (1905) and the Murray Bridge Railway Office (1906). There are now more than 90 refurbished buildings here, including a house made of cow dung, lime and sand. Old Tailem Town also has one of the country's biggest historic engine collections, open daily, 10 am–5 pm. In Tailem Bend itself the hotel, licensed in 1902, is still serving customers 100 years later.

In Tantanoola's [F4] hotel is the

stuffed remains of the 'Tantanoola tiger'. The first sighting of the 'tiger' occurred in the late 19th century, when a young man riding near Tantanoola claimed he saw a large, shaggy animal leap over a fence with a sheep in its jaws. This led to local hysteria. Children were escorted to school by men with guns. People refused to leave their homes at night. Eventually local bushman Tom Donovan, assisted by three others, shot what appeared to be a large wild dog in 1895. The beast was declared to be the Tantanoola tiger. Donovan had it stuffed and toured around with it as a travelling exhibition. The animal was then placed in a private museum in Nelson, but returned to Tantanoola in 1905 and placed in a glass display case in the hotel. In fact, the animal was an Assyrian wolf.

Tintinara [C3] is on the edge of the

desert, providing information and access to surrounding parks such as the **Ngarkat Conservation Park**, which is only accessible to 4WDs and has abundant wildlife. To camp in the park you will need a permit and plenty of your own supplies. **Coorong National Park**, to the south, features the **Younghusband Peninsula**, a ninety-mile stretch of isolated and therefore largely untouched land. The landscape of flowing sand dunes is well worth a look. Check with the Heart of the Parks Tourist Information Centre in Becker Terrace, the main street of Tintinara, before setting out.

Victor Harbor [B1] has Australia's

only horse-drawn tram service, one of only two worldwide. It operates along the causeway (constructed 1878–82) that links Victor Harbor with **Granite Island**. The island, just 630 m offshore, is home to a colony of fairy penguins. Glacier Rock, 14 km west of Victor Harbor, is a 500-million-year-old boulder carved out by the glaciers that once covered the entire south coast. The Cockle Train, a steam train service, runs between Victor Harbor and Goolwa. Two of the finest PGA courses on the Fleurieu Peninsula are the Victor Harbor Golf Club on Yankalilla Road and the McCracken Country Club on McCracken Drive, McCracken. Snorkellers and scuba divers will enjoy the underwater life around Victor Harbor among leafy sea dragons and crayfish. At Waitpinga, Parsons Beach and Petrel Cove there's excellent surfing but be warned that the strong currents and powerful swells are unsuitable for beginners. Whales cruise close to the Victor Harbor foreshore from June to September. The South Australian Whale Centre is a good starting point for any sea- or land-based whale watching in the area, with up-to-date information on the whales' location, open seven days, 11 am to 4.30 pm.

DON'T MISS: Get out your blue suede shoes in August for the National Elvis Festival in Victor Harbor. Call 08 8552 5738 for details.

Vivonne Bay [F1] on

Kangaroo Island is the base for a crayfishing fleet and is used for other commercial and game fishing. Recreational fishers can fish or launch a boat from the beach, and barbecue their catch on return.

The Walker Flat [A3] ferry

transports about 250 vehicles across the River Murray every day of the year. It is 18 m long and has a capacity of 50 tonnes. It operates 24 hours a day and is free. Other ferries across the Murray are at Wellington, Tailem Bend, Mannum, Purnong and Swan Reach.

Willunga [A1] is the state's main

almond-growing centre. The Almond Blossom Festival is in late July and early August.

Woodside [D2] was built on the

banks of the Onkaparinga River. Like many of the towns in the Adelaide Hills region, its buildings date back to settlement days and evoke the charm of the period. The National Trust has classified its police station and courthouse for preservation.

Yankalilla's [B1] Christ

GAZETTEER

Church has a marble font that once stood in Salisbury Cathedral, England, dating back to 1650. It was given to the church around 1880 and so far they have refused all requests to send it back. While the old schoolhouse, at 48 Main Street, is not open to the public, it claims to be the first place where Mary MacKillop's order of nuns, the Sisters of St Joseph, taught. On the outskirts of town, on the road to Victor Harbor, there is a strange and charming collection of garden gnomes in a place known, not surprisingly, as Gnomeland.

Diary of Events

Town	Event	Date	Contact
Birdwood	Rock'n'Roll Rendezvous	March	08 8568 5006
	Bay to Birdwood Run	September, last weekend	08 8250 6140
Currency Creek	Jet Sprint Races	April	0413 818 162
Goolwa	Wooden Boat Festival	biennial, March 2003	08 8555 3488
Karoonda	Gum Leaf Playing	April	08 8572 4707
Macclesfield	Strawberry Fete	November	08 8388 9414
McLaren Vale	Sea and Vines Festival	June	08 8323 8999
Mannum	Big Fishing Competition	February	08 8569 1303
Milang	Freshwater Classic	January long weekend	08 8555 5444
Mount Compass	Compass Cup	February, 2nd Sunday	08 8556 9115
Murray Bridge	Back-to-Back Competition	June	08 8532 3289
Penola	Penola Festival	May	08 8737 2855
Rapid Bay	Fleurieu Fishin' Fest	March	08 8558 2999
Strathalbyn	Glenbarr Gathering	October	08 8537 0451
Victor Harbor	National Elvis Festival	August	08 8552 5738
Willunga	Almond Blossom Festival	July/Aug	08 8556 2407

SA

We make
you feel like
Australian
royalty.

At Best Western you get excellent accommodation, without paying a king's ransom.

Each and every Best Western is put through a rigorous 200 point quality evaluation test. So you can be sure good standards are standard.

We offer free entry into our Gold Crown Club International (which gives members a range of special benefits and deals).

Qanatas Frequent Flyer members can earn Qantas Frequent Flyer points and we're also the only accommodation chain that offers Fly Buys points.

And Best Western makes booking a cinch, with a central reservations number and website directory.

It's services like these that will make you feel like a king or queen. Even if you're just a bloke or a sheila.

Just call 131 779 or visit www.bestwestern.com.au

 Frequent*flyer*

 Best Western®

We'll take care of you

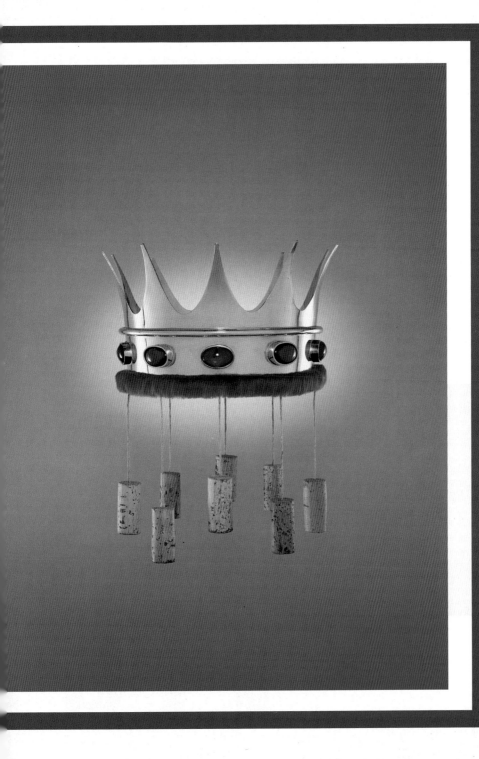

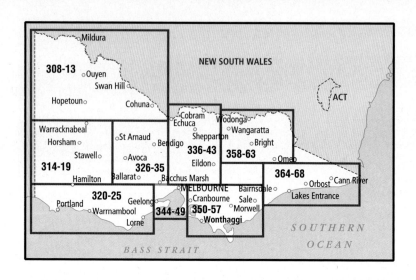

vict

With the discovery of gold in 1851, Victoria's population exploded as thousands of prospectors flooded the goldfields, first at Clunes and Anderson's Creek and then at Buninyong, Ballarat, Mt Alexander and Bendigo. Victoria is often described as 'Australia in One'.

The state offers the best of Australia—forests, wildlife, mountains, windswept coastlines, perfect beaches, meandering rivers and even deserts—in 227,600 sq km, and all within a day's reach of its capital city.

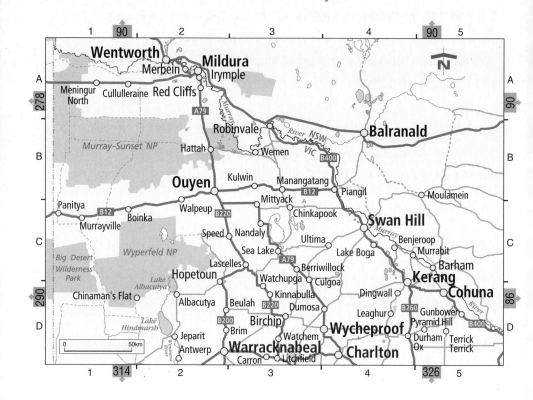

get off the beaten track

mooch

around mildura and

the murray outback

Mildura and the Murray Outback

Mildura and the Murray Outback is a land of stark contrasts: a desert with Australia's mightiest river running through it; remote national parks surrounded by rich cities; and deserts covered with banksia, red-flowered correa and holly grevillea.

Antwerp

Antwerp's [D2] Ebenezer Mission, on the south side of town, was established by missionaries in 1854 and operated until 1904. The buildings went to ruin but now have National Trust classification and are being restored. The mission church and cemetery belong to the Goolum Goolum Aboriginal Cooperative. The Aboriginal graves are mostly unmarked but there is an Aboriginal monument at the town's cemetery. The cemetery also gives a fascinating insight into the mix of European residents—the predominance of German names is quite extraordinary.

Benjeroop

Benjeroop [C4] might be a small town but there's a lot going on there—at least on the water. Being at a site where three rivers converge, the Loddon, the Murray and the Little Murray, there is good fishing, water skiing and swimming. The town's history, compiled by a local resident, dates back to 1836, with Major Mitchell's expedition. This can be viewed in the Public Hall on Easter Sunday or by appointment (call 03 5457 5290).

Birchip [D3]

Birchip [D3] has the largest amateur radio tracking station in Australia. Its radio telescope has followed the Apollo series, and used the Moonbounce Principle to explore communication technology. West of town, beyond the paddocks of wheat and sheep, are **Lake Albacutya** and **Wyperfeld National Park**. Outlet Creek, which flows out of Lake Albacutya, rarely has water in it, but **Lake Hindmarsh**, further south, is supplied with water from the Wimmera River. Two remote trails cut across the south-west extension of

VIC

LAMB RACK SERVED WITH SWEET CHILLI AND NECTARINE GLAZE

Swan Hill, where the Murray meets the Mallee, is in the centre of one of the most productive and diverse agricultural regions in Australia, famous for its beef, sheep, grain, citrus, stone fruits and more. This is why it is so important to not take fruit fly along on your travels. Watch out for the 'Fruit Fly Exclusion Zone' signs on the road and eat up before entering. There are plenty of roadside stalls in these riverside towns selling superb fresh produce to restock the snack pack.

2 lamb racks, each with 6 chops
olive oil
salt and pepper to taste
2 tsp brown sugar
6 firm nectarines, thinly sliced
sambal olek, to taste
1 cup water

Preheat oven to 200°C. Rub lamb racks with olive oil and season with salt and pepper. Seal in baking dish over a high heat, then place in oven and bake until cooked to taste (about 30–45 minutes). Remove from oven and keep warm (covered with foil) while you make the glaze. Remove any excess fat from baking dish, place on a high heat and add sugar, nectarines, sambal olek and water. Cook for 5 minutes, or until nectarines are tender and pulpy. Stir and adjust seasoning and add water if necessary. Cut lamb racks in half and serve with the glaze. Serves 4.

Sally Hardy, SWAN HILL

this park, one via Chinaman's Flat and the other, longer one via Milmed Rock. Both end up on the road between **Nhill** [see Grampians] on the Western Highway and **Murrayville** on the Mallee Highway to the north.

The **Charlton** [D4] golf course is designed in the shape of a clover leaf, with three arms of six holes radiating out from the centre. Between games you could visit Charlton's Golden Grain Museum, which has a collection of local historical artefacts. It's in the former mechanics' institute, built in 1882, and is open by appointment (03 5491 1755).

Cohuna's [D5] casein factory supplied its dried milk protein to the Apollo space mission for inclusion in the astronaut's diet during their flight to the moon. North of Cohuna (8 km) is **Gunbower Island**, a section of land between the Murray River and its anabranch, Gunbower Creek. At 60 km long, it is reputedly the world's largest inland island, extending from Koondrook to Torrumbarry Weir. The island is characterised by swamps, river red gums and box forest.

Jeparit's [D2] most famous son is Sir Robert Menzies, born here in 1894. His father was a local shopkeeper. Menzies won his first scholarship at the local school and became prime minister of Australia from 1939–41 and 1949–66. The Robert Menzies Spire at the corner of Charles and Sands Streets is an 18 m column of grey steel surmounted by a thistle and is illuminated at night.

Kerang's [C4] symbol is a flying ibis. The area around the town contains about 50 small lakes, swamps and lagoons, and the most populous ibis rookeries in the world—an estimated 200,000 straw-necked, white and glossy ibis breed in the area each year. In town, the Lester Smith

Murray area have turned the soil salinity problem to advantage by producing gourmet salt. Just south of Mildura is **Irymple**, where the Everleigh Lavender Farm is open to the public, between 15th and 16th Streets at 1589 Irymple Avenue.

Murrabit [C4] market is one of

Victoria's largest country markets, attracting more than 300 site holders selling fresh produce, arts and crafts, clothing, plants and bric-a-brac. It is held from dawn on the first Saturday of every month.

DON'T MISS: The Victorian Hotel in **Ouyen**, built in 1902, hosts the Vanilla Slice Contest every year on 17 August.

Pyramid Hill [D5] is a remarkably

exact triangle of stone, climbed by explorer Thomas Mitchell in 1836. He named it for its similarity to 'the monuments of Egypt'. It is a half-hour climb to the top, from where there are fine views of the irrigated wheat and sheep plains surrounding the town. A Braille trail for the visually impaired goes halfway up the hill.

Red Cliffs, [A2] 'Big Lizzie' was

invented and built by Frank Bottrill in Melbourne in 1914–15, and was intended to cart wool from outback stations. Hauling two wagons (each 9.1 m long), the machine

Lookout Tower offers fabulous views of Kerang and the surrounding lakes; it's also a visitor information centre. It was built in 1883 as a water tower, and is open 10 am to 3 pm Monday to Friday and on Saturday mornings.

Near **Kinnabulla** [D3] is the '221-mile peg', a remnant of the Dog Fence constructed in 1883 to keep dingoes, rabbits and other pests out of the area. The wire-netting fence ran south from Swan Hill, then west along the 36th parallel of latitude to the South Australian border.

At **Lake Boga** [C4] a well-restored Catalina flying boat in Jacaranda Crescent marks the site of the Flying Boat Museum in the secret communications bunker on the original RAAF depot site. All types of flying boats were serviced here during World War II, and are represented in the museum. The Catalina Motel features the Imperial Egg Gallery, consisting of over 100 jewelled, carved, painted and unusual eggs.

GAZETTEER

The **Leaghur** State Park [D4] comprises some 1,580 ha of blackbox forest. The trees were used by local Aborigines to make canoes, shields and shelters.

Mildura's [A2] art gallery has at least

one surprise—a Degas painting. The Grand Hotel is reputed to be the first Victorian hotel to have installed a lift. The Murray Valley has risen to prominence in recent years with Stefano de Pieri and his *Gondola on the Murray* book and television series. Downriver at Pyramid Hill the growers of the Loddon

VIC

FLOURLESS ORANGE AND ALMOND CAKE

Deliciously easy, simply delicious and a rich reminder of the abundance of the Murray Outback region thanks to the perfect matching of oranges and almonds. Better still, this cake is ideal for people on the lookout for gluten-free recipes.

3 small navel oranges, including the skin
7 eggs
325 g caster sugar
375 g almond meal
1¹/₂ tsp baking powder

Preheat oven to 180°C. Line a 25–26 cm spring-form pan with baking paper. Boil oranges until soft (approx. 1 hour), then drain and process (including skin) in a blender until smooth to make a pulp. Allow to cool. Beat together the eggs and sugar until thick and very pale. Add the almond meal, orange pulp and baking powder and beat until well combined. Pour into prepared pan and bake for approximately 1 hour or until firm to the touch.

Togs Café,
CASTLEMAINE

set off from Melbourne in 1916, carrying the Bottrill family (it was also their home). Despite scepticism concerning Big Lizzie's ability to navigate the Mallee's sand hills, it reached Mildura without trouble, only to be stopped by the flooded Murray River. It subsequently was used around **Merbein** for carting wheat, once with a load of 899 bags. When land

clearing at Red Cliffs began in 1920, the Victorian government hired the machine to uproot trees. In all, it cleared 1,500 ha, helping to create arable land. It was abandoned in 1929. In 1971 the town of Red Cliffs bought it as a memorial to the area's European pioneers. Big Lizzie is 10.7 m long, 3.4 m wide, 5.7 m high and weighs 45 tonnes. It was powered by a 60-horsepower, single-cylinder crude oil engine and had a carrying capacity of 80 tonnes. Its maximum travelling speed was about 3 km/h, and it had a turning radius of 60 m. With its two wagons attached the whole train was nearly 30 m in length. It is now in Barclay Square in the centre of town.

In **Robinvale** [B3], the largest windmill in the Southern Hemisphere, standing 18.3 m high, was erected in 1948 to supply the town with water. To find it, turn down River Road toward the caravan park on the southern bank of the river. Robinvale is a 'soldier settlement' town; a few houses and shops prior to World War II, a thriving multicultural agricultural town today. Watered by the mighty Murray, vast orchards of grapes, almonds, pistachios and olives (one of Australia's oldest and biggest plantations) abound, plus many hectares of potatoes bound for Smith's crisping industry.

The town of **Sea Lake** [C3] is nowhere near the sea, but it is near a lake. Lake Tyrrell produces 200,000 tonnes of salt each year. The lake can be seen from a viewing platform 7 km north of Sea Lake. On clear nights there is a spectac- ular view of the stars reflected on the water.

For nearly 100 years **Swan Hill** [C4] was the only point at which the Murray could be crossed—the punt here began operation in 1847. When

GAZETTEE

the first punt sank, the wood was salvaged and used to build the town's first hotel.

The Swan Hill Pioneer Settlement is an open-air historical museum covering 4 ha on the banks of the Little Murray. Australia's first such display, it recreates a 19th-century river port, with employees in period attire. There are several curios, among them a Stereoscopic Theatre (1895), which was a popular entertainment in the late 19th century. It creates a three-dimensional impression when pictures within the large cylindrical chamber are viewed through special binoculars. The bridge, built in 1896, was the first lift-span bridge on the Murray (take a look at the large counter-balancing weights). The central span was lifted to allow passage to paddle steamers. The giant cod in Curlewis Street, next to the railway station, is 11 m long and 6 m wide, and signifies the local popularity of fishing. Children can sit inside the mouth of this old movie prop for a photograph. In the same street, opposite the bowling green, the Burke and Wills Tree is an enormous Moreton Bay fig planted from a seed by a Dr Gummow, who played host to the explorers when they passed through the town in 1860 on their ill-fated excursion to the centre of Australia.

and the log smithy used by Hugh McKay to build the first horse-drawn stripper-harvester. Hugh McKay eventually left a great portion of his estate to his friend John Flynn, who used the funds to start the Royal Flying Doctor Service in 1928. A Vintage Machinery and Vehicle Rally is held every Easter Weekend.

Wycheproof [D4] is home to the world's smallest mountain, Mt Wycheproof, at only 43 m above sea level. Trains still run through the town's main street. This section of the highway is known as Broadway. Supposedly an American-born chemist came up with the name in the 1880s, as it reminded him of New York's Broadway.

Warracknabeal's [D2]

Wheatlands Agricultural Machinery Museum is at the southern end of town on the Henty Highway. It has 16 ha of machinery collected from the wheat farms of the Mallee and Wimmera districts, including giant steam-powered chaff cutters, steam engines, early tractors, 1,500 varieties of wheat

GAZETTEER

VIC

Diary of Events

Town	Event	Date	Contact
Mildura	International Balloon Fiesta	July	03 5021 4424
Ouyen	Vanilla Slice Triumph	September	03 5092 2392
Warracknabeal	Vintage Machinery and Vehicle Rally	Easter	03 5398 1632

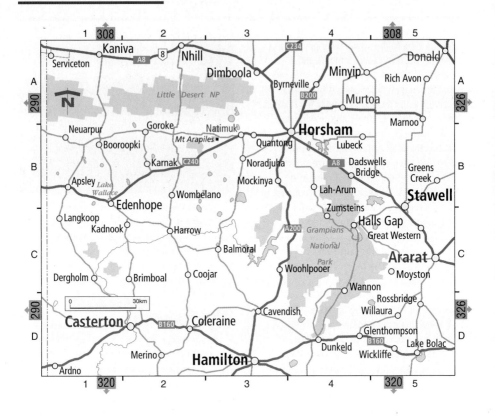

Archaeologists have dated charcoal from ancient Aboriginal campsites in the Grampians as being at least 10,000 years old.

get off the beaten track
tramp about
the grampians

In **Ararat**'s [C5] Girdlestone Street is the old Ararat County Jail built in 1860–61. Three people were hanged for murder before the jail was closed in 1887 and are buried in the

grounds. The complex reopened in 1888 as 'J Ward', an institution for the criminally insane until it closed in 1991. The gallows and other reminders of the past have been restored and the building is open to the public. The night tour is especially chilling. In Barkly Street West, opposite the courthouse, is a grapevine that was planted by GWH Grano, who established the Vine Tree Store in the late 1850s to supply the early miners with building materials. More mining memories are recalled at the $3.2 million Gum San Heritage Centre. The centre includes a museum of Chinese artefacts, dragons and costumes, and allows visitors to try their hand at gold panning.

DON'T MISS:
In March the Ararat Jailhouse Rock Festival.

Casterton [D2] was the birthplace
of controversial literary figure and swindler George Henry Cochrane, aka Grant Hervey and Hervey G Madison. He moved to Sydney, became a contributor to the *Bulletin* and, in 1914, perpetrated an unsuccessful fraud upon local newspaper the *Casterton News*. After imprisonment for forging and uttering he moved to Mildura, where he was tarred and feathered and run out of town. In 1941

the Scouts carved a fleur-de-lys with a 91 m circumference into the hill above the town. It was originally lit at night by setting fire to drums of old rags soaked in kerosene. Electric lighting has since been installed. About 11 km north of Casterton is **The Hummocks**. This unique rocky outcrop is dissected by the narrow gorge of the Wando River. More than 150 million years old, The Hummocks was originally an island standing in

a great lake. Bilstons Tree is thought to be the largest river red gum in the country. Estimated at 800 years old, it stands more than 40 m high, with a girth of 7 m. The tree is about 30 minutes drive from Casterton on the Edenhope Road).

Cavendish

[D3] has the state's eighth National School, opened in 1852—it is the only one in the state to have continuously operated on its original site to the present day. It's on the corner of Barker and Churnside Streets.

Coleraine's [D2] Peter Francis Points
Arboretum is on a hill 3 km south of town via the Portland Road. It contains more than 12,000 native plants, including more than 400 eucalypt species, and is said to be the largest such collection in Australia. There are four walking tracks leading from the shelter shed at the picnic area. Call the Eucalyptus Discovery Centre for details (03 5575 2222).

At **Dadswells Bridge** [B4]
stands the Giant Koala, which is 14 m high and cast in bronze. The town is named after an engineer and timber cutter named Dadswell

VIC

who built three bridges over Mount William Creek in 1867.

Dergholm [C1] State Park

is home to rare species of birds, such as the red-tailed black

cockatoo, swift parrot and powerful owl, Australia's largest owl. The park includes Baileys Rocks, huge granite boulders that are some 500 million years old.

LEMON MYRTLE AND COCONUT MUFFINS

The Brambuk Aboriginal Cultural Centre on Grampians Road, Halls Gap, has a café that specialises in contemporary recipes to give visitors a taste of something different, including kangaroo, emu, crocodile, native herbs and berries. The café and centre are open daily from 9 am to 5 pm excluding Christmas Day (call 03 5356 4452).

2 cups self-raising flour
1/2 cup caster sugar
1 cup desiccated coconut
2 tsp finely grated lemon zest
1 tsp lemon myrtle (bush herb)
1 cup milk
2 eggs
2 tsp vanilla essence
100 g unsalted melted butter

Preheat oven to 200°C. Grease muffin pan. Sift flour into a bowl and add sugar, lemon myrtle and coconut. Place lemon rind, milk, eggs, vanilla and butter in a jug. Whisk and pour into dry ingredients. Mix well (mixture should be a little bit lumpy). Spoon the mixture evenly into the muffin tray. Bake for 20–25 minutes. Let stand for 5 minutes and transfer to a wire rack. Serve warm with whipped cream.

Kimberley Gehan, Brambuk Aboriginal Cultural Centre Café, HALLS GAP

Between **Dimboola** [A3] and Nhill on the highway is the aptly named Pink Lake. On overcast days in particular it reflects a deep pinkish hue. It has been worked for salt since 1981.

In **Donald** [A5] it is worth driving down Byrne Street, parallel to the Sunraysia Highway, to have a quick look at the Bullock's Head—a growth on a tree in the Richardson River that closely resembles a bullock's head, complete with horns. At **Rich Avon**, south-west of Donald, take a signposted turn-off to **Lake Batyo Catyo**, which is stocked with cod, redfin, golden perch and rainbow trout. Water skiing and camping are other options.

At **Edenhope** [B1] High School in Lake Street a cairn commemorates the first Australian cricket team to tour England in 1868. This all-Aboriginal squad trained next to **Lake Wallace** before their departure. While away they won 14 games, lost 14 and drew 19. Their coach was Tom Willis, who founded Australian Rules football.

Goroke [B2] is a jumping-off point

for **Little Desert National Park**, the second-largest national park in Victoria. Despite its name it is not a true desert and supports a range of fauna and plant species. Wildlife includes possums, the black-faced kangaroo, the silky desert mouse, the bearded dragon, the short-tailed snake and 220 bird species including the mallee fowl, which is indigenous to this semi-arid portion of Victoria.

Hamilton [D3] calls itself the Wool Capital of the World, thanks to the superfine merino wool grown in the district. On Ballarat Road on the shores of Lake Hamilton is the Sir Reginald Ansett Transport Museum. Sir Reg Ansett launched his airline in 1937, overcoming the law that forbade competition against Victorian railways by making the flight free—but charging for the fruit that was served.

Harrow [C2] is a small and picturesque hamlet of 90 people, which claims to be the oldest inland town in Victoria. It was the birthplace of Johnny Mullagh and other members of the Aboriginal cricket team, the first Australian team to tour internationally. Their achievements are the subject of the Harrow/Johnny Mullagh Interpretive Centre (for details call 03 5585 9900). The Hermitage

Hotel, built in 1846, is the site of the Harrow By Night experience, for which the locals dress up and enact the parts of 19th-century figures associated with the town. The night starts with a lively dinner at the hotel. Troopers then burst in and order the party out. They are transferred to a Cobb & Co. coach for a trip through the town, its features and its colonial history.

DON'T MISS: The National Bush Billy Cart Championships are held in Harrow each year on the Victorian Labour Day weekend in March.

Horsham's [B4] Wathe Flora and Fauna Reserve is a breeding ground for the Mallee fowl. Its presence is indicated by a mound up to 5 m in diameter and 1 m high in which the fowl lays eggs, adjusting the size of it daily to maintain an incubating temperature of 33°C. The reserve is signposted off the Hopetoun–Patchewollock Road. Several lakes in the Horsham area offer good fishing; the most famous is Lake Toolondo, home to trout, redfin perch and yabbies.

Minyip's [A4] streetscape of country town architecture and wrought iron lacework was the setting for the television series *The Flying Doctors* in 1984. Many of the early selectors in the area were German Lutherans fleeing persecution in their homeland. One such congregation developed at **Kirchheim**. They built St John's Lutheran Church in 1889. Because the congregation gradually spread north, the entire 50 tonne structure was transferred in 1935, by means of a steam traction engine, to its present site at the corner of Church and Carrol Streets, Minyip. The move took three days, the entire structure nearly toppling over when the ground collapsed because of rabbit holes. St John's retains its fine octagonal steeple with belfry, 19th-century pipe organ, stained-glass lancet windows and pews.

Moyston [C5] is the birthplace of Australian Rules Football. Although no specific date is known, in or around 1856 Thomas Wills and his cousin Henry Harrison amused the local Aboriginal kids by kicking around a stuffed possum skin. Rules for the new game were adopted in 1866.

Just east of **Murtoa**'s [A4] boundary is a most surprising and unusual sight—the Stick Shed. This remarkable structure, built in

VIC

1941, used 560 unmilled tree trunks. It was used for storing grain, as wheat could not be exported during World War II. It is 260 m long, 60 m wide and 20 m high. It is not open to the public but you can ask the permission of local landowners to inspect it (outside only). Opposite the Stick Shed are the massive and unique Wimmera Inland Freezing Works engines, built in 1911. Each engine weighs 20–30 tonnes and is driven by an enormous flywheel. They have been restored and are in working order (03 5359 6284).

Around 10 km west of **Natimuk** [B3] is **Mt Arapiles**, known as the 'Ayers Rock of the Wimmera'. The sheer rock face of this 356 m sandstone monolith is widely considered Australia's finest abseiling and rock climbing venue. West of town (about 4 km), on the Goroke Road, is Mott's dummy hut, a tiny weatherboard room sitting on logs. Built in 1872, it is a testament to the flaws in the Victorian Selection Act, which was meant to broaden land ownership in the colony by offering smaller allotments to the less prosperous. This process threatened to break up the vast properties of squatters who protected their holdings by taking up 'dummy'

selections. That was the case with this minimal 'residence', erected by David Mott to maintain his father's estate.

Nhill [A2]

can mean either white mist over the water, place of spirits, or red clay, depending on

RABBIT WITH BRANDIED PRUNES

Until the 1930s, the 'rabbitoh' was a common sight in cities and towns. While a menace on the land, the rabbit was long an important part of the Australian diet and a source of income. Rabbits also provided the basis for substantial commercial industries—during World War I rabbit skins were used for making military felt hats.

1 rabbit, jointed and soaked in salt water for 1 hour	1 tbsp plain flour
	1/2 cup dry white wine
1 tbsp olive oil	1/2 cup water
100 g bacon, diced	1 bouquet garni
3 onions, sliced	6 prunes, soaked in 1/2 cup brandy
salt and pepper to taste	

Remove rabbit from salt water and dry. Heat oil in pan and brown the bacon, then remove and reserve. Sauté the meat and onions in the pan until well browned. Season with salt and pepper. Sprinkle meat with flour and cook until lightly browned again. Add wine and water, bacon and bouquet garni. Bring liquid to the boil and simmer until tender—about 45 minutes. Add prunes and brandy to the pan. Bring to the boil and simmer a further 30 minutes. Discard bouquet garni before serving. Serves 4.

Staff at West Wimmera Shire Council, EDENHOPE

who's doing the translation from the original Aboriginal term used for a meeting place here. It boasts the largest single-bin grain silo in the Southern Hemisphere and was the state's first country town to have its streets electrically lit.

Serviceton [A1] developed when

the railway came through in 1886, serving as a border station where engines and crews could be changed, because the different colonies had adopted different rail gauges. The station had two stationmasters, two engine sheds and separate installations for each state. Today the enormous 70 m platform (possibly the state's longest) seems out of place. Alongside it are the old customs offices, a mortuary and a lock-up used to hold prisoners being transported interstate.

Stawell [B5] hosts

one of the world's oldest foot races. The Stawell Gift began in 1878 for the entertainment of the miners, and now offers prize money of $30,000 for the fastest runner over 120 m. It is run on Easter Monday each year and attracts 20,000 spectators. At the corner of Main Street and Joyce Lane is the town hall (1872). The main hall and clocktower are later additions.

On the hour, Westminster chimes accompany the appearance of two animated bronze diggers operating a gold-washing cradle. At 8.58 am, 11.58 am, 2.58 pm, 5.58 pm and 8.58 pm the clock plays 'With A Swag Upon His Shoulder'. The annual Orchid Show is held in September. South-east of Stawell, the town of **Great Western** became famous for making sparkling wine using the French method.

Near **Woohlpooer** [C3], **Rocklands Reservoir** is the largest dam of the Wimmera–Mallee water scheme, which itself is one of the largest water supply systems of its kind in the world. It has more than 16,000 km of open channels transporting water over much of the western section of the state. Rocklands and the other lakes of the scheme are popular fishing and water recreational areas and there's plenty of bush camping allowed around the shores of the reservoir.

Zumsteins [C4], in

the heart of the **Grampians National Park**, is a wildlife reserve set up by Walter Zumstein when he returned from World War I. A walking track leads to McKenzie Falls and there are plenty of wild kangaroos to be seen.

Diary of Events

Town	Event	Date	Contact
Ararat	Jailhouse Rock Festival	March	03 5352 4466
Casterton	Kelpie Festival	June	03 5581 2070
Harrow	National Bush Billy Cart Championships	March	03 5588 1242
Moyston	Boxing Day Sports	Boxing Day	03 5358 2314
Stawell	Stawell Gift	Easter Monday	03 5358 1326
	Annual Orchid Show	October	03 5358 1076

VIC

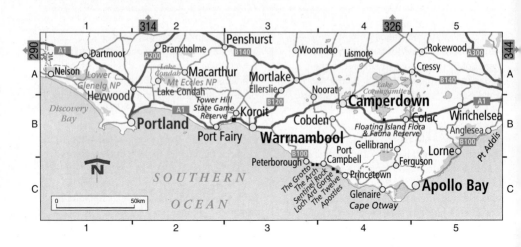

The **Great Ocean Road** is rightfully famous as a dramatic drive with spectacular vistas. From the South Australian border to Warrnambool there are equal attractions, including the gloriously historic towns of Port Fairy, once known as Belfast, and Koroit, which hosts the joyous Australian Danny Boy Championship.

get off the beaten track

drive the great ocean road and the south-west

East of **Anglesea** [B5] is a pleasant coastal walk that passes through forests and along the cliffs to **Point Addis**, a popular spot for hang-gliding, surfing and swimming. The walk takes about an hour. Turn off the Great Ocean Road 7 km north-east of Anglesea and drive 3 km to the carpark where a walking trail leads to the beach. The Great Ocean Road is a spectacular route along the southern coastline of Victoria from Anglesea to Warrnambool. It was initially a project to provide work for soldiers returning from World War I, and later for the unemployed during the Depression. It was hewn by pick and shovel from the cliff face and offers possibly the most

dramatic range of views in Australia, from surf beaches to rainforests to the massive rock formations of the Twelve Apostles (there are, in fact, only eight), which have been carved by the raging Great Southern Ocean.

Apollo Bay's [C5] Bass Strait Shell

Museum is at the eastern end of Noel Street, and is open most days. It features one of the most impressive collections of shells in Australia. The Apollo Bay Music Festival is held in March.

Camperdown's [B4] Botanic

Gardens are home to a statue of Scottish poet-icon Robbie Burns, which once stood at Tydenham Castle, near London. The Gardens also contain some rare Himalayan oaks. There is excellent fishing at **Bullen Merri Lake**, 3 km west of town. Bullen Merri is more than 80 m deep and is stocked with trout and Quinnat salmon.

The lighthouse at **Cape Otway** [C4] is the oldest on the Australian mainland. Built on the 90 m headland in 1848 after more than 600 people died in major shipwrecks through the previous decade, it stands 15.6 m high and can be seen from 22 km out at sea. It was decommissioned in 1994. The many shipwrecks along Victoria's south-west coast are due to the narrow entrance to Bass Strait between Cape Otway and Cape Wickham on King Island; it's only 50 nautical miles across and mariners refer to it as 'the eye of the needle'.

At **Colac**'s [B4] Floating Island Flora and Fauna Reserve, more than 70 bird species, koalas, possums and sugar gliders occupy an 80 ha reserve of swampland where six small peat 'islands' appear to float. There are two short walking trails leading to the islands. The islands can change position quite rapidly (some estimates suggest shifts of up to 20 m in a few minutes)—but don't hold your breath waiting to see them move. They move first from the north-east to the south-west, then 100 m in the opposite direction. Wind is thought to cause their motion, though another theory suggests that currents move them. The currents are caused by the difference in temperature between the groundwater and the lake water. Nearby **Lake Corangamite** has no outflow, and is therefore three times as salty as the sea. It is the largest lake in Victoria.

In **Ellerslie** [A3] there are more than 300 varieties of fuchsia on display at the Ellerslie House Fuchsia Display Garden, in Cook Street (behind the stone church).

VIC

BACKPACK CHINESE STUFFED CRAB

There's a lot of good eating to be had along the Victorian coastline, which is probably why it is known as the state's gourmet smorgasbord. At Portland in the west, the deep-sea boats bring in plenty of orange ruffy, blue warehou, blue grenadier, ling and blue eye. To do justice to the number of coastal eateries serving fine fish and seafood you'll simply have to extend your holiday. If you can't and you are home alone, try this delicious East–West offering.

1 King Island crab, cooked	125 g pork mince, cooked
2 cups fresh breadcrumbs	1 egg
125 g mushrooms, diced	30 g scallops, finely chopped
	salt to taste

Remove top of shell from crab and take out meat. In a bowl, mix all ingredients together, add salt and pack back into top shell of crab. Bake or grill until heated through—do not overcook. Serves 1.

The Portland Stuffing Book, Beppie Hedditch, Pat and Bren Jarrett, PORTLAND

Heywood's [A1] 'weird, wild and wonderful' Bower Bird's Nest Museum is a remarkable place. The owner, collector, historian, sculptor and painter at the museum is a delightful and energetic woman named Vanda. She has developed thousands of thematic collections of materials, which are set in 90 rooms of the

GAZETTEER

homestead and outbuildings. The museum includes a portable jail from the 19th century and the oldest church in Portland shire (1851), which now houses religious items relating to more than 100 denominations. The extensive gardens feature some magnificent trees planted by Vanda in her youth as well as her innumerable sculptural works based on legends and mythology. The museum is at a property known as 'The Trees', and is signposted off the Princes Highway, 3 km from town. The bridge across the Fitzroy River at Heywood is Victoria's oldest.

In High Street **Koroit** [B3] is the former Tower Hill Lake National School, built of sandstone in 1857. It is one of the oldest intact national schools in the state. It features two classrooms as projecting wings from a central section that served as the teacher's residence. Also in High Street are the Botanic Gardens. William Guilfoyle, curator of the Melbourne Botanic Gardens, developed a plan for the gardens in 1880. Five conifers remain from the original plantings. Six of the gardens' trees are registered with the National Trust. The Dragon's Blood Tree is included on the World Rare and Endangered List.

DON'T MISS: The Australian Danny Boy Championship, a singing competition where all the contestants sing 'Danny Boy'. It is held in Koroit each April as part of the town's Irish Festival. For details call 0428 658 155.

Lake Condah [A2] has sophisticated Aboriginal fish traps, some 8,000 years old, at the head of

GAZETTE

Darlots Creek. Aboriginal people lived here on a more or less permanent basis, because there was a reliable food supply, and there are old camp ovens near the edge of the lake. The site of the Lake Condah Aboriginal Mission, closed in 1918, is now managed by the local Aboriginal community; it is not open to visitors.

Lorne [B5] is host to the Pier-to-Pub,
the world's biggest blue-water swim, in early January, followed the next day by the Mountain to Surf.

To the west of **Macarthur** [A2] is **Mt Eccles National Park**, site of Mt Eccles, the youngest of the three volcanoes active here 19,000 years ago. The huge lava flows they produced ran all the way to the coast. Mt Eccles last erupted 7,000 years ago and you will find fascinating geological features in the park, including a scoria cone, lava canal, craters and stony rises and a scenic lake at the bottom of the main crater.

Noorat [B3] is the birthplace of
popular fiction writer Alan Marshall (1902–84), whose autobiography, *I Can Jump Puddles* (1955), told the story of his childhood battle with polio, which he contracted in 1908. A commemorative cairn has been erected in the park opposite the Beehive Store, where Marshall was born.

Penshurst [A3] hosts Easter
and Boxing Day horse races. The annual Rodeo and Campdraft, as well as a Country and Western Weekend, are held on the second weekend of February.

Past **Peterborough** [C3], heading 6 km east on the Great Ocean Road, is a turn-off to four viewing platforms over what used to be London Bridge— a natural archway and tunnel in an

offshore rock formation caused by waves eroding a portion of softer rock. Unfortunately the arch collapsed in 1990. There is no access to the beach.

East of **Port Campbell** [C4], a turn-off about 7 km along the coast road leads to **Loch Ard Gorge**, named after the iron clipper the *Loch Ard*, which left England for Melbourne in March 1878 with 37 crew and 17 passengers. On 1 June the ship was caught in a heavy mist near Port Campbell. The wind and waves drove it toward Muttonbird Island, where it hit the cliffs with such force that the wooden top deck was ripped from the hull and the mast collapsed. A huge wave swept over the vessel, and only two survived—Eva Carmichael and a ship's apprentice, Tom Pearce, both aged 19. Pearce swam to shore, then returned to save Eva, who was clinging to part of the ship's spar. He managed to get her to a cave on the beach where, because she was wearing only a nightdress, he covered her in grass then searched for other survivors. As

morning came, Tom climbed out of the gorge and followed horse tracks until he met two Glenample Station workers. The station is still standing and is open to the public. The wreck and the dramatic rescue were widely reported, and Tom Pearce became 'the hero of Loch Ard'. He was awarded a gold medal from the Humane Society in Melbourne, a gold watch and £1,000 from the Victorian government, and a set of nautical instruments from the people of Sydney. The people of Warrnambool gave him new clothes. Having seen Eva Carmichael in her nightdress, he felt it only right and decent to propose marriage to her. She declined and went back to Ireland.

VIC

In **Port Fairy** [B2], at the end of East

Beach, is Mills Reef, which is, according to local legend, used by southern right whales to scratch off their barnacles. Port Fairy, once

known as Belfast, also has a beach called Pea Soup, where Australia's only mainland colony of shearwaters live. They also live on Griffith Island.

CHOCOLATE BISCUIT CAKE

Arnott's is an Australian icon. The brand is part of our history and culture. Founded in 1865 by William Arnott, who opened a small bakery on Hunter Street in Newcastle, the company today has seven factories in Australia, Indonesia and the South Pacific. They tell us that every second of every day, 28 packs of Arnotts are sold in Australia alone. For this recipe, you simply need one— a packet of Arnott's Coffee biscuits.

250 g icing sugar mixture
2 dsp cocoa
1 egg
1 tsp vanilla
150 g butter, melted
1 packet Arnott's Coffee biscuits

Line a 16 cm square tin with baking paper. In a bowl, place icing sugar mixture, cocoa, egg and vanilla. Pour melted butter over. Mix thoroughly until smooth and beginning to thicken. Arrange alternate layers of chocolate mixture and biscuits in prepared tin, commencing and finishing with the chocolate mixture. Stand in a cool place till set. Remove from tin and slice.

Karen Small, ANGLESEA

Portland [B2] was Victoria's first

permanent European settlement, generally regarded as being established by the Henty family. Thus the state's 150th anniversary celebrations began there in November 1984. At 4 Percy Street is the Portland Inn (1840), said to be the oldest building in Victoria still on its original site—the Geelong Customs House (still in operation) is another contender. In Cliff Street is the courthouse, one of a group of very early bluestone public buildings on the cliff above the port. Built in 1845, it is still in operation and is apparently the state's oldest courthouse. The judge used to come by sea from Melbourne. The Gordon Hotel, at 63 Bentinck Street, was built in 1890 to replace an earlier building dating from 1842, when the publican's licence was first issued. It is a contender for the oldest continuous licence held in Victoria. Portland is the only deepwater port between Melbourne and Adelaide. Walk south-east along the coast from the Blowholes to the seal-viewing platform; the route takes in the highest coastal cliffs in Victoria (130 m) and the Petrified Forest, thought to have developed when a moonah forest was smothered by a large sand dune, creating unusual sandstone formations around the decaying tree trunks. West of Portland, among the tall steep dunes of Discovery Bay, is

the Portland Dune Buggy Club. This venerable establishment has been running for more than 25 years; club members race their buggies or test out their 4WD vehicles in

this wild windswept patch of dunes. The rugged coastline around Portland and its deep offshore waters are a mecca for recreational anglers pursuing snapper, flathead, snook, sweep and trevally (known locally as 'haddock'). During late April, May and June schools of southern bluefin tuna and some large sharks—especially makos—also visit these fishing grounds. The Great South Walk starts and ends at Portland, winding 250 km through farmland and the Lower Glenelg National Park and along the coastline via Discovery Bay.

Warrnambool [B3] is home to the

Fletcher Jones Gardens and a beach, Logans, where southern right whales come to give birth during the winter months. There is a whale-viewing platform at Logans Beach, appropriate enough when you consider that the town was founded as a whaling station. Flagstaff Hill Maritime Village recreates Warrnambool's early days. The small theatre sometimes shows

the 1929 classic, *Around Cape Horn*, still well worth viewing. **Tower Hill State Game Reserve**, 15 km west of Warrnambool, is in the crater of an extinct volcano. A detailed 1855 painting of Tower Hill by Viennese artist Eugene Von Guérard depicted a variety of flora and fauna that had virtually disappeared by the end of the 1860s because of the clearing practices of European settlers. Remarkably Von Guérard's painting (now in the Warrnambool Regional Art Gallery) was used as the basis of a revegetation program entailing 300,000 plantings since 1961. This process encouraged the return of wildlife.

The town of # Winchelsea [B5] was

the childhood home of international opera star Marjorie Lawrence, who was born on a farm in Deans Marsh, 24 km south-west of the town. Lawrence made a spectacular debut in Monte Carlo in 1932. Only 10 years later, a victim of polio, she made her first wheelchair appearances on stage. She was the inspiration for the Susan Hayward film *Interrupted Melody*. At Barwon Park mansion, home of the Austin family, 24 wild European rabbits were

let loose for sport in 1859. Seven years later 14,253 rabbits were shot on the property, and the venture was considered a roaring success.

Diary of Events

Town	Event	Date	Contact
Apollo Bay	Music Festival	March	03 5237 6761
Koroit	Irish Festival	April	0428 658 155
Lorne	Pier-to-Pub Race	January	03 5289 1152
	Mountain to Surf	January	03 5237 6761
Port Fairy	3YB Moyneyana Festival	January	03 5568 2682
	Folk Festival	March	03 5225 1232
Warrnambool	May Racing Carnival	May	03 5562 2211
	Melbourne to Warrnambool Classic	September	03 5562 5115

VIC

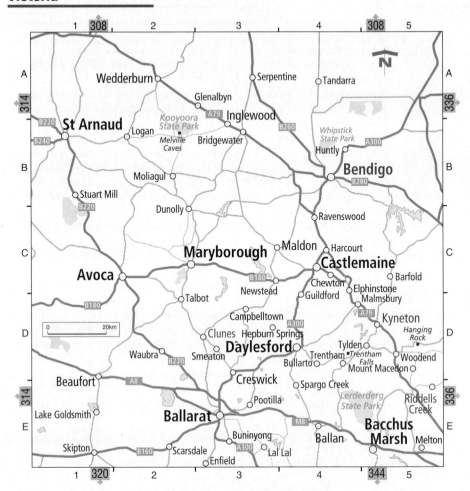

get off the beaten track

strike

it rich

in the goldfields

and macedon ranges

Avoca [C2] claims to have the oldest chemist shop in Victoria. Lalor's Pharmacy in High Street opened in 1854. The Avoca picnic races in March are a celebration of country hospitality and the place to sample the local speciality of 'pink lamb and purple shiraz'. Call 03 5465 3767 for details.

If approaching **Bacchus Marsh** [E5] from the east, you'll drive down the Avenue of Honour, considered one of the most significant remaining elm avenues in the world. Consisting of 281 North American elms, it was created to honour local citizens who fought and died in World War I. The Holy Trinity Church of England, built of local sandstone in 1877, was the town's second Anglican church. Andrew Scott, who later became the notorious bushranger Captain Moonlight, conducted services as a lay preacher in the original church in the early 1870s. Town founder Captain Bacchus, who died in 1849, is buried in the graveyard—his tomb has been restored. North of Bacchus Marsh is the **Lerderderg State Park**. A number of good trails meander through the forest, and a couple of harder 4WD tracks cross the Lerderderg River upstream from the gorge.

In front of **Ballarat**'s [E3] Information Centre is the Gold Monument, commemorating the first gold strike in the area, on 21 August 1851 at Poverty Point. A replica of the Welcome Nugget crowns the monument. Found in 1858 by the Red Hill Mining Co, the Welcome Nugget is the second-largest solid gold nugget in the world (the Welcome Stranger Nugget [see Moliagul] is the largest). A cairn on the corner of Mair and Humffray Streets marks the exact spot of the find. For more alluvial examples visit the Gold Museum in Bradshaw Street. This is also the regional museum of Ballarat and houses the noted Simon Collection of

gold nuggets and the Fitzgerald Postcard Collection. The Ballarat Fine Art Gallery at 40 Lydiard Street was established in 1884 and is Australia's largest and oldest purpose-built provincial gallery. It boasts a major collection covering the history of Australian art, with particularly strong collections of material from the Heidelberg School and the Lindsay family. In 1895 the gallery acquired the original Eureka Flag that flew over the stockade until it was attacked by

government forces in 1854. Prime Ministers Avenue in the Botanical Gardens features a handcrafted bronze bust of every Prime Minister of Australia since Federation. Grapes were first grown for wine around Ballarat in the 1850s, thanks to the Europeans who came here in search of gold. But when the gold ran out wine making also stopped. It wasn't until the 1970s and 1980s that vineyards such as Yellowglen and Mount Beckworth got the wine flowing again. Yellowglen's Ian Home originally planted red grape varieties, but the cool climate was far better suited to white wine varieties, and it was produced for the first time at Yellowglen in 1982. After hooking up with Champagne-born Dominique Landragin, the winery produced its classic yellow label Brut in 1984. More than 3,000 visitors come to Ballarat over the Queen's Birthday long weekend for the National Basketball Championships and the Winter Classic Car Rally, but the highlight of the year is Ballarat's Begonia Festival in early March. For more information call 03 5320 7444.

VIC

Victoria

Bendigo

Bendigo's [B4] magnificent Sacred Heart Cathedral is the state's largest cathedral outside Melbourne. The Joss House, at Emu Point, is Australia's earliest traditional Chinese temple. It was constructed during the 1860s by Chinese gold diggers, who lived in large numbers on the goldfields around Bendigo. Golden Dragon Museum is at 5–9 Bridge Street and houses two famous ceremonial dragons: the Loong dragon and the Sun Loong dragon. The Loong dragon is thought to be the world's oldest imperial dragon (about 110 years old).

It was part of the first Federation celebrations in 1901, and also made an appearance at the 2001 festivities. The Sun Loong dragon is the world's longest imperial dragon. At more than 100 m long it requires at least 52 men to carry it in procession, with another 52 taking over part way through. In 1873, wines from Bendigo were entered in the Vienna Wine Exhibition. The wines were so good that the judges insisted they were actually French with false labels and they withdrew in protest. Eventually a certificate of authenticity was given to the winemakers, the Acclimatisation Society of Victoria, which still has the original. For decades this framed canvas certificate adorned the walls of the Zoological Society's offices at Royal Park. Hartland's Eucalyptus Oil Factory was established in 1890 and is still operating, using the original methods. Factory tours by appointment (03 5448 8227). Head north along the Midland Highway and turn left at Huntly. The factory is next to **Whipstick State Park**. The Whipstick is mallee-covered country criss-crossed by

---

BUNINYONG BEETROOT CAKE

Here's something different for those who only think that beetroot is the dark-red slippery vegetable that comes from a can and slides out of a hamburger. This recipe is made with freshly cooked beetroot. And nothing needs to go to waste as you can use the tops as 'spinach', and the small leaves can be refreshed in cold water and used in salad. Cook the beetroot whole in a steamer or bake in a slow oven. Cool, peel, slice and bake the cake.

2 cups caster sugar	1 tsp salt
4 eggs	1¹/₂ cups cocoa
2 tsp vanilla essence	2 cups cooked, grated, drained beetroot
1¹/₂ cups light oil	icing sugar, for dusting
2¹/₄ cups plain flour	whipped cream, for serving
¹/₂ cup almond meal	
2 tsp bicarbonate of soda	

Preheat oven to 180°C and line a 24 cm springform pan with baking paper. In a bowl, beat sugar, eggs and vanilla thoroughly until light and creamy. Beat in oil. Add dry ingredients and fold through. Finally, add beetroot and mix well. Pour into prepared tin and bake for about 45 minutes, or until cooked. Dust with icing sugar and serve with whipped cream.

Jean Vagg, BUNINYONG

4WD tracks leading to small camping spots and gold fossicking areas. Its main claim to fame, however, is songbirds—the area is reputed to have Australia's greatest concentration of songbirds, such as grey-crowned babblers and swift parrots.

At **Bridgewater** [B3] you can head off into goldrush territory on your own horse-drawn wagon. Colonial Way (call 03 5437 3054) operate 'self-drive' holidays in a traditional covered wagon drawn by a Clydesdale. Someone rides with you until you're confident to take the reins, then checks on your camp daily and helps map out your travel plans.

Buninyong [E3] is the site of the first inland town in Victoria. Here in 1842 the first licence for an inland hotel was issued to the newly established Crown Hotel. It is one more contender for the oldest continually licensed premises in the state, although the present building dates from 1885—a fire destroyed the original.

Castlemaine [C4] proved to be one of the world's richest alluvial goldfields. In just six months in 1852 the Gold Escort shipped out 16,600 kg. A confectionery known as Castlemaine Rock was first produced by TS Barnes and sold in a tent on these goldfields in 1853. It is still being manufactured today by his descendants. The Theatre Royal was built in 1855, then rebuilt in 1857 after a fire—it is one of Victoria's oldest entertainment venues in continuous operation. The present façade dates from the 1930s. The town's

Botanical Gardens were established in 1856 on the site of some worked-out alluvial diggings on Barkers Creek. A number of the original trees are on the National Trust register, including a large English oak planted by the Duke of Edinburgh in 1867. It is one of the oldest cultivated trees in the state. The Indian bean tree, also in the gardens, is the largest. In Goldsmiths Crescent is a gnarled old red gum once used by the local constabulary—they passed a chain around its trunk and handcuffed offenders to it when the small lock-up was full. Opposite, set back from the street at Number 7, is a simple, single-storey red-brick house with a timber verandah, which was once a courthouse (1852). The original shingles still lie beneath the corrugated iron roof. It is thought to be the oldest surviving building from a Victorian goldfield.

DON'T MISS: Every April Castlemaine hosts the Clydesdale Foal, Filly and Mare Feature Show and All Breeds Goat Show. A tongue-in-cheek example of affirmative action for animals, it is the only 'girls' event of its type in Australia. Show organisers have restricted male entrants because they tend to take the lion's share of prizes in other shows.

Chewton [C4] has the Dingo Farm, a sanctuary for pure-bred dingoes, where you can observe Australia's native dogs (although they arrived only about 5,000 years ago) running wild in 8 ha of their natural habitat.

Clunes' [D3] claim to fame is as the site of Victoria's first gold strike. The Clunes Bottle Museum, at 70 Bailey Street, contains the largest public bottle collection in the Southern Hemisphere, with more than 6,000 rare and

GAZETTEER

VIC

interesting bottles dating back to the early days of the goldrushes. The historic museum building dates from 1882 and was originally the local schoolhouse. It functioned as a knitting mill from 1922 until the mid-1980s when it was converted to the museum.

Creswick [D3]

Historical Museum (open Sundays and public holidays), in the Town Hall on Albert Street, boasts a permanent exhibition relating to artist and

writer Norman Lindsay, who was born in the town in 1879. His novel *Redheap* (1930) evokes the Creswick of the late 19th century. It outraged some Creswick residents, who successfully petitioned the government to have it banned—the ban lasted until 1958. One of the few remaining gold batteries in the state is in Creswick. It was built to crush basalt ore in 1918 and now operates during the Spring Fiesta in October and at other times by appointment (03 5345 2892). Just outside of Creswick is the Tangled Maze, a garden maze grown from hundreds of different climbing plants. To focus visitors' attention on the various goodies within the maze, a treasure hunt is supplied a the gate. There is also a specialist nursery where many varieties of climbers can be bought.

Daylesford [D4] and Hepburn Springs

form central Victoria's spa country. It boasts around 65 mineral springs accounting for more than 80 per cent of Australia's known mineral springs. The water flows deep underground through volcanic basins, where iron, magnesium and sulphur

have been leached from the 450-million-year-old rock. Daylesford used to be called Wombat. The original Swiss–Italian settlers, who stayed after the 1850s goldrush because the area reminded them of home, left a legacy of vineyards, olive groves and stone farmhouses still evident in the surrounding area, including Lavandula lavender farm. The old macaroni factory at Hepburn Springs, a large handmade brick structure on Main Road, reflects the architectural traditions of northern Italy. It was erected in 1859 by the Lucini family.

Elphinstone [C4]

is home to the Australian Heritage Farm, a 'rare breeds' poultry farm. There are 20 different breeds, including several that arrived in New South Wales with the First Fleet. It is open during local garden festivals and state open garden days. The farm is signposted on the Calder Highway.

Harcourt's [C4]

Skydancers Butterfly Sanctuary, Native Gardens and Nursery claims to be Australia's only sanctuary devoted to temperate climate butterflies. In the 19th century Harcourt gained a reputation for its quality granite—used for Parliament House in Canberra, the John Flynn Memorial at Alice Springs, the pedestal of the Burke and Wills statue in Melbourne and local memorials.

On **Inglewood**'s [B3] main road is St Mary's, a Gothic Revival stone church dating from 1870–71, but the main reason for coming through town is to turn off west to Melville Caves. They're not really caves in the conventional sense of the word, rather a collection of huge boulders arranged to form a series of cave-like cavities atop a granite tor in **Kooyoora State Park**. The bushranger 'Captain Melville' (Frank McCallum) is thought to have used the caves as a camp and a vantage point—their height provides excellent views of the flat plains across which gold-bearing coaches travelled.

Kyneton [D5] was home to

Caroline Chisholm in the late 1850s. She was the catalyst for a scheme to **GAZETTEER** construct overnight shelters for travellers on the Mt Alexander Road (now the Calder Highway), the route to the central goldfields. One shelter still stands on the highway 1 km from Carlsruhe (if approaching from Melbourne). Kyneton Historical Museum, by the corner of Piper and Powlett Streets, is housed within the bluestone Bank of NSW building (1856)— the oldest surviving bank building in the state. By the corner of Piper and Ebden Streets is the four-storey Willis brothers' bluestone-and-timber flour mill (1862). It is apparently the only working 19th-century steam-operated mill in Australia.

DON'T MISS: The remains of the state's only surviving stone windmill (built in 1855) are at **Green Hill**, beside the Metcalfe Road.

The **Lal Lal** [E3] Blast Furnace is an industrial site listed by the National Trust. It is the only extant 19th-century blast furnace in the Southern Hemisphere and one of the best representatives of its type in the world.

SMOKED TROUT RILLETTE

Regional produce and wines are served throughout the Daylesford area and are available through farmgate and cellar door sales. Chestnuts, wild mushrooms, berries, honey, fresh or smoked trout (from Tuki Springs) and yabbies are just an example. At Lake House this dish is served with a plate of grilled local yabbies and a garlic and leek custard.

300 g smoked trout, filleted and boned	3 sprigs thyme
	2 tbsp soft butter
	salt and pepper
1 sheet gelatine	to taste
100 ml fish stock	$^1/_2$ clove garlic,
1 bay leaf	finely chopped
4 peppercorns	

Place sheet of gelatine in a small bowl of cold water, to soften. Remove gelatine and wring dry, discarding water. Heat fish stock with bay leaf, peppercorns and thyme. Add gelatine to hot fish stock and stir until dissolved. Allow stock to cool a little, then remove and discard bay leaf and thyme. In a bowl, flake smoked trout, shredding into very small pieces with 2 forks. Gradually add gelatine stock and continue to shred the trout until stock is absorbed and the trout is very finely textured. Allow to cool. Once trout is cool, add the soft butter and combine well (if trout is too warm, the butter will melt and the rillette will not set). Season with salt and pepper. Refrigerate in a covered container. Serve simply with warm toast. Serves 6.

Lake House Restaurant, DAYLESFORD

VIC

Victoria

The National Trust describes **Maldon** [C4] as Australia's best-preserved town of the goldrush era. It is also the starting point for a scenic steam train ride through forests to Muckleford and return (03 5475 2598).

At **Malmsbury**'s [D4] Botanic Gardens there are good views from the south-west corner of the impressive old railway viaduct, and a walking track right

to it. The viaduct was built of local bluestone by around 4,000 men in 1859, to carry the Bendigo railway line over the Coliban River. It is one of the largest 19th-century engineering structures in the state, and a fine illustration of the massive scale of colonial railway projects. The bridge section consists of five arched spans, each 18.5 m; the structure is 153.8 m from end to end.

In the 1890s **Maryborough** [C2] was described by American writer Mark Twain as 'a railway station with a town attached'. Anyone who has seen the 25-room station will appreciate that this was not a derogatory remark about the town but a comment on the size and magnificence of the station, which is far and away Maryborough's finest building.

Melton [E5] Shire has been a major centre of thoroughbred horse breeding since the 1850s, producing a number of race winners. Stud properties and equestrian centres are open to members of the public by appointment. For details call Melton Visitor Centre on 03 9746 7290. The Mt Atkinson Olive and Nut Grove is just out of Melton at 261 Greigs Road. The grove is set on 400 ha and produces olives, oils and almonds. A café is open on weekends. Witness the art of beekeeping at the Honey Shack at Raglan Cottage on High Street.

In **Moliagul** [B2], two Cornish miners found the Welcome Stranger Nugget in 1869 under the roots of a tree. The Goldfields Historical and Arts Museum (1880) in Dunolly has a replica of the nugget. It is still the world's largest nugget of pure gold, weighing in at just over 71 kg. Also at the museum is the Welcome Stranger Anvil, upon which the nugget was cut, and the fossilised jaw of a wombat that lived 4 million years ago.

Mount Macedon's [D5] 21 m Memorial Cross is a local landmark. It has a tiled exterior, is emblazoned with a bronze sword, and is set picturesquely amid trees and gardens. The original crucifix, gardens and access road were established by local resident William Cameron as a tribute to those Australians (including his son) who died in World War I.

In **Riddells Creek** [E5], a small township, is Dromkeen Homestead, a rather special place devoted to children's literature and book illustration. There is a bookshop, a reference library, an extensive collection of original works by notable artists such as Norman Lindsay, Dorothy Wall, Elizabeth Durack and Peg Maltby. The homestead's historical book collection includes first editions of May Gibbs' *Snugglepot and Cuddlepie* (1918), Norman Lindsay's *The Magic Pudding* (1918) and Dorothy Wall's *Blinky Bill* (1939). Call 03 5428 6799 for further information.

Near **Serpentine** [A3] is the historic woolshed at East Loddon station. Thought to be the largest woolshed built in Australia, this 28-stand structure was commissioned by noted inventor and pastoralist John Ettershank and built in 1871. It is in Longs Road and is currently private property. Australia's first official air race was held at Serpentine on 27 August 1920.

St Arnaud's [B1] Historical Society Museum is in the town's first fire station (1883). It is the oldest original fire station in the state and retains the adjoining residence of the stopcock operator (who controlled the supply of water) and the original hand-pulled ladder cart. The old hand-pumped stopcock is outside.

Just south of **Skipton** [E1] are the **Mt Widderin Caves**, on Mt Widderin Station, just off Lismore Road, the largest volcanic caves in Victoria. The main chamber is 55 m long, 20 m wide and 5 m high. The 200 m walk leads to a subterranean lake. The caves were formed when the outer crust of a lava stream solidified, creating a tunnel through which lava flowed.

LAVANDULA'S LAVENDER SCONES

Lavandula lavender farm is a legacy of the original Swiss–Italian settlers of Daylesford and Hepburn Springs, who also developed vineyards and olive groves in the area. Today we mostly think of lavender as something to put in potpourri. Try it in these scones and you'll be back for seconds.

4 cups self-raising flour
$1/2$ cup icing sugar
1 tbsp lavender flower heads, finely chopped
1 cup cream
$1^1/4$ cups milk
beaten egg, for glazing

Preheat oven to 225°C. Grease a scone tray or line with baking paper. Mix dry ingredients together in a large bowl, add cream and enough milk to mix to a firm dough. A little extra milk may be needed. Knead dough lightly on a floured surface and cut into scones. Place on scone tray, brush with a little beaten egg and bake for 20 minutes or until golden. Makes 12 large scones.

Carol White, Lavandula,
HEPBURN SPRINGS

VIC

They are open most days, but call 03 5340 2018 to check.

The main attraction at **Smeaton** [D3] is a 19th-century industrial complex with a well preserved four-storey bluestone flour mill, possibly the largest ever built in Victoria. The remarkable waterwheel measures 8.5 m in diameter and weighs 5.5 tonnes. It is probably the most intact water-powered mill in Australia. The complex was

established in the early 1860s by the Anderson family, who made their fortune in the Victorian goldrush.

Near **Talbot** [D2] are some Aboriginal drinking wells and a birthing tree—a large hollowed-out gum tree where Aboriginal women gave birth. Ask for directions at the post office on the corner of Camp and Heale Streets.

Woodend [D5] is home to the Insectarium of Victoria, on the Calder Highway. The Insectarium features what is alleged to be the world's largest captive crayfish, along with other Australian

creepy-crawlies. In the 1930s and 1940s the students of the rather ornate Braemar College (originally Clyde Girls' Grammar) attended picnics at nearby **Hanging Rock**,

BOY'S CAKE

This recipe was enjoyed by a Victorian family of eight children at the turn of the 20th century. It was 'lost' for half a century before one member of the family living in the United States reintroduced it on a visit home. Great for hungry kids.

2 cups self-raising flour	1 egg, beaten
1/4 cup butter	3/4 tsp vanilla essence
1/4 cup sugar	milk
1/2 cups mixed fruit	

Preheat oven to 190°c and lightly flour a baking tray. Place flour in a large bowl and rub through the butter. Add the sugar and mixed fruit. Mix in the egg (reserving a little to brush top of cake), vanilla and enough milk to form a scone dough. Turn out onto a floured board, knead lightly and form into a ball. Place on baking tray and bake for approximately 40 minutes or until golden brown and cooked through. Cool on a wire rack and serve warm, cut into thick slices with lashings of butter.

Betty Osborne, MARYBOROUGH

the base of Hanging Rock, where more than 100 food and wine producers set up stalls. On New Year's Day the running of the Hanging Rock Gold Cup is held at Woodend racecourse (call 132 842 for details of both events). Hanging Rock is actually a small extinct volcano rising 105 m above the surrounding plain. It was formed by lava emerging from a vent in the earth about six million years ago.

north-east of Woodend, thought to have inspired Joan Lindsay's novel *Picnic at Hanging Rock*. The college is about 7 km east of Woodend on Mount Macedon Road. The novel is commemorated every February with the Harvest Picnic held at

Nearby, **Trentham Falls** is Victoria's longest single drop waterfall. The falls are best viewed from the Northern Lookout (there is a short track from the falls), where you can witness the Coliban River plunging 32 m over ancient basalt columns.

Diary of Events

Town	Event	Date	Contact
Avoca	Pyrenees Pink Lamb–Purple Shiraz Picnic Race Meeting	March	03 5465 3231
	Taltarni Avoca Cup	October	03 5465 3231
	Blue Pyrenees Petanque Tournament	November	03 5465 3202
Ballarat	Begonia Festival	March	03 5320 7444
Bendigo	Heritage Uncorked	October, 2nd weekend	03 5447 7995
Castlemaine	Clydesdale Foal, Filly and Mare Feature Show and All Breeds Goat Show	April	03 5470 6200
	Fringe Festival	Mar/Apr	03 5476 2662
	Mt Alexander Autumn Billy Cart Bash	May	03 5472 2849
Harcourt	Applefest	March, Labour Day weekend	03 5474 2351
Maldon	State Heavy Horse Shoeing Competition	May, last weekend	03 5475 2216
Talbot	Yabby Festival	April	03 5464 7212
Woodend	Hanging Rock Gold Cup	New Year's Day	132 842
	Harvest Picnic, Hanging Rock	February	03 9286 9571

VIC

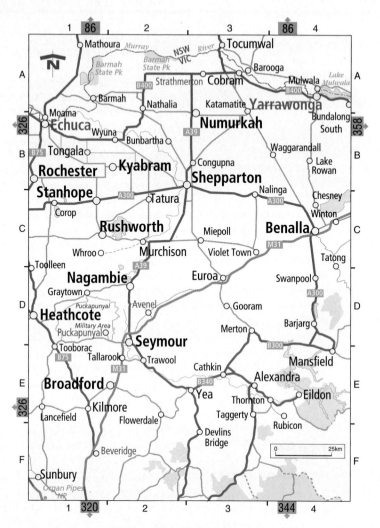

get off the beaten track

dive into goulburn and murray waters

It is here that the mighty river is at its most impressive. It's also the lifeblood of towns such as Echuca and to the west, Swan Hill and Mildura [see Mildura and Murray Outback region], which once made their money from servicing the paddle steamers that plied the river transporting wool and other produce. Today the paddle steamers bring visitors who have come to drink in the local history and take advantage of the great recreational opportunities the Murray offers.

Avenel [D2] was bushranger
Ned Kelly's childhood home from the age of 8 to 12, when his father died. Kelly senior is buried in the town cemetery. Ned was responsible for recording his father's death at the local courthouse. While living at Avenel, Kelly saved a boy from drowning in the local creek and received a sash as a reward.

Barmah [A1] State Forest (29,500 ha)
is part of the floodplains of the Murray River. In conjunction with Moira State Park (across the border) it forms the largest red gum forest in the world, and has World Heritage listing. Some of the trees rise to 40 m and are 300 years old. Canoe trees and middens bear testimony to thousands of years of Aboriginal occupation. Its second-most important product, after timber, used to be leeches, which were collected and exported to England for use by doctors. Barmah has the only pub in Victoria north of the Murray River.

At **Benalla** [C4], the Costume and Pioneer Museum at 14 Mair Street features The Ned Kelly Story, an exhibition in a portable cell where Ned was once imprisoned. The museum also displays memorabilia relating to Benalla's favourite son, the remarkable war hero Sir Edward 'Weary' Dunlop. Kelly gang member Joe Byrne is buried in the local cemetery. In Tanwell Street (250 m north of the railway line, on the left) is a rare ombu tree, listed by the National Trust and one of only six in Victoria. The Golden Vale Nursery claims to have the world's largest collection of Australian roses.

Beveridge [F1] was the
birthplace of legendary bushranger Ned Kelly, whose impoverished father, John, had settled in the town. The Kelly family home still stands. The town's most impressive building is the

VIC

BREAD AND BUTTER PUDDING

The Goulbourn Valley's first orchards were planted on the banks of the mighty Murray near Shepparton in 1884. Rich soils together with an ideal climate make the area Australia's largest deciduous fruit-growing region, often referred to as Australia's 'fruit bowl', and home of SPC, originally the Shepparton Preserving Company, which was founded in 1918. This pudding is tasty on its own and absolutely delicious served with poached fruit and a dollop of cream.

2 tbsp sultanas	3 eggs, beaten
2 tbsp Cointreau	2 tbsp sugar
plain white bread,	1 cup milk
sliced and crusts	1/2 cup cream
removed (enough	1 tsp vanilla
to fill dish)	essence
soft butter	1 tbsp almond
apricot jam	flakes

Preheat oven to 180°C and grease an ovenproof dish (approx. 18 cm square or similar). Soak sultanas in Cointreau for 10 minutes. Butter the bread and make up into sandwiches with the jam. Cut into triangles and arrange overlapping in prepared dish, sprinkling sultanas between sandwich layers. In a bowl, combine eggs and sugar, then add milk, cream and vanilla. Pour this over bread triangles and allow to soak for 10 minutes. Sprinkle with the almond flakes and bake for 20–30 minutes, or until pudding has risen, custard has set and is golden on top. Serves 6.

Alessandra Whitwell, SHEPPARTON

former Roman Catholic Church where the Kellys worshipped.

Cobram [A3] hosts the Peaches and Cream music festival every second January (in odd-numbered years), so-called because this is peaches and cream country, known for its fruit and dairy produce. Call for details on 03 5872 2132. Cobram's sister town of **Barooga**, across the Murray River in New South Wales, makes boomerangs guaranteed to return. The Murray River, from Yarrawonga Weir downstream past Cobram and on to Echuca and beyond, is popular for recreational anglers after Murray cod, golden perch, silver perch and redfin, not to mention the delicious Murray crayfish—the world's second-largest freshwater lobster. This stretch of the Murray River is also home to the rare and endangered trout cod, a smaller

cousin of the Murray cod. These fish are protected by seasonal fishing closures so check with local authorities before fishing.

Echuca and **Moama** [B1] are twin towns on opposite sides of the River Murray. Home to the Yorta-Yorta Aborigines, the area was first settled by Europeans when an ex-

convict named James Maiden established a punt service and inn on the northern banks of the river around 1845. It was the first cattle crossing on the Murray River and quickly became a major access route. Along Echuca's Murray Esplanade, in the old Bond Store (1858), is Sharp's Magic Movie House and Penny Arcade, recreating the kind of entertainment venue that drew crowds at the end of the 19th century. Here you can play more than 60 antique penny arcade machines and watch archival footage, newsreels, early Australian films and old silent comedies. Nearby is the former Star Hotel (1867), which features an old underground bar and escape tunnel for illicit drinkers.

DON'T MISS:
On Warren Street, Echuca, is the National Holden Motor Museum, containing more than 40 immaculately restored Holdens and rare prototypes as well as historic film footage.

The main attraction of **Eildon** [E4] is the vast lake of the same name, which holds five times the water of Sydney Harbour (or 5 Sydharbs). This is the place to come for waterskiing, jetskiing, sailboarding, canoeing, sailing and fishing. Trout can be fished all year round and there are plentiful supplies of redfin, roach, carp and Murray cod. House boating is an option.

For aerial sports enthusiasts **Euroa** [D3] might be worth a stop. Book a balloon excursion at Balloon Flights Victoria, 10 km south-west of the town. Parachuting is on offer at Skydive Euroa on Drysdale Road. Ask directions in the town if you want to see the memorial to Eliza Forlonge, who introduced the first fine-wool Saxon merino sheep into Victoria. They were handpicked in Saxony, shipped to Australia, and overlanded to Seven Creeks station, near Euroa, in 1851.

Kilmore
[E1] lays claim to being Victoria's oldest inland town (although the claim is disputed by Harrow in western Victoria). Squatters arrived here around 1837, attracted by the rich volcanic soil. However, the town really got underway in 1841, when William Rutledge surveyed 21 sq km and established a community of mostly Irish tenant farmers. In 1854 it became the first Roman Catholic parish in Victoria outside Melbourne—it retains a strong Catholic community to this day. The Kilmore Celtic Festival is held in July. Kilmore is home to some major horseracing events such as the Kilmore Cup in February and the Kilmore Pacing Cup and Harness Racing Carnival in October. Call the tourist information centre for more details on 03 5781 1319.

Lake Mulwala
[A4] is crossed by an unusual bridge at Yarrawonga. The dip in the bridge is said to have been caused when the New South Wales and Victorian work teams met in the middle and neither group could make the bridge meet. Lake Mulwala is famous in angling circles for its abundant population of Murray cod. While most of the cod caught here today are modest specimens weighing 2 to 6 kg, the odd giant (40 kg or more) is still encountered every season. Happily, more and more anglers are now choosing to unhook and release these important breeders.

Mansfield
's [E4] imposing Highton Manor, in Highton Lane, was the town's first two-storey brick home, built in 1896 and

VIC

JUICY MORSELS OF EMU

Often harvested in the wild, but increasingly cultivated in horticultural enterprises, bush foods are bringing new spice to old recipes as they possess unique flavours that are unavailable in other products. Some of the most sought after include bush tomatoes, Davidson's plum, lemon myrtle, riberries, quandong, warrigal greens, wattleseed and the mountain pepper used in this recipe.

750 g emu steak, diced	salt to taste
500 ml red wine	15 g ground mountain native pepper leaf
4 large white onions, diced	homemade damper, for serving
2 tbsp oil	
2 bay leaves	tomato chutney, for serving
1/4 tsp freshly ground black pepper	

Marinate emu in red wine for 4 days (this tenderises the meat). Fry the onions in 1 tbsp oil in a large pan, browning them a little. Keep warm. Drain the meat, reserving the liquid. In a large, very hot frying pan, seal and brown meat in remaining oil. Transfer meat to a large saucepan, adding onions, salt, bay leaves, black pepper and wine. Heat rapidly, then simmer gently over a low flame, covered, for about 2 hours. The liquid will reduce, and be thickened by the onion. Add ground pepper leaf. Cook for 5 minutes and serve with homemade damper and tomato chutney. Note: Mountain pepper is a native Australian ingredient. It loses its flavour if added too early or cooked too long. Serves 4.

Fred Thies, HEATHCOTE

featuring impressive stained-glass windows. Its original owner, Francis Highett, was a Victorian tennis champion. Also a notable singer, he performed duets with Dame Nellie Melba and sang in St Paul's Cathedral in London. At the corner of High and Highett Streets is a marble monument (within the roundabout) erected in 1880 as a tribute to Constables Lonigan, Kennedy and Scanlon, who were killed by Ned Kelly at Stringybark Creek in 1878. A popular destination from Mansfield is Craigs Hut, built on the Clear Hills for the *Man from Snowy River* movies. It has a spectacular view, and is reached by a reasonable dirt road and a steep walk, or a couple of 4WD tracks. Mansfield is also a stepping-off point for numerous 4WD trips, horse-riding, camel treks and ballooning excursions across the Victorian High Country. You can ride with the mountain cattlemen who starred in the *Man from Snowy River* movies, enjoy fishing in the mountain streams or just take pleasure in the remote camping spots and mountain vistas. Wilderness skiing is on offer in winter. The High Country Festival in November includes Cracks Cup, a mountain race for cross-country horse riders. The Hot Air Balloon Festival is held in April.

At Murchison's [C2] nearby

garrison, 4,000 Italian, German and Japanese POWs were detained during World War II. The camp was surrounded by three barbed wire fences, each 2 m high and 1.8 m wide, and in 1942 was manned by 64 officers and 611 other personnel. Guard towers were equipped with Vickers machine guns. In 1943 the Italian prisoners were used to pick fruit locally, because there was a shortage of farm labour (the Germans were not trusted out of sight of the guards). Those prisoners who died at Murchison were initially buried in the local cemetery. However, Luigi Gigliotti petitioned Italian families living in the Goulburn Valley to finance a mausoleum, the Ossario, for all the Italian POWs and detainees who died in Australian prison camps. The cemetery is at the southern end of town, by the Goulburn River along the Murchison–Nagambie Road.

Puckapunyal [D1] is the

largest military training centre in the state. While on a trip to Australia in 1910 British general Lord Kitchener inspected a major encampment at the nearby Seymour racecourse and recommended it as a permanent military training area. This was set up a few years later when World War I broke out. Seymour Shire's military camp ultimately led to the establishment of the Puckapunyal camp during World War II, when the army realised it needed more training areas.

Puckapunyal's Army Tank Museum was established to commemorate the Australian Light Horse and the Royal Australian Armoured Corps. It features the Southern Hemisphere's largest display of vintage tanks, said to be the third largest in the world. The museum is in Heraklion Street—the route is clearly signposted from the Hume Freeway near Seymour.

In Rushworth [C1], at the corner of

High and Hyde Streets, is an old steam

engine whistle post (1906). It was used to remind steam engine drivers (hauling logs from Rushworth Forest to Risstroms Sawmill) to sound their whistle as a warning to horse-drawn traffic.

DON'T MISS: The mallee-covered forest country to the south of Rushworth hides the abandoned goldmining town of **Whroo**. Little remains, but there are walking trails leading to the old cemetery, an Aboriginal rock well, abandoned goldmining sites and an old gold puddling machine. Fossicking is allowed in certain areas. Ask at the Visitor Centre for more information.

In Seymour [D2], on the corner of

Emily and Manners Streets, is the Royal Hotel, dating from 1848. The original structure forms the rear (and larger) portion of today's Royal. This older section attracted Australian artist Russell Drysdale, who used it as the background for his painting *The Cricketers* (1941). A sign in the painting declares that the pub is Moody's Hotel—the name by which the Royal was then known—and the sign in question still adorns the awning. Seymour is also the finishing point for the hundreds of rafters competing in the annual Raft Race, held on the long weekend in March in nearby **Trawool**.

Shepparton [B3] is the source of

the word 'furphy'. In 1873 John Furphy set himself up in Shepparton as a blacksmith and wheelwright. He established a foundry in 1878, and in 1880 began manufacturing metal water carts. Widely used throughout Australia and in World War I Australian army camps, they quickly became centres of gossip; hence a 'furphy'—a rumour or false story—has entered common parlance. In 1883 John's brother Joseph moved to Shepparton after drought ruined his prospects in the Riverina. He worked at the

VIC

foundry for 21 years. While there he wrote the manuscript for the famous Australian novel *Such Is Life*, published in 1903 under the pseudonym Tom Collins. The foundry, still owned by the Furphy family, is in Drummond Road and has a museum with old equipment, memorabilia and photographs.

In Strathmerton [A3]

the major attraction is Cactus Country, the largest land-scaped cactus garden in Australia.

GAZETTEER

Sunbury [F1]

has one of Australia's oldest girder bridges, the Jackson Creek Bridge, built in 1861. The oval next to the Rupertswood mansion in Macedon Street is where the first Ashes cricket match was played. After Australia won an 1882 match at The Oval in England, *The Times* announced the death of English cricket, asserting: 'The body will be cremated and the ashes taken to Australia.' Thus, when an English team toured Australia and played in Sunbury, Lady Janet Clarke asked her servant to burn the bails, and presented the ashes to the English captain, Ivo Bligh, in a pottery urn. In the 1920s, Bligh's widow presented the ashes to England's MCC (Marylebone Cricket Club). They are still kept at Lords. 'Emu Bottom' is a group of colonial buildings of local stone that was begun in 1836 by the original European settler in the area, George Evans, a founding father of Melbourne. It is probably the state's oldest homestead still in existence. To the south-east of town is

Organ Pipes National Park.

The main feature of the park, the 'pipes', are columns of volcanic basalt beside Jackson Creek. They formed around a million years ago when lava flowed over the Keilor Plains into the valley from Mt Holden and other cones, slowly cooling and cracking into remarkably regular hexagonal columns. Other formations of interest are Rosette Rock and the Tessellated Pavement. The entry road heads east off the Calder Highway 6 km south-east of **Digger's Rest**.

South of Tatong [C4]

the Tolmie Road climbs up into the forests of the Toombullup Plateau. Turn right into Stringybark Creek Road and after 800 m you will see a signpost pointing to the 'Kelly Tree'. The inscription says '1878 Kelly shot Lonigan'. Sergeant Kennedy and Constables Lonigan, McIntyre and Scanlon camped nearby on 25 October 1878, while searching for Ned and Dan Kelly. Ned killed Lonigan, Scanlon and Kennedy. McIntyre escaped to report the killings, which resulted in the gang being outlawed, meaning they could be shot on sight. The original tree that marked the site of Lonigan's death is long gone, but the killings of Lonigan and Scanlon did occur in the immediate vicinity. Kennedy's body was found on the other side of the creek, 400 m away.

Outside Tatura [C2]

is one of the largest station homesteads ever built in Australia. Start at the Hogan and Ross Street intersection and head south along the Murchison road for 8 km. On your left you can see Dhurringile, a 65-room mansion erected in 1871 for James Winter, who died in England before he could take up residence. Dhurringile served as a detention centre for German officers being held as POWs in World War II and later as a Presbyterian home for Scottish children. It is now a minimum security prison. If you head toward Rushworth (west from the Hogan–Ross Street intersection), you will soon come to a signposted turn-off on the right leading directly past the Tatura public cemetery. Next to it is the German War Cemetery containing the graves of 239 civilian internees and a number of POWs.

Yarrawonga's [A4] Tudor

House Clock Museum, at 21 Lynch Street, has an outstanding collection of about 400 clocks from all over the world. It's the largest public display of mechanical clocks in Australia. Junolan Stud displays its miniature horses in a large all-

weather barn and display area. There is an informative talk on the history of miniature horses, which are no taller than 86 cm. The stud is at **Bundalong South**, 4 km off the Murray Valley Highway. Byramine Homestead, the first in the area, was built by explorer Hamilton Hume's sister-in-law, Elizabeth Hume. It is open Thursday to Monday.

South-west of the town of **Yea** [E3] is **Mt Disappointment**, named by explorers Hume and Hovell in 1824 after they had climbed 800 m, hoping, but failing, to see Port Phillip Bay. East of Yea along the Goulburn Valley Highway, turn off the road at **Thornton** and drive to **Rubicon**, the smallest privately owned town in Victoria. It not only boasts the first power station in Australia, but the longest section of wooden water pipe as well. The state's longest tunnel is east of Yea. Travel 2 km along the Goulburn Valley Highway, then turn right onto the Limestone Road—6 km along is the old railway tunnel. The Goulburn River between Lake Eildon and Seymour (but especially above Yea) is immensely popular with trout anglers, who cast their lines throughout the open season (from about September to May). Check with the local authorities.

Diary of Events

Town	Event	Date	Contact
Cobram	Peaches and Cream Festival	January 2003, biennial	03 5872 2132
Kilmore	Kilmore Cup	February	03 5781 1319
	Celtic Festival	July	03 5781 1319
	Pacing Cup and Harness Racing Carnival	October	03 5781 1319
Mansfield	Balloon Festival	April	03 5775 7000
	High Country Festival	November	03 5775 1464
Trawool	Raft Race	March, long weekend	03 5799 0233

VIC

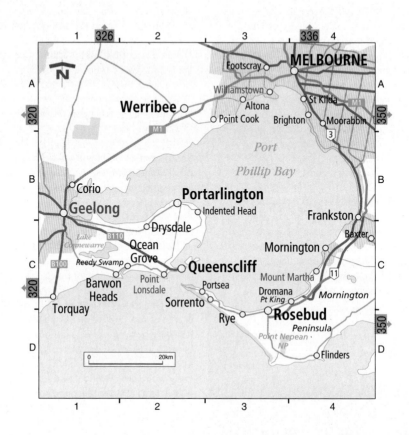

get off the beaten track

wander

the melbourne bays and peninsulas

Barwon Heads [C1] is very

familiar to most Australians, even if they don't realise it. This pretty, unspoilt coastal town was the setting for the popular television series *Sea Change*. Reinforcing its identity as a 'village by the sea', Barwon Heads has undergone a major facelift, with streets remodelled, building facades repainted and old-fashioned street lighting reinstalled. The refurbished Barwon Heads Hotel is the centrepiece. The Barwon River is arguably the best place in Victoria for hopeful anglers wishing to do battle with a large mulloway or jewfish. Specimens of 30 kg and more have been landed here, mostly by hardy souls fishing in the dead of night with live mullet or 'bay salmon' as bait. The Jirrahlinga Koala and Wildlife Sanctuary on Taits Rd is open daily from 10 am to 5 pm (03 5254 2484).

The town of **Baxter**'s [C4] Eurutta (Sage's) Cottage, one of the oldest farmhouses in

Victoria, dates from 1841 and is a rare surviving example of a quality home constructed from vertical sawn slabs. It was built by John Edward Sage, who overlanded cattle in the 1840s for Captain Benjamin Baxter's Carrup Carrup station, which he managed. The cottage is on the corner of Moorooduc and Sages Roads.

DON'T MISS: 'Mulberry Hill' (open on Sundays) is the home of author Joan Lindsay, who wrote *Picnic at Hanging Rock*.

West of **Dromana** [C3], at **Point King**, the newly created Union Jack (adding Ireland's St Patrick's Cross to those of

England and Scotland) was raised for the first time in Australia in 1802. The flag was unfurled by Lieutenant James Murray and his party during their 25-day exploration of Port Phillip Bay aboard the *Lady Nelson*. Dromana was named by Irish gold prospectors.

Just west of **Flinders** [D4] is the start of the Blowhole Walk, winding around huge bluestone boulders to the ocean. At low tide the rock platforms are accessible, and lucky fossickers might find garnet sand sapphires.

Frankston's [B4] McClelland Art

Gallery has a permanent collection of Australian sculpture arranged throughout an immense outdoor park. There are also works by notable Australian artists such as Russell Drysdale, Fred Williams, Hugh Ramsay, Rupert Bunny, E Phillips Fox, Lenton Parr, Inge King and Norma Redpath. The gallery, open from 10 am to 5 pm, Tuesday to Sunday, is a short distance out of Frankston on McClelland Drive.

Geelong's [B1] first customs

house, in the Botanic Gardens, is a
GAZETTEER small square timber Gothic pavilion with a steeply pitched shingled roof (thatched until 1854). Prefabricated in Sydney and erected in 1838, it is the oldest timber building still standing in Victoria and contains displays from its days as a telegraph station. At the corner of Eastern Beach Road and Fitzroy Street is Corio Villa, considered the most ornate prefabricated house in the country. It was ordered by the colonial land commissioner of Geelong in 1854, but he died before it arrived and the package was sold at a bargain price to magistrate and bank director Alfred Douglass, who later bought the Geelong *Advertiser*. By the time the building was assembled in 1856 the plans

VIC

had been lost, so the builders just started welding it together—they did a pretty good job as it turned out. The building's uniqueness was assured soon after, when a fire destroyed the Edinburgh factory that had made it, including all the moulds. The *Advertiser*, established as a weekly in 1840, was the first newspaper outside Melbourne in the Port Phillip district. It is now the state's oldest morning paper. Australia's oldest surviving town hall is in Gheringhap Street. This grand two-storey classical structure, with its imposing Ionic portico, was built in 1855, although additional work was carried out in 1917.

DON'T MISS: Pakington Street in Geelong West bursts into life on the last weekend of the summer for the Pako Festa, billed as one of Australia's premier multicultural festivals. Call 03 5221 6044 for dates and program of events.

At Indented Head [B2] a stone

cairn in Batman Park adjacent to The Esplanade marks the spot where John Batman landed in May 1835 to establish a British settlement. He made camp before proceeding to the head of Port Phillip Bay, where his party selected the site for what is now Melbourne. Batman did a deal with the Wurundjeri people to acquire 23,000 ha, about half of their total land holdings.

Mornington's [C4] National Antique

Centre covers 5,574 sq m of floor space with antiques, bric-a-brac and collectibles, including a motorcycle display. There's also a tearoom. The Old Post Office Museum has displays of old telecommunications equipment and items pertaining to local history. Housed in the former post office at the corner of Main Street and The Esplanade it is open Sundays and public holidays from 2 pm to 5 pm but closed from mid-June to August.

At Mount Martha [C4] is The

Briars Historic Park. The property was taken over in 1846 by Alexander Balcombe. He named it The Briars after his ancestral home on St Helena, where his family had befriended the exiled Napoleon in 1815. In gratitude for the family's kindness Bonaparte gave them gifts, now preserved in the historic 12-room homestead, built between 1848 and 1851.

GAZETTEER

North-west of Ocean Grove [C2],

Reedy Swamp and **Lake Connewarre** are

important habitats for migratory birds such as bitterns, swamp hens, ibis, spoonbills, egrets, cormorants and herons.

From the Point Lonsdale [C2]

lighthouse a cliff-top walk leads to Buckley's Cave, thought to have been the home of the remarkable convict escapee William Buckley. He was one of three convicts who escaped in April 1803 from the penal settlement at **Sorrento** on the tip of Mornington Peninsula. He lived with the Wathaurong people in the Geelong area for 32 years, learning the indigenous language and customs, before giving himself up to white settlers at Indented Head in 1835. He may be the origin of the phrase 'Buckley's chance', which means no chance at all. Just offshore from Point Lonsdale the reef is exposed at low tide dropping into deeper, dangerous water. Here on the edge of 'The Rip' is a graveyard of ships that sailed all the way

GAZETTEER

TO COOK A CRAY

Kill the cray by placing it in the freezer for about 1 hour. To cook, boil in highly salted water—the best is half seawater and half freshwater, if you have access to clean seawater. Use about 30 g of salt per litre. Cooking time is 6 minutes per kilogram and 6 for the pot after it comes back to the boil. Cool in a plastic bag on ice in the fridge. If you wish to BBQ, grill or bake the cray, cut it in half with a large, sharp knife and cook on moderate heat, basting with olive oil, salt, pepper and any herbs you like. A good BBQ technique is to first roast the cray, basted, and then finish it on the coals for flavour. Try not to burn the shell, as the burnt flavour will permeate the meat.

A GOOD CRAY MAYONNAISE
2 egg yolks
1 tsp Dijon mustard
1 clove garlic, crushed
coral from cooked cray (optional)
salt and pepper to taste
300 ml good quality extra virgin olive oil
juice of 1/2 lemon
1 tsp sherry vinegar
1 tsp of cold water

Mix the egg yolks (you can use cooked yolks if you want to keep it longer) with mustard, garlic, coral, salt and pepper. Slowly add the olive oil, whisking as you go (or use a hand beater). When the mixture is thickened and most of the oil is used up, add the lemon juice and vinegar slowly. Add the rest of the oil slowly. If mayonnaise is still too thick, add a little cold water. Taste, season and set aside. Serve a half cray per person (remember to remove the intestinal tract), with mayonnaise, a small salad and extra lemon. Makes 6 portions.

George Biron, Pettavel Vineyard, GEELONG

from England, only to be wrecked within sight of their destination. The Riptide Lookout south of the town offers an excellent view of the bay's entrance and the rip.

Portsea [C2] has always been a
popular destination for Melbourne's social set. One of their haunts is the renowned Portsea Golf Course, rated Victoria's number two public access course.

Point Nepean National Park is the most visited national park in Victoria. Of the excellent surfing spots around the area Blackbeach is the surfers' favourite.

In 1967 Australian Prime Minister Harold Holt disappeared while swimming off Cheviot Beach at Point Nepean, to the immediate west of Portsea.

Queenscliff [C2] has Australia's
only black lighthouse (and has a guided tour). The Boat Bar at the Ozone Hotel has a terrific collection of historical maritime photos. Steam train buffs will enjoy the ride on the Bellarine Peninsula Railway, which runs along 16 km of restored track from Queenscliff, skirting the shores of Swan Bay to **Drysdale**. The return trip takes under two

VIC

CEVICHE OF WESTERN PORT GAR FILLETS

The Mornington Peninsula is one of Australia's newest and most exciting wine regions. Paringa Estate is an award-winning winery located at 44 Paringa Road, Red Hill South. It was established by Lindsay and Margaret McCall in 1985 and has 4 ha of vines. The Estate's chef, Simon West, uses European influences as a base for his recipes, then gives them an original twist using local produce.

400 g fresh garfish	50 g blackcurrants
4 tbsp virgin olive oil	50 g toasted pine nuts
2 tbsp sherry vinegar	50 g sea salt
juice of 1 lime	50 g cracked pepper
1 clove garlic, finely chopped	sprigs of coriander and flat leaf parsley, for garnish
50 g flat leaf parsley and coriander, chopped	

Fillet the garfish or ask your fishmonger to do it. Lay the fillets in a glass or china dish. In a bowl, combine all other ingredients except pine nuts, salt and pepper. Pour marinade over fillets, cover with cling film and allow to marinate for 2 hours in the fridge. Fillets should now have changed colour from opaque to white. Place fillets on a serving plate, drizzling some of the marinade over them. Season with salt and pepper. Top with toasted pine nuts, sprigs of coriander and flat leaf parsley.

Simon West, Paringa Estate Restaurant, MORNINGTON PENINSULA

hours. An alternative excursion from Queenscliff is the ferry ride across the bay to Sorrento and Portsea. Dolphins often join the boat for the 40-minute crossing.

Torquay [C1] is a surfing mecca and

home to the country's only surfing museum, a tribute to nearby Bell's Beach, which hosts national and international surfing competitions.

Werribee's [A2] Park Mansion is

considered Victoria's finest colonial homestead. The state's largest private residence was built between 1874 and 1877 by two of Victoria's most substantial landholders, Thomas and Andrew Chirnside. The opulent 60-room mansion and its outstanding grounds give a good indication of the wealth and extravagant lifestyle of Australia's pastoral elite in the colonial era.

DON'T MISS: The RAAF base at Point Cook was established in 1914 to house and train the Australian Flying Corps. It is the birthplace of the Australian Air Force and the country's oldest continually operating airfield. The associated aviation museum (at the end of Point Cook Road) is considered the finest in Australia, featuring the largest collection of military aircraft and aviation artefacts in the Southern Hemisphere. Some of the vintage aircraft are still operating, with demonstration flights staged for visitors. One of the numerous special exhibits focuses on World War I flying ace Baron von Richthofen

(The Red Baron). The waters east of Point Cook are popular with trailer boat anglers pursuing the annual run of snapper. Snapper fishing normally kicks off in earnest soon after the AFL Grand Final on the last Saturday in September and peaks in November or December, with a secondary burst in February, March and even April. Expect good catches of flathead, whiting and garfish, and snapper up to 10 kg.

Williamstown [A3] emerged at

the same time as Melbourne, and for a while it was thought the site would prove the principal settlement. As a result of this early start it holds a number of state 'firsts'. The first cemetery in Victoria was established at Point Gellibrand, and St Mary's Catholic School (1842) is now the state's oldest continuously operating school. The Time Ball Tower at the bottom of Nelson Place was built as a time-keeping device that would be visible to offshore sailing vessels. A large sphere

at the top of the tower was lowered each day at exactly 1 pm so that ships' navigators could set their chronometers accurately. The square bluestone base section was built by convict labour. A cylindrical brick upper extension was added in the 1930s.

NAN'S RED CAPSICUM RELISH

Relish—there couldn't be a better word to describe this delicious chutney. It's certainly something 'appetising or savoury added to a meal' as the *Macquarie Dictionary* says. But this is a relish one can truly 'relish' with absolutely 'pleasurable appreciation'. And what's the difference between a relish and a chutney? Well, chutney is usually a 'relish' of Indian origin that's made with fruit or vegetables cooked with sugar, spices, lime juice or vinegar.

2 cups chopped red capsicum
2 cups minced white onion
1 cup white sugar
2 cups white wine vinegar
salt and pepper to taste

In a saucepan, combine capsicum and onion. Stir in the sugar, vinegar, salt and pepper. Mix well and bring to the boil. Lower heat and simmer till reduced to a jam-like consistency. Store in sterilised jars and refrigerate when opened.

Sandra O'Mara, GROVEDALE

VIC

Diary of Events

Town	Event	Date	Contact
Geelong	Pako Festa	Feb/Mar	03 5221 6044
Ocean Grove	Apple Fair	January	03 5255 1340

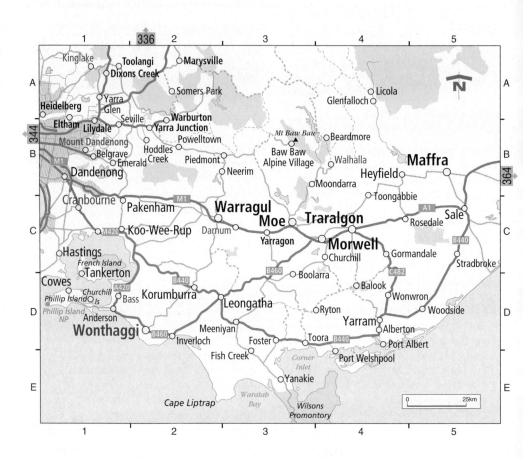

get off the beaten track

roam

the yarra valley

to gippsland

Two of **Alberton**'s [D4] early settlers, the Martin Brothers, ensured a place for themselves in the local annals when they imported an elephant from Ceylon to clear their property. Unfortunately, it escaped one evening and, weakened by cold and hunger, died not far away. Hawthorn Bank, 7 km north of Alberton at Yarram, was built in 1846 as a farm residence and is one of Victoria's few remaining wattle-and-daub structures.

At **Bass** [D1] there is a wormery with live specimens of giant earthworms—it boasts a roadside display worm more than 90 m long. The giant Gippsland earthworm, which the display celebrates, can grow up to 4 m long—Gippsland is the only region in the world where these giant worms live, in the hills between Bass and Korumburra. They are now a protected species. The town's main attraction is the Giant Worm Museum, where you can 'see the world's largest earthworms on display'. This gargantuan structure allows visitors to crawl through a worm burrow and walk through a giant simulation of a worm's stomach.

In **Belgrave** [B1] is Horatio's Amazing Home, an unusual cottage built by Horatio Jones in 1917. It is made of flattened four-gallon kerosene tins on a frame of roughly hewn eucalyptus trees. Jones was a handyman and inventor who, at the age of 17, won a prize for a self-adjusting windmill at the 1888 Melbourne International Exhibition. Jones returned to the site of his old bush hut

and built the present cottage for himself and his sisters. There they were visited by the likes of CJ Dennis and John Shaw Neilsen, who also built cottages in the area. The CJ Dennis Wilderness Hideaway is the cottage built in 1913 by the noted Australian literary figure, who wrote much of his most famous work, *The Sentimental Bloke*, here. Both houses are open by arrangement—call 03 9754 4936.

At the entrance to **Churchill** [C4] is the Big Cigar, testament to the fact that the town was named after the British wartime leader famous for his passionate speeches, his V for Victory sign and his cigars.

Churchill Island [D1], part of

the **Phillip Island Nature Park**, was named after John Churchill by his friend Lieutenant James Grant, who constructed a simple cottage here in 1801 and established Victoria's first European 'settlement'. Churchill supplied him with seeds to plant Victoria's first crops—corn, wheat, peas, onions and potatoes—as well as a small garden. Samuel Amess, who purchased the island in 1872, built a symmetrical weatherboard homestead. In his garden is a cannon from the US Confederate Civil War ship *Shenandoah*, given to Amess by the ship's officers in appreciation of his hospitality when the ship visited Melbourne in 1865.

The area around **Cranbourne** [C1] has yielded an extraordinary haul of meteorites, found between 1850 and 1982. One of the meteorites weighed 1.5 tonnes and was considered the world's largest until another was found, weighing in at 3.5 tonnes (now exhibited at the British Museum). Miniature replicas of 12 meteorites are on display at the corner of the South Gippsland Highway and Camms Road.

VIC

POTATO COCONUT ROUGHS

These taste just like coconut roughs—amazing what you can do with potatoes. Thorpdale is right in the heart of Victoria's rich potato-growing region. In fact Thorpdale is famous for its potatoes. Nearby on the Princes Highway at Trafalgar you can drop by the Spud Shed (there's a spudman out the front so you can't miss it) and stock up on fresh fruit and vegetables, local produce, free-range eggs and of course those famous potatoes.

1 cup mashed potato, cold
30 grams butter
1 ²/₃ cups icing sugar
1 ¹/₄ tablespoons cocoa
1 ³/₄ cups desiccated coconut
1 tsp vanilla essence

Beat butter into potato, gradually beat in sifted icing sugar and cocoa. Add coconut and vanilla, mix well. Spoon teaspoonfuls of this mixture onto greaseproof paper, refrigerate until firm. Makes approx. 30.

Val Murphy, THORPDALE

The **Darnum** [C3] Musical Village features a display of hundreds of musical instruments, including a single-string cello and a 15th-century clavichord, collected by Albert Fox while he travelled around the Gippsland region as a piano and organ restorer, tuner, manufacturer and teacher.

GAZETTEER

Eltham's [B1] Heidelberg School Artists Trail is designed to take visitors to the sites depicted in the paintings of artists associated with the Heidelberg School—Arthur Streeton, Walter Withers, Louis Buvelot, Tom Roberts,

Clara Southern, David Davies, Emanuel Phillips Fox, Charles Conder, Tudor St George Tucker, Eugene Von Guérard, May Vale and Jane Price. There is a reproduction of the relevant painting at each site, providing insight into the artist's interpretation of the landscape and showing how the landscape has changed since that time. The trail passes largely along the Yarra River and takes in nearby Heidelberg. A guidebook can be obtained from Banyule Council phone 03 9490 4222. The Montsalvat Artists' Colony in Eltham is also worth a look, both for the art exhibits and for the buildings themselves. The land was bought by Justus Jurgensen in 1938 as the site for an artists' retreat. There are several handsome European-style

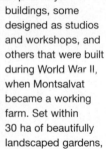

buildings, some designed as studios and workshops, and others that were built during World War II, when Montsalvat became a working farm. Set within 30 ha of beautifully landscaped gardens, the buildings are now used for art classes, exhibitions and receptions. The annual Montsalvat Poetry Festival is held on the first weekend of December and showcases the work of Australia's famous and not-so-famous poets. Call 03 9439 7712 for details.

In **Emerald** [B1] is the largest model railway display in the Southern Hemisphere. It features 2 km of HO-scale track, detailed scenery, approximately 35 working models and push-button participation. The display is in Emerald Lake Park at the end of Emerald Lake Drive, next to the **Lakeside** train station (on the Puffing Billy Line). This park was once part of the historic Nobelius Heritage Nursery, now a recreational area. At

the start of the 20th century, the nursery was one of the largest in the Southern Hemisphere, with 80 employees and about 200,000 trees on 180 ha. It was started by Carl Nobelius, allegedly a relative of Alfred Nobel, the founder of the Nobel Prize awards.

Foster [D3] is lyrebird

country, although they're more likely to be heard than seen.

French Island

[C1] supports Australia's largest koala community, now exporting koalas to the mainland and to international zoos. They

can be seen throughout the island,

including in the recreation hall and post office at **Tankerton**, where the ferries dock.

Near **Heidelberg** [A1], at 77 Burke Road, Ivanhoe, is historic Charterisville, one of the earliest surviving houses in the state. A famous 100-minute film about the Kelly Gang was filmed in 1905 in the area. A three-minute remnant of the film was rediscovered in the 1980s.

In **Kinglake**

GAZETTEER

[A1], at 8 Parkland Road, is the House of Bottles, which is constructed entirely of bottles (13,569 of them), carefully arranged with an eye to colour contrasts. Next door is a Dutch windmill built from 5,000 bottles. Both were built by Joseph Eykenbaum between 1969 and 1972. Inside is a vast bottle collection, with examples from around the world

dating back to the early 19th century. There are also fossils, minerals, rocks, memorabilia and a collection of 6,000 ornamental shoes, made of everything from leather to glass, metal to pottery. The Doll and Carnival Glass Museum is at 1205 Whittlesea Kinglake Road, Kinglake West, and is open daily. It has 2,000 dolls and teddy bears on display, and 1,000 pieces of carnival glass, a type of lustrous glassware popular in the 1920s, which became so common it was given away at carnivals.

At **Koo-Wee-Rup** [C1] you

can take an Asparagus Tour, and perhaps sample some asparagus ice-cream (call 03 5997 2202 for details). The name of the town is derived from

VIC

Victoria

YUMMY GREEN SPEARS

Asparagus has been grown in Koo-Wee-Rup since the early 1900s and now covers nearly 1,600 ha. The town grows 80 per cent of Australia's asparagus. It's Victoria's biggest-earning agricultural export. For more information and cooking ideas using asparagus, log on to the Australian Asparagus Council at www.australianasparagus.com.au

ASPARAGUS WITH MACADAMIA NUTS
Blanch, microwave or steam fresh asparagus until just tender. Serve with chopped and toasted macadamia nuts, fresh mango, finely chopped salad and onion, and lots of freshly cracked pepper.

ASPARAGUS AND SESAME
Roughly chop asparagus spears and stir fry until just tender. Add soy sauce, sesame oil, honey and toasted sesame seeds, lightly toss and serve while hot.

The Australian Asparagus Council

the Aboriginal word meaning 'blackfish swimming'. This makes sense when you realise that the area was once swampland. It was drained in the 1870s to allow settlement and farming.

The Firelight Museum in **Leongatha** [D3] has a fascinating collection of antique lamps from the 1860s to the 1940s, as well as pocket watches, coins, firearms and jewellery housed in a Tudor-style building. It is open for viewing on weekends and school holidays (call 03 5668 6272 for hours). The Daffodil Festival is a Leongatha institution, launched in 1956. Held in September it features more than 1,000 entries (for details call 03 5668 6334).

Lilydale's [B1] cemetery is where Dame Nellie Melba is buried.

DON'T MISS: About 30 km east of Lilydale, in Hoddles Creek, the Upper Yarra Draught Horse and Old Time Festival is held at the end of January every year. Whip-cracking demonstrations and ferret racing are among the highlights.

In **Marysville** [A2] the cross-country skiing is considered among the best in the world. The town's major attraction is **Steavenson Falls**, 4 km south-east of town along Falls Road. It is only a short walk from the carpark to the base of the falls. Another track leads up the side of the mountain to a more elevated perspective. These are the highest falls in Victoria, dropping 82 m in three stages. The falls and the path are floodlit each evening by a hydro-electric generator.

Moe [C3] has Gippsland Heritage Park's Pioneer Township, a living museum that recreates a 19th-century township, including 'Loren', an original building from the Gippsland area.

Morwell [C4] has one of the world's largest deposits of brown coal. The Powerworks Visitor Centre has displays and models of mining and power-generating equipment and activities. It can also arrange visits to the mine and power stations, with tours daily between 11 am and 2 pm.

Mount Dandenong [B1] is the site of the William Ricketts

GAZETTEER

354

Sanctuary, where life-sized clay sculptures of Aboriginal figures are set among rocks, tree ferns and mountain ash. Ricketts spent time living with the Pitjantjatjarra and Arrernte people of Central Australia and his work integrates his Christian tradition with their culture.

On Phillip Island [D1] is one of

Australia's most famous tourist attractions—the nightly parade of fairy penguins that walk to their burrows across Summerland Beach after a day spent fishing for whitebait. Chicory was grown on Phillip Island for the first time in 1870. The root of the plant is dried and converted into powder as a coffee additive. It was claimed that chicory had

medicinal properties. By the late 1940s nearly three-quarters of Australia's chicory crop was being grown on Phillip Island, but chicory growing eventually faded owing to high labour costs and declining demand. There are still a few chicory kilns about the island, with their strange towers and pitched roofs. One is located on Back Beach Road (the main road to the Penguin Parade).

DON'T MISS: Phillip Island is also the venue for the annual Australian Motorcycle Grand Prix, held in October (call 03 9258 7100 for details).

The rugged **Port Albert** [D4] Hotel, licensed in 1841, claims to be the oldest pub continually in operation in Victoria, although other contenders exist in Buninyong and Portland. The current brick structure dates from 1858.

While exploring **Port Welshpool** [E4], Bass and Flinders recorded a flock of an estimated 133 million mutton birds. They reported that the flock was 80 yards deep, 300 yards wide and travelling at around 50 mph; it took 90 minutes to pass overhead. The birds return every November, although now in significantly reduced numbers.

The RAAF base at **Sale** [C5] is home to the famous Roulettes aerobatic team. The Roulettes are a part-time team, made up of QFIs (Qualified Flying Instructors) from the CFS (Central Flying School) based at Sale. They fly Pilatus PC-9/As.

Seville [B1]

is the site of the Victorian Strawberry Festival, held annually in November on the Sunday after Melbourne Cup Day. The Yarra Valley Orchid Festival is held in the Seville Public Hall in late October. There is a large display of different orchids and demonstrations of potting methods.

Toolangi [A1] was the home of

the poet CJ Dennis. Dennis lived at 1694 Healesville–Kinglake Road from 1908 until his death in 1938. His last book, *The Singing Garden* (1935), was inspired by the garden he and his wife created. It now covers 1.5 ha, featuring rhododendrons and exotic trees,

VIC

including a copper beech planted by English Poet Laureate John Masefield, who visited Dennis during the state's centenary celebrations.

Walhalla

[B4] was the last town in Victoria

to get mains electricity. There is no television reception, no mobile phone service and very little radio signal. The Walhalla cricket ground is unique in that the lack of even ground forced the community to level off the top of a hill. The long trip to the town and the half-hour climb up the knoll just before the match was said to ensure a home advantage. The town's cemetery is another spot with site problems—it is on the side of a hill, and is one of the steepest cemeteries in the world. Stories abound about people being buried standing up; they are, in fact, buried feet first into the side of the hill.

Near **Warburton** [B2], about 8 km north-east along Acheron Way at the intersection with Donna Buang Road, is a spot known as Cement Creek. Its Aerial Sky Walk allows visitors to explore the canopy of a rainforest consisting of 200–300-year-old trees, from a platform about 30 m above the ground. **Mt Donna Buang**, just up the road, has the closest snow to Melbourne in winter.

Wonthaggi

[D2] came to prominence as a coalmining town when the state could no longer take coals from Newcastle. The Newcastle miners' strike in 1909 forced Victorian Railways, which ran on steam, to import wood and

coal from Japan and India. The people of Wonthaggi rapidly developed a coalmining industry from reserves they had known about since 1850. The mining complex became the first electrified mining operation in the Southern Hemisphere when a power station was built in 1912 to run the mine and supply the town with electricity. In 59 years, 17 million tonnes of coal were extracted from 12 separate mines. In 1937 a methane gas explosion killed 13 men. It was so powerful it catapulted a 2 tonne iron cage 20 m—from the mouth of the shaft to the top of the poppet head. On the front verandah of the Wonthaggi Hotel are the huge jawbones of a 22 m whale that washed up on the beach in 1923. An unemployed butcher boiled it down and sold the jaws to the hotelier for £25.

Just past **Woodside** [D5] a 432 m tower and helix building marks the site of the Omega Radio Navigation Facility, part of a worldwide network of transmitters designed to secure the safe coordination of the world's nautical and aerial traffic. It is open daily for inspection.

Yarragon

Village's [C3] inhabitants pride themselves on the local crafts. In 1999 they went so far as to knit a

BLOW-AWAY SPONGE

This traditional sandwich sponge recipe brings back memories of afternoon teas around the table and cut-throat CWA cake competitions. With this recipe it's no contest. See if you can limit yourself to just one slice, especially if it's made with local strawberries (you can pick your own) and cream.

³/₄ cup cornflour
1 heaped tsp plain flour
1 flat tsp cream of tartar
¹/₂ flat tsp bicarbonate of soda
4 eggs, separated
pinch of salt
³/₄ cup caster sugar
whipped sweetened cream
1 punnet strawberries, sliced
icing sugar, for serving

Preheat oven to 180°C and grease and flour 2 x 20 cm cake tins. Sift together three times cornflour, flour, cream of tartar and bicarbonate of soda. In a bowl, beat egg whites with salt until light and fluffy. Add caster sugar gradually, while still beating. When mixture is stiff and glossy add egg yolks one at a time. Continue beating until mixture is thick enough to hold the figure 8 when dropped from the beaters. With a metal spoon, gently fold in the flours. Divide mixture evenly between the two prepared cake tins. Bake for 16 minutes, or until cooked. Turn out immediately onto a wire rack to cool. Sandwich sponges together with whipped cream and strawberries, and dust the top with icing sugar.

Val Murphy, THORPDALE (via Moe)

giant patchwork beanie for the rotunda in the centre of town. The original idea was to raise money for charity and to promote the area's wool by covering the rotunda with something warm and colourful. The beanie has since been taken down and made into rugs for donation to local communities.

At Yarra Junction

[B2] the Vintage Engine Crank Up is held on the first weekend in April at the old Yarra Junction Railway Station. For details call the Upper Yarra Valley Historical Society on 03 5964 8230.

Diary of Events

Town	Event	Date	Contact
Eltham	Montsalvat Poetry Festival	December	03 9439 7712
Leongatha	Daffodil Festival	September	03 5668 6334
Lilydale	Upper Yarra Draught Horse and Old Time Festival	January	03 5961 5302
Phillip Island	Australian Motorcycle Grand Prix	October	03 9258 7100
Seville	Yarra Valley Orchard Festival	October	03 9431 3657
	Victorian Strawberry Festival	November	03 9758 7522
Warburton	Warburton Winterfest	Jun/Jul	03 5966 5544
Yarra Junction	Vintage Engine Crank-Up	April	03 5964 8230

VIC

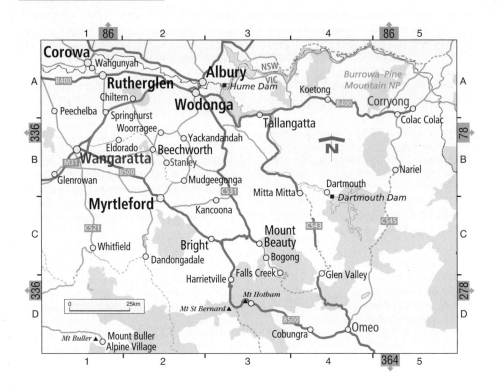

The vast roof of Australia is fast gaining a reputation as a year-round destination. Designated the 'High Country', it really can boast of having the highest, the biggest, the oldest, the prettiest, and just about the best of anything you care to name apart from a desert and an ocean shoreline.

get off the beaten track

hit the high country

Beechworth [B2] has strong

associations with Ned Kelly, his gang and family, who were regulars at the town's jail and courthouse (now a museum). The Burke Museum was established as early as 1863 in honour of explorer Robert O'Hara Burke, who served as superintendent of police at Beechworth from 1854 to 1858. The pistol that lay beside his body when it was found at Cooper Creek was inscribed: 'Presented to Captain Burke by the residents of Beechworth, Victoria.' The museum houses one of the largest collections in the country relating to Ned Kelly, including the surcingle of Joe Byrne (a Kelly gang member), the dock from the courthouse in which Ned Kelly once stood, a replica of the famous armour worn by Ned at Glenrowan, one of the five death masks made in Melbourne at the time of Kelly's death, an original reward poster, and the steps of Aaron Sheritt's hut, where Ned Kelly stood while Joe Byrne gunned down Sheritt, a former friend believed to be a police informer.

In Chiltern [A2], at the corner of Main

and Conness Streets, is the former Star Hotel and Theatre (1866). In the courtyard is a grapevine planted in 1867. With a trunk that measures 1.84 m around the base, it is recorded as the largest in the Southern Hemisphere.

Corryong's [A5] pretty hillside

cemetery is at the top of Pioneer Avenue. It contains the simple grave of Jack Riley, who is generally agreed to have been the inspiration for AB 'Banjo' Paterson's 'Man from Snowy River' (1890). Riley emigrated from Ireland in 1854 and worked initially as a tailor but then as a stockman, nourishing his interest in horses. He became known as a mountain rider, horse-breaker, bushman and tracker of wild horses. While working as the manager of the Tom Groggin cattle station in the Upper Murray Valley he undertook the ride that lies at the centre of Paterson's epic. The poet apparently met Riley on a camping trip and was inspired by his tales of adventure. The Bush Festival in April includes a re-creation of the ride. An information board in the town centre reserve details its background. The Man From Snowy River Museum's collection includes wooden skis dating back to the 1870s and a pram on skis owned by Olympic skiers Thomas and Elyne Mitchell. **Burrowa–Pine Mountain National Park**, to the north-west, boasts a monolith one-and-a-half times the size of Uluru. The upper Murray River near Corryong and its two major tributaries, the Swampy Plains and Indi Rivers, are home to brown and rainbow trout and offer superb angling opportunities during the open season, especially for fly-fishers.

Dartmouth Dam [B4], built in the

1970s, has the state's largest dam wall (670 m long and 180 m high), and is

VIC

MY FATHER'S BRAWN

'This is my late dad's recipe—it's a good one.' *The Gazeteer*'s kitchen test team agrees wholeheartedly with Edna's verdict. 'Brawn' is the medieval term for dark, heavy and slightly fatty meat of poultry or boar. In Victoria's pioneering days, long before refrigerators and iceboxes and far from the corner shop, vinegar and spices would be used to pickle or preserve meats and fresh foods to make them last.

2 veal knuckles	1 tsp mixed dried
250 g pickled pork	herbs
750 g gravy beef	1 dsp gelatine
2 cups beef stock	2 tbsp water
1 ltr water	1/2 cup vinegar
salt and pepper	1 tbsp
to taste	Worcestershire
1 bay leaf	sauce
3 cloves	

Grease a 23 cm x 13 cm (or similar) loaf pan. Place meats in a large saucepan, cover with liquid and add salt, pepper, bay leaf, cloves and herbs. Cover saucepan with a firm lid and simmer on low heat until meat breaks away from bone (this may take about 3 hours). Remove meat from saucepan, dice finely, pack into greased pan. Soften gelatine in water, then dissolve in the hot stock. Add vinegar and Worcestershire sauce, then strain and pour over meat to just cover. Refrigerate until set firmly. Unmould onto serving plate.

Edna M Stein, RUTHERGLEN

Australia's highest rock-fill dam. The dam's surface area is 62,000 sq km and it holds 4 million megalitres. Dartmouth Dam is a popular trout fishing destination and

also holds good stocks of Macquarie perch— a native fish species now rare in most other areas. There are special restrictions on taking Macquarie perch, or 'Maccas', from these waters, and anglers should check on these regulations before casting a line. The dam itself is remote, though. Only a couple of 4WD tracks (steep mountain trails off the Corryong–Omeo road) come within cooee of the shoreline.

Eldorado [B2], a former goldmining

town, retains a huge dredge (on the Register of the National Estate) built in 1935. It was reputedly the largest in the Southern Hemisphere and continued to operate until 1954, yielding 2.3 million grams of gold and 1,475 tonnes of tin. By the time it was decommissioned it had dredged 30 million m^3

from the river flats of the Eldorado Plain. A pleasant road, normally open to 2WD cars driven with care, runs from Eldorado parallel to Reedy Creek, crossing it a couple of times before coming to **Woolshed Falls**. Here the miners of old chopped a gash through the solid rock to divert the creek so they could get at the gold at the bottom of the falls.

Glenrowan [B1], 15 km from

Wangaratta, is the site of the capture of Ned Kelly and his gang in 1880. There is a giant Ned Kelly effigy overlooking the township and there are a variety of attractions, museums and historic walks that relate to the Kelly history.

In **Mitta Mitta** [B4] the Mighty Mitta Muster is held on the long weekend in March (Victoria's Labour Day). It features show jumping, world championship wood chopping, dog jumping, whip cracking and gumboot throwing.

Mount Hotham [D3], at 1,861 m,

is the highest village in Victoria, sitting just below the summit of the mountain. European settlement of the area began when several women set up cabins and shanties to house miners in transit between the area's goldfields. 'Mother' Morwell, for example, established a log cabin near **Mt St Bernard** in 1884. Legend has it that because the St Bernard hospice was only 3.5 m high, the mailman occasionally fell down the chimney while searching through very heavy snowfall for the building. South of Hotham is the mountain road (closed in winter) to Dargo [see Lakes and Wilderness map] and the Blue Rag Range track. This dead-end 4WD track offers some of the finest scenery in the Australian Alps—and some very exposed driving along a ridgeline.

Not far from the centre of **Omeo** [D4], on the Great Alpine Road to Mount Hotham, is the Memorial, a very practical war memorial in the form of a bridge spanning Livingstone Creek, which was built by returning diggers after World War I. On the far side of the old bridge is a parking area with a sign pointing to a walking track. The track crosses a footbridge and follows the river, continuing past the brick pumping station that supplies water to the town to reach the 'oriental claims', where the then world's largest hydraulic sluicing operations for gold were carried out, largely by Chinese workers. (The 1,800 kg of gold discovered would be worth $23 million at today's prices.) The site, now preserved as an historic area, is surrounded by large man-made cliffs, up to 30 m tall, that retain traces of gold. Old tunnels pockmark the hillside. The entrance to one of these burrows is accessible from the path (enter at your own risk) leading to the main area of the claims. Omeo once had a newspaper with a masthead that must rank as one of the country's longest: *The North Gippsland Mountaineer, and Swift's Creek and Wombat Reporter*.

Rutherglen [A1] is in the centre

of one of Australia's oldest wine-growing regions—vines were first planted here in 1858. The townspeople have added a steel mesh statue of a wine bottle to the top of the old 300,000 ltr water tower in Hunter Street to celebrate the liquid they depend on.

In the centre of **Stanley** [B2] there is a rare cork tree classified by the National Trust.

Tallangatta [A3] was

relocated to its present site in 1954 to allow the expansion of the **Hume Dam**. 'Old' Tallangatta (which was settled in the 1850s)

VIC

disappeared beneath the water, but not before the hospital building and Tallangatta Butter Factory were moved across the causeway to **Toorak**, and more than a hundred other buildings moved to 'New' Tallangatta. The town was officially launched in June 1956, the same year as the

POLKA-DOT PRUNE CAKE

You can replace the prunes with dates if you prefer in this delicious shortcake-type cake, although prunes will make a moister product. It's just the sort of cake to pack in the picnic basket for a day at Wangaratta's world-renowned annual Festival of Jazz; or something sweet to look forward to after a long day in the nearby snowfields.

1/3 cup caster sugar	1 tbsp milk
1 egg, beaten	1/2 cup butter, melted and warm
1 1/2 cups self-raising flour	about 26 dessert prunes, seeded
1/2 tsp salt	1 tbsp chopped walnuts
2 tbsp cornflour	

Preheat oven to 180°C and line a 21 cm x 11 cm loaf tin (or similar) with baking paper. In a bowl place sugar, egg, half the flour, half the salt and half the cornflour. Add milk to melted butter and pour onto ingredients in bowl. Beat for 3 minutes. Add remaining dry ingredients and beat for another minute. Mould a small portion of mixture around each prune to cover it completely. Arrange in layers in loaf tin. Sprinkle nuts on top and bake in oven for 30–35 minutes.

Damien Silvestri, WANGARATTA

Melbourne Olympics. A 1950s festival is held each November to celebrate the town's relocation (call 03 5756 2345 for details).

In **Wahgunyah** [A1], All Saints Estate was established in 1864, one of the state's oldest wineries. It is 4 km north-east of town on All Saints Road. The original owner, George Smith, was the first Australian to win an international gold medal for wine at Vienna in 1873. The main building, classified by the National Trust, dates from 1878 and is modelled on the Castle of Mey in Scotland. The Rutherglen Keg Factory is located in the grounds of the estate. There you can watch a cooper plying his trade in the traditional manner.

Wangaratta [B1] is the final resting place of Dan 'Mad Dog' Morgan, whose headless body lies in the town cemetery at the corner of Tone Road and Mason Street. Morgan was a violent bush-ranger, and had an enormous reward of £1,100 on his head by 1865, the year he was killed at **Peechelba Station**. He was decapitated, and his head sent to the University of Melbourne for phreno-

GAZETTEER

logical studies. What remained of his body was buried outside the cemetery's boundary. The fence was later relocated and the grave can now be found inside the small gate at the cemetery's northern end, near the toilet block. The town's main attraction is Airworld, an aviation museum. If you stop at the Visitor Information Centre don't miss the one-sixth scale house constructed by a Mrs Stell, who was 70 years old when she began the task.

Wodonga [A2] is the Victorian half of

the twin border towns of Albury–Wodonga. On Melrose Drive is Australia's largest outdoor tennis centre. East of Wodonga are the old army camps of Bandianna and Bonegilla, through which many of Australia's postwar migrants passed.

Yackandandah's [B2] Isaacs

Avenue is named after Sir Isaac Isaacs, a local boy who became Australia's first home-grown governor-general. On the north-eastern corner of Williams Street and Isaacs Avenue is one of the town's first brick residences (c 1866).

NAN'S BAKED RICE PUDDING

'Not rice pudding again' was Mary Jane's cry in AA Milne's much-loved poem. But Mary Jane had obviously never tasted Nan's version of this family staple for filling hungry tummies, which is so deliciously creamy the hands fly up for seconds.

1 tbsp sugar	1 tbsp butter
2 tbsp rice	1/2 tsp vanilla
600 ml milk	nutmeg

Preheat oven to 160°C and grease a small (4-cup capacity) casserole dish. Put sugar, rice and milk in the casserole dish, then add vanilla. Dot with butter and sprinkle with nutmeg. Bake for 1 1/2–2 hours, or until most of the milk is absorbed into the rice. Serves 1 (if greedy), or 2 or 3.

Ann Sigalla, MANSFIELD

Diary of Events

Town	Event	Date	Contact
Bright	Autumn Festival	May	03 5755 2275
Corryong	Bush Festival	April	02 6076 9012
Dartmouth	Dartmouth Alpine Fishing Classic	February	02 6072 4255
Falls Creek	A Taste of Falls Creek	January	1800 033 079
Mansfield	Balloon Festival	April	03 5775 7000
Mitta Mitta	Mighty Mitta Muster	March, Labour Day weekend	02 6072 4213
Myrtleford	Tobacco, Hops and Timber Festival	March, Labour Day weekend	03 5752 1808
Tallangatta	1950s Festival	November	03 5756 2345
Whitfield	King Valley Petanque Competition	May, 1st weekend	03 5729 8270

VIC

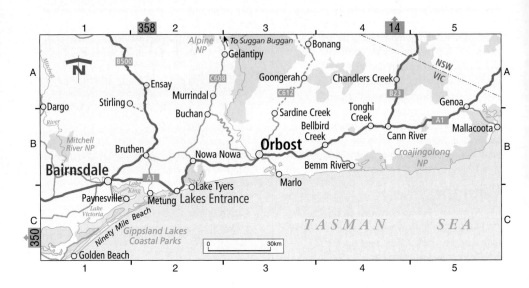

The Lakes and Wilderness region of Victoria has the most amazing diversity of nature, including the UNESCO world biosphere reserve of Croajingolong and the Great Alpine Road through Victoria's highest mountains.

get off the beaten track

lounge around
the lakes
and wilderness

Bairnsdale's [B1] ornate

and well-preserved Court House in Nicholson Street, opened in 1894, is one of Victoria's finest examples of late 19th-century architecture. St Mary's Roman Catholic Church has the unusual distinction, for an Australian church, of elaborately painted murals, sanctuary, Stations of the Cross and a ceiling featuring hundreds

of figures in its depiction of heaven and hell. The paintings were done by Francesco Floriani, an Italian painter who worked as a labourer in the area during the 1930s.

Bruthen [B2] is on the Great Alpine

Road, which essentially follows the route of the first European travellers, passsing a number of curiously named historic sites as it heads north alongside the Tambo River toward Omeo [see High Country map]. Heading north of Bruthen (7 km), **Monkey Creek** was named by Angus McMillan after the 'monkey bears' (koalas); **Walsh's Cutting** (15 km) after a coach driver who died when a brake failure caused his vehicle to plummet down the hill; and **Piano Bridge Creek** (27 km) after the tendency of the old bridge's panels to bounce up and down like piano keys. In the same area is the **Pig and Whistle**, said to be the spot where railway surveyors collected their liquor when their boss denied them access to the local hotel. **Jew's Pinch** (30 km) immortalises a Jewish hawker whose vehicle met with difficulties here. **Snake's Back** (35 km) recalls the old

road's curvature. **Haunted Stream** (35 km) is named after its connection with the murder of Ballarat Harry. **Name Stone Point** (36 km) is named after a stone, now gone, which was adorned with travellers' doodlings, and **Devil's Backbone** (45 km) after the tortuous nature of the country. **Gypsy Point** is a small piece of paradise, especially if you fish.

Four-wheel-drivers can take a more arduous run along the Haunted Stream track—it crosses the stream more than 40 times before arriving in the once rich gold town of **Stirling**. From here you climb the steep hills to meet the Angora Range Road.

Buchan [B2] is a source of black

marble, and items made from it can be bought at the Black Marble Hut in town. The black marble outcrop 12 km south-west of Buchan South provided the 16 huge pillars for Melbourne's Shrine of Remembrance. Some 900 tonnes were also shipped to London for inclusion in Australia House. The Buchan Caves were discovered by Europeans in 1907 and opened to the public a year later—the highlight is the 400-m long Fairy Cave.

The small mountain town of # Dargo [A1]

is a famous stepping-off point for the mountain trails that radiate from here. The Crooked River goldfields, the 'Hidden Valley of the Alps' (the famous Wonnangatta River valley) and the spectacular **Alpine National Park** are within striking distance of Dargo. Dog's Grave, north-east of town, lies in a hidden valley and is a magnificent monument to man's best friend. The annual Dargo Walnut Festival takes place on Easter Sunday (call 03 5155 3766 for details).

Genoa [A5] marks the start of the

Wingan Nature Walk in **Croajingolong National Park**. The one-and-a-half-hour walk leads through stands of bloodwoods, melaleucas, swamp paperbarks and wild

VIC

cherry trees, before reaching Fly Cove. George Bass anchored here in 1797, lending his name to Bass Strait. Visible from this point are the Skerries Islands, home to fur seals and penguins.

North of **Golden Beach** [C1] at

Ninety Mile Beach is the wreck of the *Trinculo*, best seen after a king tide. This 318-tonne barque was 41 m long. In 1879 it struck a sandbar 30 m offshore. All the crew reached land, including the captain's wife and 16-month-old baby, and one crew member, a Mr Lefèvre, was awarded a silver medal by the Royal Humane Society. The monument at Golden Beach was built from a water tank salvaged from the wreck. Ninety Mile Beach offers fine surf-casting opportunities for anglers after Australian salmon, mullet, flathead and gummy sharks.

Gippsland Lakes and their feeder streams are famous for their hard-fighting and delicious black bream, which bite especially well from July to October.

At **Lake King** [C1] the Mitchell River empties to form silt jetties that stretch 8 km into the lake. They are the second largest silt jetties in the world after those of the Mississippi delta. The Mitchell River, which winds south from Dargo through the **Mitchell River National Park** and Bairnsdale until it reaches Lake King, also offers excellent fishing opportunities for black bream, yellow-eye mullet and the highly prized estuary perch. In one of the national park's rainforest gullies is the Den of Nargun, a place of great cultural significance to the Gunai/Kurnai Aboriginal community. Tradition has it that the female deity Nargun was able to deflect spears and boomerangs back at the thrower. The story is thought to have served the dual purpose of keeping children close to their camp and protecting this sacred women's site from unwanted visitors.

Along **Lakes Entrance**

[C2] foreshore a wood carver has converted the stumps of trees into images of Australia at war, including famous scenes from World War I such as Simpson and his donkey, and a nurse looking after wounded soldiers. The Griffiths' Sea Shell Museum and Marine Display, at 125 The Esplanade, features 90,000 shells; the head of one of the largest marlin ever caught (162.7 kg); exotic corals; a 91.5 m model railway; and a large aquarium complex containing sea snakes, giant crabs, blue-ringed octopuses, squid and many rare or unusual marine organisms.

GAZETTEER

BRAISED OXTAIL WITH ORANGES AND WALNUTS

Long before the roadtrain, the bullocks hauled goods to market along rough roads. Marjorie Barnard in her *History of Australia* says: 'It was slow travelling, but the great-hearted beasts could be relied on to surmount all obstacles, and the bullocky's verbal encouragement was proverbially lurid.'

- **1.5 kg oxtail, cut into portions (where the joints are) and trimmed of fat**
- **1 tbsp butter**
- **1 tbsp olive oil**
- **125 g bacon, chopped**
- **1 large onion, chopped**
- **150 g large mushrooms, chopped**
- **3 cloves garlic, crushed**
- **2 tbsp tomato paste**
- **1 carrot, diced**
- **1¹/₂ cups red wine**
- **3 bay leaves**
- **1 tsp dried thyme**
- **salt and pepper to taste**
- **2 large tomatoes, peeled, seeded and diced**
- **water**
- **1 tbsp parsley, chopped, for serving**
- **2 tsp fresh orange zest, for serving**
- **2 tbsp chopped walnuts, for serving**

Preheat oven to 150°C. In a large flameproof casserole dish (with a lid) brown the oxtail in the butter and olive oil. When well browned remove meat, add bacon and cook until browned. Remove bacon and add onion, mushrooms, garlic, tomato paste and carrot. Cook for 5 minutes, then return oxtail and bacon to pan. Add the wine, bay leaves, thyme, salt, pepper and tomatoes. Top up with enough water to just cover. Cover with lid and bake in oven for about 3 hours, or until meat is tender. During cooking skim surface to remove any excess fat or oil. Sprinkle meat with chopped parsley, orange zest and walnuts to serve. Serves 4–6.

Sarah Cory, BAIRNSDALE

West of **Lake Tyers** [C2], at Stony Creek, is a railway bridge built in 1916 of local grey box and red ironbark. At 276 m long and 18.6 m high, it is one of the largest wooden bridges in Australia.

Every Easter **Mallacoota** [B5] hosts the Festival of the Southern Ocean, which began in 1981 as the Carnival in 'Coota' but took on its current name in 1996. The aim is to foster cultural connections with other coastal towns and cities lying near the 38th Parallel South. Events include a parade, theatre, cabaret, music and jam sessions, sporting events, workshops, exhibitions and films.

The alluvial river flats around **Orbost** [B3] are said to be among the most fertile in the world, beaten only by those of the Nile Delta. The historic Slab Hut in town has a cottage garden planted in period style.

VIC

SPICY SEAFOOD STIRFRY

The Lakes and Wilderness region is great for country cuisine and all things fishy. It is famed for the vast array of seafood available. Tuck in at one of the many restaurants and cafés that specialise in serving the freshest local seafood, or try this recipe from Viva, the sole Australian brand of olive oil products.

12 green king prawns, shelled with tails left intact	2 spring onions, sliced
4 small fresh squid, cleaned and cut into narrow rings	1 clove garlic, crushed
	12 scallops
	1 tbsp fish sauce
2 tbsp Viva Late Harvest Extra Virgin Olive Oil	2 tbsp sweet chilli sauce
1/2 red or green capsicum, cut into fine strips	handful small leaf spinach or fresh basil leaves

Heat oil in wok and add capsicum, onion, garlic and prawns; stirfry for 2 minutes. Add squid and scallops; stirfry for 1 minute. Add fish sauce and sweet chilli sauce, stir over high heat to coat ingredients, then add spinach or basil. Heat briefly and serve over rice. Serves 2–3.

Viva, INGLEWOOD

Paynesville's [C1] St Peters-by-the-Lake is an Anglican church with a nautical theme. The spire resembles a lighthouse tower and has a light that is used as a navigational aid. The pulpit, built by well-known Metung boat builder Joe Bull, is an exact model of the prow of a fishing vessel and even has copper-head nails. The sanctuary lamp is fashioned from a ship's riding light, and the font is in the shape of a ship's bollard. It holds the upturned bell of the SS *Dargo*, the last

trading steamer to operate on the Gippsland Lakes. The large windows behind the altar give a panoramic view over **Lake Victoria**. On the exterior of the church is a mosaic, in the form of four fish.

Suggan Buggan [A3], see also NSW Alps and Foothills] on the Barry Way, got its unusual name from a combination of Gaelic and Aboriginal words, both meaning basket or

GAZETTEER bag. When the O'Rourke family came to this area in 1858 they carried their children in baskets, or 'suggan' in Gaelic. Added to this was the similar Aboriginal word for a bag made from grass, 'buggan'. The two-room schoolhouse at Suggan Buggan was built in 1865 by Edward O'Rourke and is still standing.

Diary of Events

Town	Event	Date	Contact
Dargo	Walnut Festival	Easter Sunday	03 5155 3766
Mallacoota	Festival of the Southern Ocean	Easter	03 5158 0890

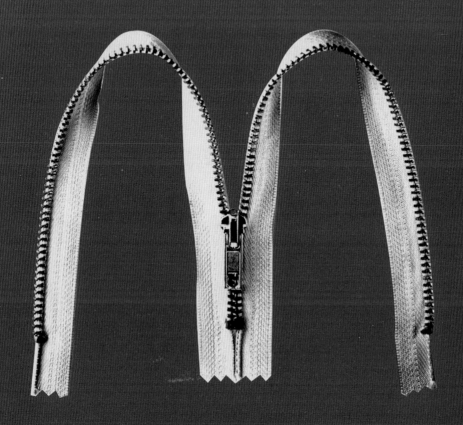

Zip into McDonald's.

McDonald's has over 700 restaurants Australia wide. That makes them the perfect road side stop to grab a coffee, stretch your legs and take a rest before the next leg of your journey.

Where will you crash?

It's been estimated that tiredness contributes to one in five deaths on Victorian roads. So if you're driving, pull over every two hours for a break or as soon as you feel tired. It's no substitute for a good night's sleep but a 15 minute powernap could save your life. Visit www.tacsafety.com.au   arrive alive!

A 15 minute powernap could save your life. TAC

Drive Right

TAC

and help reduce Victoria's **road toll**

How to **drive right.**

✓ Drive or ride appropriately for the road conditions, and always within the speed limit.

✓ Indicate well in advance of turning or changing lanes.

✓ Ensure all vehicle occupants are appropriately restrained, and riders wear protective gear.

✓ Keep to the left unless overtaking or turning right.

✓ Drive courteously: let other vehicles merge, and be patient at pedestrian crossings.

✓ Follow the vehicle in front at a safe distance.

See www.tacsafety.com.au for more information

Mmmm-morning, Sunshine!

Pace Farm Eggs

Available in all supermarkets.

Phone 1300 653 447

King I

Flinders I

BASS STRAIT

Stanley
Burnie
Devonport
Gladstone
Deloraine
Launceston
376-87
Ross
Strahan
Queenstown
388-97
Bothwell
New Norfolk
Strathgordon
HOBART
Huonville
Dover
Port Arthur

SOUTHERN

OCEAN

| Northern Tasmania | 376 | Southern Tasmania | 388 |

tasm

The sea that separates Tasmania from the mainland has protected its ancient natural environment and nurtured a unique island lifestyle. It is Australia's smallest and most remote state. The cities of Hobart and Launceston are gateways to a land of rugged mountain landscapes, temperate rainforests, open plains and unspoiled beaches.

Tasmania is often described as a well-kept secret and, when it comes to food and wine, there are many famous Australian chefs who source their ingredients from Tasmania's natural larder. With an amazing array of fresh produce, Tasmania is becoming known to food lovers worldwide. The clean air, pure waters and deep rich red soils provide the perfect ingredients for growing produce.

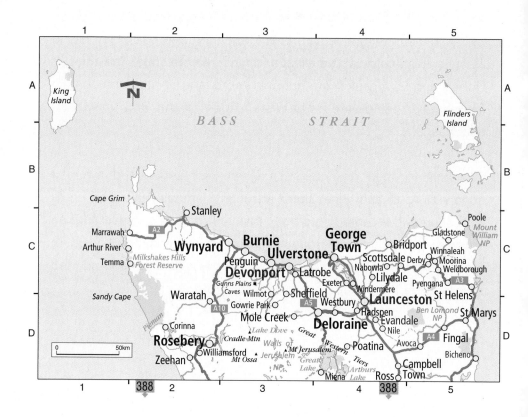

1   2   3   4   5

King Island

BASS   *STRAIT*

Flinders Island

Cape Grim

Stanley

Marrawah
Arthur River

A2

Wynyard   Burnie   George Town

Bridport   Gladstone

Poole
Mount William NP

Temma

Milkshakes Hills Forest Reserve

Penguin   Ulverstone

Scottsdale   Winnaleah

Devonport   Latrobe

Derby   Moorina
Weldborough

Nabowla

Sandy Cape

Gunns Plains   Exeter

Lilydale

A3

Waratah

Caves   Wilmot   Sheffield

Windermere   Pyengana

St Helens

Gowrie Park   Westbury   Launceston

A10

A5

Hadspen

Ben Lomond NP

St Marys

Pieman

Corinna

Mole Creek   Deloraine

Evandale

Nile

A4

Fingal

Rosebery

Lake Dove   *Great*

Cradle Mtn   *Walls*   *Mt Jerusalem*

Poatina   Avoca

Bicheno

0   50km

Williamsford   *Jerusalem*

Western

Zeehan

Mt Ossa   *NP*

Greats Lake

Tiers

Campbell Town

Arthurs Lake

Miena   Ross

388   388

get off the beaten track

know all about

northern

tasmania

Arthur River [C1] is a small settlement in the far north-west of the state on the stream of the same name. There's some great four-wheel-driving around here, the hardest and the best being the drive south to **Sandy Cape**; the last 25 km from **Temma** is especially tough. Another good but challenging 4WD trip is from Temma inland to **Balfour**. Locals aren't entirely sure how the nearby **Milkshakes Hills Forest Reserve** got its name, but it's thought the hills were so called because they resembled old-fashioned milkshake cups.

In **Avoca** [D5], at the back of St Thomas' Anglican Church (1842), visitors will find a very special pew, dating from the days before standardised mass production. It was custom built to accommodate the portly church warden of the day.

GAZETTEER

The Bass Strait Islands

[A1–A5] are all that's left of a land bridge that joined Tasmania to the mainland 12,000 years ago. The numerous small islands in the Bass Strait now provide a habitat for the migratory short-tailed shearwater, or muttonbird, known as yolla to the Aboriginals. A traditional food for the Aboriginal people of the region, yolla is regarded as a gourmet item. The Tasmanian Aboriginal community harvests yolla each March during a five-week season and the rich meat is sold fresh, salted or frozen. **King Island** is one of the best-known islands in the Strait. It not only has a world-famous dairy industry but is becoming known for kelp harvesting, beef, abalone and cray fishing. It is also attracting professional surfers who come from all over the world to try the huge breaks off the island's coast. It's not only the big waves that are the big attraction here, it's the fact that the waves are so fast because of the strong winds known as the Roaring Forties. The Roaring Forties have

Northern Tasmania is where the first free settlers built elegant properties on their sheep and dairy farms. Throughout the rural expanse are hawthorn hedges, lush gardens and towns that resemble their British counterparts.

TAS

also made King Island a popular destination for intrepid divers; it has more known shipwrecks than any other part of Australia. More than 100 vessels have sunk off the shore, including the *Cataríqui*, which killed 399 people when it went down in the 19th century, making it Australia's single worst civil disaster. Although there is much for divers to explore, the rough seas coming through Bass Strait can make conditions far from ideal. Other activities on King Island include fishing, horseriding and bushwalking in the nature reserve at Yarra Creek Gorge. **Flinders Island** is renowned for the Killiecrankie diamonds found in the north of the island. This is a form of topaz released by decomposing granite rocks. You can search for them in the creek bed and on the beach at **Killiecrankie Bay**. Flinders Island is now home to around half the world's population of the second-rarest goose species, the Cape Barren goose (*Cereopsis novaehollandiae*), which is no longer considered endangered. Between **Bridport** and Flinders Island there is only one mode of public transport (other than by air)—a cattle punt that makes the crossing once a week. Once a month it continues to Port Welshpool in Victoria.

Bicheno [D5] is home to the Sea

Life Centre, on the north side of town. The centre has a number of unusual

GAZETTEER

attractions, including the anchor from the barque *Otago*, the only vessel ever commanded by the great Polish-English novelist Joseph Conrad. Bicheno provides one of the finest temperate-water diving spots in the world. Visibility can exceed 50 m, allowing a superb view of the Giant Kelp Forests, huge underwater jungles that are unique to Bicheno. Down the coast (follow the signs to the south of the town)

is Bicheno's famous Rocking Rock, a huge 80 tonne piece of granite balanced so delicately that it rocks with the movement of the waves.

The Burnie [C3] Inn (now in beautiful

Burnie Park) was built in the early 1840s to cater for the growing population of the north-west coast. The inn was granted a licence in 1847 and is the oldest building still standing in the city, though it is just a café today.

DON'T MISS: The Lactos cheese tasting and sales centre in Old Surrey Road is worth a visit.

Campbell Town [D4] is a

historic and beautiful township, and its locals proudly claim it is home to the oldest agricultural show in the British Commonwealth; its first sheep show was held in 1839.

Corinna [D2] is one of the last places

where the purportedly extinct thylacine, or Tasmanian tiger, used to roam. The very last thylacines captured were caught further north, but in the wilderness around Corinna it is possible, at least according to the locals, that a few might survive. The interesting home-built ferry that takes vehicles across the **Pieman River** at Corinna is called the *Fatman*. The river gained its name from the notorious convict Alexander 'The Pieman' Pearce, who was responsible for one of Australia's few recorded instances of cannibalism. Pearce, formerly a pieman in Hobart, and seven other convicts attempted to cross the island from Macquarie Harbour to Hobart, where they hoped to catch a merchant ship to freedom. Poorly provisioned, they lost their way. Some weeks later Pearce, alone, was recaptured, with no trace of his fellow escapees. The following year Pearce escaped again, accompanied by another convict, Thomas Cox. Once again Pearce

found himself without food. When he was finally recaptured he admitted to killing and eating Cox, as well as his companions during his first escape. He even produced a still-bloody gobbet from his pocket as proof. Pearce was subsequently executed in Hobart.

Deloraine [D4] has a large multi-panelled artwork in silk called 'Yarns' in the Community Complex, and holds the Tasmanian Craft Fair, said to be Australia's largest, on the first weekend in November. The town claims to have the oldest continuously used racecourse in Australia, dating from 1853.

Derby [C5] has a Tin Mine Museum and a reconstructed Shanty Town with a collection of original buildings from the district, including two cells of the old jail.

In # Devonport [C3], on Mersey Bluff (on the western shore of the Mersey River), is the Aboriginal art site Tiagarra. It is one of the few Tasmanian sites where Aboriginal rock carvings are still well preserved. Consequently, it is very important as a record of the Aboriginal settlement of Tasmania's northern coast. The Tiagarra Art Centre houses more than 2,000 artefacts in 18 displays, including dioramas and exhibits showing the lifestyle of the original inhabitants of the area. A more recent historical attraction of Devonport is Home Hill, once the home of Dame Enid and Joseph Lyons. He was the only Australian to have been both premier of his state and prime

minister of the Commonwealth. Dame Enid Lyons, elected in 1943, became the first woman member of the House of Representatives. In 1949 she was sworn in as the first woman federal minister of the Crown. Home Hill is a superbly maintained 1916 building with exquisitely kept gardens. Follow the signs on the highway for the turn-off at the Devonport Overpass. From January to April the house is open Tuesday, Thursday and Saturday, 12–4 pm, and on Wednesday and Sunday, 2–4 pm. From May to December it's open Tuesday to Thursday and Sunday, 2–4 pm, and Saturday, 12–4 pm. At other times the house is open by appointment (03 6424 3028). About 90 km south of Devonport is Australia's most famous bushwalk, the 83 km Overland Track linking **Cradle Mountain** with **Lake St Clair** to the south. Near its beginning at Cradle Mountain, blending pleasantly with the bush, are the old buildings of Waldheim, a lodge built in 1912 by Gustav Weindorfer, who was largely responsible for the gazetting of the surrounding national park in 1922. The lodge has recently been renovated. About halfway along the trail between Cradle Mountain and Derwent Bridge is **Mt Ossa**, at 1,617 m, Tasmania's tallest mountain.

Evandale's [D4] National Penny Farthing Championships are usually held on the third weekend in February (call 03 6391 8223 for details). Up to 70 cyclists race around the centre

GAZETTEER

TAS

Tasmania

TAMAR COMMUNITY TASTE TREATS

Each year the Tamar River Festival Committee puts together a calendar featuring recipes donated by local Windermere residents from both sides of the river, as well as photographs of the glorious Tamar scenery. Here are a few that we can thoroughly recommend.

WHITE CHRISTMAS CAKE
This is a lovely cake, especially for those who don't like a dark, rich fruit cake.

- 125 g each glacé pineapple, cherries and preserved ginger
- 60 g each glacé figs, apricots and mixed peel
- 125 g walnuts
- 1 tbsp marmalade
- 1 tbsp grated lemon rind
- 1 tbsp honey
- 1/4 cup Grand Marnier or sherry
- 1 tsp glycerine
- 1 tsp vanilla essence
- 250 g butter
- 1 cup brown sugar
- 4 eggs
- 2 cups wholemeal plain flour
- 1 tsp ground ginger

Chop all fruits and nuts coarsely and combine with the marmalade, lemon rind, honey, Grand Marnier, glycerine and vanilla. Cover and stand overnight. Preheat oven to 150°C and line a 20 cm deep cake tin with baking paper. Beat the butter and sugar together until light and fluffy. Add the eggs one at a time beating after each addition. Fold through the fruit mixture and finally add the dry ingredients and mix well to combine. Spoon into prepared tin and bake for 2 hours or until cooked.

SHARON'S TAMAR NASHI CAKE
- 4 nashi fruit, peeled, sliced and poached with a little sugar to taste
- 1 1/2 cups self-raising flour
- 1/2 cup caster sugar
- 2 tsp cinnamon
- 125 g butter
- 1 egg, beaten
- 1 cup milk

Preheat oven to 190°C and line a round 20 cm tin with baking paper. Rub the butter into the dry ingredients until it resembles breadcrumbs. Add the egg and milk and mix well to combine. Spread half the mixture into prepared tin, then add a layer of fruit and lastly the remaining batter. Bake for 35–40 minutes or until cooked. Serve warm with cream or ice-cream.

DORA'S QUICK PAVLOVA
- 1 1/2 cups icing sugar
- 2 egg whites
- 1/3 cup boiling water
- 1 tsp white vinegar
- 1 tsp vanilla

Preheat oven to 180°C and line a baking tray with baking paper. Beat all ingredients together for 7–10 minutes or until stiff (the boiling water starts to cook the egg whites, increasing their volume.) Spoon onto baking tray and shape into a large round with the sides higher than the centre. Bake for 10 minutes at 180°C and then 150°C for a further 45 minutes. Turn off oven, leaving the pavlova to cool in the oven with the door open. To serve, fill with whipped cream and selection of berries.

Tamar River Festival Committee, WINDERMERE

380

of Evandale, the final event being a four-lap circuit where speeds build to such an extent that as they come round the pub corner the riders lean the bikes into a 45° angle. The day before the event the nearby Launceston airport is closed and the tarmac used for a Measured Mile race. Speeds up to 45 km/h have been recorded. If you miss the event itself you can still get into the spirit by taking a half-day penny farthing cycle tour around the town's historic sites, held Wednesday to Monday throughout the year.

Exeter
[C4] is a small town in the Tamar Valley, surrounded by farms growing apples, pears, grapes and cherries. Further north along the West Tamar Highway is Beaconsfield Point, where the Grubb Shaft Gold and Heritage Museum tells the story of Tasmania's largest gold mine. The museum was built from the ruins of massive, ornate brick engine houses. It's a hands-on experience where you can try using a horse works, an ore truck, a gold cradle and water pumps. The pumps used in the mine are said to be the largest of their type ever built. At nearby **Beauty Point** you can visit the world's first seahorse farm, a working farm and aquarium. To view the mystical seahorses you enter a cave with a pool that lets you see them up close. The nearby aquaculture museum and theatrette displays the history and the future of aquaculture.

Fingal
[D5] was the site of Tasmania's first payable gold find, discovered in 1852 at The Nook. The town is now the centre of Tasmania's coal industry. In March (on Tasmania's Eight Hours Day long weekend) Fingal plays host to the Fingal Valley Festival, which includes World Championships for both Coal Shovelling and Roof Bolting. The Fingal Hotel, in Talbot Street, is a two-storey hotel built in the 1840s. In the spirit of the town's name, it has a fine collection of Scotch whiskies, reputedly the largest in the Southern Hemisphere. Head east to **St Marys** to see the magnificent isolated beaches where it is possible to be the only person on the beach. Continuing north along the coast, the road passes through **St Helens**, a fishing village that also has good surfing beaches, particularly the Bay of Fires about 10 km north-east of St Helens. In April each year St Helens holds an international tarmac rally, Targa Tasmania, which is an invitation-only road rally for the best touring and sports cars in the world. It is the modern version of the Targa Florio, the annual road race run along winding roads in Sicily from 1905 to 1974. Call 03 6224 1512 for details.

DON'T MISS: Near Fingal, at the **Evercreech Forest Reserve**, is the world's tallest white gum—it stands 89 m and is 10 m around.

George Town
[C4] is Australia's oldest town (aside from those that grew into cities). It was settled in 1811 and named for King George III. At **Low Head**, 5 km north of George Town, is the oldest pilot station in Australia, set up in 1805; the existing building dates from 1835. Today the station houses a maritime museum of memorabilia salvaged from the many north coast shipwrecks, as well as some early diving equipment. Also at Low Head is the Penguin Observatory, situated in Lighthouse Road. The fairy penguins can be seen as they come ashore just after dusk. Guided tours run from November to March each evening.

If you reach # Gowrie Park [D3]
 by nightfall you can go platypus watching at the weir at O'Neill's Bridge. Nearby you can climb Mt Roland and also visit the huge Devils Gate Dam with walls 82 m high. The town has a collection of pioneer buildings including the biggest shingle-roofed structure in Australia.

TAS

KING ISLAND BRIE AND FIG TART

Time was Australians shunned home-produced cheeses out of inverted snobbery. These days only the woefully insecure would consider serving up a platter of imported cheeses. This renowned gourmet island in Bass Strait started Tasmania's run for glory with superb bries, camemberts and cheddars, thanks to pastures that produce cream so rich you just about need to take a knife to it, and cheesemakers with a commitment to excellence.

2 cups plain flour	2 eggs
125 g very cold butter, grated	1/2 cup cream
1/2 cup pecans or walnuts, finely chopped	salt and pepper to taste
1–2 tbsp cold water	4–5 slices pancetta, very thinly sliced
300 g fresh ricotta	6–8 fresh figs, halved
400 g King Island Brie	1 tbsp marmalade, warmed

Preheat oven to 200°C. Grease a 22–24 cm flan tin with removable base. In a bowl work together the flour, butter, nuts and enough water to form a stiff dough. Form into a ball and refrigerate for 30 minutes. Roll out and line the base and sides of flan tin and blind bake for 10 minutes by covering pastry shell with baking paper and filling with dried beans. Remove beans and bake for a further 5 minutes. Mix together the ricotta, brie, eggs, cream, salt and pepper until well combined. Spoon into flan. Top with a layer of pancetta and then the fig halves. Brush lightly with the marmalade and bake at 180°C for 50–60 minutes. Serves 6–8 as an entrée.

Janet Banks, LAUNCESTON

Hadspen

Hadspen [D4] was first settled in the early 1820s, and was the home of Thomas Reibey III, grandson of Sydney's famous convict-turned-businesswoman, Mary Reibey. Thomas III also earned some notoriety when he was fired from his post as the first archdeacon of the Church of England in Launceston for his 'dubious morals'. He then became Premier of Tasmania in 1876. The main historic attraction of Hadspen is Entally House, Thomas Reibey's original home and one of the most impressive and earliest historic homes in Tasmania. Built on the banks of the South Esk River in 1819 and named after a suburb of Calcutta, India, Entally House stands on the outskirts of the town.

Latrobe

Latrobe [C3], 9 km south-east of Devonport, is the only place in Australia where legal crops of opium-grade poppies are grown for the pharmaceutical industry. There is very tight security surrounding the poppies. The town also hosted the world's first axeman's carnival for woodchopping events in 1888. Latrobe claims a number of other firsts: the local brass band, formed in 1872, is the oldest band in Australia still playing; and the Latrobe Bicycle Race Club, established in 1896, is one of the oldest in Australia. Every December Australia's biggest cycling carnival, the Latrobe Wheel and Latrobe Gift, takes place here—call 03 6426 1041 for details.

Launceston

Launceston [D4] has been breaking new ground since it was established in the early 19th century as Australia's third city. In 1835

Launceston put on the first production of an Australian play, *The Bandit of the Rhine*. In 1851 the city hosted the first inter-colonial cricket match, when Tasmania played Victoria.

Just minutes from the city, you can cross the **Cataract Gorge** in a chairlift with the longest single span in the world. West of Launceston (6 km), in the **Trevallyn State Recreation Area**, is Australia's only cable hang-gliding simulator. Morton House, a two-storey Georgian structure originally known as St John's Hospital, is where, in 1847, anaesthetic was first used in Australia. **Grindelwald**, Tasmania's one and only 'Swiss village', is 14 km from Launceston along the West Tamar Highway. Grindelwald came about when local businessman Roelf Vos and his wife returned from holidaying at a quiet lakeside village in Switzerland, and were so inspired that they decided to create a similar one overlooking the Tamar Valley. Building started in 1981 on about 405 ha of land with a 7 ha man-made lake called Lake Louise. Today Grindelwald has grown into an extensive resort including self-contained chalets and a 9-hole golf course. For a more thrilling alpine experience, the drive up to the **Ben Lomond** ski field, 50 km south-east of Launceston features six hairpin bends on a very steep unsealed road with no safety barriers, but it is worth it for the views across north-eastern Tasmania. For the faint-hearted there is also a shuttle service from the bottom of Jacobs Ladder. The great ancient blockfields of the sides and floor of the plateau are remnants of glaciation. Some of the park's features have telling names: Misery Bluff and Little Hell are two worth pondering.

Lilydale

[C4] has an outstanding floral attraction in the form of Walker's Rhododendron Reserve, on the road to Lalla, established by Englishman Frank Walker in the 1890s. Two oak trees at Lilydale Falls, propagated from acorns collected near Windsor Castle in England and planted on 12 May 1937, commemorate the coronation of King George VI.

Marrawah

[C1] is a base for the 8 km drive north to one of the most important Aboriginal art sites in Tasmania, the Mount Cameron West Engravings. Discovered in 1933 by a Devonport schoolteacher, they are recognised as the finest example of Tasmanian Aboriginal art and one of the best displays of hunter-gatherer art in the world. They are located on a beach about 3 km from Mount Cameron West and have been returned to Aboriginal custodianship. The whole area is known by the Aboriginal name of Preminghana. Access to the site is strictly prohibited. Marrawah itself offers great surfing on the pounding swell created by the Roaring Forties.

Miena

[D4] is a fishing village on the southern shores of **Great Lake**, which has the distinction of being the highest lake in Australia. At 22 km long, it was also the country's largest freshwater lake until the Hydro Electric Commission drowned Lake Pedder in 1972. While the trout fishing in Great Lake itself is excellent (as it is in most waterways in this central highlands region), nearby **Arthurs Lake** is claimed by many to be the pick of the crop. Renowned for its summer 'hatches' of Highland Dun mayflies and the fat, speckled brown trout that dine greedily upon them, Arthurs Lake attracts fly-casting visitors from across the country and around the world, and supports several full-time fishing guides. To the west of Great Lake is the **Walls of Jerusalem National Park**, a series of sheer dolerite cliffs. It was first named in 1849, with some features following the biblical theme, such as Mt Jerusalem, Lake Salome and Herods Gate.

Near **Mole Creek** [D3], at Trowunna Wildlife Park, you can meet a living cartoon character—a Tasmanian devil. These

beasts bear a remarkable resemblance to their namesake on the Bugs Bunny Show, although they have not yet learned to emulate his whirling run.

The Tasmanian devil allegedly has more powerful jaws than a Doberman dog. They are not a major threat to living humans, being mostly carrion eaters, but they can be intensely aggressive.

Mole Creek is also the starting point for exploring the **Great Western Tiers** and the **Mole Creek Karst National Park**, which includes more than 200 limestone caves. This underground labyrinth was formed around 30 million years ago from layers of ancient coral and other marine debris, laid down when the area was covered by ocean, about 450 million years ago.

In the area around **Moorina** [C5], in the state's north-eastern corner, Tasmania's largest sapphire was found. Moorina's 9-hole golf course is uniquely located in the rainforested hills west of town.

Nabowla [C4] is world famous for its lavender. Because it exists in complete isolation, it cannot be contaminated by cross-pollination. The best time to visit is at harvest time, which begins on Boxing Day and runs for three or four weeks. The Bridestowe Lavender Farm is one of the

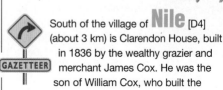

largest producers of lavender oil in the world and the only one of its kind outside Europe.

GAZETTEER

South of the village of **Nile** [D4] (about 3 km) is Clarendon House, built in 1836 by the wealthy grazier and merchant James Cox. He was the son of William Cox, who built the first road across the Blue Mountains in New South Wales.

Penguin [C3], named after the large penguin rookeries nearby, has taken its name to heart. There's a large model penguin (reputedly the largest in the world) in the beachfront park; there are penguin garbage bins in the streets; and even the Penguin Meals on Wheels has a picture of a penguin on the side of the building. The main tourist attraction is the parade of Fairy penguins (*Eudyptula minor*) across the beach, arriving home with dinner for their offspring each evening between November and March. Penguin also has a replica Dutch windmill in Hiscutt Park, presented to commemorate Penguin's Dutch settlers and the Dutch explorers who were the first Europeans to find Tasmania.

Just south of **Poole** [C5] is **Mount William National Park**, the place to go for a glimpse of Tasmania's only kangaroo, the forester. There's some pleasant four-wheel driving and camping along the coast north of Eddystone Point, itself the most easterly point in Tasmania and site of an impressive lighthouse.

Pyengana

Pyengana [C5] is tiny but the wilderness nearby is beautiful, especially the Columba Falls. It was around here in 1995 that a forest ranger sighted what he believed was a Tasmanian tiger (thought to be extinct).

Scottsdale

Scottsdale's [C4] St Barnabas' Church of England, erected in King Street in 1892, was Tasmania's first example of an apsidal building (an apse being a semi-circular or hexagonal recess commonly at the end of a church choir). It is a small, attractive wooden building.

The **Sheffield** [C3] murals attract an estimated 120,000 people every year. The murals are credited with reviving the town, which had deteriorated after a boom period during the construction of Lake Barrington. Not only are the murals a very obvious tourist attraction but, according to many locals, they have also given the town a sense of purpose and raised its self-esteem, all the while providing a visual insight into the history of the region. The murals have been a project for the entire town. The children from the local school even painted the rubbish bins with mini-murals. Pick up a map of the murals at the Diversity Murals Theatrette, which screens a documentary about their creation. Just down the road is **Paradise**, a locality on the map with nothing more to show than a lopsided barn. Still, a photo of the sign will go to prove that you have, indeed, been to Paradise.

Stanley

Stanley [C2] was the first settlement in north-west Tasmania, and home to the VDL (Van Diemen's Land Company), set up in 1825 to establish a merino wool industry. Lyons Cottage, birthplace of Australian Prime Minister Joseph Lyons, is open to the public. At the eastern edge of town is Circular Head, better known as **The Nut**, a lava plug rising 150 m above sea level. You can catch the chairlift to the top, although the arduous 20-minute climb gives a more righteous feeling.

Ulverstone

Ulverstone [C3], on the banks of the Leven River, is where buckwheat is grown for the production of soba—Japanese noodles. Nearby is the Small Concern Whisky Distillery, which uses pure Tasmanian water and newly developed Franklin barley to produce the triple-distilled Cradle Mountain Single Malt Whisky. Cradle Mountain Double Malt Whisky is a blend of the single malt whisky with the Springbark Single Malt Whisky from Campbelltown, Scotland. They have even managed to sell it in Scotland.

Waratah

Waratah [D2], about 60 km south-west of Burnie, is where the world's richest tin deposit was found in 1871. The mine, established in 1888, was the first plant in Australia to use electric lighting, with hydro-electric power supplied by a waterfall. In 1889 the mine manager, HWF Kayser, had the electric light connected to St James' Church in Smith Street, which thus became the first church in Tasmania to be lit by electricity.

Weldborough

Weldborough's [C5] original hotel, built in the 1890s, burned down in the 1920s. The current building dates from 1928 and, courtesy of its landlord's warped sense of humour, is known as 'the worst little pub on the coast'—it is nowhere near the coast. The humour extends to the menu, with such offerings as 'maggot mornay' and 'leeches and cream'.

TAS

In **Westbury** [D4], turn west off the main road at Lonsdales Prom and you will come to the Village Green, said to be the only true village green in Australia. In the 1830s, with soldiers stationed nearby, it was used for parades and archery competitions. Prisoners were put in the stocks on the green and it would have been alive with fairs during the summer months. These days a Maypole Festival is held each March as part of the town's St Patrick's Day festivities (call 03 6424 4466 for details). Pearn's Steam World, on the Bass Highway (between the Village Green turn-off and Fitzpatrick's Inn),

has over 100 steam engines ranging from locomotives to complex pieces of agricultural equipment. This is reputedly Australia's largest collection of steam engines. Also on the Bass Highway is Tasmazia, the world's largest maze complex. It includes eight mazes, among them a replica of Hampton Court Maze in England. Within the maze is Australia's only reported memorial to a plumber—Thomas Crapper, the British inventor of the flush toilet.

Williamsford [D2], just south of

Rosebery, is the access point for Montezuma Falls, which tumble 104 m, the highest falls in Tasmania. An easy 4WD track follows the old railway line through rainforest to a point where vehicle access is impossible. From there it's a relatively short walk to the falls.

Windermere's [C4] St Matthias'

Church, completed in 1842, claims to be the oldest continuously used church in Australia. Its setting on the Tamar River is inspirational and it is popular for weddings. The jetty nearby is used not only by enthusiastic anglers but also by wedding parties who, looking for something relatively original, make their way across the river to the Rosevears Hotel directly opposite.

Winnaleah's [C5] clean environment

makes it ideally suited to the production of wasabi—Japanese horseradish—a new crop now being commercially produced in the state. The root of the plant is crushed to produce the wasabi, and the leaves can also be eaten as a salad vegetable.

Near **Wynyard** [C3], at the mouth of the Inglis River, is Fossil Bluff, where Errol Flynn's father found the oldest known marsupial fossil. Known as *Wynyardia bassinia*, it is exhibited in the Queen Victoria Museum in Launceston.

The explorers Bass and Flinders had some foresight when they named the nearby **Cape Grim** as it is now an international air pollution monitoring station, part of a series around the world used to help scientists understand global atmospheric conditions. Fortunately, the news for the locals is not so grim—the air at the Cape's baseline station is consistently measured as the cleanest in the world.

DON'T MISS: In spring Wynyard turns on a spectacular tulip display to complement the Dutch windmill at Penguin to the south-east.

When **Zeehan** [D2] was a roaring boom town, in the late 19th and early 20th centuries, the Gaiety Theatre, which seated 1,000 people, was Australia's largest concert hall and theatre. Such was its prestige that during that time it saw Enrico Caruso, Dame Nellie Melba, Harry Houdini and the infamous Lola Montez all treading the boards and entertaining the wealthy miners. When silver and lead deposits were found in Zeehan in 1882 it became Tasmania's third-biggest

town. By 1901 it had 11,000 people and 26 pubs. During the boom about $8 million worth of ore was recovered. From 1908 the ore began to play out, the mines eventually closed and the population moved on. The reopening of a tin mine at Renison Bell, just to the north, has brought the town back to life and it now serves as a dormitory community for the mine. Take a drive out to the coast at **Trial Harbour**, or further north to **Granville Harbour**, both important ports in their day but racked by southerly storms. You'll need to be a very experienced four-wheel-driver to tackle the beach drive.

DON'T MISS: The most impressive sight in Zeehan is its well-designed West Coast Pioneers' Memorial Museum in the attractive School of Mines.

Diary of Events

Town	Event	Date	Contact
Burnie	Burnie Burns Festival of Fire	October, last weekend	03 6431 9675
Carrick (Launceston)	Agfest	May, 1st weekend	03 6334 0262
Deloraine	Tasmanian Craft Fair	November, 1st weekend	03 6362 3471
Evandale	Penny Farthing Championships	February, 3rd weekend	03 6391 8223
Fingal	Fingal Valley Festival	September	03 6374 2165
Latrobe	Grande Fiesta Filipino	February	0407 504 578
	Latrobe Wheel and Latrobe Gift	Christmas	03 6426 1041
Launceston	Annual Night at the Gorge	February	03 6323 3215
Rosebery	Rosebery Miner's and Axemen's Bush and Blarney Festival	February	03 6473 1132
Ross	Festival of the Arts	March	03 6391 2352
St Helens	Targa Tasmania	April	03 6224 1512
	Suncoast Jazz Festival	June	03 6373 6151
Westbury	St Patrick's Day and Maypole Festivals	St Patrick's Day	03 6424 4466

TAS

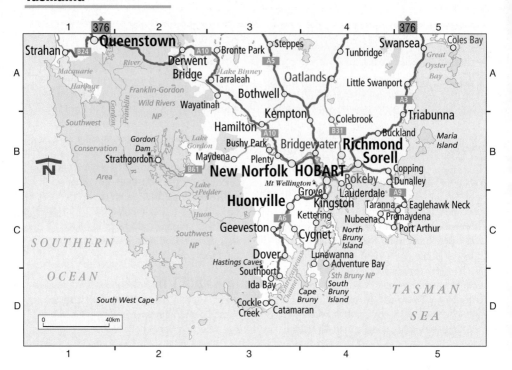

Southern Tasmania covers the capital city of Hobart; the historic village of Richmond; the convict past at Port Arthur; the southern wine region; and the waterways, fish farms and orchards of the lush Huon Valley and D'Entrecasteaux Channel.

■ get off the beaten track

swing through southern tasmania

Bothwell

Bothwell [A3] is a classified historic town, with 53 buildings that have National Trust listing or recognition. The Australasian Golf Museum is in the old schoolhouse. It is claimed that the first game of golf in Australia was played in 1828 at Alexander Reid's property, Ratho, 2 km west of the town on the A5. The course is still in use. Thorpe Farm produces what many consider the best goat's cheese in Australia— Tasmanian Highland Cheeses. Owner John Bignell also produces old-fashioned rye flour marketed under the name Tasmanian Highland Watermill and has just started commercial production of the Japanese condiment wasabi, rivalling Winnaleah in the north.

Bridgewater

Bridgewater [B4] has long provided the gateway for the most direct route from Hobart to Launceston. In 1816 James Austin and his cousin John Earle established the first trans-Derwent ferry service there, which operated until the completion of a causeway in the 1830s. Austin's Cottage, one of Australia's oldest

buildings, is a basic structure built by the ex-convict in 1809 on his release from custody. The causeway itself was built by convicts. At its southern end, at **Granton**, is the Old Watchouse, where convict labourers not pulling their weight are said to have been sentenced to solitary confinement in one of the building's 'upright' cells, 2 m high and only 50 cm square. At the tiny settlement of **Austin's Ferry**, about 5 km back toward Hobart on the old Hobart Road, is Hestercombe Chapel (ask for directions), built in 1833 by Hobart merchant Henry Hopkins. The oldest Congregational Church in Australia, it has a

fireplace and a minuscule organ. It is easy to miss as it is grey and unremarkable, characterised by a simple asceticism.

Bronte Park

Bronte Park [A3] is close to the geographical centre of Tasmania, which lies to the east and is marked by a monument on the Lyell Highway. Originally built to house Hydro Electric Commission workers, the town now caters for the many anglers who come here for the excellent trout fishing. The Commission huts have been transformed into chalets, each named after a European country.

Bruny Island

Bruny Island's [C4–D4] north and south 'islands' are joined by a narrow isthmus of sand. Cape Bruny lighthouse, at the southern end, dates from 1838. It was built after three shipwrecks (including that of the *George III* in 1835, which went down when prison guards fired into the convict-filled hold to quell a panic) convinced authorities that the marker buoys in the **D'Entrecasteaux Channel** between the island and the mainland weren't able to keep shipping safe. The Bligh Museum of Pacific Exploration at **Adventure Bay** (on the north-east coast of South Bruny) was built from handmade convict bricks from the 1840s. Its collection of artefacts includes a remnant of a tree, found not far away, into which Captain Cook had carved 'Cook 26th January 1777' when he landed on the island; and a globe of the world dating from 1799.

Buckland

In **Buckland** [B4] is St John the Baptist Church—the age of its East Window is the subject of much speculation. Some people

GAZETTEER

claim the window was designed for Battle Abbey in England, a church dating from 1094. The story is that before the famous Battle of Hastings in Sussex, William the Conqueror vowed that if he won he would build an abbey to commemorate his victory, which he did, purportedly where the English King Harold II had fallen. The church was pulled down during the Reformation and it is argued that the window subsequently found its way out to Australia. The problem, however, is that experts believe the window in St John the Baptist Church was made in the 14th century (some 300 years after the Battle of Hastings). What is certain is that the Reverend FH Cox, rector of the church in 1846–48, brought the window to Australia when he emigrated from Sussex. It is still remarkable to see a 14th-century window in a church that wasn't built until 1846.

Just behind **Bushy Park** [B3], the largest hop-producing town in the Southern Hemisphere, is a 3 km water race that takes water from a dam on the Styx River and channels it to Oast House (now Australia's only museum devoted to hops). The water once drove a huge waterwheel generating electricity to dry the hops. It is claimed that Bushy Park

had electricity before Hobart. In the middle of a field of hops is the famous Text Kiln, a building constructed by E Shoobridge in 1867. Shoobridge, who was helped by his wife, three sons and five daughters, was committed to the motto 'Union is Strength', and believed that the words of the Bible would inspire his workers. Hence a series of biblical quotations on the walls of the Text Kiln. Ebenezer Shoobridge,

son of William Shoobridge (credited with being the first person to grow hops in Tasmania), made Bushy Park a centre of hop production.

Colebrook [B4] was once called
Jerusalem, thanks to the explorer Hugh Germain, who travelled through Tasmania in the early 1800s giving religious or exotic names to towns in the area. Some places, such as Bagdad and Jericho, have kept their names, but Jerusalem was renamed Colebrook in 1894 when the railway was built. The History Room in Colebrook Park has a display of memorabilia from the convict era and the late 19th century. It is housed in a Georgian-style cotttage, built in 1996 from sandstone that was reclaimed from Colebrook's first substantial house, Jerusalem Park, built in 1824. The History Room is open by appointment (03 6259 7263).

Near **Coles Bay** [A5] is one of the most famous natural spots in Australia, **Wineglass Bay**. American magazine, *Outside*, has rated it as one of the best

10 beaches in the world. It was also selected as the place for the royal yacht, *Britannia*, to anchor during Queen Elizabeth's 1981 visit to Tasmania. It's in the **Freycinet National Park**. There is good climbing and abseiling in The Hazards, the pink and grey granite mountains above Coles Bay and Wineglass Bay.

The town of **Copping** [B4] is the latest site producing truffles beneath its walnut trees.

Perigord Truffles harvested its first truffles at Deloraine in 1999 and now has 27 sites.

Cygnet [C3] was named Port de Cygnet
Noir by French Admiral Bruni D'Entrecasteaux because of the number of swans in the bay (he sailed through the area in 1791–93). It is now known just as Cygnet. Part of the house of the first white settler, William Nichols, is still standing and dates from 1834.

Derwent Bridge [A2], surrounded
by extensive highland eucalypt forests, is a good base from which to explore the nearby national parks and go trout fishing in the lakes.

Dover [C3] can legitimately claim to be the
southernmost town 'of significance' in Australia. There is a longstanding argument between the hotel in Alonnah on Bruny Island and the Dover Hotel as to which is the most southerly hotel in Australia.

In **Dunalley** [B4], just before the Dunalley High School, is a sign directing visitors to the Tasman Monument. It was erected in 1942 to mark the 300th anniversary of Abel Tasman's landing from the *Heemskerck* and *Zeehaen*. Tasman's party landed 5 km east of Dunalley at the entrance to Blackman Bay. A small pyramid was erected there in 1923 but it's virtually inaccessible, other than by boat. The Dennison Canal in Dunalley is Australia's only purpose-built sea canal. Originally mooted in 1854, it was finally opened in 1905, allowing

POTATO BABA

Jenny Williams arrived in Tasmania in 1969, a refugee from Czechoslovakia, where she lived through the ravages of World War II and the takeover of Communism (which she has written about in her recent autobiography *Yenni*). Her memories of traditional Hungarian and Slovakian cooking stayed with her and she opened a restaurant on Lauderdale's infamous 'canal' in 1992 (now trading as Eating on the Edge). She remembers that many Slovakian villages were poor. Because of their very mountainous country they grew mainly potatoes, and their national dishes reflect this. Baba (also called Harula) is very widely known and popular and is served on its own or with a hearty soup as a main course.

4 medium to large unpeeled potatoes
1/2 cup milk
2–3 tbsp plain flour
1 egg
1/2 tsp each, salt, pepper, garlic powder
chopped parsley or marjoram (optional)
oil for frying

Wash potatoes thoroughly. Grate potatoes and squeeze out half the moisture. Work together the milk, garlic, pepper, parsley or marjoram and egg and pour over the potatoes. Add flour to make a sluggish mixture. In a frypan heat the oil and fry portions to resemble thick pancakes. Drain on paper and serve. Serves 4–6. Note: The mixture can be refrigerated, but fried baba is not suitable for the fridge or freezer. Variations on baba include salmon baba (a glorified peasant dish topping the baba with smoked salmon, a spread of sour cream, chopped onion, parsley and paprika) and cheese and ham baba (under the grill).

Jenny Williams, LAUDERDALE

TAS

OYSTERS OCHRE

It takes 18 months–2 years to grow an oyster of marketable size. Cameron of Tasmania specialises in prime Pacific oysters, and their hatchery and nursery on the Dennison Canal at Dunalley produce more than 60 million oyster spat (spawn) each year. What started out as a small family-owned business in 1971 now has products in demand all over Australia and exported to Asia, including Japan. If you can't wait to try this recipe buy fresh oysters opened to order at the Dunalley Fish Market.

2 dozen Tasmanian Pacific oysters, in shells	**125 g wedge Cradle Mountain Yellow Ochre cheese, grated**
60 g (3 tbsp) butter	**1/2 tsp salt**
1 clove garlic, crushed	**2 drops tabasco sauce**
4 tbsp plain flour	**1/2 tsp dry mustard**
1 1/4 cups milk or 1 cup evaporated milk with 1/4 cup water	**Tasmanian caviar or lumpfish roe (optional)**

Place the oysters on a wire rack (this makes them more stable) over a baking tray. Melt the butter in a saucepan, add garlic and flour, and cook for 1 minute, stirring constantly. Gradually add the milk, stirring constantly until the mixture boils and thickens. Add the cheese and seasonings, stir until cheese melts. Divide the thick cheese sauce equally (about 2 tbsp) between the oysters and, using the back of a teaspoon, spread it over the oysters. Place the oysters under the preheated, medium to hot grill until the cheese sauce is a light golden brown. Serve immediately, garnished with caviar or lumpfish roe if desired.

Lactos, BURNIE

boats to travel between Dunalley Bay and Blackman Bay. Sydney-to-Hobart yachts returning to Sydney after the race still use the canal as a shortcut.

At **Eaglehawk Neck** [C5] is a sombre reminder of the Tasman Peninsula's history—a bronze sculpture of a dog marks the spot where chained attack dogs were stationed on the narrow isthmus. They formed a line of defence to prevent convicts escaping from Port Arthur via the **Forestier Peninsula**. The town is the starting point for the Tasman Peninsula Convict Trail. To follow this, look for the yellow Convict Trail signposts that begin at the Officers' Quarters. The other stops on the trail are the terminal of the convict-powered tramway at Taranna, Port Arthur, Nubeena, **Premaydena**, **Koonya**, the probation station at **Saltwater River** and the nearby coalmine where the worst offenders were sent as punishment. Eaglehawk Neck has a remarkable tessellated pavement, a geological formation giving the impression that the rocks have been rather neatly tiled by a fastidious giant. The phenomenon is natural; the fracturing of the rocks is actually caused by geological movements. A few kilometres southeast of the isthmus at **Doo Town** (itself quaintly containing houses and streets with names associated with the word 'do') is the **Tasman Arch Reserve** with the dramatic rock formations known as the Tasman Blowhole and Devil's Kitchen.

Geeveston's [C3]

most immediately obvious symbol is the huge trunk of a swamp gum (*Eucalyptus regnans*) logged in Arve Valley on 10 December 1971. A sign on the side of the trunk proudly declares

that its length is 15.8 m, its girth 6.7 m, its weight 57 tonnes and its volume 56.7 m³. Out on the Arve Loop Road you can still see living examples. It is interesting to note that St Peter's Church (built 1834–37) has only one door. The reason was almost certainly to stop members of the congregation, in the early days about 50 per cent convicts, attempting to escape. The Old Schoolhouse, a huge two-storey sandstone structure, was built by convict stonemasons in 1858. It is an interesting comment on the times that, unlike the church, it has two doors—so that the children could enter the school from different directions, according to their gender. On the Huon Trail, 26 km from Geeveston, is the **Tahune Forest Reserve**, where you can walk at treetop level. The Airwalk is a canopy walkway, suspended up to 45 m high, that meanders through the rainforest with one section extending to glimpse the meeting of the Huon and Picton Rivers.

Grove

[C3] is home to the oldest jam makers in Australia. Doran's jam factory opened in 1834, and is now housed in modern premises in Pages Road, incorporating a museum with old jam-making equipment.

Hamilton

[B3] is a charming village with many historic buildings including St Peter's Church erected in 1834, a post office built in 1835, and a schoolhouse dated 1858. Accommodation is available in a number of the original cottages. This is also a great area for fishing with trout, blackfish, redfin and tench in abundance in the Clyde River. Within half an hour's drive of Hamilton is one of Tasmania's prettiest waterfalls, **Russell Falls**.

North of **Hobart** [B4] is a series of towns that are virtually suburbs of the capital. **Glenorchy** was proclaimed a city

in 1964, its growth assured by the establishment of the Cadbury Chocolate factory at **Claremont** to the north. Based in an area of old churches, colonial houses and riverside parks, the factory began in 1921. More than 63 farms supply it with more than one million litres of milk a week. In between the two is **Berriedale**. Its $11 million Moorilla Museum has one of the world's finest collections of antiquities, including an Egyptian sarcophagus dated 600 BC.

Kempton

[B4] is classified as a historic town and has a number of charming old buildings including St Mary's Church, built around 1840, and the Wilmot Arms Inn (1843). About 50 years after it opened the inn was closed by the landlord, who turned to religion and fed the last of his beer to the pigs. The inn has since been restored and is part of Tasmania's colonial accommodation circuit.

At **Kettering**'s [C4] Oyster Cove Marina you can hire your own kayak or join a number of spectacular guided kayak tours of the local waterways. For the adventurous, the Wilderness on Water tour includes a flight to and from the World Heritage area of Melaleuca.

South of **Kingston** [C4] (2 km on the Channel Highway) is the Australian Antarctic Headquarters. It is open for inspection weekdays between 9 am and 5 pm. The displays include some fascinating photographs and Antarctic artefacts, such as Sir Douglas Mawson's sledge. To the north of Kingston, also on the Channel Highway, is the remarkable 66 m Shot Tower, erected by builder and engineer Joseph Moir in 1870. The building is said to

TAS

have used more than 8,000 curved and tapered sandstone blocks. As its name suggests, the Shot Tower was used to produce lead shot, by pouring molten lead through perforations inside the top of the tower. The resulting droplets fell into water, hardening into spherical shot. Visitors keen to see the view can climb the 291 steps to the top.

Lauderdale's [B4] lack of a canal is

the stuff of history. In 1911 the residents petitioned for a canal, pointing out that fruit, much of which was grown to the east of the

river, could reach markets in better condition if a canal was built. They said that a canal would reduce the return journey between Hobart and Clarence from three days to one. Further deputations followed and in 1913 the House of Assembly voted £5,000 to 'investigate' the project. Tenders were called, dredging commenced and in 1923

with some £60,000 down the drain, work was abandoned, commemorated only by a half-finished canal and the following verse.

'Not a drum was heard, not a funeral note / As the dredge home from Ralp's Bay we hurried / Not a steamer, nor yacht, neither dinghy, nor boat / Shall go through that canal we've buried / We Buried it darkly at dead of night / The sods with our southern votes turning / By the Upper House Council's electric light / And the wish of the Assembly spurning … ('The Burial of The Canal Project', 'Critic', 18 April 1923).

Inala, at # Lunawanna [C4], is a 600 ha

property offering accommodation, tours, bushwalking and exceptional birdwatching with almost 90 different

bird species to see. It is also near the **South Bruny National Park**.

The forestry town of # Maydena [B3] is

at the beginning of the Gordon River Road. The great attraction in the area is the **Styx Big Tree Reserve** in the Styx Valley. A huge 92 m mountain ash (*Eucalyptus regnans*) is the largest eucalypt in Australia.

New Norfolk's [B3] famous Bush

Inn, although not as charming as the Old Colony Inn down the road, which is now a café, is still a pub. During a visit in 1927 Dame Nellie Melba stood on the balcony and sang to the crowds below. In Burnett Street is Willow Court, a superb stone building built as a military barracks in 1827–30 by Major Kelsall. It is a remarkable and simple building of great elegance and character. St Matthew's, in Bathurst Street, is the oldest surviving Anglican church in Tasmania, with parts dating back to 1823. All that remains of the original structure are the walls and flagged floor of the nave and part of the western transept. About 3 km downstream from New Norfolk are the huge newsprint mills at **Boyer**. Opened in 1941 they were the world's first to manufacture newsprint from hardwood.

Oatlands [A4] has the largest

collection of pre-1837 buildings in Australia, with 87 stone buildings in the main street and a total of 138 within the town boundaries. The Midlands Highway between Oatlands and Tunbridge is enlivened by the topiary creations of Jack Cashion. Beginning in the early 1960s while working as a highway patrolman, Cashion clipped his creations from roadside hedges: first a rooster, subsequently a steam train

complete with tender, a giraffe, a gorilla (shaped after a car ran into the original elephant) and a kangaroo. It is reported that a stag he had created was so lifelike that a passing motorist tried to shoot it one night.

In 1864 **Plenty** [B3] was the first town in the Southern Hemisphere to raise brown and rainbow trout in ponds. Farming of Atlantic salmon began here in 1986. You can visit the Salmon Ponds where the first brown trout were hatched in the 19th century, and keen anglers might want to add the Museum of Trout Fishing to their itinerary.

Port Arthur [C5] is the best known of

Tasmania's penal settlements and is the most significant of the sites on the Tasman Peninsula Convict Trail [see Eaglehawk Neck]. The peninsula provided a natural prison, connected to the mainland by only a narrow strip of land. Port Arthur's major cell block, known as the Penitentiary, at 75 m long and four storeys high, was the largest building in Australia when it was completed in 1844. The Penitentiary was originally built as a huge granary and flour mill but, after a decade, was converted to house prisoners transferred from Norfolk Island. Those with strong nerves and a taste for the supernatural will enjoy the Ghost Tour, a lantern-lit walk at night around the Port Arthur Historic Site, with spooky stories about strange sightings in the area from convict times to the present. Golfers will enjoy the thrill of playing the par 3 eighth hole at the Tasman Club, near Port Arthur. The tee shot has to reach a very small green on the far side of a gorge of vertical cliffs that plunge hundreds of metres to the ocean.

At **Queenstown** [A1] you can take a ride on the only operating rack-and-pinion rail system in Australia, the Abt Wilderness Railway, which goes to Strahan. The trip goes past rainforest and the **King River**.

Richmond [B4] is Tasmania's most

important historic town, and the ghosts of its convict past are still present. Richmond Bridge, Australia's oldest, was built by prison chain-gangs between 1823 and 1825. The jail in Bathurst Street was built in 1825. The original building, now the northern side of the complex,

was designed to house convict work gangs and local petty criminals. St John's Church, beside the Coal River, across the bridge from the town, is Australia's oldest Roman Catholic church, designed by ex-convict and architect Frederick Thomas. The nave, completed in 1836, opened on 31 December 1837. The church is still in use.

Rokeby [B4] is where Reverend

Robert Knopwood, the first chaplain in Van Diemen's Land, is buried, in the graveyard of St Matthew's Church. Knopwood arrived in Hobart Town in 1804 with the first European settlers, and Rokeby was to be his last parish. He died here in 1838. Inside the church is an organ from the old St David's Church in Hobart, Tasmania's first organ having arrived in Van Diemen's Land in 1825. There are also some chairs carved from wood used in the ships from Nelson's fleet.

GAZETTEER

Sorell [B4] was once almost declared

Tasmania's capital city and now has one of the island's most varied berry productions. The Sorell Fruit Farm's amazing range includes strawberries, raspberries, tayberries, boysenberries, loganberries, silvanberries and blackcurrants. In the warmer months visitors can pick their own berries and vegetables.

Southport

Southport [D3] is yet another settlement, along with **Cockle Creek**, **Catamaran** and Dover, which claims to be the southernmost in Australia. Back on the highway a road around the bay leads to Lune River—the local post office here is recognised as the southernmost in Australia—and on to Southport Bluff. The little **Ida Bay** Railway runs for a scenic 6 km from the bay to Lune River. Nearby, on the Huon Trail, are the **Hastings Caves** and thermal pools in the heart of the forest. You can tour the cave chambers, formed more than 40 million years ago, and take a swim in the pools which stay at a comfortable 28°C all year round.

The Steppes

The **Steppes** [A3] Historic Site consists of a number of historic buildings, including a homestead built in 1888, a post office dated 1897 and an art studio. Call 03 6391 2352 for information on open days. A short walk away is Steppes House, which has a grove with sculptures themed around highland life by Tasmanian artist Stephen Walker.

Strahan

In January 1999 **Strahan** [A1] was named 'Best Little Town in the World' by the *Chicago Tribune*'s travel editor Randy Curwen, who had this to say: 'With fewer than 1,000 year-round residents, this is the only settlement on the entire south-western coast of Tasmania. Downtown is a one-block postcard shot and the only real nightlife is the spectacular sunset over Australia's largest bay.' Included in Strahan's tiny downtown is one of the finest examples of Federation architecture in the country, Ormiston, in Bay Street off The Esplanade. Built in 1902, its grounds are large and impressive. North of Strahan the vast sandy expanse of the Henty Dunes blankets the coastline, which you can drive in four-wheeled motorcycles. Beware when driving the long stretches of Ocean Beach; quicksand is quite common and has swallowed many vehicles. Strahan is the base for the Gordon River cruises, now restricted to the river's lower reaches because of the erosion caused by the wash of the boats. The cruise first crosses the vast Macquarie Harbour, the world's largest natural harbour, covering an area of 285 sq km. Its entrance was named Hells Gate, because of its danger and because it gave access to one of the most feared places in the colony, Australia's most remote convict settlement, Sarah Island.

DON'T MISS: Piners' Festival in Strahan in March celebrates the traditions of pine felling and boat building. Traditional piners' punts race down the Huon River and there are races for an assortment of other boats.

Strathgordon

Strathgordon [B2] is surrounded by extraordinary wilderness, with the World Heritage-listed **Southwest National Park** to its south and the **Franklin-Gordon Wild Rivers National Park** to its north. The drive to the town from Maydena takes you along the Gordon River and Scotts Peak roads through bush, forest and moorland. Strathgordon sits between Lake Gordon and Lake Pedder, which, between them, hold more water than any other body of water in Australia. During the late 1970s and early 1980s, Lake Pedder gained national exposure for the massive brown trout it was regularly producing for keen anglers. Many specimens weighed more than 5 kg and at least a few over 8 kg, most taken at night using an unlikely wooden surface lure called a 'fish cake'. By the end of the 1980s, the boom was largely over and the fishery had declined.

Swansea [A5] and **Cranbrook** are in the Municipality of Glamorgan, the first rural council in Australia. Residents elected their first council early in 1860.

Taranna [C4] gained its status as the terminus of the dreaded human railway from Little Norfolk Bay to Long Bay. This was the first railway in Australia and was operated by four convicts pushing the carriages along the 7 km line. Prisoners then rowed the passengers to their final destination at **Carnarvon Bay** at Port Arthur. The closest you can get to the railway today is to ask someone at the Tasmanian Devil Park to point out the mound on the far side of the road, its only remnant.

Tarraleah [A3] is a hydro-electric town, built by 'the Hydro' to service one of its facilities. The views of the hydro-electric pipes as they tumble down the hill, diverting water from two of the state's largest lakes, are spectacular.

Triabunna [B5] got its first taste of wakame, a sea vegetable, accidentally. The ballast from Japanese woodchip boats in the 1980s introduced the first spores. Triabunna now exports it to Japan and the United States.

HONEY HEALTH CANDY

Tasmania is renowned for its honey, from the full-bodied leatherwood of the west coast to milder flavours such as bush honey, river red, blue gum, white box and prickly bush. The Huon Valley, famous for its apples, has a way with honey. Drop by Dorans Fine Foods on Pages Road, Huonville, and try some. It's Australia's oldest jam factory (1834).

1 cup honey
1 cup sunflower seeds
4 tbsp sesame seeds
2 cups coconut

Boil honey in a saucepan for 4 minutes. Add seeds and boil for 1 minute more. Remove from heat and add coconut. Press into well-oiled tray and refrigerate until cool. Cut into squares. Makes 12.

Varina Clark, HUONVILLE

At **Tunbridge**'s [A4] northern end, spanning the Blackman River, is the oldest surviving, wooden, single-span bridge in Australia. Built in 1848, it is particularly important because it is a rare example of a sandstone bridge with timber decking.

Diary of Events

Town	Event	Date	Contact
Hamilton	Heritage Tour and Open Garden	November	03 6286 3276
Hobart	Taste of Tasmania	Dec/Jan	03 6230 8383
	Tulip Festival	Sept/Oct	03 6230 8383
	Finish of the Sydney-to-Hobart Yacht Race	December	03 6230 8383
Huon Valley	A Taste of the Huon	March long weekend	03 6264 8400
Strahan	Piners' Festival	March	

TAS

Important first steps.

When your kitten's tummy is barely the size of a thumbnail, you need to make sure his meal is full

of nutrients. Whiskas® Kitten food has been designed to give growing kittens all the vitamins and minerals they need,

including a unique blend of natural antioxidants. Antioxidants are known to help improve the body's resistance

to disease. So, make sure he puts his best foot forward and gets a healthy start to life with Whiskas Kitten food.

*Now available in an
easy-pour, reclosable box*

Part of every healthy relationship

Protection from the start of life.

Top breeders recommend **Pedigree® Puppy** because its unique blend of quality ingredients and natural anti-oxidants strengthens the immune system and protects your puppy from the start of life.

MUB556

Accor
www.accorhotels.com.au

Best Western Australia
www.bestwestern.com.au

Breville
Better ideas sooner

Breville Pty Ltd

McDonald's Australia Limited
www.mcdonalds.com.au

The National Road and Motorists' Association
Limited
www.nrma.com.au

index

Index

Index

Index

Index

Recipe Index

Index

Broken Hill Regional Tourist Association

"The real Australia is in the Outback towns and in the mountain ranges; it's in the broad sweep of a ninety-mile beach and the primitive palm grove of a rainforest; it's in this country's culture and its character; its produce and its people.

Looks aren't everything.
Especially when you earn $3 million a year.

We admit, it's no oil painting. Fortunately there's more to the pickle than meets the eye. Just ask Griffith farmer, Tony Parle. He's been growing the things for ten years. You'll find his handiwork inside most McDonald's burgers. That's because Tony is our sole supplier of sliced pickles in Australia.

Tony started his business with a patch of land and some big plans. Thanks to McDonald's support, Tony's pickles now add $3 million a year to the Australian economy.

In fact his pickle business is growing so fast, he recently built a new processing plant. Parle Foods has even been able to expand into frozen vegetables, exporting them to countries all over the world. While a thriving